Intercultural Communication

Building Relationships and Skills

Helen Acosta | Mark Staller | Bryan Hirayama

Kendall Hunt

publishing company

Cover image © Shutterstock, Inc. Used under license.

Kendall Hunt
publishing company

www.kendallhunt.com
Send all inquiries to:
4050 Westmark Drive
Dubuque, IA 52004-1840

Copyright © 2014 by Helen Acosta, Bryan Hirayama, and Mark Staller

ISBN 978-1-4652-5292-0

Printed in the United States of America

Contents

Preface

This textbook is one in a series of Communication textbooks written by faculty members of the Communication Department at Bakersfield College (located in Bakersfield, California) in collaboration with Kendall Hunt publishers. The goal of the writers has been to provide readable, accessible textbooks that offer clear explanations of relevant communication theories and practical advice for improving communication skills.

Intercultural Communication: Building Relationships and Skills is not an upper-division college textbook designed to present the finer points of complex intercultural communication theories to budding communication specialists: rather, it is a lower-division college textbook designed to introduce students to the most important concepts, theories, and strategies related to intercultural communication so that they can improve their intercultural communication skills and establish and maintain satisfying relationships with people from other countries and cultures.

Here is what you can expect from this textbook. There are a total of 10 chapters. Chapters 1 to 3 provide a solid foundation for understanding intercultural communication. Chapters 4 and 5 are pivotal chapters that help you come to an understanding of who you are and how your culture and co-cultures have influenced and formed your personal identity. Chapters 6 to 9 are skill-centered chapters, and Chapter 10 presents advice about intercultural communication in very specific contexts (travel, education, health care, and romantic relationships).

The first two skill-centered chapters (Chapters 6 and 7) focus on verbal and nonverbal communication, obvious communication skills. The last two skill-centered chapters (Chapters 8 and 9) focus on less obvious intercultural communication skills—adapting to other cultures and practicing empathy (Chapter 8) and managing conflict (Chapter 9).

Some people may claim that you either have the attitudes and character traits that make you a good intercultural communicator, or you do not. We, the authors of this textbook, believe that there are mental skills you can practice that allow you to develop the necessary attitudes and character traits that are needed for effective intercultural communication. In Chapter 2, we introduce "cognitive restructuring," a psychological skill that you can develop in order to make attitudinal and behavioral changes. Through cognitive restructuring and other mental skills you can develop the necessary attitudes for intercultural communication, attitudes like openness, curiosity, relational interest, and positive regard.

To help you process the ideas in your textbook and to develop the skills suggested by your textbook, the authors have also written a workbook that provides reading guides, journal assignments, activity sheets, and self-tests. If you use this workbook, you will be able to check your basic understanding of the concepts and theories in the textbook, you will be able to analyze and evaluate your own intercultural communication strengths and weaknesses, and you will be encouraged to use your higher critical thinking faculties to apply the textbook theory to your own life.

Here is what you can expect from a college course in intercultural communication. Expect to learn about other national cultures and about some of the co-cultures that exist in your own country. Expect moments of confusion and uncomfortableness that may lead to important insights into yourself and into your home culture. Expect to gain a deeper understanding of, and appreciation for, who you are and for the cultural influences that have helped to form your personality. Expect to develop a greater sensitivity to other people groups and a greater desire to interact with people from other cultures.

We hope that this textbook is a valuable part of your learning experience in your Intercultural Communication course and a useful aid in developing your intercultural communication skills. However, this textbook, and your Intercultural Communication instructor, can only help you along the way in your educational journey. You are responsible for your own development as an intercultural communicator. As people who are taking the same journey, we wish you great success, satisfying intercultural relationships, and many positive, enriching experiences with people from other cultures.

About the Authors

Since the subtitle of this textbook is "Building Relationships and Skills," we the authors would like to establish a relationship with our readers by disclosing some of our own cultural backgrounds. Rather than pretending that someone else is sharing our personal background information, we will speak to you using our own voices.

Helen Acosta

From my earliest memories college was an important co-culture in my life. When I was in preschool my dad was in college. First, he studied at Orange Coast College, and then he transferred to Long Beach State to complete his Bachelor's Degree as well as his Master's Degree in Communication. Once he completed his degree he was hired as an instructor and Speech and Debate coach at Bakersfield College. From 2nd grade through 10th grade I lived less than a mile from Bakersfield College, I grew up playing in the hallways where I work today. While college has always been part of my life, and an expected destiny, my own academic journey was one of struggle. As a dyslexic, even after a year of tutoring with a reading specialist, I often felt less intelligent than other students at school. I struggled with the work. My teachers were often disappointed because my large vocabulary and verbal skills gave them the expectation that I was above average but my written academic skills were far lower than many of my peers. I never saw myself as an academic but I knew that I loved learning new things and making new connections between ideas. My joys in school were always performance based: band, choir, and drama. Music was my major when I enrolled in college. In my first semester I also joined my dad's Speech and Debate team. I struggled in my music classes and I excelled on the Speech and Debate team. I became a national champion and I learned to support the work of my teammates as a peer coach. I decided to become a Speech and Debate coach and became a Communication major when I entered my junior year of college. While I continued to struggle in courses outside of my major I thrived in my Communication courses, earning first a Bachelor's Degree in Communication and then a Master's Degree, both from CSU, Northridge. While in school I coached the Speech and Debate team at Los Angeles Valley College. A few months after graduation, I was hired as an instructor and Speech and Debate coach at Bakersfield College. After years in Southern California it felt good to return home.

17 years ago, Mark Staller joined me as a coach and instructor in the Communication department at BC. On the surface it appears that Mark and I are exact opposites: I am extremely liberal, he is extremely conservative; I am a secular atheist, he is a devout Christian; I have no interest in ever having children, he has two wonderful adult children. Even our brains work differently. His ability to categorize ideas, ponder philosophical constructs, and conceptualize complex ideas simply astounds me. My understandings of the world do not tend toward the philosophical. I tend toward concrete understandings of the world.

All those difference do not hold a candle to the similarities that have kept our friendship harmonious for nearly 2 decades. We are both in love with learning, we are passionate about our work, we both have "absentminded professor" tendencies, and we both put family at the center of our lives. These similarities balance our differences.

Well into my 40s, I remained the youngest faculty member in the Communication Department at Bakersfield College. Luckily, 2 years ago we hired Bryan Hirayama. Bryan's youth belies by his wide-ranging experience and expertise. Bryan gives me a glimpse of many experiences of the world that are far from my own. He and his active young family have a lifestyle that might be featured in a fitness magazine. Bryan has traveled and lived outside of the US, neither Mark or I share his global understanding. Beyond Bryan's athleticism and cosmopolitan experiences, he has a drive and determination that inspires me.

Today, after 18 years at Bakersfield College, I have a wide variety of communities of which I am a part. I discuss these communities in the chapter titled, "Our Multifaceted Selves." For my entire career I have taught between three and five public speaking courses per semester. I authored two chapters of the textbook Contemporary Public Speaking: How to Craft and Deliver a Powerful Speech. A decade ago, I also began teaching Persuasion and I began teaching Intercultural Communication 6 years ago. Intercultural Communication, more than any other course I have ever taken or taught, has changed my approach to all of my interactions. When any instructor I meet says they would like to start teaching Intercultural Communication I always say "Get ready! It will change you!" . . . and it does! The skills necessary to be an effective intercultural communicator are all learnable and, as authors, we hope that this text will help you recognize, practice and begin to master them.

The relationship in my life that has taught me more about Intercultural Communication than any other is my relationship with my husband, Enrique. Enrique has provided me a window into a world entirely unlike my own. Together, over the last 23 years, we have created a two-person culture of our own. Without him my life would be far less exciting. Enrique has introduced me to more co-cultures than I ever imagined: Comic book and Science Fiction (and their conventions), Medieval Recreation Societies, Community Theatre, Hard Rock musicians, actors, composers, theater companies, and coffee aficionados. Together we have been poets, play producers, and members of a community chorus we co-founded. His life before we met was my polar opposite. He pushes me toward adventure and helps me check my perceptions when I would not notice the need on my own. . . . and he keeps me from wandering out into traffic . . . which is tremendously helpful.

I wrote Chapter 4 (History vs. Histories), Chapter 5 (Our Multifaceted Identities), Chapter 6 (Verbal Communication), and Chapter 8 (Adaptation and Empathy).

Bryan Hirayama

There are so many events and experiences that have shaped me as a person and driven me to become more aware and conscientious of my communication with others, especially with those who might not come from a similar background. Many of these experiences I wear like badges of honor like being raised in a single-parent home by a woman, despite having four growing children, took full advantage of the support and generosity from family and friends to go back to school and become a credentialed teacher. Although some badges were apparent, chosen, and intentional, some of the badges that decorate my life are worn more proudly than others. There are three in particular that color me as an individual, a scholar, an author, as a professor, and as a husband and father.

I come from humble beginnings, much like many of the students who will read this text. Despite not always having the things I wanted and needed growing up, my participation in sport culture gave me a social capita that was worth its weight in gold. As I excelled in a number of sports within my community, the disparities of being someone without certain luxuries disappeared on some level. My involvement with sports and the culture of athletics propelled my life in ways that will forever be understood as nothing short of life changing. My friend groups and the way I was treated by others were often a direct product of my involvement and skills in sports. Even the friendships I was able to build with others from different sports were unique from the friends from other sports. Each sport culture is so different and rich. It is really the interplay between the sports, sport teams, and fandom of the sports I played that acted as my first training grounds for intercultural communication. The language and behaviors in one sport make very little sense on different fields and venues. It was not until college that I really started to understand just how different and special the culture of sports was. During my community college days I was a two-time All-American in water polo and swimming. Although I consciously made a decision to not continue after two very successful years at the community college level, Water Polo is still very much a part of my life. This culture has and continues to shape the way I see the world and how I understand others.

Secondly, another co-culture that has impacted and continues to impact my life is related to my ethnic identity. As a Japanese American I take great pride in my heritage and being part of a co-culture of racial mixed people. My minority status is often called into question because of my subtle Japanese features but ideologically I have always felt more in-line with other co-cultures that are on the fringes of society. As a fourth-generation Japanese-American, or yonsei, the experiences I share with others within my co-culture creates a bond that is very important for me to nourish and a bond I hope to pass onto my racially mixed children. My love for Japan and Japanese culture helps me to stay connected and grounded within my co-culture and since many of my students are interested in Japanese culture, I am often given a soapbox to share this love with them. Following graduate school, I took a visiting professorship position teaching at a private University in Japan. My two years teaching, studying, living, and learning in Japan has forever solidified my love for my father-land, as I call it, and my family that made the difficult journey to America a few generations ago. My affiliation and inclusion within this co-culture is something I have to work hard to maintain at times but it is through the struggle of reaching out to others, travel, and study that makes this membership so much more meaningful.

Lastly, I belong to a co-culture of loss. Without going into too much detail, my father died when I was eleven. A consequence of his death was in fact my initiation into a co-culture of survivors. At times I hide the fact that I am a part of this co-culture. It is not easy to talk about with others regardless if they too have experienced this kind of loss. It has shaped me in ways that I am still making sense of today in my early thirties. Although co-cultural groups for survivors exist out there, I have always been wary about making my membership known. It is not that I am ashamed or embarrassed, it is just that I reserve my communication about my inclusion in this co-culture to the people that I trust and with students when it is appropriate. This co-culture has helped to shape my goals, values, and in many ways helps me stay true to other co-cultures that I am a part of. Each of these three co-cultures has made and continues to make its imprint on me as a person, a community member, and a family member. I value each of these co-cultures despite my openness about them.

Mark Staller

I belong to several academic co-cultures. As a student in a Great Books program at Saint Mary's College in Moraga, California, I earned a BA in Liberal Arts and was the recipient of the Thomas Aquinas Award for outstanding achievement in the Liberal Arts. At the University of California at Berkeley I earned an MA and PhD in Rhetoric. My doctoral areas of concentration were rhetoric and philosophy in the classical world, modern rhetorical theory, and the rhetoric of philosophy. After completing my doctoral work, I taught for about 4 years at several Central Valley colleges in three different academic disciplines, English, Philosophy, and Speech. I taught courses in basic writing, research writing, technical writing, public speaking, critical thinking, and Introduction to Philosophy. Some of my academic identities, therefore, are writing instructor, speech instructor, liberal arts generalist, rhetorician, and philosopher.

For the past 17 years, I have taught full-time as a Professor of Communication at Bakersfield College. For my first 5 years, I alternated with my colleague Helen Acosta as coach and assistant coach of the Bakersfield College Speech and Debate Team, so Helen and I first developed our professional relationship as members of the California Speech and Debate community. For the past 12 years, I have been teaching Communication courses at Bakersfield College, including Public Speaking, Rhetoric and Argumentation, Intercultural Communication, Interpersonal Communication, and Small Group Communication. Collaborating with my colleagues in the Communication Department, I am a principle coauthor of three Communication textbooks: <u>Contemporary Public Speaking: How to Craft and Deliver a Powerful Speech</u>; <u>Small Group Work in the Real World: A Practical Approach</u>; and, now, <u>Intercultural Communication: Building Relationships and Skills</u>.

In addition to my academic co-cultures, the primary co-culture I am involved in outside of my college career is the conservative Christian co-culture. I have been an active member of my church denomination since I was a small child, and I have pastored a small church in Tehachapi, California, for about the past 15 years. For a large part of my life, I have travelled back and forth between this traditional religious co-culture and the secular academic co-culture. Studying and teaching Intercultural Communication has helped me to clarify and claim both of these major parts of my personal identity.

Studying and teaching intercultural communication has also helped me to discover my German roots. Although my last name is "Staller," until 6 years ago (when I first started teaching Intercultural Communication) I only thought of myself as American—I had almost no ethnic identity. On an unconscious level, I had disassociated myself from anything German because I primarily thought of Adolf Hitler and Nazis when I thought of German culture. After researching my family background and my German heritage, I can now write proudly that I am German-American. The Stallers, I have learned, were German Lutheran farmers who immigrated to the eastern part of the United States in the late 1800s. I hope that my Intercultural Communication students can have similar experiences getting in touch with their own co-cultures and their own personal identities.

I wrote Chapter 1 (The Foundations of Intercultural Communication), Chapter 2 (Appreciating Both Sameness and Difference), Chapter 3 (Values and Worldviews), Chapter 7 (Nonverbal Communication), and Chapter 9 (Approaches to Conflict).

Dedication

Helen Acosta would like to dedicate this book to her parents, Norm and Lucille Fricker, her husband, Enrique Acosta, her sisters, Matie Fricker and Cari Fricker-Hische, and all of her friends near and far.

Bryan Hirayama would like to dedicate this book to all his brothers and sisters around the world. Love you and miss you always.

Mark Staller would like to dedicate this book to his wife, Sylvia.

Chapter 1

Foundations of Intercultural Communication

Mark Staller

Chapter Learning Objectives

1. Develop a basic vocabulary related to intercultural communication in order to understand the connection between communication and culture.
2. Gain a deeper understanding of culture by learning the functions of culture, some similes for culture, and some important characteristics of culture.
3. Know the general history of the study of culture and the specific history of Intercultural Communication studies.
4. Understand and appreciate the major reasons to study Intercultural Communication.
5. Learn the essential information one needs to know in order to become more cosmopolitan.
6. Develop the ability to evaluate intercultural communication competence.

© Dmitry Zamorin, 2014. Used under license from Shutterstock, Inc.

Introduction

A building lacking a solid foundation is on shaky ground: similarly, an area of study lacking clear foundational concepts and principles is on questionable footing. In this introductory chapter, we lay a solid foundation for your understanding and practice of intercultural communication.

We first provide some basic definitions related to culture and communication and explore some of the connections between communication and culture. We then deepen your understanding of culture by presenting some of the major functions of culture, some similes related to culture, and some of the important

Figure 1.1   A building needs a solid foundation.

characteristics of culture. Next, after giving a brief history of Intercultural Communication studies, we present to you 15 reasons to care about and study intercultural communication. We then reveal that this textbook is designed to make our readers more "cosmopolitan." Finally, we end this chapter by presenting two approaches to evaluate intercultural communication competence.

After reading through this introductory chapter, you should have a solid grasp of the essential definitions and details related to Intercultural Communication studies, and you should be motivated to engage in intercultural communication after gaining a better understanding of its utility and its many purposes.

Some Foundational Definitions

To effectively engage in the intelligent study of intercultural communication, you must understand the terms used in this field of study. First and foremost, what is this thing called "culture?" Culture is actually not a physical "thing" at all. Culture is a nonmaterial component of human society. A human **society** is a group of people that live together in a (more or less) ordered community.

Human beings are, in part, physical entities, and since the term "society" refers specifically to a group of human beings, it is more closely related to the physical world than the term "culture." Since the term "culture" often refers to some of the immaterial elements that help to form and organize human societies, it has, over time, generated a large number of definitions.

We define **culture** as *the learned beliefs, values, attitudes, and behaviors that bind a group of people together*. Note that these four components of culture—beliefs, values, attitudes, and behaviors—are not physical, material things. Thus, the term "culture" refers less to the physical, and much more to the mental life of human beings.

Beliefs are ideas and propositions that are held to be true. Beliefs are at the core of human culture because they generate the values, attitudes, and behaviors of human beings. **Values** are important beliefs shared by members of a culture about what is good or bad, desirable or undesirable, important or unimportant. **Attitudes** are settled ways of thinking and feeling that are usually manifested in people's behavior. **Behaviors** are the ways people in a society act or react to internal and external stimuli. Behaviors are the observable elements of culture—what we see or hear other people do or say.

We can also observe the cultural artifacts that people produce. **Cultural artifacts** are physical objects made by human beings that transmit and give information about human cultures. We can analyze cultural artifacts to gain an understanding of the beliefs and values of a people group.

© ermess, 2014. Used under license from Shutterstock, Inc.

Some people groups are bound together by physical geography. **Indigenous cultures** are cultures that exist among people groups living in a particular geographical area. The original inhabitants of a geographical area are labeled "indigenous" or "native," and the culture they create and transmit is labeled "indigenous" or "folk" culture.

Another type of culture related to geography is "national" culture. A **national culture** is composed of the common beliefs, values, attitudes, and behaviors that exist within the population of a sovereign nation. There are approximately 200 nation-states, and these nation-states or countries lay claim to different geographic areas. Within the borders of each country, sovereign nations establish their own laws and institutions.

Figure 1.2   Cultural artifacts help us to gain an understanding of the beliefs and values of a people group.

Deep-structure institutions are the social organizations of family, church, and state that have created, transmitted, maintained, and reinforced the basic elements of every traditional human culture. The **family** is the primary social group that transmits and maintains cultural beliefs, values, and behaviors in any society. (A **nuclear family** is composed of one or both parents and their children. An **extended family** includes grandparents, grandchildren, aunts, uncles, and cousins.)

Figure 1.3   The family is the primary social group that transmits culture.

More complex societies also develop the institutions of "church" and "state." The term "church" refers to the organized religions established in a society. A **religion** is an organized system of beliefs, ceremonies, and rules attempting to answer basic questions and solve fundamental problems related to the human condition. (We will explore some of the major religions of the world in Chapter 3 when we focus on cultural values and worldviews.) The term "state" refers to the many different institutions created by a society's government, including public schools and universities.

As human beings are integrated into the deep-structure institutions of family, church, and state, they become "enculturated." **Enculturation** is the process whereby people learn their group's culture through observation and instruction. Enculturation begins at a very early age.

In addition to enculturation into their family and national cultures, human beings also experience **acculturation**, a process in which members of one culture adopt many of the beliefs, values, and behaviors of another cultural group. Acculturation occurs when a person immigrates from one country to another, but it also occurs when a person moves from one part of a country to another part and becomes a member of the new regional culture, and it occurs when a person who is part of a dominant national culture becomes a member of one of the many "co-cultures" that exist within and alongside of the dominant culture.

A **dominant culture** (also called an "umbrella" culture or a "mainstream" culture) is a culture created by those who have the greatest influence on the beliefs, values, and behaviors of a people group. Often the ethnic group with the greatest numerical advantage in a country creates the dominant national culture of that country, but this is not always the case: sometimes people with the greatest influence in or on a dominant or mainstream culture are not the people with the greatest numerical advantage, but the people who control the tools and institutions of enculturation. For example, a company's culture is not created by its rank-and-file employees (who have the greatest numerical advantage), but by the owners and leaders of the company who have the authority and power to create the company culture.

In the modern world, in addition to the traditional deep-structure institutions, culture is transmitted by popular culture products. **Popular culture** is cultural products and artifacts that are widely disseminated and consumed, including television shows, movies, recorded music, video clips, and other mass media products. In the modern world, the people who create and control mass media popular culture products are largely responsible for the dominant or mainstream culture of a country or region.

A subgroup within a larger dominant or umbrella culture that has beliefs and behaviors that differ from the dominant culture was in the past referred to as a **subculture**. However, the prefix "sub" carries a negative connotation of inferiority or subservience, so the term "co-culture"

Figure 1.4   Mass media popular culture products greatly influence modern cultures.

is now the preferred term in intercultural studies. A **co-culture** is an interdependent and equal cultural group that exists within and alongside of a dominant national culture.

Although there are only about 200 national cultures in the modern world, there are thousands of co-cultures that exist. Most human beings are members of only one national culture while simultaneously belonging to dozens of co-cultures. Whereas national culture is determined by *space* (the geographical borders of the country in which you live), your co-cultures are primarily determined by *time*. The people groups with which you spend a lot of time develop their own beliefs and values, behaviors and rituals, and language and slang expressions—these are the crucial elements of a co-culture, and not necessarily a particular cultural space.

An Alphabetical List of the National Cultures of the World
(The 193 Member States recognized by the United Nations in 2013)

Afghanistan, Albania, Algeria, Andorra, Angola, Antigua and Barbuda, Argentina, Armenia, Australia, Austria, Azerbaijan, (The) Bahamas, Bahrain, Bangladesh, Barbados, Belarus, Belgium, Belize, Benin, Bhutan, Bolivia, Bosnia and Herzegovina, Botswana, Brazil, Brunei, Bulgaria, Burkina Faso, Burma (Myanmar), Burundi, Cambodia, Cameroon, Canada, Cape Verde, Central African Republic, Chad, Chile, China, Colombia, Comoros, (Democratic Republic of the) Congo, (Republic of the) Congo, Costa Rica, Cote d'Ivoire, Croatia, Cuba, Cyprus, Czech Republic, Denmark, Djibouti, Dominica, Dominican Republic, East Timor, Ecuador, Egypt, El Salvador, Equatorial Guinea, Eritrea, Estonia, Fiji, Finland, France, Gabon, (The) Gambia, Georgia, Germany, Ghana, Greece, Grenada, Guatemala, Guinea, Guinea-Bissau, Guyana, Haiti, Honduras, Hungary, Iceland, India, Indonesia, Iran, Iraq, Ireland, Israel, Italy, Jamaica, Japan, Jordan, Kazakhstan, Kenya, Kiribati, (North) Korea, (South) Korea, Kuwait, Kyrgystan, Laos, Latvia, Lebanon, Lesotho, Liberia, Libya, Liechtenstein, Lithuania, Luxembourg, Macedonia, Madagascar, Malawi, Malaysia, Maldives, Mali, Malta, Marshall Islands, Mauritania, Mauritius, Mexico, (Federated States of) Micronesia, Moldova, Monaco, Mongolia, Montenegro, Morocco, Mozambique, Namibia, Nauru, Nepal, Netherlands, New Zealand, Nicaragua, Niger, Nigeria, Norway, Oman, Pakistan, Palau, Panama, Papua New Guinea, Paraguay, Peru, Philippines, Poland, Portugal, Qatar, Romania, Russia, Rwanda, Saint Kitts and Nevis, Saint Lucia, Saint Vincent and the Grenadines, Samoa, San Marino, Sao Tome and Principe, Saudi Arabia, Senegal, Serbia, Seychelles, Sierra Leone, Singapore, Slovakia, Slovenia, Solomon Islands, Somalia, South Africa, South Sudan, Spain, Sri Lanka, Sudan, Suriname, Swaziland, Syria, Tajikistan, Tanzania, Thailand, Togo, Tonga, Trinidad and Tobago, Tunisia, Turkey, Turkmenistan, Tuvalu, Uganda, Ukraine, United Arab Emirates, United Kingdom, United States, Uruguay, Uzbekistan, Vanuatu, Venezuela, Vietnam, Yemen, Zambia, and Zimbabwe.

An Alphabetical List of Some Co-Cultures in America

A.A. Members, Air Force Pilots, Arab-Americans, Army Grunts, Atheists, Automotive Mechanics, Ballroom Dancers, Baptists, Barbers, Bartenders, Beauticians, Beauty Contestants, Bloggers, Body Piercers, Bouncers, Boy Scouts, Boys Club Mentors, Buddhists, Burning Man Participants, Calligraphers, Campers, Canadian-Americans, Cancer Survivors, Carnies, Cat Lovers, Catholics, Cellists, Cement Workers, Cheerleaders, Chinese-Americans, Chiropractors, Choir Members, Cigar Smokers, City Council Members, Civil War Re-Enactors, Clarinet Players, Cloggers, Clubbers, Coast Guard Members, Comic-Con Groupies, Community College Students, Computer Programmers, Cos-Players, Country Music Fans, Crossword Puzzle Players, Democrats, Dental Assistants, Diabetics, Disciples of Christ, Dog Lovers, Drum Corps Members, DMV Employees, EMTs, Episcopalians, Facebookers, Fantasy League Participants, Fast Food Workers, Fetishists, Figure Drawers, File Clerks, Firefighters, Flautists, Fraternity Members, French-Americans, Gang Members, German-Americans, Girl Scouts, Grease Monkeys, Greek-Americans, Green Berets, Guitar Players, Gym Rats, Gymnasts, Habitat For Humanity Volunteers, Harmonica Players, Hip Hop Dancers, Househusbands, Irish-Americans, Italian-Americans, Japanese-Americans, Jehovah's Witnesses, Jugglers, Knitters, Libertarians, Lottery Players, Lutherans, LVNs, Magicians, Manicurists, Marching Band Members, Masons, Meth Addicts, Mexican-Americans, MLB Fans, Mormons, N.A. Members, NAACP Members, NASCAR Fans, Navy Seals, NBA Fans, NFL Fans, NRA Members, Nudists, Nurses, Office Managers, Oil Field Workers, Oil Painters, Orthodox Jews, Parking Valets, Pentecostals, Philologists, Phone Solicitors, Photographers, Pianists, Poker Players, Police Cadets, Polish-Americans,

(*Continued*)

Postal Employees, Pot Smokers, Presbyterians, Pro Wrestling Fans, PTA Members, Quilters, Ravers, Realtors, Receptionists, Republicans, Restaurant Hosts/Hostesses, Retail Sales Clerks, Rowers, Royal Rangers, RPG Players, Russian-Americans, Salon Workers, Saxophonists, Scrabble Players, Secretaries, Secular Humanists, Seventh-Day Adventists, Shia Muslims, Shriners, Sikhs, Skateboarders, Social Workers, Soccer Fans, Sorority Members, Spa Enthusiasts, Street Ballers, Street Performers, Street Racers, Strippers, Sunni Muslims, Survivalists, Swing Dancers, Tattooists, Tax Preparers, Theater Performers, Toastmasters, Tour Guides, Trekkies, Trumpeters, Tweeters, UPS Drivers, Vegans, Violinists, Waiters/Waitresses, Whovians, Wiccans, Wine Enthusiasts, Wolf Pack Members, Wrestlers, and Yoga Studio Members.

Culture and Communication

Since there are two main areas of emphasis in the study of intercultural communication—1) culture and 2) communication—we need to provide you some basic definitions related to communication. Although human communication has existed as long as human beings, the study of human communication as a modern social science only developed in the twentieth century. As twentieth century communication technologies developed, a scientific understanding of communication was developed and refined.

The modern transactional model of human communication gives us a standard vocabulary which allows us to describe and discuss any communication interaction. **Communication** can be defined as *a transactional process whereby two or more communicators share meaning*. A **communicator encodes** a **message** and sends it through a communication **channel**. Another communicator receives and **decodes** this message and then sends **feedback**. While the communication transaction unfolds, the communicators must deal with communication **noise**.

Channel: A communication channel is the medium that carries a message.

Communicator: A communicator is someone who either sends or receives a message.

Decoding: Decoding is the mental process of transforming messages received back into ideas and concepts. The communication symbols used to communicate a message must be interpreted and assigned meaning.

Encoding: Encoding is the mental process of transforming ideas and feelings into symbols (words, sounds, actions, etc.) and then organizing these symbols into a message.

Feedback: Feedback is any response, verbal or nonverbal, that a receiver gives to a message. Feedback indicates to the sender whether and how the message was received and understood.

Message: A message is the content of a communication, the ideas and emotions people wish to share.

Noise: Noise is anything that interferes with the transmission of a message. Noise can be external or internal. External noises are sights, sounds, and other stimuli that can draw attention away from the message being transmitted. Internal noises are thoughts, feelings, and physical conditions in the communicators that interfere with the communication process.

The transactional model of communication helps us understand why communication is difficult, and why intercultural communication can be especially difficult. **Intercultural communication** is *communication between people from substantially different cultural groups.* Intercultural communication occurs when people from different national cultures interact, but it also occurs within a single society when people from different co-cultures interact.

Although human communicators from different cultures may want to communicate with one another, to send and receive messages, cultural differences can complicate the communication process. People from different cultures may focus on different communication channels. (For example, people from some cultural groups focus on verbal messages, whereas people from other cultural groups focus more on the nonverbal messages sent through the visual channel.) People from different cultures may also encode and decode messages very differently. Sometimes people from different cultural groups may not even share the same basic concepts and ideas that are being encoded and decoded.

Knowing that human communication is a negotiated transaction, however, can help you persevere in your intercultural interactions, even when they are frustrating and confusing. If you want to build a successful relationship with someone from another culture, you both must be willing to hang in there even when your communication partner prefers a different communication channel or encodes and decodes messages differently. And if you discover that miscommunication is occurring because you and your communication partner possess different ideas and values, you both have an opportunity to gain insight into what makes another person tick.

Within the field of Communication Studies, several subfields of human communication have been identified. **Interpersonal communication** is the study of one-on-one, dyadic communication and its impact on personal relationships. **Small group communication** is the study of communication that occurs in groups of 3-12 people. **Public speaking** is the study of the one-way verbal communication that occurs when a speaker addresses an audience. **Organizational communication** is the study of communication within an organization and of communication between an organization and other outside entities. **Mass communication** is the study of mass forms of communication such as print, radio, television, and the internet and how these forms of communication influence societies.

Intercultural communication traverses all of these subfields of human communication. You can experience intercultural communication in a one-on-one interpersonal interaction, in a small group environment, in a public speaking situation, within an organization, and as a producer or consumer of mass communication products. Whereas other subfields of communication are marked off primarily by how many people are involved in a communication situation, intercultural communication is identified primarily by the fact that the communicators involved in a communication transaction belong to substantially different cultural groups.

Although intercultural communication traverses all the subfields of communication, we will focus in this textbook on intercultural communication at the interpersonal level. The concepts and principles laid out in this textbook are presented primarily with the interpersonal communication context in mind. We want you to learn to build successful relationships with people from other cultures— friendships, working relationships, and even romantic relationships. We want you to build effective communication skills so that you can build satisfying relationships with people from around the world.

Figure 1.5 Effective intercultural communication skills can help you build satisfying relationships with people from all around the world.

© bikeriderlondon, 2014. Used under license from Shutterstock, Inc.

The Culture–Communication Connection

Although several academic areas study human culture, it is especially appropriate that culture is studied in the Communication field. Put simply, human culture would not exist without communication, and human communication would not exist without culture. Let us consider both of these assertions further.

First, what do we mean when we assert that human culture would not exist without communication? We are referring specifically to *verbal* communication, that is, to human language. Other animals communicate primarily through nonverbal signals, but we human beings are distinguished by our ability to transform our thoughts and feelings into verbal symbols and to share these verbal symbols with other human beings who can decode them in order to comprehend the thoughts and feelings we wish to share.

Language allows human beings to form and share ideas and beliefs, and beliefs are at the core of culture. We do not refer to "dog culture" or "cat culture" or any other animal culture because only human beings, through human language, are capable of forming and sharing abstract thoughts and beliefs. (We focus on human language and verbal communication in Chapter 6.)

Second, what do we mean when we assert that human communication would not exist without culture? Since the signs and signifiers used in human language are arbitrary, human beings must agree upon and assign common meanings to these signs and symbols, and this agreement could not occur if human beings did not come together and form cultural groups. Cultural groups allow individuals to agree upon and share common meanings for words and other language symbols. Cultures are, among other things, language communities that share common symbol systems.

© VLADGRIN, 2014. Used under license from Shutterstock, Inc.

Figure 1.6   Culture is communication, and communication is culture.

Deepening Our Understanding of Culture

Now that we have gained a basic understanding of culture and of intercultural communication, let us go even deeper by tracing the historical development of the concept of culture and by considering some of the major functions of culture, some useful similes for culture, and some important characteristics of culture.

The Development and Spread of the Concept of Culture

The term "culture" can be traced back to the Latin noun "cultura," which was probably formed from the past participle stem of "colere," which means "to tend, guard, cultivate, or till." Thus, the term "culture" was originally associated with agriculture, or the tilling of land.

In his *Tusculan Disputations*, the Roman orator and educator Cicero gave the term "culture" a new meaning when he used the phrase "cultura animi," or "cultivation of the soul." This non-agricultural use of the term "culture" reappeared in Europe in the Middle Ages when people emphasized the cultivation of the mind through education. Over time, the noun "culture" came to refer to the betterment or refinement of individuals, and a "cultured" person was a person who had been educated or civilized. In the eighteenth and early nineteenth century, a distinction thus developed between "low" and "high" culture.

In the late nineteenth century, British anthropologist Edward Burnett Taylor used the term "culture" in its modern sense to refer to a diverse set of activities characteristic of all human societies. In the twentieth century, culture became a central concept in Anthropology. Two major fields of Anthropology were recognized—Physical Anthropology and Cultural Anthropology—and the term "culture" is now used in Anthropology to refer to the range of human phenomena that cannot be directly attributed to genetics. Culture is now an important concept and field of study in six different academic areas—Anthropology, Communication, Cultural Studies, Geography, Psychology, and Sociology.

The Major Functions of Culture

When we explored the connection between communication and culture, we pointed out that culture binds people together in social groups and makes human communication possible. In addition, culture gives meaning to events and actions. Cultural groups create and relate histories that teach their members what events and activities are important or unimportant, laudable or worthy of censure. (The importance of history is explored further in Chapter 4.)

Culture also gives people their identities. As we are enculturated into different people groups, these groups become an important part of who we are—we identify with, and are identified by, our cultural affiliations. (Identity is the primary focus of Chapter 5.)

Finally, culture provides people with a pattern for living and teaches people how to adapt to their surroundings. The Nature/Nurture distinction reveals that genetic programming may be responsible for some human actions and behaviors, but many of our behaviors are a result of cultural conditioning.

The positive functions of culture demonstrate that you cannot "escape" from culture, nor should you. Your status as a human being is a result of the cultures that have nurtured and created your social relationships and your interior intellectual world. You are in large part a product of the many cultures to which you have belonged or do belong.

Similes for Culture

To gain a deeper understanding of culture, we can compare culture to other elements in the world around us. As you consider the following similes for culture, remember that all comparisons eventually break down. If two things being compared were identical, you would end up with a straight identification, rather than a simile or an analogy. We are not claiming that culture is *exactly* like a fishbowl, or a pair of glasses, or a computer operating system, or an iceberg, but that each of these comparisons is based on a similarity that helps us more fully grasp an important feature or aspect of culture.

Culture is Like a Fishbowl.   This simile emphasizes the unconscious nature of culture. A fish in a fishbowl does not realize that it is in a fishbowl—it is unaware of the environment in which it lives and of how this environment is different from other environments outside its familiar surroundings. Similarly, people who grow up in isolated cultures are often unaware of the cultures outside their borders, and they do not realize that their way of living is only one way of living among many others.

Figure 1.7   Culture is like a fishbowl.

Culture is like a pair of glasses.   This simile emphasizes the way that culture influences our perceptions. Wearing a pair of glasses affects the way you see things. Reading glasses help you to see printed words more clearly. Sunglasses make things seem darker than they actually are. Similarly, the "cultural lenses" that you look through affect the way that you perceive and interpret the world around you. Cultures form our worldviews and create perceptual filters. Our cultural values make us pay attention to and focus on certain things while we ignore or downplay other things.

Figure 1.8   Culture is like a pair of glasses.

Culture is like a computer operating system.   This simile emphasizes the differences between cultures. Computers cannot function without both hardware and software. In addition to motherboards and processing chips and hard drives, computers need to be programmed with a software operating system. Similarly, human beings have bodies and brains (hardware), but they cannot function without a worldview, without a way of viewing and interpreting the world around them (software). Cultures provide people with worldviews that give people a way to understand and interpret the events and behaviors around them. Like computer operating systems, cultures can differ significantly. Human beings may have the same "hardware" (bodies and brains), but the "software" that guides human thought and behavior can be very different.

Figure 1.9 Culture is like a computer operating system.

© liunewind, 2014. Used under license from Shutterstock, Inc.

Culture is like an iceberg. This simile is ubiquitous in the field of Intercultural Communication—it is the most common, most popular comparison used to help people understand that culture has hidden, unseen elements. Just as a large part of an iceberg is below the waterline, so a large part of culture is below the observable surface. We can observe the behaviors of people from other cultures (what they do and what they say), but to understand what is motivating their behaviors, we must go deeper to discover their attitudes, values, and beliefs. Let us develop this comparison more fully, overlaying the four basic elements of culture—behaviors, attitudes, values, and beliefs—on the iceberg image:

Behaviors

Attitudes

Values

Beliefs

© leonello calvett, 2014. Used under license from Shutterstock, Inc.

Figure 1.10 Culture is like an iceberg.

- **Behaviors:** What people say and do can be observed. This is the part of culture that is "above the waterline." To learn about other cultures, you first need to become a keen observer of the behaviors of others.
- **Attitudes:** The attitudes that people have are close to the conscious, observable surface. We often can tell when someone "has an attitude." People's attitudes directly affect their behaviors.
- **Values:** What people value, what people think of as important, is harder to determine. Values are often below the conscious surface—people are often not "tuned in" to their own values. To discover the motivations and causes behind peoples' behaviors and judgments, you need to determine their values.
- **Beliefs:** At the core of a culture, often way below the conscious surface, are the master thoughts and beliefs that create the values, attitudes, and behaviors of a cultural group. Thoughts create feelings that lead to actions. To truly understand a culture at a deep level, you must reverse the process and observe actions in order to discover and uncover the underlying attitudes, values, and beliefs that create these behaviors.

Some Important Characteristics of Culture

Let us end this section designed to deepen your understanding of culture by pointing out three important characteristics of culture: 1) culture is passed from one generation to the next; 2) culture is dynamic; and 3) culture is an integrated system.

Culture is passed from one generation to the next.   Cultures endure over time because cultural beliefs and practices are passed not only from person to person, but also from generation to generation. Some thoughts and behaviors are idiosyncratic and ephemeral—they are spoken or performed by only one individual, and they are not necessarily repeated. The core beliefs and behaviors of a culture, however, are repeatedly expressed and acted out. This repetition and reinforcement of core beliefs and expected behaviors perpetuates culture from one generation to the next. Some elements of culture are remarkably stable and persist over time.

Culture is dynamic.   Although some elements of culture persist over time, culture is not static and unchangeable. As you identify the core beliefs and values of different cultures, be aware that some of these beliefs may be modified or rejected in the future, and that certain cultural values may be de-emphasized or replaced by other values. The younger generation of a culture does not always adopt *all* the beliefs and values of the older generation. That is why culture is dynamic, and that is why Americans distinguish between baby-boomers, the "me generation," "generation x," and so on.

Culture is an integrated system.   Although we can distinguish between different basic elements of culture, it is important to recognize that culture operates as an integrated system. Some of the basic elements of culture are human language and communication, memory and history, worldviews and values, family, church, state, and popular culture products. Although these elements of culture can be mentally isolated and distinguished, they are constantly interacting in the world around us to create the complex phenomenon we have identified as "culture."

A Brief History of Intercultural Communication Studies

I became personally aware that Intercultural Communication is a fairly young academic discipline when I attended a memorial service for a long-time attendee of the Summer Institute for Intercultural Communication at Reed College in Portland, Oregon. One of her colleagues claimed that she had taught the first college course in Intercultural Communication at Portland State University in the 1970s. She had combined together a cohort of American athletes and a cohort of Arab exchange students to create a college classroom where people could study and experience intercultural communication together.

I have not been able to verify this claim, but the fact that it seems reasonable reveals how relatively recent the study of Intercultural Communication is. The academic study of public speaking, another subfield of Communication, can easily be traced back almost 2,500 years. Intercultural Communication studies, by contrast, have post-World War II beginnings.

Most scholars trace the beginning of the study of Intercultural Communication to anthropologist Edward T. Hall and other social scientists working for the United States Foreign Services Institute (FSI) in the early 1950s. The FSI was established after WW II to train officers and support personnel of the US foreign affairs community, and E.T. Hall and others developed the first theories and concepts related to cross-cultural communication, which they used in their training sessions with FSI attendees.

Hall published the first magazine article on intercultural communication in *Scientific American* in 1955, and in 1959, Hall used the term "intercultural communication" in his popular book The Silent Language. The Silent Language was a best-seller that introduced intercultural communication to a wide audience, including many scholars from various academic fields. Hall focused in his book on nonverbal communication, including proxemics (the study of the use of space in cultures) and chronemics (the study of the use of time in cultures). He is now recognized as the founder of these subfields of Intercultural Communication studies.

In 1961, the Peace Corps, an international volunteer public service organization, was founded by the US government. Many young Americans began traveling to other countries on short-term assignments, so training and experience in intercultural communication expanded beyond diplomatic personnel. Many Intercultural Communication concepts and theories were tested in the field throughout the 1960s.

In the late 1960s and early 1970s, Intercultural Communication as a formal academic discipline took root in American colleges and universities. In 1969, an International Communication program was established at the American University. In 1972, Intercultural Communication: A Reader (the first collected writings on intercultural communication) was published by editors Larry A. Samovar and Richard E. Porter. In 1973, the first textbook, Intercultural Communication, was published by L.S. Harms. By the beginning of the 1980s, hundreds of college courses in intercultural communication were being offered across the United States.

We should note that Intercultural Communication studies were not founded or developed by Americans alone. Many of the Intercultural Communication scholars developing the field in the 1950s had ties to Japanese culture, and very fruitful cross-cultural exchanges in Intercultural Communication studies occurred between American and Japanese scholars throughout the 1970s. The International Association for Intercultural Communication Studies, founded in 1985, has expanded the interaction between American and Asian scholars by holding alternating international conferences in the US and various Asian countries. Through the IAICS, Intercultural Communication studies have become very much a matter of East/West collaboration.

Many professional organizations, divisions, and journals related to Intercultural Communication have been established. In 1970, the International Communication Association established a Division of Intercultural Communication. In 1974, the Society of Intercultural Education, Training, and Research (SIETAR) was founded. In 1975, the Speech Communication Association (now the National Communication Association) established a Division of Intercultural Communication. Around 1976, the first summer session of the Intercultural Communication Institute was held, and in 1998, the International Academy of Intercultural Relations was founded.

© kazoka, 2014. Used under license from Shutterstock, Inc.

Figure 1.11   Intercultural Communication studies are a result of East/West collaboration.

As the new millennium unfolds, you are entering into a fairly new academic field that has become solidly established, but in many ways is still quite young. We hope that this textbook enhances your study of Intercultural Communication, and that it adds useful insights and practical skill-building exercises to the growing body of knowledge related to Intercultural Communication.

What Is Your Motivation? (Reasons to Study and Care About Intercultural Communication)

If you are reading this textbook, you are probably enrolled in a college-level Intercultural Communication course. You may have enrolled in this course to earn a Communication certificate or degree or to fulfill a general education "multicultural" requirement. In this section, we provide you with 15 other reasons to study Intercultural Communication.

We want to convince you that Intercultural Communication is a relevant field of study and that intercultural communication is almost inevitable in our modern world. (We will use a capital "I" and a capital "C" when we are referring to IC as a formal field of study, and we will use lower-case letters when we are referring to the general activity of intercultural communication.) As you read through the 15 reasons why intercultural communication is important, we want you to decide for yourself why this particular subfield of Communication is important to you—why do you care about intercultural communication as an activity and Intercultural Communication as an academic field of study?

(Note: We do not have time or space to present specific evidence or specific examples for the 15 reasons listed below. If we did, we would have to write at least a page per reason. Instead, we present to you one paragraph with very general assertions for each reason.)

Fifteen Reasons to Care About Intercultural Communication

1. Advances in Transportation Technologies

Before the advent of modern transportation technologies, many people lived their entire lives without ever leaving their town or village, and much fewer people traveled from one country to another. There was much less intercultural communication because travel from one nation to another was slow, arduous, and hazardous. Modern transportation technologies have now made international travel quick, convenient, and safe. You can travel the globe by ship in a few months, by car or train in a few weeks, and by plane in just a few days. As you travel from country to country, you need good intercultural communication skills in our modern world.

© Pablo Scapinachis, 2014. Used under license from Shutterstock, Inc.

Figure 1.12   Modern transportation technology has made the world a much smaller place.

2. Advances in Communication Technologies

Thanks to advances in communication technologies, you do not even have to travel to other countries to engage in intercultural communication. Just as innovations in travel technologies have sped up and improved international travel, advances in communication technologies have sped up and improved communication between people in different countries. Audio, text, and video transmissions using satellite systems and the computer internet have made communication between people almost anywhere in the world possible. Messages that in the past took weeks or months to be delivered now travel information superhighways and are delivered in seconds. Intercultural communication using modern communication technologies is almost instantaneous, so you need to quickly learn effective intercultural communication skills.

Figure 1.13   Modern communication technologies allow you to speak to almost anyone anywhere.

3. Globalization

Globalization is the tendency toward worldwide integration of economic systems. The world economic markets are now intertwined, and many businesses are international, going beyond national borders. You are likely to encounter people from many cultures at your work and in your business. Thanks to globalization, intercultural communication is not only possible, but necessary. Without intercultural communication, companies cannot operate, products cannot be produced, shipped, or marketed, money cannot be borrowed, lent, or invested, and goods and services cannot be bought or sold.

Figure 1.14   Globalization makes intercultural communication imperative.

4. Travel and Tourism

International travel is no longer an activity for intrepid adventurers and explorers or unfortunate refugees. Millions of people now regularly travel to other countries on vacation. The success of their vacation trips depends in large part on their ability to communicate with people from other cultures. Travelers need to care about intercultural communication, and people in host countries need to care about intercultural communication.

A good chunk of the current global economy is money generated through travel and tourism. Tourism is now one of the major industries in many modern countries, and their economic health and survival depend on effective intercultural communication as foreign travelers interact with their native populations.

© Maridav, 2014. Used under license from Shutterstock, Inc.

Figure 1.15   Successful travel depends on effective intercultural communication.

5. Education and Study Abroad

Many people travel to foreign countries on vacation in order to broaden their horizons and to experience more of the world. Those who wish to intensify their learning experience may elect to get some or all of their formal education by studying abroad. These foreign exchange students need adequate intercultural communication skills to successfully complete their programs of study. A solid understanding of intercultural communication will help them succeed in their academic endeavors, which will in turn help them succeed in their careers and chosen professions.

© chuckstock, 2014. Used under license from Shutterstock, Inc.

Figure 1.16   Some people enhance their education through studying abroad.

6. Governmental Work and Diplomacy

In addition to enhancing their vacations and educational experiences, tourists and international travelers with good intercultural communication skills can also build successful relationships with people in their host countries. However, people involved in governmental work and diplomacy need good intercultural communication skills not just for their interpersonal relationships: ambassadors, diplomats, and embassy workers need good intercultural communication skills in order to establish successful international relationships between their country and the other countries of the world. A diplomat or government representative lacking an understanding of the theory and practice of intercultural communication can do more harm than good when it comes to establishing and maintaining formal country-to-country relationships.

Figure 1.17 Diplomats and government representatives need good intercultural communication skills.

7. World Peace

Technology has its dark side. In the twentieth century, in addition to advances in transportation and communication technologies, there were also great "improvements" in war technologies. In WW I and WW II, human beings created weapons of destruction that efficiently killed and maimed millions upon millions of people. Hostile relationships within and among the nations of the modern world should be of great concern to anyone not wanting to see WW III. Establishing and maintaining good international relationships through effective intercultural communication is an important component of world peace.

Figure 1.18 People who want to avoid WW III care about effective intercultural communication.

8. Social Welfare and Social Justice

Social workers and social activists are drawn to the field of Intercultural Communication because they want to make sure that the voices of disenfranchised and oppressed cultural groups can be heard and that more powerful and privileged cultural groups truly listen to the messages that can promote social reform. Their desire for social justice makes them truly passionate about intercultural communication.

© EvrenKalinbacak, 2014. Used under license from Shutterstock, Inc.

Figure 1.19   Social activists use intercultural communication skills to give a voice to oppressed peoples.

9. Immigration and Domestic Diversity

The inscription in the pedestal of the Statue of Liberty that stands on Liberty Island in New York harbor reads, in part, "Give me your tired, your poor, your huddled masses yearning to be free. . . ." America is largely a nation of immigrants, so although the US is geographically isolated (with only two bordering countries), we Americans need good intercultural communication skills because of our great domestic diversity. We do not have to travel to other countries or become diplomats to engage in intercultural communication: many of us engage in intercultural communication every day with our neighbors, coworkers, and customers who have roots in, and ties to, other countries and national cultures.

© iko, 2014. Used under license from Shutterstock, Inc.

Figure 1.20   Many Americans engage in intercultural communication every day with their neighbors, coworkers, and customers.

10. Effective Healthcare Communication

Due to America's great domestic diversity, your health, even your very life, depends on effective intercultural communication. Many US doctors, nurses, and other healthcare workers have immigrated from other countries, and many patients are first- and second-generation immigrants. Different cultural beliefs, values, and practices related to health and healthcare make intercultural communication skills crucial for healthcare workers and proactive patients who want to effectively manage their healthcare experiences.

Figure 1.21 Your health, even your very life, depends on effective intercultural communication.

11. Communication Between Co-Cultures

You learned earlier in this chapter that in addition to about 200 national cultures, thousands of co-cultures exist. Although the interactions between different national cultures were the initial impetus for the development of the Intercultural Communication field, many of the insights that have been gained by observing the interactions between national cultures can also be applied to interactions between co-cultures. The concepts and skills developed in the field of Intercultural Communication that allow you to understand and improve your interactions with people from other countries can also be used to help you understand and improve your interactions with people who belong to different co-culture groups.

12. Enhanced Interpersonal Relationships

Because the world has become so much smaller through the mixing and intermingling of different cultural groups, people increase their chances of finding fulfilling interpersonal relationships when they become effective intercultural communicators. When people become more adept in their intercultural interactions, they can enlarge their circle of foreign friends. If they learn to break down cultural barriers, they may even find the romantic partners they have been seeking. (We explore intercultural communication in the dating context in Chapter 10.)

Figure 1.22 Better intercultural communication increases your chance of romantic success.

13. Increased Sensitivity to Others

Employees in companies are sometimes required to take "sensitivity training": much of this training is connected to the theories and concepts developed in the field of Intercultural Communication. In addition to enhancing interpersonal relationships, Intercultural Communication studies can also increase people's sensitivity to how they think about, talk about, and treat people who are different from themselves. In other words, Intercultural Communication studies can help decrease bigotry and prejudice. (We focus on stereotyping, ethnocentrism, prejudice, and discrimination in the following chapter.)

14. Increased Self-Awareness

Many people enter into Intercultural Communication studies hoping to learn about other cultures, but in addition to knowledge about other cultures, Intercultural Communication studies provide people with a much better understanding of their own culture. Effective Intercultural Communication studies transform unconscious cultural influences into conscious self-awareness. As people learn about the different beliefs, values, and practices of other cultures, they become aware of the deep-seated beliefs and values of their own culture, and of how these beliefs and values have influenced their own attitudes and behaviors.

15. Greater Ability to Avoid Embarrassing Situations

Some people want to study Intercultural Communication not for the grand goals of world peace and social justice, but for the much more modest goal of avoiding embarrassing intercultural situations. Intercultural Communication textbooks usually contain many anecdotes and examples of the social faux pas that occur when people are unaware of different cultural rituals and expectations. Studying Intercultural Communication decreases the likelihood that people will make fools of themselves during intercultural interactions.

Now that you have read through the 15 reasons for studying and caring about intercultural communication, what are your top reasons for studying Intercultural Communication and for improving your intercultural communication skills? If you keep these reasons in mind, you should have plenty of internal motivation and drive to propel you forward in your own study and practice of intercultural communication.

Becoming More Cosmopolitan

In addition to the 15 reasons we have provided for studying and caring about Intercultural Communication, I will now present one reason why I am personally motivated to teach Intercultural Communication: one of my pedagogical objectives is to make my students more "cosmopolitan."

Before reading this textbook, you may have associated the term "cosmopolitan" with an alcoholic beverage (a cocktail made with vodka, cranberry juice, and lime juice) or with a woman's magazine (given its modern format by American editor Helen Gurley Brown in the 1960s and now published in many international editions by Hearst Magazine).

After reading this chapter, you will also associate this term with its original ancient Greek roots. The term "cosmopolitan" is a compound word formed from the Greek words "cosmos" (meaning "world" or "universe") and "polites" (meaning "citizen"). In the Greek language, a "cosmopolitan" is a person who, like Diogenes the Cynic, identifies themselves as a "citizen of the world."

George Santayana (a Spanish-American philosopher and poet) expressed a cosmopolitan notion when he said, "A man's feet (sic)

Figure 1.23   A "cosmopolitan" is more than a cocktail or a woman's magazine.

must be planted in his own country, but his eyes should survey the world." I want my students to become more cosmopolitan and to accept the idea that all human beings are citizens in a single world community. This idea really hit home in the late 1960s when astronauts traveled to outer space and sent back pictures of our planet—for the first time in human history, human beings literally saw that they were travelers on "spaceship earth" hurtling through the solar system.

Figure 1.24 All human beings are traveling through the universe on spaceship earth.

We are citizens of our respective countries, but we are also part of the human family that inhabits various regions of the globe. Because dual citizenship is possible, patriotism and cosmopolitanism are not incompatible: you can be a proud citizen of your home country, but you can also be a (figurative) citizen of the world. As you study and learn about the national cultures of the world in order to become a more effective intercultural communicator, you can also become a citizen of the world who is concerned about international, worldwide issues.

For several years I have asked the students in my Intercultural Communication courses to turn in brief handouts that contain what they think is the essential information a human being needs to know in order to become more cosmopolitan. The following Cosmopolitan Primer is based, in part, on their research and thought. This primer is designed to give you the basic information you need to be an informed citizen of the world. Numbers have been rounded off. Use the Primer to learn some of the very basic facts and issues a person should know in order to develop a worldwide vision.

A Cosmopolitan Primer

Facts About the Planet We All Share: Earth is the third planet from the sun. Its average distance from the sun is about 93,000,000 miles, and it takes about 575,000,000 miles and 365.25 days to complete its solar orbit. It is tilted on its axis at about 23.5 degrees, which creates the seasons. It revolves on its axis in about 24 hours, which creates night and day. It has one large satellite, the moon, which orbits the earth in approximately 28 days. The moon's gravitational pull creates earth's tides. The earth is about 8,000 miles in diameter, and its circumference is about 25,000 miles. Part of earth's core is molten, resulting in volcanic activity. About 30% of the earth is covered by land and 70% of the earth is covered by water. The earth has seven major continents (Africa, America, Asia, Australia/Oceania, Europe, North America, and South America) and five major oceans (Arctic, Atlantic, Indian, Pacific, and Southern). Three percent of earth's water is fresh, and 2% of this fresh water is frozen in glaciers. The earth has two large polar climates and a wide equatorial band of tropical to subtropical climates. The atmosphere of the earth is 77% nitrogen, 21% oxygen, 1% argon, and 1% water vapor. Free oxygen is created by earth's flora, allowing for the sustainability of life. Earth is the only planet in the solar system known to contain liquid water, moving tectonics plates, and biological life forms.

Facts About the People Groups Who Inhabit Our Planet: Large ancient human civilizations arose in fertile river areas that allowed for extensive agriculture. Although traditional racial groups are associated

(Continued)

with geographic areas (American Indian/Americas, Asian/Asia, Black/Africa, Pacific Islander/Pacific Islands, and White/Europe), different racial and ethnic groups have spread and intermingled (to greater and lesser extents) through voluntary and involuntary migration (colonization, exploration, diasporas, and so on). In the modern world, human beings have organized themselves into large, self-governing nations (or countries) with geographic borders. There are about 200 countries (and 200 national cultures) in the modern world (54 in Africa, 44 in Asia, 14 in Australia/Oceania, 47 in Europe, 23 in North America, and 12 in South America). The major languages and religions of the world extend beyond national borders. Although there are about 6,000 spoken human languages, half the world population speaks the 13 most spoken languages (Mandarin, Spanish, English, Hindi, Arabic, Portuguese, Bengali, Russian, Japanese, Punjabi, German, Javanese, and Wu). The major world religions are Christianity, Islam, Hinduism, Buddhism, Confucianism, Taoism, Sikhism, Judaism, Baha'i Faith, Jainism, and Shintoism. About $1/7^{th}$ of the total world population (1 billion people) are secular/nonreligious/agnostic/atheist. Two of the most important facts of modern history are human population growth and the rise of modern science and technology. First, the human population of the earth has increased dramatically in the last 200 years: 1820, 1 billion; 1930, 2 billion; 1960, 3 billion; 1974, 4 billion; 1988, 5 billion; 2000, 6 billion; 2013, 7 billion. At the current growth rate, the human population would double to 14 billion by the year 2075. Second, although art, religion, and philosophy have been a part of human civilization for thousands of years, modern science and technology have just come on the scene in the last few hundred years. Science and technology can help humanity to solve some of the problems associated with human population growth, but they have also created new problems like weapons of mass destruction.

WorldWide, International Issues and Concerns: Border disputes, crime syndicates, depletion of forest areas and wetlands, depletion of nonrenewable resources, disease and pandemics, drug trafficking, economic instability, energy shortages, ethnic conflicts, extinction of animal and plant species, food hording and food shortages, fresh water shortages, genocide, global climate change, human rights abuses, human trafficking, illiteracy, industrial disasters (chemical spills, oil spills, nuclear plant meltdowns),international conflicts, loss of vegetation (deforestation, desertification, overgrazing), malnutrition, natural disasters (earthquakes, floods, meteor strikes, solar flares, tsunamis, volcanic eruptions), pollution (air, water, and soil), poverty, prejudice and discrimination, proliferation of weapons of mass destruction, severe weather (cyclones, droughts, hurricanes), social injustice, soil degradation and erosion, terrorism, unequal distribution of wealth, and war.

Attitudes and Attributes to Become a Citizen of the World: Compassion, courage, creativity, curiosity, empathy, honesty, humility, intelligence, kindness, knowledge, openness, respect, self-discipline, sense of responsibility, sensitivity, tolerance, vision, and wisdom.

Actions to Take:
- Acknowledge and appreciate the similarities and differences between people and cultures.
- Actively work to make the world a better place. (Join an international non-governmental organization. Serve in the Peace Corps. Participate in a micro-lending program.)
- Communicate and interact with people from other cultures. (Find a foreign pen pal. Host an exchange student. Study abroad. Travel.)
- Immerse yourself in other cultures to better understand, appreciate, and empathize with the peoples of the world. (Eat food from around the world. Listen to music from around the world. Read books written by authors from different parts of the world. Watch movies and television shows from around the world.)
- Inform yourself by reading news sources from different countries.

- Learn to read, to write, and to communicate verbally and nonverbally with others. Also learn how to use modern communication technologies that will allow you to more easily communicate with people in other countries.
- Learn one or more foreign languages.
- Learn from wise people, and pass on what you learn to others.
- Listen carefully and deeply.
- Obey the just laws of your country, and work to change those which are unjust.
- Resist and react against ethnocentrism, xenophobia, intolerance, prejudice, and discrimination.
- Suspend judgment when learning about different cultural worldviews and values.

Actions to Avoid:
- Do not assume that your culture is superior to or better than other cultures.
- Do not perpetuate stereotypes or negative judgments of people or cultures based on stereotypes.
- Do not use unnecessary force or violence to gain your objectives or to get your way.
- Do not verbally or physically abuse others.

An Important Cosmopolitan Document: The United Nations' Universal Declaration of Human Rights. Visit http://www.un.org/en/documents/udhr/

Evaluating Intercultural Communication Competence

As you begin to consciously think about your intercultural interactions, you need some conceptual tools to help you analyze and evaluate the effectiveness of your intercultural communication. We will present to you three different evaluative tools you can use to assess your intercultural communication competence: 1) the AACU Intercultural Knowledge and Competence VALUE Rubric, 2) the Intercultural Effectiveness Scale by the Kozai Group, and 3) the Developmental Model of Intercultural Sensitivity or The Bennett Scale, developed by Dr. Milton Bennett.

Since the Developmental Model of Intercultural Sensitivity emphasizes difference, and since Chapter 2 focuses on appreciating both sameness and difference, we will introduce the Bennett Scale in the second chapter of this textbook. We will end this first chapter with brief introductions to, and explanations of, the AACU VALUE Rubric and the Intercultural Effectiveness Scale (or IES) by the Kozai Group. These evaluative tools will guide you in the evaluation and development of your intercultural communication skills, attitudes, and knowledge areas.

The AACU VALUE Rubric

In 2008 and 2009, the Association of American Colleges and Universities had Rubric Development Teams develop rubrics to help evaluate essential learning outcomes in undergraduate general education areas. The project was called VALUE, Valid Assessment of Learning in Undergraduate Education. The Intercultural Knowledge and Competence Rubric was developed by lead faculty in Intercultural Communication representing colleges and universities from around the nation. It is based in part on Milton Bennett's Developmental Model of Intercultural Sensitivity and D.K. Deardorff's intercultural framework.

The rubric is intended for institutional-level assessment of student learning, but can be modified and used at the campus, discipline, and course level. It is composed of two knowledge areas, two skill areas, and two attitude areas. In addition, for each area, the rubric places students at a benchmark level (level 1, the lowest level), two milestone levels (levels 2 and 3), and a capstone level (level 4, the highest level). Individuals can be assigned a score of zero if they have not yet reached the benchmark level.

The full Intercultural Knowledge and Competence Rubric is posted on the official AACU website (visit www.aacu.org/value/rubrics/pdf/InterculturalKnowledge.pdf). One strength of the AACU VALUE Rubric is that it distills down into six areas the essential knowledge, skills, and attitudes you need to be an effective intercultural communicator. Here are the six areas, with a summary of the "capstone level" description on the rubric:

> **Knowledge area: Cultural self-awareness** (Can articulate insights into one's own cultural rules and biases).
>
> **Knowledge area: Knowledge of cultural worldview frameworks** (Has a sophisticated understanding of the complex elements important to members of other cultures in relation to their history, values, beliefs, and practices).
>
> **Skill area: Empathy** (Can interpret intercultural experiences from the perspective of different worldviews and can act in a supportive manner that recognizes the thoughts and emotions of other cultural groups).
>
> **Skill area: Verbal and nonverbal communication** (Has a complex understanding of cultural differences in verbal and nonverbal communication and is able to skillfully negotiate a shared understanding based on these differences).
>
> **Attitude area: Curiosity** (Asks complex questions about other cultures and seeks out answers to these questions that reflect multiple cultural perspectives).
>
> **Attitude area: Openness** (Initiates and develops intercultural interactions with others and suspends judgment when analyzing and evaluating these interactions).

If you understand the terminology and descriptions on the VALUE Rubric, you have six specific areas you can consider when you evaluate your own intercultural communication competence or the competence of others.

Six Areas of Intercultural Communication Competence	
Knowledge Area #1:	Knowledge of your own culture
Knowledge Area #2:	Knowledge of other cultures
Skill Area #1:	Empathy
Skill Area #2:	Verbal/Nonverbal communication
Attitude Area #1:	Curiosity
Attitude Area #2:	Openness

Figure 1.25   Six areas of evaluation suggested in the AACU VALUE Rubric for Intercultural Knowledge and Competence.

The Intercultural Effectiveness Scale by The Kozai Group

The Intercultural Effectiveness Scale (IES) is an assessment tool that evaluates the competencies that are critical for effective interaction with people from other cultures. The instrument is used primarily by nonprofit organizations and educational institutions. The IES is administered by The Kozai Group (visit www.kozaigroup.com/inventories/the-intercultural-effectiveness-scale/).

The assessment consists of a series of questions about yourself that you answer based on your perception of your own behaviors. You do not need to prepare for the assessment. To get accurate results, you just answer the questions as honestly as you can.

The IES focuses on three dimensions of intercultural effectiveness, 1) Continuous Learning, 2) Interpersonal Engagement, and 3) Hardiness. Each of these three areas is further broken down into two subcategories. The IES breaks down the dimension of Continuous Learning into the subcategories of Self-Awareness and Exploration. The dimension of Interpersonal Engagement is broken down into the subcategories of Global Mindset and Relationship Interest. The dimension of Hardiness is broken down into the subcategories of Positive Regard and Emotional Resilience.

For each dimension area, and for each subcategory, you are assigned a score of low (1 or 2), medium (3 or 4), or high (5 or 6). All of these scores are added together to yield your overall IES score. In addition, the IES describes eight different profiles that can be mapped out on a profile graph. After filling out the profile graph, you will be able to identify the particular type of intercultural communicator you are.

If you take the IES, you will receive an individual feedback report that will give you your overall intercultural effectiveness score, your score in each dimension area and each subcategory area, explanations of each score and what it means, your intercultural profile, and a personal development plan for improving your intercultural communication effectiveness. The personal development plan provided by The Kozai Group lets you identify your weakest areas of intercultural effectiveness and develop an action plan to strengthen those areas.

The IES is one of many tools available for assessing intercultural communication competence, but it provides you with some objective results that have been averaged with the data of thousands of other participants. A strength of the IES is that it gives you a more objective evaluation of your intercultural communication effectiveness by a third party.

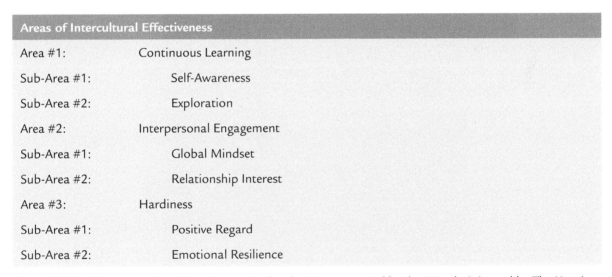

Areas of Intercultural Effectiveness	
Area #1:	Continuous Learning
Sub-Area #1:	Self-Awareness
Sub-Area #2:	Exploration
Area #2:	Interpersonal Engagement
Sub-Area #1:	Global Mindset
Sub-Area #2:	Relationship Interest
Area #3:	Hardiness
Sub-Area #1:	Positive Regard
Sub-Area #2:	Emotional Resilience

Figure 1.26   Three areas (and six sub-areas) of evaluation suggested by the IES administered by The Kozai Group.

Comparing the AACU VALUE Rubric and the IES

There are many different things that you could focus on when evaluating your intercultural communication competence. When I attended a workshop on evaluating intercultural communication competence, the workshop leaders asked me and the other workshop participants to make a list of the characteristics of an effective intercultural communicator. In 20 minutes, we generated a list of about 50 different characteristics or traits!

The AACU VALUE Rubric and the IES administered by The Kozai Group help us to quickly identify some of the most important characteristics or traits of an effective intercultural communicator. First, we should note the overlap between the two evaluation tools. Both the AACU VALUE rubric and the IES point out the importance of knowing about your own culture and knowing about other cultures. You need to develop self-awareness of your own cultural beliefs, values, and practices, and you need to understand and appreciate the beliefs, values, and practices of other cultures.

Both evaluation tools also emphasize that intercultural communication competence goes beyond possessing knowledge and skills—a large part of intercultural communication competence relates to your attitudes. The VALUE Rubric points out that you need to develop your verbal and nonverbal communication skills and your ability to empathize with others, but it also highlights the need for the attitudes of curiosity and openness. The IES points out that you need self-awareness and the awareness of other cultures that come from a global mindset, but it also emphasizes that you need to have an interest in relationships, positive regard for the people with whom you interact, and emotional resilience to bounce back when intercultural interactions do not go smoothly.

To develop the knowledge, skills, and attitudes you need to be an effective intercultural communicator, you must do more than read this textbook. This textbook presents theories, concepts, and facts related to intercultural communication, and if you read it carefully, you will gain a lot of important knowledge. However, to develop intercultural communication skills, and to develop the attitudes you need for effective intercultural communication, you need to engage with people from other cultures. Intercultural communication is an *activity*. Thank you for reading this chapter carefully, and thank you in advance for the attention you will pay to the chapters that follow. We appreciate your desire to learn from us and from this textbook. However, much of your intercultural communication competence will be developed when you put this textbook aside and enter into intercultural interactions and conversations.

© a katz, 2014. Used under license from Shutterstock, Inc.

Figure 1.27 To progress as an intercultural communicator, you must have intercultural experiences.

We wish you great success in your development as an intercultural communicator. As you engage with people from other cultures, let us suggest a few more attributes and character traits not mentioned by the AACU VALUE Rubric or the IES. Be courageous, and initiate conversations and dialogues with others despite your fears. Be patient and forgiving, both with yourself and with others. Communication is difficult, and intercultural communication is especially difficult. Finally, develop a good sense of humor. Missteps and faux pas are likely to occur when you attempt to communicate with people who are substantially different than yourself. Having the ability to laugh at yourself can make even embarrassing situations enjoyable.

Competent intercultural communicators, you now know, are courageous, curious, empathetic, forgiving, open, patient, resilient people who are interested in relationships, have positive regard for others, and possess the ability to laugh at themselves.

Summary

After reading this chapter, you now have a solid foundation for your study and practice of intercultural communication. You have a basic vocabulary for discussing the connection between culture and communication. You have gained a deeper understanding of culture by learning some elements of culture, some similes for culture, and some characteristics of culture. You now know the general history of the study of culture and the specific history of the study of intercultural communication. You know 15 reasons why people study and care about intercultural communication, you know some basic facts that can help you become more cosmopolitan, and you know the important knowledge, skills, and attitudes you need to be an effective intercultural communicator. You are on solid footing to begin building intercultural relationships and skills.

Glossary

Acculturation   A process in which members of one culture adopt the beliefs, values, or behaviors of another cultural group.

Attitudes   Settled ways of thinking and feeling that are usually manifested in a person's behaviors.

Behaviors   The ways people in a culture act or react to internal or external stimuli. Behaviors are the observable elements of culture; what we see or hear other people do.

Beliefs   Ideas that are held to be true or real. Beliefs are at the core of human culture because they generate the values, attitudes, and behaviors of human beings.

Co-culture   An interdependent but equal cultural group that exists in a dominant or national culture. In intercultural studies, this term has come to replace the term "subculture."

Communication   The process of sending and receiving messages through verbal or nonverbal symbols.

Cosmopolitanism   The idea that all human beings are citizens in a single world community.

Cultural artifacts   Objects made by human beings that give information about a culture.

Culture   Learned beliefs, values, attitudes, and behaviors that bind a group of people together.

Curiosity   The desire to learn and know more about something or someone. One of the two essential attitudes for competent intercultural communicators identified by the AACU VALUE Rubric.

Deep-structure institutions   The social organizations of family, church, and state that have created, transmitted, maintained, and reinforced the basic elements of every traditional culture.

Dominant culture   (Also called *umbrella culture* or *mainstream culture*) The culture created by those who have the greatest influence on the beliefs, values, and customs of a people group.

Emotional resilience   The ability to cope with stress and adversity. One of the subcategories of effective intercultural communication identified by the IES.

Empathy   The ability to understand and relate to the thoughts and feelings of others. One of two essential skills of competent intercultural communicators identified by the AACU VALUE Rubric.

Enculturation   The process whereby people learn their group's culture through observation and instruction. Enculturation begins at a very early age.

Family   One of the three primary deep-structure institutions that transmit and maintain cultural beliefs, values, and behaviors. A fundamental social group usually consisting of one or two parents and their children.

Globalization   The tendency toward worldwide integration of economic and communication systems.

Intercultural communication   Communication between people from substantially different cultural groups. Intercultural communication occurs when people from different national cultures interact, but it also occurs within a single society when people from different co-cultures interact.

Language   The system of words and signs that people use to communicate thoughts and feelings. Language is a foundational element of culture. Human culture would not exist without human language.

Popular culture   Cultural products and artifacts that are widely disseminated and consumed, including television shows, movies, recorded music, video clips, and many other mass media products.

National culture   The common beliefs, values, and behaviors that exist within the population of a sovereign nation.

Openness   Receptiveness to new or different ideas, experiences, and people. One of the two essential attitudes of competent intercultural communicators identified by the AACU VALUE Rubric.

Positive Regard   Basic acceptance, support, and respect of other people. One of the subcategories of effective intercultural communication identified by the IES.

Subculture   A subgroup within a larger culture that often has beliefs or behaviors that differ from the dominant culture. The term *co-culture* avoids the negative connotation of inferiority attached to the prefix "sub," so *co-culture* is now the preferred term in intercultural studies.

Values   Important beliefs shared by the members of a culture about what is good or bad, desirable or undesirable, important or unimportant.

Chapter 2

Appreciating Both Sameness and Difference

Mark Staller

Chapter Learning Objectives

1. Recognize two contrasting approaches for dealing with people and cultures: focusing on sameness and focusing on difference.
2. Understand the role that cognitive restructuring can play in developing intercultural communication competence.
3. Learn to appreciate sameness and difference by understanding the positive consequences of both and the negative consequences of overemphasizing either.
4. Learn to balance between contrasting or complementary concepts or values.
5. Understand and explain the difference between valid generalizations and invalid stereotypes.
6. Develop an awareness of the negative effects of stereotypes, ethnocentrism, prejudice, and discrimination.
7. Recognize the symptoms and stages of culture shock, and develop the capacity to adjust to new and different cultural experiences.

© Rawpixel, 2014. Used under license from Shutterstock, Inc.

Chapter Pretest

Sameness   **Difference**

⬅━━━➡

When interacting with other human beings and with people from other cultures, what is most important, focusing on similarities (sameness) or differences (difference)? Place an "x" on the line above to indicate which of these basic elements you value the most. If you value sameness and difference equally, place your "x" in the middle of the line. The stronger your preference for one of these basic elements, the farther your "x" should be placed to the left end or the right end of the line.

Introduction

Did you complete the chapter pretest above? If you do not want to mark up your textbook, please use your power of imagination to mentally place the requested "x" on the sameness/difference continuum. Before you read this chapter, we want you to carefully consider how much you value sameness and how much you value difference.

This chapter begins by contrasting the United Nations' Universal Declaration of Human Rights (UDHR) to the Developmental Model of Intercultural Sensitivity (DMIS) in order to point out two different approaches to human interactions that focus on sameness and difference, respectively. After asking which approach is most fruitful, we assert that a sophisticated understanding of people and cultures requires the recognition and appreciating of *both* sameness and difference.

After explaining how cognitive restructuring can help people develop an appreciation for contrasting or complementary concepts and values, we then demonstrate how cognitive restructuring works in practice by attempting to develop in you, our reader, the appreciation of both sameness and difference that we recommend.

First, we use the positive approach and present five reasons to appreciate sameness and five reasons to appreciate difference. Second, we use the negative approach and point out five negative consequences of privileging sameness at the expense of difference and five negative consequences of privileging difference at the expense of sameness. (You will learn that an overemphasis on either sameness or difference can lead to unfortunate consequences like culture shock, xenophobia, stereotyping, ethnocentrism, prejudice, and discrimination.) Third, we present five examples that will help you balance between an appreciation of sameness and an appreciation of difference.

If you agree with the observations and arguments made in this chapter, after reading this chapter you should have a balanced appreciation for both sameness and difference, and you will be motivated to pay attention to both the similarities and differences between people and cultures.

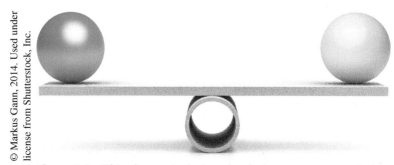

© Markus Gann, 2014. Used under license from Shutterstock, Inc.

Figure 2.1   This chapter is designed to balance your appreciation for sameness with your appreciation for difference.

The "Sameness" Approach (The United Nations' Universal Declaration of Human Rights)

The Universal Declaration of Human Rights (UDHR) was adopted by the United Nations General Assembly on December 10, 1948. After the atrocities of World War II, members of the United Nations felt it was important to clarify the fundamental human rights that they pledged to uphold in the United Nations Charter. The UDHR contains a preamble that begins with the assertion that the recognition of universal, inalienable rights of all members of the human family ". . . is the foundation of freedom, justice, and peace in the world," and ends with the assertion that the UDHR sets ". . . a common standard of achievement for all peoples and all nations."

The UDHR is a great example of an important international document that espouses moral universalism and asserts that every human being has the same rights and responsibilities. In Article 1, the UDHR claims that all human beings are endowed with reason and conscience and that they ". . . should act toward one another in a spirit of brotherhood." In Article 2, it makes clear that everyone is entitled to all the rights and freedoms set forth in the Declaration, ". . . without distinction of any kind." The UDHR emphasizes, again and again, that the differences among people have no effect on their common rights, freedoms, and responsibilities.

In the 28 articles that follow the first 2, the declaration sets forth the universal rights that pertain to all human beings, including the right to life, liberty, and the security of person (Article 3), the right to freedom of movement (Article 13), the right to a nationality (Article 15), the right to marry (Article 16), the right to own property (Article 17), the right to work (Article 23), the right to rest and leisure (Article 24), and the right to education (Article 26). (The full text of the UDHR can be found at the official UN website. Visit http://www.un.org/en/documents/udhr/.)

The UDHR is one of the most translated documents in the world. It is referenced in most national constitutions written after 1948, and it plays a foundational role in international law. Although the countries of the world have different national cultures, those countries that have ratified the UDHR recognize that all persons have a common humanity and the same fundamental human rights and freedoms.

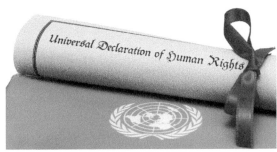

© Corgarashu, 2014. Used under license from Shutterstock, Inc.

Figure 2.2 The UDHR emphasizes what is the same about human beings.

The "Difference" Approach (The Developmental Model of Intercultural Sensitivity)

The Developmental Model of Intercultural Sensitivity (or The Bennett Scale) was developed by Dr. Milton Bennett (a founder of the Intercultural Communication Institute) in the late 1980s and 1990s. The DMIS provides a way to evaluate a person's progress in developing effective intercultural communication attitudes and behaviors. We give a fuller explanation of The Bennett Scale in Chapter 8 (where we focus on cultural adaptation), but we introduce it here because it emphasizes the importance of dealing with difference.

Bennett sets up a six-stage model to help track the progress (or regress) a person makes when interacting with people from different cultures. Bennett labels steps 1 to 3 "ethnocentric" stages and steps 4 to 6 "ethnorelative" stages. As a person encounters people from other cultures and learns to deal with the differences between cultures, he or she (hopefully) makes some progress through these different stages of sensitivity. Here are the six stages, from lowest to highest:

The Six Stages of Intercultural Sensitivity

6. Integration of difference.

5. Adaptation to difference.

4. Acceptance of difference.

3. Minimization of difference.

2. Defense of difference.

1. Denial of difference.

Figure 2.3   The Bennett Scale helps track a person's progress in dealing with difference.

Bennett claims that it can take months or years to progress from one stage of intercultural sensitivity to the next, so do not expect to reach the sixth stage (integration of difference) by the end of this one-semester course in Interpersonal Communication. However, The Bennett Scale provides even new students of Intercultural Communication with a conceptual model that emphasizes the importance of recognizing and appreciating difference.

© Anson0618, 2014. Used under license from Shutterstock, Inc.

The Best Approach

Figure 2.4   The DMIS emphasizes that difference must be recognized and appreciated.

The UDHR emphasizes what is the same about human beings, and the DMIS emphasizes the importance of recognizing the differences between people and cultures. Which approach is the best or most fruitful approach if you want to be an effective intercultural communicator and if you want to establish solid intercultural relationships? Should you emphasize and appreciate what people have in common (as the UDHR does), or should you focus on and appreciate the differences between people and cultures (as the DMIS does)?

Our answer: if you want a sophisticated understanding of people and cultures, if you want to build solid relationships with people from other cultures, and if you want to be a highly effective intercultural communicator, then **you should recognize and appreciate** *both* **sameness and difference,** *both* **similarities and differences.**

Merely recognizing similarities and differences between people and cultures is not good enough: you need to recognize and *appreciate* both sameness and difference. As you learned in Chapter 1, competent intercultural communicators need more than just knowledge and skill—they also need to develop appropriate attitudes. When dealing with sameness and difference, you need to develop an appreciative attitude for both—that is why this chapter is titled "*Appreciating* Both Sameness and Difference."

What can you do if you value and appreciate sameness more than difference, or difference more than sameness? Attitudes are defined in Chapter 1 as "settled ways of thinking and feeling." How can you change your negative attitude toward either sameness or difference if you deep down prefer one over the other? If you have settled ways of thinking and feeling about sameness and difference, then what can you do to develop an appreciation for both? In the next section, we describe a process called **cognitive restructuring** that can and does help people change their attitudes and behaviors.

Cognitive Restructuring

There are many therapeutic processes used in the field of psychology, but one of the most fruitful processes used in cognitive behavioral therapy is the process of cognitive restructuring. People with emotional or behavioral problems are taught to identify and dispute irrational or inaccurate thoughts that are causing emotional or behavioral dysfunctions. Once an irrational or inaccurate thought is identified, it can be replaced by a more rational, more accurate thought that can lead to more facilitative emotions and more beneficial behaviors.

For example, some people who have high public speaking anxiety are caught in a vicious cycle of negative speech performances based on negative thinking. They fear public speaking because they think they will give a terrible speech. Their negative thinking about "giving a terrible speech" becomes a self-fulfilling prophecy that increases their anxiety and actually causes them to perform poorly. With the help of a good speech coach, they can break the cycle of negative thinking and learn to envision themselves as competent speakers capable of delivering excellent speeches. Their new, positive thinking creates a mental environment that allows them to decrease their anxiety and to succeed in their public speaking efforts.

Reviewing the "iceberg simile" from Chapter 1 can help clarify the process of cognitive restructuring. In Chapter 1, we asserted that just as a large part of an iceberg is below the waterline, so a large part of culture is below the observable surface. We superimposed the four basic elements of culture—behaviors, attitudes, values, and beliefs—on an iceberg image.

We will repeat here what we said in Chapter 1 about the importance of beliefs: "At the core of a culture, often way below the conscious surface, are the master thoughts and beliefs that create the values, attitudes, and behaviors of a cultural group. Thoughts create feelings which lead to actions. In order to truly understand a culture at a deep level, you must reverse the process and observe actions in order to discover and uncover the underlying attitudes, values, and beliefs which create these behaviors."

The iceberg simile also applies to individual human minds: much of what we think and feel is below the conscious level. Although our thoughts create feelings which lead to behaviors, many of our thoughts and feelings (and even our behaviors) are unconscious. E.T. Hall and the earliest developers of Intercultural Communication studies realized that this was the case as they began to study nonverbal communication. People do not usually consciously think about how close they should stand to others or what expressions they should put on their faces. A large percentage of our nonverbal communication behaviors (and many other behaviors) are unconscious and motivated by unconscious thoughts, values, and attitudes.

People who study intercultural communication have the opportunity to become consciously aware of the thoughts, values, and attitudes that underlie and motivate the behaviors manifested by people from other cultures. With this deeper knowledge, they can fully adapt to other cultures not only by modifying their behaviors, but also by modifying their thoughts and values. They can consciously "reprogram" their minds and adopt the thoughts and values of other cultural groups. Instead of merely mimicking the behaviors of people in other cultural groups, they can enter into intercultural interactions with new ways of thinking that allow the correct cultural behaviors to flow naturally.

In cognitive behavioral therapy, cognitive restructuring usually involves replacing one thought with another thought: an irrational thought is replaced with a rational thought, or an untrue thought is replaced with a true thought. However, in intercultural interactions and intercultural communication, a different kind of cognitive restructuring needs to occur: instead of replacing one thought with another thought, you need to expand your mind and make room for more beliefs and values than the core beliefs and values operating in your home culture.

To become an effective intercultural communicator, you do not need to abandon or replace the core beliefs and values of your home culture, but you do need to supplement and enrich these beliefs and values with other ways of thinking about and

Figure 2.5   Effective intercultural communicators expand their minds in order to view the world in different ways.

viewing the world. If you are curious, you will want to learn about and know what makes other people tick. You will ask "Why do people in other cultures do what they do? What are the core beliefs and values that are driving their behaviors?" Openness to these beliefs and values will allow you to entertain these ideas and incorporate them into your own mind. Instead of having only one "operating system" to guide your behaviors and your interactions with others, you can develop multiple "operating systems" for different cultural interactions.

If what we are suggesting seems radical to you, then realize that you have been adjusting to different cultures and co-cultures your entire life. You were enculturated into your family culture at a very young age, but after a few years you entered into and became part of other co-cultures—your school culture, your church culture, your work culture, and so on. Sometimes the core beliefs and values of these different cultures or co-cultures conflicted or were in tension—what did you do then? If you did not abandon one culture for the sake of the other, you somehow learned to navigate between the two cultures and to integrate their conflicting or contrasting beliefs and values in your life and mind even though they were in tension.

In the remainder of this chapter, we will demonstrate that it is possible to integrate contrasting values by developing an appreciation for both sameness and difference. Sameness and difference are in opposition, but you do not have to choose between the two. You do not have to devalue sameness in order to value difference, or vice versa. You can (and should) value and appreciate both sameness and difference. We will first take the positive approach by presenting five reasons to appreciate sameness and five reasons to appreciate difference. We will focus your mind on sameness and difference at a very general level, and we will also focus specifically on similarities among, and differences between, people and cultures.

Five Reasons to Appreciate Sameness

REASON #1: Patterns and Pattern Recognition

Sameness is esthetically pleasing. As evidenced in much of our folk and traditional visual art, we humans enjoy making and viewing patterns. We like to combine shapes and colors in repeating patterns. Similarly, traditional musical pieces are built up out of repeating patterns that exploit tonal and rhythmic similarities.

In part, our appreciation for patterns arises from the fact that pattern recognition helps us to organize our experience and make sense of our world. If nothing was the same, if there were no underlying similarities, everything which exists, all reality, would be chaotic and incoherent.

Similarities among cultures help us organize our knowledge and understanding of the many different people groups in the world. Although there are distinctive, unique elements in almost every culture, there are also important similarities that provide an underlying coherence. Cultures can be contrasted for differences, but they can also be compared for similarities, and this search for sameness yields some fascinating cultural patterns.

Figure 2.6   Human beings enjoy making and viewing visual patterns, which repeat similar colors and shapes.

Here are four patterns to be aware of when studying the national cultures of the world. First, the countries of the world can be classified by their political or economic systems. Some countries are democracies, some are monarchies, and some are dictatorships. Some countries are capitalist, some are socialist, and some are communist. These political and economic systems can create similar values and behaviors in different countries.

Second, the countries of the world can be classified by their dominant religion(s). The majority of the human population is Christian in North and South America, Europe, Southern Africa, and Australia. The majority of the population is Muslim in the Middle East, Northern Africa, and Indonesia. The majority of the population is Hindu in India. The majority of the population is Buddhist in Eastern Asia. Thus, common religious beliefs and values bind many different people groups in many different countries together.

Third, the countries of the world can be classified by the East/West historical division. The people groups of the world consider themselves (and others) to be "eastern" or "western" depending on their geographical location or historical ties. There are important similarities among Eastern/Asian countries and Western/European countries. Many Western European countries have a history of colonialism, and the countries that they colonized in the "New World" have become part of the "western" historical tradition.

Fourth, the countries of the world can be classified by their Northern/Southern geographical locations. Similar cultural patterns can be found among very different countries depending on their distance from the equator. Countries closer to the equator are often high-contact countries, whereas countries farther from the equator are often low-contact countries. Countries closer to the equator often have populations that are more emotionally expressive, whereas countries farther from the equator often have populations that are more emotionally restrained. Countries closer to the equator often have populations that prefer softer rock music, whereas countries farther from the equator often have populations that prefer harder rock music.

Although there are close to 200 national cultures in our world, when you recognize similarities in political and economic systems, dominant religions, historical groupings, and geographical locations, you can gain general insights that help you to organize your understanding of these many different cultures.

REASON #2: Abstract Thought and Language

Our ability to recognize sameness makes abstract thought and human language possible. Human language is a symbol system, and in order for the symbol system to operate, and in order for meaning to be shared, the same symbol must be associated with the same object or element of reality. A powerful scene from the biographical movie *The Miracle Worker* illustrates the transformative power of human language. A young deaf and blind girl, Helen Keller, is unable to communicate with others, and she is trapped in an animal-like existence until she realizes that the finger-spelled word *w-a-t-e-r* her teacher has traced on the palm of her hand over and over is the language symbol for water. When Helen Keller realizes that the same language symbol can be used whenever she wants to refer to water, she gains the ability to share meaning and to communicate with others through language.

Helen Keller was able to make a generalization because of her ability to recognize sameness. An "inductive leap" occurs when a person realizes that two or more things always or often go together or can be associated together. Our ability to make generalizations about culture is possible because we recognize that different people share the same beliefs, values, and behaviors.

If people did not share the same beliefs, values, and behaviors, we would not be able to generalize about people groups. We would not be able to think or talk about "American" culture or "French" culture, or any other culture. However, because similarities do exist among the individuals that make up a cultural group, we can speak intelligently about the "national character" of the people who live in a country. Although we must be careful about how we apply them, we could not think or communicate about cultures without making such generalizations.

Figure 2.7 Helen Keller and her teacher are commemorated on a US postage stamp.

REASON #3: Stability and Predictability

Although the assertion "You are so predictable" is not usually a compliment, human beings want and need stability and predictability. For example, people return again and again to chain restaurants because they know what to expect—they know exactly how to order, they know how the food will be prepared, and they know exactly how the food will taste. They want and expect the same (or a very similar) experience each time they visit.

The desire for stability and predictability extends from our gastronomical lives to our social lives. Although cultures are dynamic and changing, they are also fairly stable and somewhat predictable because the same beliefs, values, and behaviors are passed from one generation of a culture to the next. Similarity in behavior over time creates cultural traditions and rituals that pass on cultural values. Thus, the "patterns of behavior" and "rules for living" enshrined in cultural traditions and rituals have some stability and longevity.

Figure 2.8 Chain restaurants illustrate our desire for stability and predictability.

Whereas genetics and DNA give some stability in the material existence of human beings, enduring beliefs and values give some stability in the mental and social lives of human beings. Identical or similar gene sequences help to perpetuate the human species. Although genetic permutations are possible, the great majority of genes are replicated accurately with great precision. Similarly, cultural rituals and traditions help to perpetuate human cultures. Although human beliefs and values can be modified, the great majority of cultural beliefs and values are passed from one generation to the next with amazing consistency.

REASON #4: Social Cohesion

The adoption of similar beliefs, values, and behaviors allows social cohesion to extend beyond families and clans. Culture is defined in Chapter 1 as ". . . learned beliefs, values, attitudes, and behaviors that *bind a group of people together*." When people hold the same beliefs and values, they are bound together not just by "blood ties," but also by mental or psychological ties. Individuals think of themselves as part of a greater social unit because they have beliefs and values in common with others.

Religion is one of the "deep structure" social institutions that promulgate culture. The word "religion" may be derived from a Latin root word meaning "to tie or bind." As the mass of humanity swirling around the Kabba in Mecca during the annual Muslim pilgrimage demonstrates, religious beliefs do not just cause divisions among people—religious beliefs, like other beliefs, unite many different people together into a community.

Figure 2.9 Beliefs unite people together into communities.

Now that social scientists have uncovered the foundations of culture—shared beliefs, values, attitudes, and behaviors—modern businesspeople have consciously engineered "company cultures" by creating company mottos, mascots, and mission statements that bind their employees together and give them a common company identity. When the same beliefs, values, and behaviors are adopted, social groups are formed and strengthened.

REASON #5: Equality and Human Rights

As we pointed out earlier in this chapter, the UDHR demonstrates that social justice relies on the concept of a common humanity that shares the same rights and responsibilities. Although people are very different, they all share the same "inalienable" rights, rights which are absolute and cannot be taken or given away.

Article 7 of the UDHR asserts that ". . . all are entitled to equal protection against any discrimination in violation of this Declaration and against any incitement to such discrimination." In other words, the UDHR is asserting that people deserve the same treatment under the law: no one deserves to be treated differently, and no one should be subjected to different treatment. When it comes to human rights and social justice, a focus on sameness, not difference, is paramount.

Figure 2.10 A focus on sameness is paramount for human rights and social justice.

Now that we have given you five reasons to appreciate sameness, we will present to you five reasons to appreciate difference.

Five Reasons to Appreciate Difference

REASON #1: Diversity and Variety

Sameness is esthetically pleasing, but so is difference. Difference provides us with diversity and variety, and we humans take great delight in variety. We listen to different music for our different moods, we are entertained by watching "variety" shows, and we take pleasure in sampling foods with different tastes and textures.

Human beings are fascinated by difference. Exoticism (not to be confused with eroticism) is a recognized movement in art and fashion to appropriate what is different (often through "cultural borrowing"). Exoticism is sometimes defined as "the charm of the unfamiliar." We humans enjoy the contrast and stimulation that difference provides.

For example, in the 18th and 19th centuries, Europeans were fascinated both by the old "exotic" cultures of the East (in a revival of Orientalism) and by the newly discovered cultures of the Pacific islands. Many Europeans in this age of discovery were greatly interested in learning about Pacific cultures that had different ways of thinking about, and different ways of living in, the world. In the 21st century, interest in the diverse cultures of the world survives and thrives.

© Ritu Manjo Jethani, 2014. Used under license from Shutterstock, Inc.

Figure 2.11   American tourists enjoy learning about "exotic" Polynesian cultures.

REASON #2: Creative Thinking

Difference should be appreciated because creative thinking involves combining old ideas and concepts in new and different ways. The creative brainstorming process developed by advertising executive Alex Osborn in the 1940s and 1950s and widely used in modern business and industry emphasizes the generation of many different ideas, and brainstormers are given special recognition for coming up with the most unique ideas.

In the field of small group problem solving, researchers have discovered that diverse small groups get better results than small groups composed of very similar members. When different people with

© kentoh, 2014. Used under license from Shutterstock, Inc.

Figure 2.12   Cross-cultural collaboration fosters innovation and creative thinking.

different perspectives are brought together, they solve problems more creatively and more effectively than "homogenous" small groups lacking diversity.

On a larger societal scale, when different regional or national cultures mix together, these cross-cultural interactions are often fertile ground for human innovation. Inventive, creative thinking is one of the results of recognizing and appreciating difference.

REASON #3: Change, Growth, and Progress

Cultures are stable and endure over time, but they are also dynamic—they are capable of change and growth. Difference makes change, growth, and progress possible. If everything stayed the same, nothing would ever change. Because situations and things can become different, they can improve over time.

Human beings are able to adapt to different environments and historical situations. In the modern world, our ability to think creatively has led to rapid change and progress due to advances in scientific knowledge and technology. Not every change is necessarily for the better, but civilizations would not be able to progress if people did not value and allow for difference, for new and different ways

Figure 2.13 Allowing for difference makes societal progress possible.

of thinking and living in the world. New, different ways of thinking and acting have created material and societal improvements.

REASON #4: Sensitivity and Positive Discrimination

The term "discrimination" is most often used to refer to the unfair, unjust treatment of people. However, the term "discrimination" has a positive meaning—it can be used to refer to a person's ability to make fine distinctions. The ability to recognize differences, especially small differences, leads to the highest levels of human knowledge and satisfaction. Experts in any knowledge area can make fine distinctions when others cannot even recognize a difference. Wine experts with "discriminating palates" can recognize subtle differences in varieties and vintages of wine. Art experts can recognize subtle differences in materials and methods that allow them to distinguish an art masterpiece from an art forgery. Expert linguists can recognize subtle differences in pronunciation and enunciation that allow them to pinpoint a person's regional affiliation.

Intercultural experts can make fine distinctions among the people groups that exist within a national or umbrella culture. For example, there are at least 56 different ethnic groups which exist in the nation of China, and there are over 250 ethnic groups in the African nation of Nigeria.

A person who cannot recognize significant cultural differences is considered to be ignorant and insensitive. For example, a person who groups all Asians together and cannot or does not distinguish between Chinese, Japanese, Korean, and other Asian cultures is lacking in basic cultural knowledge. Similarly, a person who cannot or does not distinguish between the many different nations and cultures on the African continent lacks basic powers of discrimination. The statement "They all look the same to me" indicates a lack of recognition and respect for important cultural differences.

© ArtWell, 2014. Used under license from Shutterstock, Inc.

Figure 2.14   There are 56 ethnic groups in the nation of China.

REASON #5: Individual Personhood

© Kichigin, 2014. Used under license from Shutterstock, Inc.

The recognition and appreciation of difference has to go all the way down to the individual level. Every one of the seven billion human beings that inhabit our planet, and every one of the human beings that has ever lived on the earth, is or has been unique. Although human beings share a lot of the same DNA, each individual person is a unique constellation of biological, cultural, and historical influences.

We value and respect other human beings not only because we share a common humanity, but also because we recognize their unique personhood—everyone is "one of a kind." We may have our physical "doppelgangers," but no two human beings are exactly alike, not even "identical" twins. Our different personal histories and personalities result in unique individuals that are given the status of "persons" rather than "things." Human beings are not interchangeable widgets: they are unduplicatable persons. If you value individual persons, you value difference.

Figure 2.15   Like snowflakes, every person is unique.

To develop in you an appreciation for both sameness and difference, we have first taken the positive approach: we have given you five reasons to appreciate sameness and five reasons to appreciate difference.

Reasons to Appreciate Sameness	Reasons to Appreciate Difference
1. Patterns and Pattern Recognition	1. Diversity and Variety
2. Abstract Thought and Language	2. Creative Thinking
3. Stability and Predictability	3. Change, Growth, and Progress
4. Social Cohesion	4. Sensitivity and Positive Discrimination
5. Equality and Human Rights	5. Individual Personhood

If you see the positive value in these 10 areas of human experience and existence, then you should appreciate both sameness and difference. Now that we have tried the positive approach in our attempt at cognitive restructuring, we will take the negative approach and point out the problems and difficulties that arise when people value and privilege sameness at the expense of difference, and when people value and privilege difference at the expense of sameness.

Problems Related to Privileging Sameness (At the Expense of Difference)

PROBLEM #1: Forced Uniformity and Conformity

A common plot device in science fiction stories involves replacing human beings with robots that can be programmed to provide uniform responses and services. Instead of pesky people who think for themselves and have the ability to act and react differently, the robots always function as they are programmed to function. In most science fiction stories, this robotic uniformity and conformity is an evil that must be overcome by humanity. A defining characteristic of human beings is our ability to think and act independently.

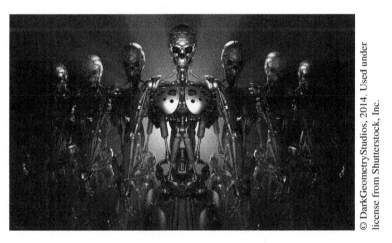

Figure 2.16   Complete uniformity and conformity is considered inhuman.

Repressive regimes that demand conformity and insist on uniform beliefs and behaviors are not just found in science fiction. An overemphasis on sameness can cause people and societies in the real world to mandate and force uniformity and conformity. Insisting on sameness at the expense of diversity leaves little room for nonconformists or eccentrics. Those who are different can be subjected to social pressures and punishments. At its worst, forced conformity can result in the elimination of those who deviate from the accepted norms, whether through incarceration, deportation, or execution.

PROBLEM #2: Monotonous Routine and Stagnation

An overemphasis on sameness can lead to monotonous routine and stagnation. In the business world, vibrant, energetic start-up companies that become successful can over time become "set in their ways," lose their edge, and stagnate. "We always do things this way" is an assertion that usually indicates a company is in trouble.

Similarly, cultures and societies that cannot or do not adapt to changing historical realities may decline and disappear. If the "rules for living" provided by a culture no longer apply, then the culture must adapt to the new realities faced by its members. Overemphasizing the need for sameness can prevent people and cultures from creating new traditions and making necessary changes in thought and behavior patterns.

PROBLEM #3: Stereotyping

Stereotypes are offensive because they assume sameness where sameness does not exist. When someone says "White people can't dance," the word "all" is implied: "(All) White people can't dance." If you are a white person who can bust a move and dance proficiently, your individual skill has been denied because you have been placed in the category of "Nondancing white people."

Even "positive" stereotypes are offensive, for the very same reason. When someone makes a positive assumption about a person based on a stereotype, they are still assuming sameness where sameness does not exist, and they are ignoring that person's individual personhood. Even the "positive" stereotype "(All) Asians are good at math" may be offensive to Asians, especially to Asians who are not good at math.

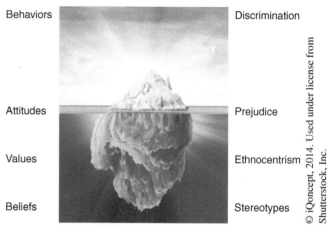

Figure 2.17   Stereotypes are at the heart of many bad attitudes and behaviors.

Stereotypes that assume sameness among a group of people are at the heart of many bad attitudes and behaviors. We will revisit the iceberg metaphor and image once more to clarify the relationship between stereotypes, ethnocentrism, prejudice, and discrimination. Stereotypes are false beliefs. These false beliefs can lead to ethnocentrism, the belief that one's own culture is superior to other cultures. Ethnocentrism can lead to prejudice, an unjustified attitude of dislike, disdain, and even hatred for other people. Prejudice often leads to discrimination, the unfair treatment of others.

Distinguishing Valid Generalizations from Invalid Stereotypes

As we pointed out earlier in this chapter, in order to talk about national cultures or co-cultures at all, you need to make generalizations about these cultures. For example, in order to talk about what Americans are like, you need to make statements or assertions that apply to the majority of Americans. And in order to talk about what American men and women are like, you need to make statements or assertions that apply to the majority of American men and women. If you could not make generalizations, you could not even begin to think or talk about cultures.

However, when you speak about characteristics or attributes that apply to a large group of people, it is very easy to fall into stereotyping. When talking about Americans, you may find yourself and others stereotyping people and saying things like "Americans are materialistic" or "Americans are religious." When talking about men and women, you may find yourself and others stereotyping people and saying things like "Men like to drink beer" and "Women like the color pink."

How can you talk about cultures without stereotyping people? You need to clearly distinguish valid generalizations from invalid stereotypes. There are two major differences. First, valid generalizations are qualified with words and phrases such as "most," "many," "the majority of," "often," "generally," and so on, whereas invalid stereotypes use or imply universal terms such as "all," "every," "always," "never," and so on.

When speaking about people groups or dominant cultures, make sure you qualify your generalizations and assertions with words like "most," "many," and "the majority of" in order to leave room for cultural "deviants"—people who violate the cultural norms and do not fit into the mental category you are creating. Generalizations about cultures are almost always a matter of probability, not certainty. Universal deductive thinking (the method used in classic Euclidian Geometry) is not a good model for thinking and talking about people and cultures. Individuals in a culture vary, and some will not be included in the generalizations you must construct in order to make sense of the world.

Second, valid generalizations are based upon evidence, whereas invalid stereotypes are assumed and applied without evidence. The valid generalization "Most Americans are acquisitive" can be backed up with plenty of evidence—just look at the plethora of material possessions found in the majority of American homes. However, even this valid generalization can lead to invalid stereotyping if it is applied to an individual American without any corroborating evidence. Just because Janice is an American, and just because most Americans are acquisitive, you should not *assume* that Janice is also acquisitive.

When you learn the general qualities or attributes of people in a culture or co-culture, do not apply these generalizations to an individual person without supporting evidence. For example, although it is true that many Japanese prefer to be indirect in conflict situations, you should not automatically assume that your classmate Yuriko prefers to be indirect in conflict situations merely because she is Japanese. Instead, you should use your general knowledge about Japanese culture as a starting point for interacting with Yuriko in a conflict situation: there is a good chance she prefers an indirect approach to conflict, but she may deviate from this cultural norm.

Remember, to avoid stereotyping, there are two steps you must take: 1) qualify your generalizations and assertions with words such as "most," "many," and "the majority of," and 2) do not apply a generalization to an individual without evidence or corroboration.

PROBLEM #4: Ethnocentrism and Xenophobia

Overemphasizing sameness can lead to ethnocentrism. "Ethnocentrism" is a broader term than "racism." Whereas the term "racism" refers to the belief in the inherent superiority of one's own racial group, "ethnocentrism" refers to the belief in the inherent superiority of one's own ethnic group or culture. If you are ethnocentric, you assume that people like you and cultures like your culture are good, desirable, and superior, whereas people that are different from you and cultures that are different from your culture are bad, undesirable, and inferior.

It is not necessarily wrong to conclude that some aspects of your culture are superior or better than some aspects of other cultures: human beings can and should make value judgments and moral evaluations. However, you are guilty of ethnocentrism when you assume that your culture is superior just because it is *your* culture.

Like stereotypes that are assumed without evidence, ethnocentric evaluations are made without undertaking the mental work of looking through different cultural lenses or attempting to understand different cultural worldview frameworks. It is unfair to judge or evaluate another culture with your own cultural criteria and without having a clear understanding of the beliefs, values, and motives that are driving the people in a culture. This is the principle behind the Native American proverb "Do not judge a person until you have walked two moons in their moccasins."

You should not assume that everyone has the same way of viewing the world, or that different cultures value the same things equally. In Chapter 3 of this textbook, you will learn about the different worldviews and the many different value orientations that exist among different people and people groups. When you have made the effort to understand people and cultures at a deep level, when you have comprehended their worldview frameworks and value orientations, then you have earned the right to make responsible value judgments and moral evaluations.

Embodied Ethnocentrism

To be an effective intercultural communicator, you need to decrease your ethnocentrism, but it is unreasonable to think that you can completely eradicate all ethnocentrism, especially "embodied ethnocentrism." Human beings feel comfortable in places that they recognize as their own—this is "embodied ethnocentrism." We often prefer and highly value our own houses, neighborhoods, and countries.

Even though there is nothing inherently superior about your house and neighborhood, you may have a strong preference for and allegiance to this physical space. In fact, according to many objective standards, your house or neighborhood may be obviously inferior to other houses or neighborhoods, and yet you may still prefer your house and your neighborhood, and you may value them highly, because they are "home."

Just as we live in a neighborhood and have a sense of belonging to our "home," we live in a country and have a sense of belonging to that country or homeland. The US national anthem refers to America as the "land of the free and *home* of the brave." The Canadian national anthem refers to Canada as "my *home* and native land." National anthems like these are played for the top-placing athletes at the International Olympics, and many Olympic athletes take great pride and pleasure in representing their respective countries. Although human beings may have a cosmopolitan perspective, they still have a need to belong somewhere on the earth—a homeland.

However, embodied ethnocentrism is no excuse for national jingoism or other forms of extreme ethnocentrism. Ethnocentrism can lead to "xenophobia," the extreme fear or hatred of strangers or foreigners. Xenophobia results in part from "othering," a mental activity whereby an individual or group is classified as different and "not one of us." Othering can lead to ostracizing people who are viewed as different or "alien."

A Literary Example of Ethnocentrism

"We and They"
(By Rudyard Kipling, from "Debits and Credits," 1919–1923)

Father and Mother, and Me,
Sister and Auntie say
All the people like us are We,
And every one else is They.
And They live over the sea,
While We live over the way,
But-would you believe it?—They look upon We
As only a sort of They!

We eat pork and beef
With cow-horn-handled knives.

They who gobble Their rice off a leaf,
Are horrified out of Their lives;
While they who live up a tree,
And feast on grubs and clay,
(Isn't it scandalous?) look upon We
As a simply disgusting They!

We shoot birds with a gun.
They stick lions with spears.
Their full dress is un-.
We dress up to Our ears.
They like Their friends for tea.
We like Our friends to stay;
And, after all that, They look upon We
As an utterly ignorant They!

We eat kitcheny food.
We have doors that latch.
They drink milk or blood,
Under an open thatch.
We have doctors to fee.
They have Wizards to pay.
And (impudent heathen!) They look upon We
As a quite impossible They!

All good people agree,
And all good people say,
All nice people, like Us, are We
And every one else is They:
But if you cross over the sea,
Instead of over the way,
You may end by (think of it!) looking on We
As only a sort of They!

PROBLEM #5: Unconscious Prejudice and Discrimination

Assuming that people are the same, or that we should act like they are the same when they are in fact different, can lead to unconscious, unintentional prejudice and discrimination. Some well-intentioned people trying to avoid or decrease prejudice and discrimination actually promote prejudice and discrimination when they assert that people are "basically the same" and that differences among people "do not really matter."

This was the approach taken by many feminists in America in the 1960s and 1970s. Many feminists advocating for equal rights for women made the mistaken claim that women were "just the same as men" and therefore should be treated equally. However, in her groundbreaking book In A Different Voice (Harvard University Press, 1982), feminist Carol Gilligan pointed out that women have different biological and cultural influences that cause them to view morality somewhat differently than men. Men are taught to follow abstract rules and seek for justice, whereas women are taught to value relationships and an ethic of care, so the path of moral development may be different for men and women.

If we impose a "male" model of moral development on women (as psychologists had done until Carol Gilligan's work was published) and assume that women's moral development is exactly the same as men's, we will evaluate female deviations from the male model as problematic, and we will view female moral development as inferior. Similarly, medical studies that use male subjects as the biological norm and that do not distinguish between male and female physiology will make female physical development seem abnormal or aberrant.

Figure 2.18   Males and females are different, but equal.

Certainly early feminists were trying to benefit women, but their insistence on sameness actually helped to contribute to the devaluation of females who deviated from the dominant male norm. It now seems much wiser to say that men and women are different, but equal. Women are not "just the same as" men: they are not biologically, psychologically, or culturally the same, and to treat them as such makes their differences seem inferior and undesirable.

When dealing with race and racism, an approach which overemphasizes sameness is the notion of **colorblindness**: some well-intentioned people assert that we should not pay attention to the color of a person's skin. We should, they claim, be "colorblind" and realize that people are, underneath their skin, "just the same."

However, skin color, and the way people are treated because of their skin color, is an important part of our lived experience that creates who we are as human beings. When we overemphasize sameness and do not recognize differences, we can assume that minority ethnic or racial groups in a culture have had the same experiences and privileges as the majority ethnic or racial group—this is clearly not the case.

Differences in race or skin color can lead to very different experiences and attitudes. Although all American citizens belong to the same national culture, they belong to different co-cultures determined in part by their age, sex, socioeconomic status, and race. These differences need to be acknowledged, or else unconscious discrimination can result. For example, minority advocates point out that standardized questions on educational aptitude tests sometimes have a "white bias" that favors students who are part of the dominant white culture. Discrimination is often motivated or caused by prejudice, but sometimes it is unintentionally caused by the assumption of sameness when important differences exist.

Now that we have presented to you five problems that can arise when sameness is privileged at the expense of difference, we will present five problems that can arise when difference is privileged at the expense of sameness.

Problems Related to Privileging Difference (At the Expense of Sameness)

PROBLEM #1: Extreme Relativism and Uncertainty

When differences are overemphasized, an extreme relativism can result that undermines the possibility and practice of rational thought and discourse. As we pointed out in the previous "positive" section, sameness (and the recognition of sameness) makes abstract thought and human language possible.

If the recognition of difference is privileged (at the expense of recognizing sameness), language and meaning disintegrate. By focusing on difference (or "differance"), French literary and social critic Jacques Derrida (and others) created the post-modern Deconstructionist movement that sought (in part) to undermine both classic literary texts and the social institutions that helped produce them. As a result, the verb "deconstruct" now has the popular meaning of demonstrating the *incoherence* of a text or position.

Overemphasizing difference can also lead to the undermining of moral thought and practice. If every culture has different values and moral standards, if there are no common moral standards that can be applied to all human beings, then a declaration of universal human rights is questionable if not impossible. Any moral pronouncement, any judgment of right and wrong, could be considered ethnocentric because "what is right for me and my culture is right for me and my culture" and "what is right for you and your culture is right for you and your culture." Such an extreme moral relativism can be used to justify very bad behavior, and it can lead to moral disorientation, confusion, and uncertainty.

PROBLEM #2: Culture Shock

Culture shock is a psychological phenomenon experienced by people who suddenly must function in a very different cultural setting. Too much difference, all at once, can be overwhelming. The term "culture shock" was first used in the late 1950s to describe the experience of sojourners who are swiftly transported from one culture to a very different culture. Culture shock can also occur when one culture is brought into sudden contact with another culture (for example, an indigenous culture suddenly confronted by modern civilization).

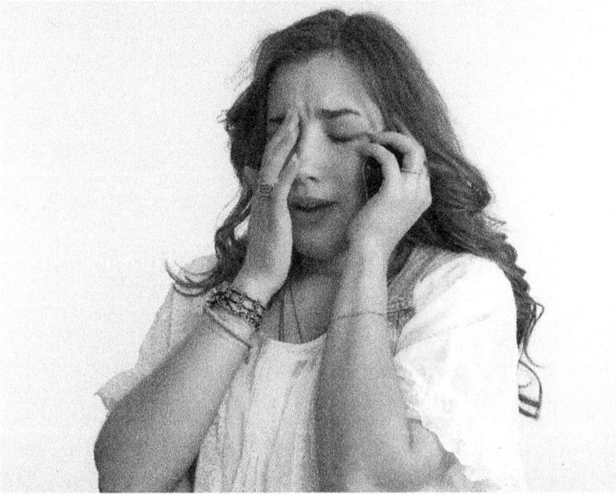

Just as an extreme moral relativism can create moral confusion and disorientation, people who are suddenly thrust into a very different culture can also experience confusion and disorientation. Some intercultural trainers want to replace the term "cul-

Figure 2.19 Culture shock is a real phenomenon that should be taken seriously.

© Toranico, 2014. Used under license from Shutterstock, Inc.

ture shock" with a term that has less negative connotations, but we think that "culture shock" is an appropriate term to describe what for many people is a fairly unpleasant, even traumatic experience.

Mild symptoms of culture shock include boredom, confusion, fatigue, feelings of insecurity, and homesickness. More serious symptoms of culture shock include feelings of helplessness, excessive sleep or insomnia, compulsive eating and drinking, headaches, obsession with cleanliness, suicidal or fatalistic thoughts, and hostility toward people in the host culture.

The U-Curve Theory

Although culture shock is a real phenomenon, the good news is that it is usually short-lived. Scholars and trainers who study cross-cultural adaptation have identified four fairly standard stages that people go through as they experience culture shock and adapt to their new host culture: Stage 1, Exhilaration (excitement and enthusiasm when entering into a new culture); Stage 2, Culture Shock (disorientation and confusion when confronted with many cultural differences); Stage 3, Adjustment (learning to adapt to the host culture); and Stage 4, Effective Functioning (the ability to function in the host culture with competence and confidence).

These four standard stages comprise what is often called **The U-Curve Theory:** Stage 1, the exhilaration stage, can be placed at the left top side of the letter "U." Stage 2, the culture shock stage, can be represented at the bottom left of the "U," when a person is at their lowest. Stage 3, the adjustment stage, can be represented at the bottom right of the letter "U," when a person is turning the corner and learning to function in the host culture. Stage 4, the effective functioning stage, can be represented at the top right side of the "U," when a person has returned to a high level of functioning.

However, we should be careful not to oversimplify the stages people go through when adjusting to a new culture. Some cross-cultural trainers argue that cultural adjustment is better represented by the letter "W," which contains several highs and lows.

We should also mention the phenomenon of **reverse culture shock**. After adjusting to a new host culture and spending some time in this new culture, people may have a difficult time adjusting when they return to their home culture. The cultural rules and rituals of their home culture may seem foreign and unusual, and they will need time to adjust to their original culture.

Ways to Reduce Culture Shock
1. Learn as much as you can about the host culture.
2. Be open-minded, flexible, and willing to learn.
3. Engage with people in the host culture and establish relationships with positive people.
4. Be patient with yourself and give yourself time to adjust.
5. Exercise, eat healthy meals, and get enough sleep.
6. Keep in contact with people from your home culture.
7. Develop and maintain a sense of humor.

PROBLEM #3: Dichotomous Thinking and Polarization

Focusing on and overemphasizing difference can lead to dichotomous thinking and polarization. When two different positions are recognized, they may be placed in opposition to one another, and people may think that they have to choose one or the other. This phenomenon is recognized in informal logic as a "false dichotomy" or the "either/or" fallacy: one is asked to choose between two options when more options or alternatives may exist, or when both options or alternatives are possible.

If people are asked to "choose a side" when different positions are contrasted, an unhealthy polarization can occur, both on an interpersonal and societal level. Interpersonal relationships can be strained when a couple polarizes and focuses on their individual differences, goals, and desires ("me" and "my" vs. "you" and "your") rather than their common goals and interests ("we" and "our").

© Dennis Owusu-Ansah, 2014. Used under license from Shutterstock, Inc.

Figure 2.20 Overemphasizing differences can lead to polarization and strained relationships.

On the societal level, different cultures and co-cultures can polarize around contrasting beliefs and values. Societal relationships can be strained when people divide into opposing camps: Eastern vs. Western, secular vs. religious, modern vs. traditional, liberal vs. conservative, masculine vs. feminine, younger generation vs. older generation.

Polarization occurs when the recognition of difference leads to the privileging of one belief, value, or position and the denigration and devaluing of a contrasting belief, value, or position. Sometimes polarization leads people to reject the values and beliefs of their own culture. This is what occurs, for example, when a Peace Corps volunteer "goes native."

When confronted with a new culture that has different beliefs and values than their home culture, some people totally reject the beliefs and values of their culture of origin and wholeheartedly embrace the beliefs and values of their new host culture. In a type of "reverse ethnocentrism," instead of assuming that their culture is *superior* to other cultures, when confronted with different ways of viewing and living in the world, some people assume that their culture must be *inferior* to other cultures.

In the next section of this chapter, we propose that a good alternative to dichotomous thinking and polarization is balance and integration. However, focusing on and overemphasizing difference can lead to unbalanced thinking and unnecessary oppositions.

PROBLEM #4: Factionalism and Societal Disintegration

Since beliefs and values drive behaviors, dichotomous and polarized thinking can lead to factionalism and societal disintegration. When people groups overemphasize their differences, they may desire to isolate and separate themselves from other groups.

This chapter section is taking the "negative" approach, so we need to consider the worst that can happen when people overemphasize their differences. At its worst, focusing on and overemphasizing differences can lead to segregation and, even worse, genocide. Segregation is the practice or policy of separating people of different races, religions, and so on. Genocide is the systematic killing and extermination of a people group because of their race, ethnicity, religion, or cultural practices.

Figure 2.21 Focusing on and overemphasizing difference can lead to segregation and, even worse, genocide.

In Figure 2.21, a black South African man sits on a bench in a park reserved for whites. Such segregation practices were common during the apartheid years in South Africa. However, prejudice extends beyond racial categories. In the Nigerian genocide that occurred in the 1960s, one to three million Igbo were killed by the Hausa and Yoruba people. In the Rwandan genocide that occurred in the 1990s, one half to one million Tutsi were killed by the Hutu people. The Rwandan government now requires its citizens to refer to themselves as "Rwandans" rather than by their tribal affiliations. Overemphasizing racial or ethnic differences can lead to very serious, violent consequences.

PROBLEM #5: Conscious, Intentional Prejudice and Discrimination

Whereas overemphasizing sameness can lead to unconscious, unintentional prejudice and discrimination, overemphasizing difference can lead to something worse—conscious, intentional prejudice and discrimination. Conscious, intentional prejudice and discrimination occurs when people believe that others' differences are a mark or indication of inferiority. These "inferior" people, they believe, deserve to be treated differently.

One historical example of conscious, intentional prejudice and discrimination is the unjust treatment of women in many different cultures and time periods. Although treating women as if they were "just the same" as men can lead to unintentional discrimination, treating women as if they were different from, and inferior to, men has often led to intentional discrimination. In the not-too-distant past it was claimed that women were less intelligent and less capable than men, and these supposed "differences" were used to justify the withholding of basic rights and opportunities from women, including the right to vote, to work, to receive an education, and to take leadership roles in society.

Figure 2.22 Since 1975, The United Nations has celebrated International Women's Day on March 8. Many countries of the world have pledged to work together to promote gender equality and equal rights for men and women.

Similarly, although "colorblindness" can lead to unintentional racial discrimination, focusing on and overemphasizing racial differences has led to conscious, intentional racism. It is a sad fact that late nineteenth and early twentieth century scientific theories were used to justify the belief that some races are inferior to others and that differential treatment of races is justified. Scientific racism was common up until WW I, and scientific theories were used to justify white Western imperialism and colonialism. It was considered to be "the white man's burden" to bring Western culture to inferior, nonwhite inhabitants of European and American colonies.

After WW II and the Holocaust, scientific racism was discredited in theory and discontinued in practice, and it is now considered pseudoscience. There is now no widely recognized scientific basis for claiming that one racial group is inferior or superior to another racial group. On May 17, 1998, the American Anthropological Association (AAA) published an official Statement on "Race" that clarified the scientific thinking about race and racial differences at the end of the twentieth century. (See the official Statement on "Race" at www.aaanet.org/stmts/racepp.htm.)

The AAA Statement on "Race" begins as follows: "In the United States both scholars and the general public have been conditioned to viewing human races as natural and separate divisions within the human species based on visible physical differences. With the vast expansion of scientific knowledge in this century, however, it has become clear that human populations are not unambiguous, clearly demarcated, biologically distinct groups. Evidence from the analysis of genetics (e.g., DNA) indicates that most physical variation, about 94%, lies *within* so-called racial groups. Conventional geographic 'racial' groupings differ from one another only in about 6% of their genes. This means that there is greater variation within 'racial' groups than between them."

The AAA Statement on "Race" ends by asserting that a "racial" worldview emphasizing racial differences has been used in the United States to discriminate against Native Americans and African Americans, and it concludes that ". . . present-day inequalities between so-called 'racial' groups are not consequences of their biological inheritance but products of historical and contemporary social, economic, educational, and political circumstances." When supposed racial differences were emphasized, the AAA claims that conscious, intentional racism was the primary result.

We will now summarize the problems and negative consequences that arise when people privilege and overemphasize either sameness or difference:

Problems Related to Privileging Sameness	Problems Related to Privileging Difference
1. Forced Uniformity and Conformity	1. Extreme Relativism and Uncertainty
2. Monotonous Routine and Stagnation	2. Culture Shock
3. Stereotyping	3. Dichotomous Thinking and Polarization
4. Ethnocentrism and Xenophobia	4. Factionalism and Societal Disintegration
5. Unconscious Prejudice and Discrimination	5. Conscious Prejudice and Discrimination

Balancing Between Contrasting Concepts or Values

There are benefits and positive consequences of recognizing and appreciating both sameness and difference, and there are drawbacks and negative consequences of overemphasizing and privileging either sameness or difference. For full human flourishing, a balance must be struck between the appreciation of sameness and the appreciation of difference.

People in collectivistic Eastern/Asian cultures (that value social cohesion and stability highly) often have a bias toward sameness, whereas people in individualistic Western cultures (that value individual autonomy and self-actualization highly) often have a bias toward difference. If you discover a bias in yourself toward either sameness or difference, you can employ cognitive restructuring to make a "mental recalibration."

Cognitive restructuring takes time and concentrated effort. When ways of thinking become habitual and attitudes become fixed, you must work hard to create new neural patterns and "mental grooves." If you have a bias toward sameness, you need to focus on the reasons to appreciate difference, and you need to remind yourself of the problems and difficulties that arise when you privilege sameness over difference. If you have a bias toward difference, you need to focus on the reasons to appreciate sameness, and you need to remind yourself of the problems and difficulties that arise when you privilege difference over sameness.

We will end this chapter with several examples that will help you to appreciate the need for balance. Our first example comes from the East, followed by five more examples more likely to appeal to a Western audience.

An Example from the East: Yin-Yang.   First, we will note that Chinese philosophy contains the principle of Yin-Yang. The principle of Yin-Yang is that opposite or contrary forces are interconnected and interdependent: as these opposing forces interact, they give rise to and create one another and the natural world.

© Svitlana Amelina, 2014. Used under license from Shutterstock, Inc.

© Archwiz, 2014. Used under license from Shutterstock, Inc.

Figures 2.23 and 2.24   The Yin-Yang principle in Chinese philosophy sees opposite or contrary forces as an interconnected duality.

Western Example #1: Masculine and Feminine.   Since this textbook is written primarily for a Western audience, we will supplement our reference to the Yin-Yang principle with an example that relates to people in both the East and the West. Wherever you go on this earth, you need to deal with the reality that half the world's population is male and half is female. Most people do not think that they have to choose between male and female, or between masculine values and feminine values.

It is unreasonable to think that either masculine characteristics or feminine characteristics are superior or inferior. Male chauvinists and radical feminists may be engaged in a "battle of the sexes," but the majority of people understand that males and females need each other: masculine characteristics and values are complemented by feminine characteristics and values. All human beings can benefit from understanding and appreciating both a male perspective and a female perspective.

American females do not have to "outmale" the males in order to succeed in business and politics. Males have something to teach females, and females have something to teach males. Over the last three decades, American business management has been improved with the incorporation of female approaches to leadership. Companies are learning that managers need to be concerned about productivity and "the bottom line," but they also need emotional intelligence and the ability to develop and sustain effective relationships. The balance between masculine values and feminine values is benefiting American business, and this balance between masculine and feminine can benefit many other areas of society.

Western Example #2: The Similarity Principle and the Complementarity Principle.   In the field of interpersonal communication, two principles of interpersonal attraction related to sameness and difference have been identified: they are the similarity principle and the complementarity principle.

The similarity principle reveals that sometimes we are attracted to people because they are similar to us. The proverb "Birds of a feather flock together" illustrates this principle. People often like to be around others who share similar interests or outlooks. Attraction between two people can be strongest when they are similar in a high percentage of important areas.

The complementarity principle reveals that sometimes we are attracted to people because they are different from us. The saying "Opposites attract" illustrates this principle. The complementarity principle goes beyond mere exoticism, the love of what is foreign or different: differences can strengthen a relationship when they are complementary—when each partner's different characteristics satisfy the needs of the other partner.

Figure 2.25   Couples in successful long-term relationships find a way to balance their similarities and differences.

© Rahhal, 2014. Used under license from Shutterstock, Inc.

You do not have to choose between these two principles of interpersonal attraction: one principle is not "wrong" while the other is "right." Couples in successful long-term relationships find a way to balance their similarities and differences. They have enough similarities to satisfy each other mentally and physically, but they also have enough differences to complement each other and to keep things interesting.

Western Example #3: Stability and Variety in Dialectical Tension.   Researchers in the field of Interpersonal Communication have also discovered that couples must manage "dialectical tensions" in their relationships: dialectical tensions are conflicts that arise when two people in a relationship are motivated or influenced by opposing or seemingly incompatible forces. For example, you may prefer privacy, whereas your partner prefers openness, or you may be wired for connection, whereas your partner is wired for autonomy.

One dialectical tension in interpersonal relationships related to sameness and difference is the desire for stability versus the desire for variety, or the desire for predictability versus the desire for novelty. People who desire stability and predictability appreciate sameness, whereas people who desire variety and novelty appreciate difference.

A quick way to determine the pole of this dialectical tension that you are closest to is to think about going out for a meal. When you have a chance to eat out, do you want to go to the same restaurant you usually go to and order the same dish you know you will enjoy, or do you want to go to a new restaurant you have never been to before and order a new dish to see what it tastes like? If you prefer the same restaurant with the same order, you are primarily wired for stability and predictability. If you prefer the new restaurant with the new dish, you are primarily wired for variety and novelty.

It is important to realize that one of these preferences is not "right" while the other preference is "wrong": human beings need both sameness and difference in their lives. The key to a successful interpersonal relationship is to learn how to manage the dialectical tensions that arise between you and your partner. You can use a poor strategy like denying the dialectical tension that exists, or you can use a better strategy like learning to love someone because of their differences, and not just in spite of their differences.

The management of dialectical tensions in interpersonal relationships can be transferred to the field of intercultural communication. As you interact with people from other cultures, you will need to identify your personal preferences for sameness and difference, and you will need to manage the tension that results when your preferences do not synch with the preferences of your relational partners.

Western Example #4: Moral Universalism and Moral Relativism.   As we noted earlier in this chapter, there are two moral or ethical worldviews that emphasize sameness and difference, respectively: moral universalism emphasizes sameness and argues that all people are subject to universal laws or standards of behavior, whereas moral relativism emphasizes difference and argues that people and cultures are different and therefore not subject to the same laws or standards of behavior.

These two ethical worldviews often come into conflict with one another. On the one hand, moral universalists often view moral relativists as undermining basic principles of human decency and fundamental moral obligations applying to all of humanity; on the other hand, moral relativists often view moral universalists as ethnocentric individuals who apply their own personal standards of right and wrong to everyone else and then claim a universalism that does not exist in reality.

Just as couples need to learn to balance similarities and differences and to manage their individual preferences for stability and variety, moral universalists and moral relativists need to work together to generate an appreciation for both the similarities and differences that exist among individuals and cultures.

Ethical matters are complicated, so it seems best to avoid the extreme moral universalist and moral relativist positions that overemphasize either sameness or difference. Instead, the master key for effective intercultural communication and strong intercultural relationships is learning to appreciate both sameness and difference. In important ways, human beings in every society and culture are the same, and in important ways, human beings in every society and culture are different.

Western Example #5: The Melting Pot Metaphor and the Salad Bowl Metaphor.   There are two contrasting metaphors that have been used to describe America as a nation: the first metaphor, "The Melting Pot," emphasizes sameness, whereas the second metaphor, "The Salad Bowl," emphasizes difference.

The melting pot metaphor is based upon metallurgy: it refers to several base metals being mixed together in a crucible or (s)melting pot to create a new metal like steel (a combination of iron and carbon).

This metaphor is used to describe a heterogeneous culture becoming more homogeneous. It was used by Hector St. John de Crevecoeur (1782), Ralph Waldo Emerson (1845), Frederick Jackson Turner (1893), and Henry James (1905) to describe the immigration, assimilation, and acculturation that occurred in America in the eighteenth and nineteenth centuries. The metaphor was popularized in Israel Zangwill's 1905 Broadway play, *The Melting Pot*. In this play, the protagonist proclaims, "Understand that America is God's Crucible, the great Melting-Pot where all the races of Europe are melting and reforming! Here you stand, good folk, think I, when I see them at Ellis Island, here you stand in your fifty groups, your fifty languages, and histories, and your fifty blood hatreds and rivalries. But you won't be long like that, brothers, for these are the fires of God you've come to—these are the fires of God. A fig for your feuds and vendettas! Germans and Frenchmen, Irishmen and Englishmen, Jews and Russians—into the Crucible with you all! God is making the American." (As quoted in Gary Gerstle's *American Crucible: Race and Nation in the Twentieth Century*, Princeton University Press, 2001, p. 51.)

The salad bowl metaphor was developed in the 1970s to suggest that immigrants to, and ethnic cultures in, the United States do not have to fully assimilate and become one new homogeneous culture. Instead, like the ingredients of a salad, each ethnic group and co-culture can keep its distinct qualities and characteristics while becoming part of a multicultural nation.

The salad bowl metaphor is sometimes replaced with the idea of a "cultural mosaic." Both the salad bowl metaphor and the idea of a cultural mosaic point out that a new entity—a whole created by combining distinct and different elements together—can only come into existence when the distinctness and differentness of the individual elements are preserved. If all the stones in a mosaic were the same, an image could not be created. If all the ingredients of a salad were minced and blended together, you would create an unappetizing sludge. Sometimes differences must be preserved in order to create something new and wonderful.

Both metaphors, the melting pot and the salad bowl, have merit. Which metaphor of America do you prefer? Why? Do you think Americans need to emphasize their similarities or their differences? At the end of this chapter, you know the answer we would propose—Americans need to acknowledge and appreciate both their similarities and their differences.

© chinahbzyg, 2014. Used under license from Shutterstock, Inc.

Figure 2.26   America the melting pot.

© MaraZe, 2014. Used under license from Shutterstock, Inc.

Figure 2.27   America the salad bowl.

Conclusion

In this chapter, we have taught you that you can learn to balance between opposing or contrasting values or concepts. You can expand your mind to make room for beliefs and values that seem to be in conflict or tension with one another. We have demonstrated that this special kind of cognitive restructuring is possible by taking one pair of contrasting elements—sameness and difference—and showing that a balanced appreciation of both is possible.

We have presented five reasons to appreciate sameness: 1) patterns and pattern recognition, 2) abstract thought and language, 3) stability and predictability, 4) social cohesion, and 5) equality and human rights. We have also presented five reasons to appreciate difference: 1) diversity and variety, 2) creative thinking, 3) change, growth, and progress, 4) sensitivity and positive discrimination, and 5) individual personhood.

Next, we presented five problems that arise when sameness is privileged over difference: 1) forced uniformity and conformity, 2) monotonous routine and stagnation, 3) stereotyping, 4) ethnocentrism and xenophobia, and 5) unconscious prejudice and discrimination. We also presented five problems that arise when difference is privileged over sameness: 1) extreme relativism and uncertainty, 2) culture shock, 3) dichotomous thinking and polarization, 4) factionalism and societal disintegration, and 5) conscious prejudice and discrimination.

We finally presented several examples that demonstrate the importance of balancing between opposing or contrasting concepts or values. One example from the East was presented—the principle of yin and yang. Five more Western examples were also presented: 1) masculine and feminine, 2) the similarity principle and the complementarity principle, 3) stability and variety in dialectical tension, 4) moral universalism and moral relativism, and 5) the melting pot metaphor and the salad bowl metaphor.

If you have carefully considered the examples and arguments related to sameness and difference that were presented in this chapter, then we believe that you now have a more balanced appreciation for both sameness and difference. When it comes to sameness and difference, you should now be a "both/and-er" rather than an "either/or-ist."

The type of cognitive restructuring demonstrated in this chapter can be put to good use in Chapter 3. In Chapter 3, we present to you more than 20 pairs of opposing or contrasting values. Just as a balanced appreciation for sameness and difference can be achieved, we believe that a balanced appreciation for each of these pairs of contrasting values is also possible.

Chapter Posttest

Sameness   **Difference**

$$\longleftarrow\!\longrightarrow$$

When interacting with other human beings and with people from other cultures, what is most important, focusing on similarities (sameness) or differences (difference)? Place an "x" on the line above to indicate which of these basic elements you value the most. If you value sameness and difference equally, place your "x" in the middle of the line. The stronger your preference for one of these basic elements, the farther your "x" should be placed to the left end or the right end of the line.

Glossary

Colorblindness   Not recognizing skin color or racial distinctions.

Complementarity principle   Interpersonal attraction based on the differences between people.

Culture shock   The disorientation and confusion a person experiences when suddenly exposed to a different culture or society.

Dialectical tensions   Opposing forces that people experience in their relationships; the tension between two desirable goals or values.

Difference   The quality or condition of being unlike or dissimilar.

Discrimination   Unfair treatment of people, often motivated by prejudice; (alternate definition) the ability to see or make fine distinctions.

Embodied ethnocentrism   The preference people have for familiar places. We feel comfortable in spaces and places that we consider to be our own.

Ethnocentrism   The belief in the inherent superiority of one's own ethnic group or culture.

Generalization   A statement or assertion applied to a large group of people or things.

Heterogeneous   Composed of different parts or people.

Homogeneous   Made up of the same kind of people or things.

Integration   The act or instance of combining things into an integral whole.

Melting pot   A metaphor that emphasizes sameness; a heterogeneous society becomes more homogeneous when the different co-cultures "melt together" and create a common national culture.

Monoculturalism   The practice of actively preserving a national culture by excluding external cultural influences.

Moral relativism   An ethical philosophy that emphasizes difference and argues that different cultures and individuals have different standards of right and wrong.

Moral universalism   An ethical philosophy that emphasizes sameness and argues that certain human behaviors are right or wrong regardless of circumstances.

Multiculturalism   The idea that several different co-cultures can coexist peacefully and equally in one national culture.

National character   A group of characteristics or behavioral traits that apply to the majority population of a whole nation.

Othering   A mental activity whereby an individual or group is classified as different, alien, and "not one of us."

Pattern   Something that repeats in a predictable, intelligible way; an arrangement or sequence regularly found in objects or events.

Prejudice   An unfavorable and unjustified feeling of dislike, disdain, or hatred for a person or group of people because of race, sex, religion, age, and so on.

Salad bowl   A metaphor that emphasizes differences. The co-cultures of a national culture are compared to the ingredients of a salad; the preserved cultural differences create a heterogeneous, multicultural society.

Sameness   The quality or state of being alike.

Similarity principle   Interpersonal attraction based on the similarities between people.

Stability   The quality or state of something that is not easily changed. Stability is in dialectical tension with variety.

Stereotype   An invalid generalization applied universally to an entire group with insufficient evidence.

U-curve theory   A theory in intercultural studies that describes culture shock, adjustment, and acculturation as stages in a process. Often four stages are recognized: 1) exhilaration, 2) culture shock, 3) adjustment, and 4) effective functioning.

Variety   The quality or state of being different or diverse. Variety is in dialectical tension with stability.

Xenophobia   Extreme fear or hatred of strangers or foreigners.

Chapter 3

Values and Worldviews

Mark Staller

"Values aren't buses . . . They're not supposed to get you anywhere. They're supposed to define who you are."
—Jennifer Cruise

"It's not hard to make decisions when you know what your values are."
—Roy Disney

Chapter Learning Objectives

1. Define values and understand the basic characteristics of values.
2. Identify common pairs of opposing values and determine your personal orientation for each pair of opposing values.
3. Identify common universal questions asked in every human culture, and list the different types of answers given.
4. Distinguish between different basic types of worldviews.
5. Develop a basic understanding of different religious and nonreligious approaches to living in the world.
6. Describe the values and beliefs of classical world religions.

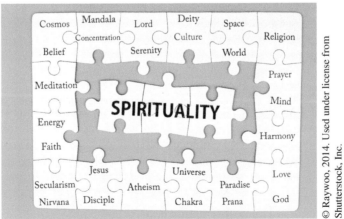

Introduction

How valuable, how useful or helpful, is this textbook chapter on values and worldviews? If you want to develop a deep understanding of people and cultures, then this chapter is "golden." Worldviews create and anchor the core beliefs of different cultural groups, and cultural values create and drive the goal-directed behaviors of people. A knowledge of cultural values and worldviews can help you understand and interact with many different types of people and with many different cultures and co-cultures.

Figure 3.1   This chapter on values and worldviews is "golden."

There are three main sections in this chapter: Section 1 will familiarize you with the most important values that motivate and drive human beings. You will learn about the dominant values in American culture and about basic human values found in every culture. After learning about different pairs of opposing values, you will complete your own "value inventory" to determine what values are most important to you.

Section 2 will provide you with a basic understanding of worldviews. You will learn some definitions of, and synonyms for, worldviews. You will learn the characteristics of worldviews. You will also learn about three different types of worldviews: 1) ontological worldviews, 2) epistemological worldviews, and 3) moral/ethical worldviews.

Section 3 will briefly review the major religions of the world. You will learn some of the major beliefs and values of about a dozen major world religions. In addition, you will also learn about secular, nonreligious approaches to living in the world.

After reading this chapter on values and worldviews, in addition to a deeper understanding of the core beliefs and values of different cultural groups, you should also gain some important insights into your personal values and beliefs. You should be able to consciously think and talk about your own value orientations, and you should be able to describe the "cultural lenses" you typically use to view and understand the world.

Section 1: Values

We will begin our discussion of cultural values by referencing a monograph titled "The Values Americans Live By" written by Robert Kohls. Robert Kohls was an American who lived and worked in Korea in the 1950s. In the 1960s, he worked for the Peace Corps and trained volunteers working in Korea, Brazil, Tunisia, and Libya. In the late 1970s and early 1980s, Kohls was the director of the U.S. Information Agency and the Meridian International Center in Washington, DC, where he taught government employees and cultural attaches how to live overseas.

In 1984, Robert Kohls published the monograph "The Values Americans Live By" to orient foreign visitors to the US national culture. He claimed in his monograph that if foreigners understood deeply ingrained American values, they would be able to understand about 95% of American actions. Although this monograph is now 30 years old, it is still widely published and excerpted because Kohls' description still holds up well. Although culture is dynamic and undergoes changes, Kohls' list of American values demonstrates that the deep structure of American culture is fairly stable. (Kohls' 17-page monograph was published in 1984 by Meridian House International, and can be accessed on many different educational websites on the internet. See: www.uri.edu/mind/VALUES2.pdf.)

Kohls' American Values

In his monograph, Robert Kohls lists 13 values that apply to a majority of Americans. He points out that although Americans like to think that they are unique individuals, foreigners observing American culture can identify common values that most Americans hold. In addition, Kohls points out that these 13 American values are often at odds with the traditional values of other countries of the world. At the end of his monograph, Kohls lists these 13 American values and their contrasting or opposing values. We will present this list of contrasting values, and then we will briefly describe the 13 American values identified by Robert Kohls.

United States Values	vs.	Values of Other Countries
1. Personal control over the environment		1. Fate
2. Change		2. Tradition
3. Time and its control		3. Human interaction
4. Equality/Egalitarianism		4. Hierarchy/rank/status
5. Individualism/Privacy		5. Group's welfare (collectivism)
6. Self-Help		6. Birthright inheritance
7. Competition		7. Cooperation
8. Future orientation		8. Past orientation
9. Action/work orientation		9. "Being" orientation
10. Informality		10. Formality
11. Directness/openness/honesty		11. Indirectness/ritual/face
12. Practicality/efficiency (pragmatism)		12. Idealism
13. Materialism/acquisitiveness		13. Spiritualism/detachment

Although Kohls' monograph was written for foreigners, its observations are very useful for Americans because it allows us to view ourselves through foreign eyes. Below is a brief description of each of Kohls' 13 American values. As you read through this list, consider the following questions:

Do you think that Kohl's list of American values applies to American culture today? Why or why not?
Which American values listed by Kohls are important to you personally?
Which American values listed by Kohls are not important to you personally?
Are there other important American values that you think Kohls has neglected to mention? If so, what are they?

1. Personal control over the environment

© aragami12345s, 2014. Used under license from Shutterstock, Inc.

Figure 3.2 Americans believe that human beings can and should control the physical environment in which they live. They seem compelled to achieve what other cultures claim is beyond human capabilities.

2. Change

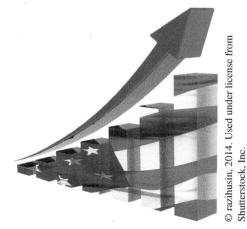

© razihusin, 2014. Used under license from Shutterstock, Inc.

Figure 3.3 In the American mind, change is good, and it leads to improvement and progress.

3. Equality and egalitarianism

© Just Keep Drawing, 2014. Used under license from Shutterstock, Inc.

Figure 3.4 Equality is one of the most cherished American values. Most Americans believe that everyone is "created equal."

4. Individualism/privacy

© Alexander Mak, 2014. Used under license from Shutterstock, Inc.

Figure 3.5 Americans tend to overestimate their ability to think and act as individuals. They think that each individual is unique, and that each individual needs and wants their own personal privacy.

5. Self-Help

© donskarpo, 2014. Used under license from Shutterstock, Inc.

Figure 3.6 Americans believe that personal achievement is important. They value and admire the "self-made" man or woman.

6. Competition and free enterprise

© bikeriderlondon, 2014. Used under license from Shutterstock, Inc.

Figure 3.7 Most Americans believe that competition brings out the best in people. They encourage competition in almost every social endeavor, including economic endeavors.

7. Future orientation

© Patrick Foto, 2014. Used under license from Shutterstock, Inc.

Figure 3.8 Americans are almost always "looking ahead." Although they may be proud of past or present accomplishments, they are almost always focused on future goals and achievements.

8. Work/action orientation

© Brocreative, 2014. Used under license from Shutterstock, Inc.

Figure 3.9 Most Americans schedule an extremely active day. Many Americans are workaholics, and even their vacations and recreation schedules are usually filled with activity.

9. Informality

Figure 3.10 Americans are much more informal than people in other cultures. They are informal in their greetings and in their clothing.

10. Directness, openness, and honesty

Figure 3.11 Americans are very direct, even when giving negative evaluations. They are likely to view anyone who is subtle or indirect as dishonest or manipulative.

11. Practicality and efficiency

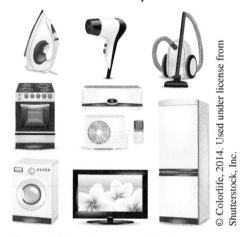

Figure 3.12 Americans are known for their practicality. They usually make pragmatic decisions and favor practical careers and professions.

12. Materialism and acquisitiveness

Figure 3.13 By any standards, Americans are materialistic. They own a large amount of material possessions, and they replace them frequently.

Schwartz' Basic Human Values

Whereas Robert Kohls identifies and describes specific, distinct "American" values, cross-cultural psychologist Shalom Schwartz has attempted to identify and describe basic human values that can be found in every country and culture group. According to Schwartz, there are at least 10 basic values that almost every person and culture holds. Schwartz' research is valuable to those who study intercultural communication because it provides this "short list" of basic human values and it helps us to clarify our thinking about values. First, we will give some background information about Schwartz' research; second, we will present 6 characteristics of values noted by Schwartz; third, we will list and describe the 10 basic human values identified by Schwartz; and, finally, we will point out how some of these values are in tension with, or opposition to, each other.

Background of Schwartz' Basic Value Theory

Shalom H. Schwartz obtained his PhD in social psychology from the University of Michigan-Ann Arbor and taught at the University of Wisconsin until he moved to Israel in 1979. He is past president of the International Association for Cross-Cultural Psychology and a recipient of the Israel Prize in psychology. In 1982, he began to search for a set of universal human values, and in the 1980s and 1990s he identified 10 basic human values that people in all cultures seem to recognize.

Schwartz' Theory of Basic Values posits that virtually all human beings recognize 10 basic, motivationally distinct values and that conflicts between opposing values are consistent among people regardless of their national culture. Furthermore, his research has shown that there is a high level of consensus regarding the relative importance of the 10 values across societies. Schwartz has collaborated with 150 researchers who have applied his theory and methods for measuring values in over 80 countries.

An overview of the Schwartz Theory of Basic Values (2012) is presented in <u>Online Readings in Psychology and Culture</u> by the International Association for Cross-Cultural Psychology. (See http://dx.doi.org/10.9707/2307-0919.1116.) Although Schwartz' work is from the field of cross-cultural psychology, we present highlights from this overview here because we believe that it is very applicable to intercultural communication and intercultural interactions.

Six Characteristics of Values

Before presenting the 10 basic human values that seem to be present across cultures, Schwartz clarifies exactly what values are by noting six characteristics of values. We will paraphrase these six characteristics.

1. **Values are beliefs that are linked to affect or emotion.** When you value something, you develop strong feelings when progress toward your value goal is impeded or enhanced. For example, if you value independence, you will be upset and feel threatened if your independence is taken away, and you will feel satisfied and happy when your independence is maintained or enhanced.
2. **Values are desirable goals that motivate human actions.** If you value justice, you will be motivated to pursue justice. If you value benevolence, you will be motivated to perform benevolent actions. If you value social order, you will be motivated to create a more ordered society.
3. **Values transcend specific actions, objects, or situations.** If you value honesty, you will be concerned about truthfulness at work, at home, at school, and everywhere else. If you value beauty, you will appreciate any beautiful object that you see. The transcendent nature of values distinguishes values from social norms that apply only in particular situations or to specific objects.
4. **Values serve as standards or criteria, which guide our actions and our evaluations of actions, policies, people, and events.** You decide what is good or bad, what is worth doing or best avoided, and what is relevant or irrelevant, based on the way it will impact your values. You are often not consciously aware of the values that underlie your decisions and evaluations until a value conflict arises.
5. **Values can be ordered by relative importance.** People do not normally rank norms or attitudes, but they do rank values and place them in a hierarchical order. How you rank different values characterizes you as an individual. Do you think achievement is more important than benevolence? Do you think conformity is more important than hedonism? Your value priorities create your character.

6. **The relative importance of multiple values guides human actions.** The give-and-play among relevant, competing values influences your attitudes and guides your behaviors. For example, if you value security and tradition more than you value hedonism or stimulation, you will have a conservative attitude and you will make conservative choices.

Figure 3.14   Your core values create your attitudes and guide your behaviors.

Ten Basic Human Values

Dozens, possibly hundreds, of human values can be identified. Shalom Schwartz' research is useful because he generates a short list of values when he attempts to identify general human values that can be found in every culture. Although there are important human values that do not appear on Schwartz' "top ten" list, we think that Schwartz' list is valuable precisely because of its brevity.

Schwartz also provides a theoretical explanation for the existence of these 10 broad values in human societies. Schwartz theorizes that these basic values are likely to be universal because they are grounded in one or more of three universal requirements of human existence: 1) the needs of individuals as biological organisms, 2) the needs for coordinated social interaction, and 3) the survival and welfare needs of groups.

What Schwartz finds astonishing is that across societies there is a surprising consensus regarding the hierarchical order of the 10 basic human values. Although individuals may differ in how they rank the 10 basic values, across representative samples the importance ranks for the 10 values are remarkably consistent. We will now present and briefly describe each of these 10 values in their rank order, from most important (number one) to tenth most important.

1. **Benevolence.** Benevolence is generally defined as the inclination to be kind and to help others, but Schwartz ties benevolence specifically to preserving and enhancing the welfare of those with whom one is in frequent personal contact (especially the family or other primary groups).
2. **Universalism.** Schwartz contrasts universalism to benevolence. Universalism is care and concern for all people and for nature. He connects universalism to the survival needs of both individuals and groups. Concern for everyone and for nature is created when we realize that the scarcity of resources and competition for these resources can lead to life-threatening consequences for everyone.

3. **Self-Direction.** Self-direction is tied to the needs of the individual. To survive and thrive, individuals require autonomy and independence. Human beings need to be capable of independent thought and action.

4. **Security.** Schwartz ties the value of security to both individual and social needs. We are motivated to protect ourselves and our social groups. We want to be safe and secure, both as individuals and as groups (e.g., national security).

5. **Conformity.** Conformity is tied to social needs, and it emphasizes self-restraint for the benefit of others, especially close others. Individuals sometimes have to inhibit inclinations that would disrupt social interactions and undermine smooth group functioning.

6. **Hedonism.** Hedonism is an individual value. Individual human beings seek pleasure and avoid pain. As biological organisms, we derive pleasure from the gratification or fulfilling of basic organismic needs.

7. **Achievement.** Although achievement is primarily an individual value, Schwartz points out that personal success is usually measured by demonstrating competence according to prevailing cultural or social standards. We have individual needs to be validated by others.

8. **Tradition.** Tradition is a social value. People who value tradition accept and respect customs and ideas provided by their social group. Tradition and conformity both involve the subordination of the self to socially imposed expectations, but tradition often entails subordination to more abstract objects, especially religious customs and ideas.

9. **Stimulation.** Stimulation, like self-direction, is related to the needs of the individual organism. Individuals need variety and stimulation for optimal performance. We need a certain amount of novelty, excitement, and challenge in order to thrive as human beings.

10. **Power.** Power is an individual value. Individuals have an inclination for dominance and control over people and resources. Schwartz asserts that since social institutions apparently require some degree of status differences, groups also treat power as a value.

Ten General Human Values Ranked By order of Importance
1. Benevolence
2. Universalism
3. Self-direction
4. Security
5. Conformity
6. Hedonism
7. Achievement
8. Tradition
9. Stimulation
10. Power

Figure 3.15 Ten basic human values are consistently ranked in a similar hierarchical order across cultures.

Contrasting or Opposing Values

Just as Robert Kohls contrasted his 13 American values to traditional values prominent in other countries, Shalom Schwartz also notes that the basic values he identifies can be contrasted or placed in opposition to each other. Schwartz places his 10 basic values on a "value wheel" that helps to reveal the relationship between different values. Values placed on adjoining spokes of the value wheel have more similarities and affinities, whereas values on opposite spokes of the value wheel are in opposition to each other. The tables below reveal some of the oppositions that exist among the values identified by Schwartz.

Individual Values	Social Values
1. Power	1. Universalism
2. Achievement	2. Benevolence
3. Hedonism	3. Conformity
4. Stimulation	4. Tradition
5. Self-direction	5. Security

Figure 3.16   Individual values can be contrasted to social values.

Values of Self-Enhancement	Values of Self-Transcendence
1. Power	1. Universalism
2. Achievement	2. Benevolence

Figure 3.17   Values of self-enhancement can be contrasted to values of self-transcendence.

Values Open to Change	Values of Conservation
1. Hedonism	1. Conformity
2. Stimulation	2. Tradition
3. Self-direction	3. Security

Figure 3.18   Values open to change can be contrasted to values of conservation.

Values Based in Anxiety	Values Free of Anxiety
Values With Prevention of Loss Goals	Values with Promotion of Gain Goals
Values of Self-Protection	Values of Self-Expansion and Growth
1. Power	1. Universalism
2. Achievement	2. Benevolence
3. Conformity	3. Hedonism
4. Tradition	4. Stimulation
5. Security	5. Self-direction

Figure 3.19   Values based in anxiety can be contrasted to values free of anxiety.

As these tables of contrasting values demonstrate, human values often come into conflict and oppose or are in tension with one another. Another social science researcher who realized this fact was Gerard Hofstede. We will now introduce to you Gerard Hofstede's value dimensions.

Hofstede's Value Dimensions

Gerard (Geert) Hofstede is a Dutch social psychologist who worked for IBM International in the 1960s and the 1970s. As a researcher for IBM, he was able to access tens of thousands of employee surveys in order to analyze and identify national values in over 40 different countries. Over the last four decades, his research has yielded six cultural value dimensions that are now widely recognized and discussed in the fields of cross-cultural psychology, international business, and intercultural communication. Anyone working in these fields should have some familiarity with Hofstede's categories and the vocabulary he developed to describe and discuss different national values.

Hofstede's biography and a list of his published work can be found on his official website, www .geerthofstede.nl. According to his official website, a revised and expanded third edition of his book Cultures and Organizations (McGraw-Hill, New York, 2010) contains the latest iteration of his cultural dimensions. We will provide a very brief, very general summary of Hofstede's value dimensions in order to acquaint you with Hofstede's value dimension categories.

Hofstede's Value Dimensions

1. Individualism	1. Collectivism
2. High-Power Distance	2. Low-Power Distance
3. High Uncertainty Avoidance	3. Low Uncertainty Avoidance
4. Masculinity	4. Femininity
5. Long-Term Orientation	5. Short-Term Orientation
6. Indulgence	6. Restraint

Figure 3.20 Hofstede has identified six different cultural value dimensions.

Individualism vs. Collectivism: In this value dimension, Hofstede is not referring to communist collectives, but to how much individuals are integrated into groups. People from individualistic societies value personal achievement and individual autonomy, whereas people from collectivistic societies value social cohesion and social stability.

High-power distance vs. Low-power distance: In cultures with high-power distance, less powerful members of organizations and institutions are likely to accept and expect that power is distributed unequally, whereas in cultures with low-power distance, members accept and expect more consultative and democratic power relations. High-power distance cultures are hierarchical, whereas low-power distance countries are egalitarian.

High uncertainty avoidance vs. Low uncertainty avoidance: In cultures with high uncertainty avoidance, people try to minimize unknown and unusual circumstances by implementing and following rules and regulations, whereas in cultures with low uncertainty avoidance, people accept and operate well in unstructured environments and changing situations with few rules or regulations. High uncertainty avoidance cultures expect an "official" voice or explanation, whereas low uncertainty avoidance cultures are comfortable with the expression of multiple viewpoints and opinions.

Masculinity vs. Feminity: Masculine cultures value competitiveness, assertiveness, materialism, ambition, and power, whereas feminine cultures value relationships, emotional sensitivity, and the quality of life. In masculine cultures, the differences in sex and gender roles tend to be more pronounced and less fluid than in feminine cultures. In feminine cultures, the differences between gender roles are less pronounced and more fluid, and both males and females value care and concern for others.

Long-term orientation vs. Short-term orientation: Cultures with a long-term orientation value the future benefits that come through persistence, saving, and the ability to adapt, whereas cultures with a short-term orientation focus on the past or present and value respect for tradition, preservation of face, reciprocation, and fulfilling social obligations.

Indulgence vs. Restraint: Indulgent societies tend to allow relatively free gratification of basic physical human desires, whereas restrained societies tend to regulate the gratification of basic human physical desires by strict norms.

Figure 3.21   Individualistic cultures value individual achievement.

Figure 3.22   Collectivistic cultures value group effort and social cohesion.

Hofstede's work has provided a framework for discussing and thinking about cross-cultural communication. Many other researchers have supplemented Hofstede's original work, so you can now access charts and graphs that place most of the countries of the world on Hofstede's value dimensions. You can also take surveys that will reveal your personal value dimension scores. Both individuals and countries can be compared to one another in order to gain a better understanding of where they fall on Hofstede's value dimensions.

Hall's Two Types of Time Orientations

Although chronemics (the study of the way different cultures view and use time) is an appropriate topic for our chapter on nonverbal communication (Chapter 7), we will introduce here E.T. Hall's distinction between two different types of time orientation because these two different time orientations lead cultures to value different things.

Robert Kohls pointed out in his monograph that Americans value time and its control. When he made this observation in the 1980s, Kohls was very likely drawing upon the groundbreaking work of E.T. Hall that was mentioned in Chapter 1 of this textbook. In Chapter 1, we noted that E.T. Hall is credited with the establishment of Intercultural Communication studies in the 1960s, including the establishment of the study of the way cultures use space (proxemics) and the study of the way cultures use time (chronemics).

When he initiated the study of the way cultures view and use time, E.T. Hall coined technical terms for two different time orientations: some cultures, Hall asserted, were "monochronic," whereas other cultures were "polychronic." This distinction is now widely accepted.

On the one hand, monochronic cultures have a time orientation that views time as linear. People in monochronic cultures view time as something that can be segmented into precise units that can be used or spent. Consequently, monochronic cultures value time and its control very highly.

Polychronic cultures, on the other hand, have a time orientation that views time as circular or reoccurring. Since time is viewed as something that reoccurs or repeats, polychronic cultures do not view time as a valuable commodity. Instead, they subordinate their use of time to their relationships with other people. Polychronic cultures value human interaction and human relationships. The following table presents some of the differences between monochronic and polychronic people.

People in Monochronic Cultures	People in Polychronic Cultures
1. Do one thing at a time	1. Do many things at once
2. Adhere to plans and schedules	2. Change plans and schedules often and easily
3. Take deadlines seriously	3. View deadlines as objectives that may or may not be achieved
4. Are committed to task completion	4. Are committed to people and to relationships
5. Value promptness and being on time	5. Value socializing

Figure 3.23 Different time orientations lead to different behaviors and different cultural values.

An Inventory of Contrasting Values

Combining the insights of Kohls, Schwartz, Hofstede, and Hall together, we can create an inventory of 23 contrasting value pairs. You can use this inventory to explore your personal values and the values of different cultures and co-cultures.

An Inventory of Contrasting Values

1. Achievement	vs	1. Benevolence
2. Acquisitiveness	vs	2. Detachment
3. Action orientation	vs	3. Being orientation
4. Change	vs	4. Tradition
5. Competition	vs	5. Cooperation
6. Directness	vs	6. Indirectness
7. Equality	vs	7. Hierarchy
8. Future orientation	vs	8. Past orientation
9. Hedonism	vs	9. Conformity
10. High-power distance	vs	10. Low-power distance
11. High uncertainty avoidance	vs	11. Low uncertainty avoidance
12. Honesty	vs	12. Saving face

13. Individualism	vs.	13. Collectivism
14. Indulgence	vs.	14. Restraint
15. Informality	vs.	15. Formality
16. Long-term orientation	vs.	16. Short-term orientation
17. Masculinity	vs.	17. Femininity
18. Monochronic time orientation	vs.	18. Polychronic time orientation
19. Personal control of environment	vs.	19. Fate or luck
20. Power	vs.	20. Universalism
21. Pragmatism	vs.	21. Idealism
22. Self-direction	vs.	22. Security
23. Self-help	vs.	23. Birthright inheritance

We have placed an arrow in the middle of this list of contrasting value pairs in order for you to analyze and record your own personal value preferences. For the first 12 pairs, place the number for each pair (numbers 1 to12) above the line at the appropriate position for your personal value preferences. For the last 11 pairs, place the numbers 13 to 23 below the line at the appropriate position for your value preferences.

For example, for the value pair "achievement vs. benevolence," place the number 1 exactly in the middle of the line if you value achievement and benevolence equally. If you believe personal achievement is more important than benevolence toward others, place the number 1 closer to the "achievement" end of the line. If you believe that benevolence is more important than achievement, place the number 1 closer to the "benevolence" end of the line. Similarly, for each value pair, place the corresponding number (2–23) at the appropriate point on the line to represent your remaining value preferences. Here is a sample completed value inventory:

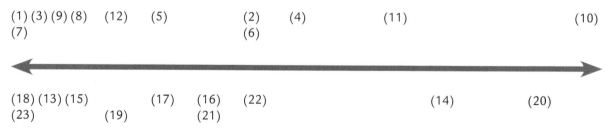

Figure 3.24   A sample completed inventory of contrasting values.

The person completing the value inventory above highly values achievement (1), action orientation (3), equality (7), monochronic time orientation (18), and self-help (23). This individual also highly values low-power distance (10) and universalism (20). However, this person equally values change and tradition (4), and self-direction and security (22).

You can use this inventory of contrasting values to gain insight into your own personal values, but you can also use this inventory to start a values conversation with people from other cultures and co-cultures. Having these discussions will help you go way below the surface of people's attitudes and behaviors in order to understand on a deeper level what is motivating them to feel and behave as they do.

Kluckhohn and Strodtbeck's Values Orientation Theory

Clyde Kluckhohn was an American anthropologist and social theorist who carried out ethnographic work among the Navajo people in the Southwest United States in the 1950s. He theorized that all cultures have value orientations based upon basic universal questions that all human beings must answer. In the early 1960s, Florence Kluckhohn, Clyde Kluckhohn's wife, and Fred Strodtbeck further developed and operationalized this values orientation theory developed by Clyde Kluckhohn.

Kluckhohn and Strodtbeck's Values Orientation Theory looks at five basic questions every human society must answer, and they posit that there are a limited number of answers to these questions. We present here the five basic questions explored by Kluckhohn and Strodtbeck because they go beyond the dual opposing values of the theorist we have presented so far. Although some values can be placed in contrasting pairs, other values may need to be fit into a more complex theoretical structure. For the five universal questions posed below, you will see that Kluckhohn and Strodtbeck offer three possible answers.

Five Universal Questions:

1. What is the nature of human nature?
2. What is the correct relationship between humanity and the natural environment?
3. What is the correct relationship between human beings?
4. What is the prime motivation for human behavior?
5. What is the correct orientation toward time?

Kluckhohn and Strodtbeck claim that there are three primary answers to each of these questions. These three answers are presented in the following chart:

Kluckhohn and Strodtbeck's Value Orientations

View of:	View Number 1	View Number 2	View Number 3
1. Human nature	Good	A mixture of good and evil	Evil
2. Humans and nature	Subject to nature	Harmony with nature	Mastery over nature
3. Social relationships	Authoritarian/lineal	Group/collateral	Individualistic
4. Motivation for behavior	Being	Being-in-becoming	Doing
5. Time orientation	Past	Present	Future

Figure 3.25 Different cultures answer basic worldview questions differently.

Kluckhohn and Strodtbeck's Value Orientation Theory is widely known and disseminated among cross-cultural psychologists and interculturalists. Many scholars feel that their approach can give us important insights into the similarities and differences between human beings from different cultures. We do not have the time or space to fully develop or explain this theory. Instead, we are using Kluckhohn and Strodtbeck's Value Orientation Theory as a transitional device to move from a consideration of simple opposing value pairs to a more complex discussion of worldviews. Worldviews, we will see, play a large role in the value orientations of human beings.

Figure 3.26   Some cultures believe that human beings should aim for harmony with nature.

Section 2: Worldviews

The English word "worldview" (first used in 1858) is derived from the German word "weltanschauung," a term coined by the German philosopher Immanuel Kant to denote a set of beliefs that underlie and shape a person's or a culture's view of the world. Synonyms for "worldview" are "metaphysical view," "meta-narrative," and "Big Picture." Definitions of the term "worldview" include the following:

1. a comprehensive conception or apprehension of the world;
2. the overall perspective from which one sees and interprets the world;
3. a collection of beliefs about life and the universe held by an individual or group;
4. a way of thinking about truth and reality;
5. a set of presuppositions or assumptions which we hold about the basic makeup of our world.

In Chapter 1, we presented four comparisons for culture: we said that culture was like 1) a fishbowl, 2) a pair of glasses, 3) a computer operating system, and 4) an iceberg. Each of these comparisons about

Figure 3.27   Your core beliefs underlie and shape how you view the world.

culture also sheds light on how worldviews operate, especially the third comparison—culture is like a computer operating system. We will reintroduce this comparison here:

> "Computers cannot function without hardware and software. In addition to motherboards and processing chips and hard drives, computers need to be programmed with a software operating system. Similarly, human beings have bodies and brains, but they cannot function without a worldview, without a way of viewing and interpreting the world around them. Cultures provide people with worldviews that give people a way to interpret the events and behaviors around them."

This computer comparison connecting worldviews to cultures leads into the first of six general characteristics of worldviews.

Six Characteristics of Worldviews

1. **Worldviews are transmitted by human cultures.** Although some elements of human nature and human behavior are very likely innate, our basic beliefs about the world are transmitted and taught to us. The process of enculturation binds us together with other people who hold similar beliefs about the basic makeup of the world.
2. **Worldviews are deep-seated and often unconscious.** Most of the time, human beings do not consciously think about or consider their worldviews. The term "worldview," remember, has only been in existence for about 200 years. Like fish unaware that they are in a fishbowl, human beings are often unaware that their thoughts are contained in a worldview framework.
3. **Worldviews are anchored by basic core beliefs, assumptions, or presuppositions.** As the iceberg comparison in Chapter 1 revealed, when analyzing people or cultures, you need to look below their surface behaviors. As you go deeper, you discover that behaviors are motivated by attitudes, and attitudes are created by values, and values are anchored by basic core beliefs. We will present three types of core worldview beliefs in this chapter section: 1) beliefs about the nature of reality, 2) beliefs about the nature of truth, and 3) beliefs about the nature of good and evil.
4. **Worldviews are fluid and dynamic (changeable).** Just as a person can put on a different pair of glasses, a person can change their "perceptual lenses" and worldview frameworks. However, shifting from one worldview framework to another is a complex psychological process. Worldviews can be changed, but not easily. People often resist any changes to their core beliefs.
5. **Worldviews can contain internal conflicts or tensions.** Worldview frameworks are belief systems, and belief systems sometimes contain internal tensions. People may undergo worldview shifts when they cannot resolve an internal worldview conflict.
6. **Worldviews can clash or conflict.** In addition to containing internal conflicts, worldviews can also conflict with one another. Sometimes the core beliefs of one worldview directly contradict the core beliefs of another worldview. Sometimes a "culture clash" is actually a worldview clash—groups of people sometimes have very different ways of viewing the world and of interpreting the events occurring in the world.

Three Types of Worldviews

A very rich discussion of worldviews can be found on the internet at the Project Worldview website (See www.projectworldview.org). Stephen P. Cook has designed an interactive, web-based experience that allows people to explore 81 different worldview themes and 320 worldview subcategories. We will aim for a much more modest introduction to worldviews in this section—we will introduce to you three basic types of worldviews: 1) ontological worldviews, 2) epistemological worldviews, and 3) moral/ethical worldviews.

Ontological Worldviews

Ontology is a branch of philosophy that studies the nature of reality. Your "ontological worldview" is your view of what is "really real." In his book Why Religion Matters (HarperCollins, 2009), Huston Smith, a well-respected scholar of comparative religion, identifies and labels three major ontological worldviews that have existed in human history: 1) the traditional worldview, 2) the modern worldview, and 3) the postmodern worldview.

Smith claims that for the bulk of human history, most human beings held a traditional, dualistic view of reality that recognized both the natural and supernatural realms. He claims that every major world religion has taught and upheld this traditional ontological worldview.

Smith traces the modern ontological worldview back to the rise of modern science. As modern science (based on the observation and quantification of the material world) arose and took hold in the western world, a monistic view of reality prevailed that recognized nature and the material world as the only reality there is. The modern, secular, naturalistic worldview was prevalent in western cultures from the mid-1600s to the early part of the twentieth century.

Smith notes that a postmodern ontological worldview (anticipated by German philosopher Nietzsche) took hold in western cultures in the 1950s and is still in operation today. Postmoderns reject the notion of worldviews and "meta-narratives" which, they claim, are used to oppress and control human beings. They reject the idea that there is any "Big Picture."

The Transformation of Ontological Worldviews in the Western World

1. The Traditional Worldview (From the beginning of human civilization to 1650)
2. The Modern Worldview (From 1650 to 1950)
3. The Postmodern Worldview (From 1950 to the present)

Figure 3.28   Three ontological worldviews (views of reality) have dominated in western cultures.

To understand modern American culture, you need to understand that all three of these ontological worldviews (traditional, modern, and postmodern) are held by different American co-cultures. Some Americans believe that there is a natural world and a supernatural world, some Americans believe that the natural world is the only reality there is, and some Americans refuse to take a stand on the ultimate nature of reality. Let us take a brief look at each ontological worldview.

Traditional Ontological Worldview: Note that the inner circle in Figure 3.29 is composed of a broken line because a diagram of the traditional ontological worldview must allow for inter-action between the natural and supernatural realms. Those who hold a traditional ontological worldview believe that the natural world is penetrated and permeated by the super- or supra-natural world: reality is a duality that consists of the natural/supernatural, material/immaterial, and physical/spiritual. The major religions of the world teach and uphold the traditional onto-logical worldview, so people who are traditionally religious can be categorized as ontological

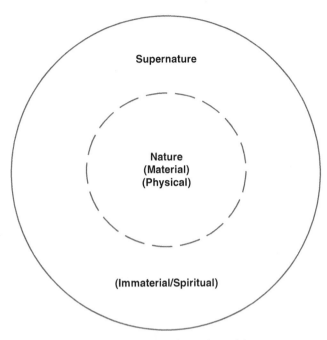

Figure 3.29 Traditional ontological worldview.

dualists. However, some people who reject organized religion still retain the traditional ontological worldview. Instead of identifying themselves as "religious," they may identify themselves as "spiritual."

Modern Ontological Worldview: There is only one circle representing the modern ontological worldview because this worldview is "monistic": nature, the modern ontological worldview holds, comprises all of reality. Since modern science gave rise to the modern worldview, people who value modern scientific knowledge tend to hold the modern, monistic ontological worldview, especially people prone to "scientism." Scientism is the belief that scientific knowledge is the only valid way of knowing.

Figure 3.30 Modern ontological worldview.

Since the modern ontological worldview does not acknowledge the reality of the supernatural, immaterial, spiritual realm, many people who hold this worldview are not traditionally religious. Most often, people who hold this ontological worldview are atheists: they do not believe in the existence of a supernatural deity or in the existence of supernatural entities of any sort.

The Postmodern Ontological Worldview: A large question mark is placed in the circle representing the postmodern ontological worldview because people who hold this ontological worldview are not willing to commit either to traditional ontological dualism or to modern ontological monism. The nature of reality, they believe, is not easily determined, so they avoid making ontological worldview claims altogether. However, people who hold the postmodern ontological

Figure 3.31 Postmodern ontological worldview.

worldview on the conscious level may, unconsciously, hold either of the other two ontological worldviews.

What is your ontological worldview? Are you a traditional dualist who believes in the interaction between nature and supernature, are you a modern monist who believes that nature is a closed system, or are you a postmodern person who eschews meta-narratives and "Big Picture" thinking? Perhaps you belong to co-culture groups that promote different ontological worldviews, so you sometimes hold to one ontological worldview, and at other times your attitudes and actions are influenced by another ontological worldview.

It is probably easiest to shift from a postmodern ontological worldview to one of the other two ontological worldviews. This particular ontological worldview shift involves primarily making a commitment to either ontological dualism or monism. Basically, a person making this worldview shift "chooses a side." Conversely, a person shifting from either a traditional or modern ontological worldview to a postmodern ontological worldview opts out of "Big Picture" thinking and refuses to be placed in either the "traditional" or "modern" category.

The ontological worldviews that are in greatest tension are the traditional and modern worldviews: you cannot be, at the exact same moment, a monist and a dualist. These two ontological worldviews conflict at the deepest level: either nature is all there is, or there is more to reality than the natural world. To help you determine whether you hold primarily either to a traditional, supernatural worldview or a modern, natural worldview, we will list some traditional supernatural realities described in many major world religions. For those who are traditionally religious (and who hold a traditional ontological worldview), at least some of the items on this list will be viewed as real. Those who hold a modern ontological worldview, however, will view most, if not all, of the items on this list as religious concepts that have no basis in reality. That is, they will admit that these items exist as concepts in the human mind, but they will believe that these concepts have no corresponding entities that exist outside of the human mind.

Allah/Jehova/God	Incorporeal, immortal soul
Angels/devils	Jins/genies
Answered prayer	Life after death
Black magic/voodoo	Miracles/divine intervention/providence
Creation of the world by a deity or deities	Purgatory/Paradise
Demon possession/exorcism	Rational glossalalia
Devil/Satan	Reincarnation
Ghosts/spirits	Resurrection
Gods or goddesses	Revealed truth/divine inspiration
Heaven/hell	Supernatural healing

Figure 3.32   Traditional supernatural realities/concepts found in major world religions.

Epistemological Worldviews

Epistemology is a branch of philosophy that studies the nature of knowledge and truth. Your "epistemological worldview" is your view of knowledge. Just as your ontological worldview causes you to believe that certain things are or are not real, your epistemological worldview causes you to believe that certain things can or cannot be known. We will present to you three epistemological worldviews: 1) the dogmatic worldview, 2) the cynical worldview, and 3) the idealistic/skeptical worldview.

While completing his doctoral work in the rhetoric of philosophy at the University of California, Berkeley, in the late 1980s and early 1990s, Mark Staller identified three different epistemological worldviews. The similarities and differences between these epistemological worldviews are illustrated in Figure 3.33.

Unlike the ontological worldviews identified by Huston Smith, Staller's epistemological worldviews are not clearly linked to different periods of history in western culture. Instead, Staller first identified the two epistemological worldviews that were in greatest tension, the dogmatic worldview and the cynical worldview, and then he developed his explanation of the idealistic/skeptical worldview that functions as a middle ground between these two contrasting worldviews. Like Kluckhohn and Strodtbeck's Values Orientation Theory, Staller marks off a middle position between two contrasting positions.

Dogmatic Worldview	Idealistic/Skeptical Worldview	Cynical Worldview
Truth exists	Truth exists	Truth does not exist
Truth can be known with certainty	It is difficult to get hold of the truth	"Truths" are constructed to persuade people
Language is used to teach the truth	Language is used to approach the truth	Language is used as a game or a power play
Certainty	Certainty/uncertainty	Uncertainty

Figure 3.33 Three epistemological worldviews.

The Dogmatic Epistemological Worldview: People who hold the dogmatic epistemological worldview believe that truth exists, and they also believe that truth can be known with certainty. Dogmatists believe that human language should be used to teach truth and certain knowledge to others. A negative example of the dogmatic epistemological worldview would be religious and other cults. A positive example of the dogmatic epistemological worldview would be Roman Catholicism. However, you do not have to be religious to hold the dogmatic epistemological worldview, as extreme scientism and the now-discredited philosophy of logical positivism illustrate. (In the early twentieth century, logical positivists argued that only self-evident or experimentally verifiable propositions had any validity.)

The Cynical Epistemological Worldview: People who hold the cynical epistemological worldview believe that absolute truth (Truth with a capital "T") does not exist, but they believe that people construct their own "truths" (in quotation marks) in order to persuade others. Cynics believe that human language is just a game or a power play—you can use language to entertain yourself and others, or you can use it to get what you want from others. Politicians, cynics claim, say whatever they need to say to get elected. Lawyers, cynics claim, say whatever they need to say to win their legal cases. People who hold a cynical epistemological worldview are often extreme relativists—nothing is certain, and everything is negotiable.

The Idealistic/Skeptical Worldview: People who hold the idealistic/skeptical worldview believe that truth exists, but they also believe that it is difficult to get hold of the truth. In other words, absolute truth exists, but it cannot be known with absolute certainty. Idealistic skeptics believe that human language should be used to approach the truth. Politicians should vigorously debate issues in order to make the best possible decisions about government policies. Lawyers should do their best to prosecute and defend clients so that the judge and jury have the best chance of arriving at a just verdict. People who hold an idealistic/skeptical worldview do not naively believe that truth, justice, and wisdom are easily reached or achieved, but they believe that people should strive to approach these ideals.

What is your primary epistemological worldview? Do you believe that truth can be known with absolute certainty, or do you believe that truth is an ideal to strive toward, or do you believe that truth does not exist? Do you believe that language can be used to teach absolute truth to others, or do you believe that language should be used to approach the truth, or do you believe that language is a game or a power play?

We should point out that Staller's epistemological worldviews are not necessarily exhaustive: there may be other epistemological worldview possibilities. For example, if you do not hold a dogmatic or cynical epistemological worldview, perhaps you can find another way besides idealistic skepticism to find a middle ground between these two opposing positions. Perhaps you may want to become a "truth agnostic" and not take a firm stand on whether truth does or does not exist. If so, you can construct your own epistemological worldview that falls somewhere between idealistic skepticism and cynicism.

We should also point out that epistemological worldviews, like ontological worldviews, can shift and change. You may hold one epistemological worldview at a certain age, or when thinking about certain knowledge areas or beliefs. You may also shift epistemological worldviews as you interact with different people and different cultures. However, because worldviews are deep-seated, you most likely have one epistemological worldview that predominates. We will give you another list that can help you determine your epistemological worldview. Here are 10 different sources of knowledge or beliefs:

1. Authority
2. Inspiration
3. Intuition
4. Introspection
5. Experience
6. Experimentation
7. Observation
8. Revelation
9. Testimony
10. Theorizing/thinking

Figure 3.34 Ten sources of knowledge or beliefs.

Questions for Consideration:

Which of these sources predominate in art? In philosophy? In religion? In science?
Which of these sources give us the most reliable knowledge and most valuable insights?
Which of these sources give us the least reliable knowledge and the least valuable insights?
Which sources do you value the most? Why?
Which sources do you value the least? Why?

If you take the time to thoughtfully answer the above questions, you will deepen your understanding of your own epistemological worldview, and you will discover what knowledge and belief sources are most important (and least important) to you. However, you also need to prepare yourself to interact and communicate with people from other cultures and co-cultures who answer these questions differently.

Moral/Ethical Worldviews

In addition to ontological worldviews and epistemological worldviews, human beings have moral/ethical worldviews: they have basic, core beliefs about the nature and reality of good and evil. The chart below created by Mark Staller illustrates four answers that can be given when considering the nature/reality of good and evil in three different areas: 1) views on the moral nature of human beings, 2) views on the moral nature of the natural, material world, and 3) views on the moral nature of the supernatural, immaterial world.

Kluckhohn and Strodtbeck, remember, identified three primary answers to the question, "What is the nature of human nature?" Their Values Orientation Theory claimed that human cultures and societies have answered that either 1) human nature is good, 2) human nature is a mixture of good and evil, or 3) human nature is evil.

Staller has added a fourth possible answer that is often given by people in modern, secular societies: human nature is neither good nor evil. The modern ontological worldview that recognizes nature as the only reality can lead to a moral/ethical worldview that is value-free or value neutral. Nature just is—it is neither good nor evil. Human beings are a product of nature whose actions are determined by nature, so they too are neither good nor evil. The supernatural world does not exist, so it too is neither good nor evil. Try to identify other past or present cultures that give the four different answers listed in the chart below.

Moral/Ethical Worldviews

Area	View #1	View #2	View #3	View #4
Human beings	Good	A mixture of good and evil	Evil	Neither good nor evil
The natural world	Good	A mixture of good and evil	Evil	Neither good nor evil
The supernatural world	Good	A mixture of good and evil	Evil	Neither good nor evil

Figure 3.35 There are four primary views of the moral nature of human beings, the natural world, and the supernatural world.

Questions to Consider:

What is your view of human beings? Are human beings basically good, evil, a mixture of good and evil, or neither good nor evil?

What is you view of nature? Is the natural world basically good, evil, a mixture of good and evil, or neither good nor evil?

What is your view of the supernatural world? Is the supernatural world basically good, evil, a mixture of good and evil, or neither good nor evil?

The way you answer the above questions is determined by your moral/ethical worldview, and your moral/ethical worldview is determined to a large extent by the cultures and co-cultures to which you belong. If you are a member of a religious culture, you may be able to quickly formulate answers to the above questions because one function of religion is to provide answers to these very general, very basic questions about life and morality.

Section 3: Religion

Why does this chapter on values and worldviews end with a section on religion? Religions often provide meta-narratives that answer "Big Picture" questions. Religions provide answers to some of the most important human questions, and these answers form worldviews from which we derive our values. Religion has been recognized as one of the "deep-structure" institutions of traditional cultures, and although secularism is an important development in the modern world, about 80% of the human population still practices some form of religion.

Although there are thousands of religions in the world, we will focus on classical major world religions that might be studied in a college course on comparative religion. We end this chapter with a brief summary of the major tenets and values of the following major world religions: Baha'i Faith, Buddhism, Christianity, Confucianism, Hinduism, Islam, Jainism, Judaism, Shinto, Sikhism, and Taoism. These major world religions cross national boundaries and create common beliefs and behaviors for people in many different

Figure 3.36 Worldviews and values are influenced by different secular and religious approaches.

countries and cultures. Since secularism is an important part of the modern world, we also consider the values and tenets of modern secular humanism, a clearly defined, nonreligious movement.

The term "religion" is notoriously difficult to define. We will present five definitions of religion, and then we will point out the drawbacks and limitations of these definitions. Here are five definitions of religion:

1. an organized system of beliefs, ceremonies, and rules used to worship a god or group of gods;
2. an organized collection of beliefs, cultural systems, and worldviews that relate humanity to an order of existence;
3. belief in and reverence for a supernatural power or powers;
4. a set of beliefs concerning the cause, nature, and purpose of the universe;
5. relation of human beings to god or the gods or to whatever they consider sacred or supernatural.

The first part of definition 1 is important because it points out that religions have an organized system of beliefs, ceremonies, and rules. However, the last part of definition one is too narrow because it excludes religions like Buddhism and Confucianism that do not necessarily worship a god or group of gods.

On the other hand, definitions 2 and 4 are too broad to clearly distinguish religion from philosophy or science. These other fields of human knowledge also provide organized collections of beliefs that "relate humanity to an order of existence." Modern science, like religion, also provides "a set of beliefs concerning the cause, nature, and purpose of the universe," but science should be clearly distinguished from religion.

Definitions 3 and 5 are on the right track because they recognize that traditional world religions uphold a "dualist" view of the world that acknowledges the supernatural. However, these definitions omit references to an organized system of beliefs and practices, so they do not clearly distinguish "spiritualism" from religion: some people reject organized religion while still believing in the supernatural or spiritual.

Four Elements of Religion

Instead of providing one unproblematic definition of religion, we will point out four basic elements of religion. Traditional religions of the world contain these four elements: 1) Creed (doctrines, teachings, and shared beliefs); 2) Code (an ethical system); 3) Cult (religious practices, rituals, and observances); and 4) Community (a group of religious believers or practitioners).

Four Elements of Religion
1. Creed (doctrines, teachings, and shared beliefs)
2. Code (an ethical system or code)
3. Cult (religious practices, rituals, and observances)
4. Community (a group of religious believers or practitioners)

Figure 3.37 Four elements of religion are creed, code, cult, and community.

Creed: Religions diverge most significantly in their doctrines and dogmas. The most basic, fundamental beliefs of one religion may conflict with, and even directly contradict, the basic, fundamental beliefs of another religion. The core beliefs of religions are often written down, transmitted through, and preserved in sacred texts or holy books. The sacred text of Judaism is the *Tanakh* or Hebrew Bible, especially the *Torah*. The sacred text of Christianity is the Christian Bible, especially the *New Testament*. The sacred text of Islam is the *Koran* (or *Quran*). Some of the major teachings and beliefs of Confucianism can be found in *The Analects*, of Taoism in the *Tao te Ching*, and of Buddhism in *The Dhammapada*, *The Pali Canon*, and *The Lotus Sutra*. Some of the major teachings and beliefs of Baha'I Faith can be found in the *Kitab-i-Aqdas* and the *Bab*, of Sikhism in the *Guru Granth Sahib* or *Adi Granth*, and of Shinto in *Kojiki* and *Nihon-gi*. Hinduism has the one of the richest traditions of sacred texts, including the *Vedas*, the *Upanishads*, and the *Puranas*. Book Six of *The Mahabharata* (an epic poem), *The Bhagavad Gita*, is also now widely recognized by many Hindus as a sacred text. Almost every major world religion also has secondary texts that help to explain and interpret the primary sacred texts.

© kamomeen, 2014. Used under license from Shutterstock, Inc.

Figure 3.37 The beliefs of major world religions are transmitted by and preserved in sacred religious texts.

Code: There is remarkable agreement in the ethical systems or codes of the major world religions. Most major world religions promote benevolence, universalism, self-sacrifice, and an ethic of care and concern for others. Whereas disagreements in religious creeds can lead to religious conflicts, agreement in religious codes can help to promote similar positive ethical behaviors in many different countries and cultures.

Cult: Religions often have daily practices and rituals such as prayer, meditation, the reading of sacred texts, sacrifices, and purification rituals. They also often have special observances that occur over the course of the calendar year such as feast days, pilgrimages, and festivals.

Community: Religion is primarily a social institution: religious believers often gather together to practice their religious faith, and sometimes they even live together in religious communities. Religious cultural spaces where such gatherings occur include temples, shrines, churches, mosques, and monasteries.

© chrupka, 2014. Used under license from Shutterstock, Inc.

Figure 3.38   The Monastery of Agia Triada in Crete, Greece.

Four Religious Stances

In addition to four basic elements of religion, when interacting with people from different religious faiths and religious traditions, you should be aware of four primary religious stances: 1) exclusivism, 2) inclusivism, 3) pluralism, and 4) syncretism. **Exclusivism** is the belief that one religion is correct, and that other religions are in serious error. **Inclusivism** is the belief that all religions, below the surface differences, are unifiable. **Pluralism** is the belief that religions are different but can coexist. **Syncretism** is the belief that different religions can be amalgamated or combined together.

Four Religious Stances
1. Exclusivism (the belief that one religion is correct, and all other religions are in serious error)
2. Inclusivism (the belief that all religions, below the surface differences, are unifiable)
3. Pluralism (the belief that religions are different but can coexist)
4. Syncretism (the belief that different religions can be amalgamated or combined together)

Figure 3.39   There are four religious stances taken by different religious traditions.

Religious syncretism is widely practiced in China and other Eastern countries. Unlike countries in the West that have different populations practicing different religions, China has the same religious population practicing several Eastern religions at once. Chinese traditional religion is a combination of Buddhism, Confucianism, Taoism, and other local customs and practices.

Figure 3.40   Chinese traditional religion is a combination of Buddhism, Confucianism, and Taoism.

A Religious and Nonreligious Primer

Although we should not discount religion and the influence of religion, we also cannot ignore the growth in secularism and in nonreligious people groups in the modern world. Modern American society is composed of religious, nonreligious, and antireligious people groups. Similar divisions can be made in many modern countries of the world.

To be an effective intercultural communicator, you need to develop a basic vocabulary that defines and describes different religious and nonreligious categories. The following terms help to distinguish some of these different categories:

Agnosticism: A philosophical or religious orientation of doubt. Agnostics do not commit to firm belief or disbelief in god.

Deism: The belief in a creator god who does not intervene in the universe. Deism was a transitional worldview (popular between 1700 and 1850) between the traditional ontological worldview and the modern ontological worldview. Thomas Jefferson and Benjamin Franklin were Deists.

Explicit atheism: The conscious rejection of theistic belief. Explicit atheists are committed to firm disbelief in god, and most explicit atheists are also opposed to belief in any supernatural element.

Implicit atheism: The absence of theistic belief without conscious rejection of it. Implicit atheists may be apathetic toward or uninterested in traditional religious beliefs.

Monotheism: The belief in a single, all-powerful god. Four monotheistic world religions are Christianity, Judaism, Islam, and Sikhism.

Pantheism: The belief that god is in all, including nature. Pantheism collapses the dualistic distinction between nature and supernature.

Polytheism: The belief in many gods or spirits. Hinduism and Shinto are world religions classified as polytheistic.

Secular humanism: Humanism viewed as a system of values and beliefs that are opposed to the values and beliefs of traditional religions.

Secularism: Indifference to or rejection of religion and religious considerations.

This religious primer should help you to communicate more effectively with religious and nonreligious people groups. To further your understanding, we will end this chapter with a list of 11 classical world religions and a brief summary of their major tenets and values. These world religions are listed alphabetically, and the number of adherents of each of these religions is adapted from the website adherents.com.

Classical World Religions and their Major Tenets and Values

Baha'i Faith: Founded by Baha'ullah in Persia in 1863.
(Adherents: 7 million) Tenets and Values:

- Unity of all religions
- Unity of humanity

- Service to humanity

- Equality between the sexes
- Baha'ullah as a divine messenger
- Elimination of all forms of prejudice

- A peaceful and integrated global Society

- Harmony of science and religion

Buddhism: Founded in India between the sixth and fourth centuries BCE by Gautama Buddha.
(Adherents: 376 million) Tenets and Values:

- Enlightenment
- Nirvana
- Release from suffering

- Detachment/renunciation
- Compassion
- Wisdom

- The Four Noble Truths
- The Eightfold Path
- The Five Precepts

Christianity: Founded in Palestine in the first century CE by Jesus Christ.
(Adherents: 2 billion) Tenets and Values:

- Love of god and neighbor
- Salvation from sin and death
- Forgiveness and mercy

- The divinity of Christ

- Unconditional love

- Self-sacrifice

- Purity/righteousness

- Resurrection and judgment

- The Apostle's Creed

Confucianism: Founded in the sixth century BCE by Chinese philosopher Confucius.
(Adherents: 394 million [Chinese Traditional Religion]) Tenets and Values:

- Practical social ethics
- Importance of family
- Cultivation of virtue

- Politeness and propriety
- Altruism and humaneness
- Loyalty and filial piety

- The perfectibility of human beings
- Harmonious relationships
- Meritocracy

Hinduism: Ancient religion founded before or by 1,500 B.C. Composed of a diverse body of ancient religion, philosophy, and cultural practice native to and predominant in India.
(Adherents: 900 million) Tenets and Values:

- Brahman as ultimate truth and reality
- Evolution of the individual personality
- Execution and achievement of dharma

- Moksha: liberation from the cycle of death and rebirth

- Divinity of human beings

- Universality/inclusiveness

Islam: Founded by Mohammed in Arabia in the seventh century CE.
(Adherents: 1.5 billion) Tenets and Values:

- The Quran as god's final revelation
- Mohammed as god's prophet
- Obedience and submission to Allah

- Alms for the poor
- The five pillars
- Day of judgment

- Protection of life, religion, knowledge, family, and wealth
- The worship of one god

Jainism: Founded by Mahavira in India in the sixth century BCE.
(Adherents: 4 million) Tenets and Values:

- Ahimsa, nonviolence to-ward all living beings
- Moksha, liberation of the soul
- Spiritual independence and equality between all forms of life

- Asceticism/self-control
- Enlightenment
- Honesty

Judaism: Tracing its origins to Abraham and having its spiritual and ethical principles embodied in the Hebrew Scriptures and the Talmud.
(Adherents: 14 million) Tenets and Values:

- Compassion
- Social justice
- Knowledge/education

- Argumentation/debate
- Unity of god
- Love of neighbor

- Humanity created in the image of god
- TORAH
- Well-being of humanity

Shinto: Native to Japan and lacking formal dogma. Characterized by devotion to deities or nature spirits.
(Adherents: 4 million) Tenets and Values:

- Essential goodness of humanity
- Purity
- kami, divine nature spirits

- Harmony
- Practical ethics
- Social order

- Loyalty to clan and state
- Ritual
- The present life

Sikhism: Founded by Guru Nanak in Northern India in the sixteenth century CE.
(Adherents: 23 million) Tenets and Values:

- Worship of one god
- Equality
- Nondiscrimination

- Peace and unity of humankind
- Hard work
- Service and sharing with others

- Religious freedom and justice
- The Ten Gurus
- The Five Articles of Faith

(Continued)

Taoism: Founded by Lao-tzu in China in the sixth century BCE.
(Adherents: 394 million [Chinese Traditional Religion]) Tenets and Values:

- Harmony with the Tao
- Naturalness
- Simplicity
- Spontaneity
- Compassion
- Moderation
- Humility
- Nonaction/effortless action
- Yin and Yang

Addendum: One-seventh of the total world population (about one billion people) is secular/nonreligious/agnostic/atheist. One well-defined secular worldview is developed in the Secular Humanist Movement. The following list of the tenets and values of secular humanism is adapted from the website secularhumanism.org.

Secular Humanism: A nonreligious outlook on life developed in the modern world. Most secular humanists uphold the following tenets and values:

- A naturalistic philosophy
- Free inquiry
- A consequentialist ethics
- The scientific method
- Freedom and democracy
- Humanist Manifesto I and II
- A cosmic outlook rooted in science
- Application of reason and science
- Rejection of and freedom from traditional religious beliefs

Summary

After reading Section 1 of this chapter, you have a better understanding of human values. You know 13 dominant values of modern American culture, and you know 10 basic values that are found in almost every country. You also now know about six value dimensions, two time orientations, and several different value orientations found among the different people and cultures of the world. In addition, you have (hopefully) analyzed and identified your own value preferences and value orientations.

In Section 2 of this chapter, you gained a better understanding of worldviews and the foundational part they play in human cultures and in your own perceptions. You can now distinguish between three basic types of worldviews (ontological worldviews, epistemological worldviews, and moral/ethical worldviews), and you can describe different worldviews that exist in each of these knowledge areas. In addition, you have had a chance to identify your own ontological, epistemological, and moral/ethical worldviews.

In the third and final section of this chapter, you gained a better understanding of some of the major world religions as well as some nonreligious ways of viewing and living in the world. You now know the four elements of religion (creed, code, cult, and community) and four religious stances (exclusivism, inclusivism, pluralism, and syncretism). You also now have a vocabulary that can help you understand and discuss some basic religious and nonreligious categories.

This chapter concludes the first unit of your textbook. You now know about the foundations of intercultural communication, you have learned to appreciate both sameness and difference, and you now understand the crucial role that values and worldviews play in intercultural interactions. With this solid theoretical and practical grounding, you are well equipped to build more satisfying relationships with people from other cultures. We encourage you to continue to expand your knowledge of intercultural communication and to improve your intercultural communication skills by reading units 2 and 3 of this textbook.

Glossary

Achievement   One of the 10 basic human values identified by Schwartz. The defining goal of achievement is personal success through demonstrating competence according to social standards.

Acquisitiveness   One of the 13 American values identified by Kohls. Characterized by a strong desire to acquire money or material things.

Agnosticism   A philosophical or religious orientation of doubt. Agnostics reserve committing to firm belief or disbelief in god.

Atheism   Disbelief in, and the denial of, the existence of god or gods.

Baha'i Faith   One of the 12 classical world religions founded by Baha'ullah in Persia in 1863 and emphasizing the spiritual unity of humankind.

Benevolence   One of the 10 basic human values identified by Schwartz. The defining goal of benevolence is preserving and enhancing the welfare of those with whom one is in frequent personal contact.

Buddhism   One of the 12 classical world religions founded in India between the sixth and fourth centuries BCE by Gautama Buddha designed to help people escape from suffering and the cycle of rebirth through the attainment of nirvana.

Christianity   One of the 12 classical world religions founded in Palestine in the first century CE by Jesus Christ and focused on salvation from sin and death.

Collectivism   One of the six value dimensions identified by Hofstede; contrasted to collectivism. People from collectivistic societies value social cohesion and social stability.

Confucianism   One of the 12 classical world religions founded in the sixth century BCE by Chinese philosopher Confucius emphasizing family, tradition, ethical behavior, and mutual respect.

Conformity   One of the 10 basic human values identified by Schwartz. The defining goal of conformity is restraint of actions, inclinations, and impulses likely to upset or harm others and violate social expectations or norms.

Cynical worldview   One of the three epistemological worldviews identified by Staller. A cynical worldview rejects the concept of absolute truth and views language as a game or power play.

Deism   The belief in a creator god who does not intervene in the universe.

Dogmatic worldview   One of the three epistemological worldviews identified by Staller. A dogmatic worldview accepts the notion of absolute truth and certain knowledge and views language as a vehicle to reveal truth to others.

Dualism   As it relates to ontology, the notion that the universe is composed of two realities, the natural and the supernatural world.

Egalitarianism   One of the 13 American values identified by Kohl. The notion that all people should have equal political, economic, social, and civil rights.

Epistemological worldview   A person's or society's view of truth, knowledge, and belief.

Femininity   One of the six value dimensions identified by Hofstede; contrasted to masculinity. Feminine cultures value relationships and the quality of life. In feminine cultures, the differences between gender roles are less pronounced and more fluid, and both males and females value care and concern for others.

Hedonism   One of the 10 basic human values identified by Schwartz. The defining goal of hedonism is pleasure or sensuous gratification for oneself.

Hierarchical   Ordered or arranged by rank, ability, or status. Hierarchy is a value contrasted to the American value of equality or egalitarianism.

High-power distance   One of the six value dimensions identified by Hofstede; contrasted to low-power distance. In cultures with high-power distance, less powerful members of organizations and institutions are likely to accept and expect that power is distributed unequally.

High uncertainty avoidance   One of the six value dimensions identified by Hofstede; contrasted to low uncertainty avoidance. In cultures with high uncertainty avoidance, people try to minimize unknown and unusual circumstances by implementing and following rules, laws, and regulations.

Hinduism   One of the 12 classical world religions composed of a diverse body of religion, philosophy, and cultural practice native to and predominant in India and characterized by the worship of many gods (including Brahma as a supreme being), a caste system, and belief in reincarnation.

Idealistic/Skeptical worldview   One of the three epistemological worldviews identified by Staller. The view that truth exists, but it is difficult to grasp with certainty; consequently, language is used to approach the truth.

Individualism   One of the six value dimensions identified by Hofstede; contrasted to collectivism. People from individualistic societies value personal achievement and individual autonomy.

Indulgence   One of the six value dimensions identified by Hofstede; contrasted to restraint. Indulgent societies tend to allow relatively free gratification of basic physical human desires.

Islam   One of the 12 classical world religions founded by Mohammed in Arabia in the seventh century CE and characterized by the doctrine of submission to Allah and to Mohammed as the chief and last prophet of God.

Jainism   One of the 12 classical world religions founded by Mahavira in India in the sixth century BCE as a reaction against Vedic religion and characterized by the core belief of ahimsa, or noninjury to all living things.

Judaism   One of the 12 classical world religions tracing its origins to Abraham and having its spiritual and ethical principles embodied in the Hebrew Scriptures and the Talmud.

Long-term orientation   One of the six value dimensions identified by Hofstede; contrasted to short-term orientation. Cultures with long-term orientation value the future benefits that come through persistence, saving, and adaptation.

Low-power distance   One of the six value dimensions identified by Hofstede; contrasted to high-power distance. In cultures with low-power distance, members accept and expect power relations that are consultative and democratic.

Low uncertainty avoidance   One of the six value dimensions identified by Hofstede; contrasted to high uncertainty avoidance. In cultures with low uncertainty avoidance, people accept and operate well in unstructured environments and changing situations with few rules or regulations.

Masculinity   One of the six value dimensions identified by Hofstede; contrasted to femininity. Masculine cultures value competitiveness, assertiveness, materialism, ambition, and power. In masculine cultures, the differences in sex and gender roles tend to be more pronounced and less fluid than in feminine cultures.

Materialism   One of the 13 American values identified by Kohls. Americans are materialistic and acquisitive; they desire property and material possessions.

Modern worldview   One of the three ontological worldviews identified by Smith. The modern, secular worldview of many modern western societies recognizes only the natural world as real.

Monism   As related to ontology, the view that the world is made of one reality. You can be a materialistic monist, believing that only the material, natural world exists, or you can be a spiritual monist, believing that only the supernatural, immaterial, spiritual world is real.

Monochronic   A time orientation that views time as segmented into precise units that can be used or spent. People in monochronic societies value their time highly because they view time as a linear continuum that can be lost or wasted.

Monotheism   The belief in a single, all-powerful god.

Ontological worldview   A person's or society's view of what is really real.

Pantheism   The belief that god is in all, including nature.

Polychronic   A time orientation that views time as circular or reoccurring. People in polychromic societies value their relationships more highly than the completion of tasks.

Polytheism   The belief in many gods or spirits.

Postmodern worldview   One of the three ontological worldviews identified by Smith. The postmodern worldview does not recognize any Big Picture concerning reality.

Power   One of the 10 basic human values identified by Schwartz. The defining goal of power is social status and prestige and control or dominance over people and resources.

Pragmatism   One of the 13 American values identified by Kohls. Pragmatism emphasizes practicality and functionality.

Restraint   One of the six value dimensions identified by Hofstede; contrasted to indulgence. Restrained societies tend to regulate the gratification of basic human physical desires by strict norms.

Secular humanism   Humanism viewed as a system of values and beliefs that are opposed to the values and beliefs of traditional religions.

Secularism   The belief that religion should not play a role in education, government, or other public aspects of society. Indifference to or the rejection of religion and religious practices and considerations.

Security   One of the 10 basic human values identified by Schwartz. The defining goal of security is the safety, harmony, and stability of society, relationships, and self.

Self-Direction   One of the 10 basic human values identified by Schwartz. The defining goal of self-direction is independent thought and action.

Shinto   One of the 12 classical world religions native to Japan lacking formal dogma and characterized by devotion to deities or nature spirits.

Short-term orientation   One of the six value dimensions identified by Hofstede; contrasted to long-term orientation. Cultures with short-term orientation focus on the past or present and value respect for tradition, preservation of face, reciprocation, and fulfilling social obligations.

Sikhism   One of the 12 classical world religions founded by Guru Nanak in Northern India in the sixteenth century that rejects caste distinctions, idolatry, and asceticism and is characterized by belief in liberation from the cycle of reincarnation by living righteous lives as active members of society.

Stimulation   One of the 10 basic human values identified by Schwartz. The defining goal of stimulation is excitement, novelty, and challenge in life.

Taoism   One of the 12 classical world religions founded by Lao-tzu in China in the sixth century BCE that advocates simplicity, selflessness, and harmony with the Tao.

Theism   Belief in the existence of god (or gods), especially in a personal god as the creator and ruler of the universe who is actively involved in the world.

Tradition   One of the 10 basic human values identified by Schwartz. The defining goal of tradition is respect, commitment, and acceptance of the customs and ideas that one's culture or religion provides.

Traditional worldview   One of the three ontological worldviews identified by Smith. Traditional societies based on traditional religions hold the view that reality is a combination of the natural and supernatural, the material and immaterial.

Universalism   One of the 10 basic human values identified by Schwartz. The defining goal of universalism is understanding, appreciation, tolerance, and protection for the welfare of all people and of nature.

Values   Principles or standards of behavior based on what one views as good or bad, right or wrong, important or unimportant. Our values guide our decisions about what we should or should not do, depending on whether or not our actions will help us reach our goals.

Worldview   A collection of beliefs about the universe and humanity's place in it. The overall perspective from which a person observes and interprets the world.

Chapter 4

History vs. Histories

Helen Acosta

"If you don't know history, then you don't know anything. You are a leaf that doesn't know it is part of a tree. "
—Michael Crichton

Chapter Learning Objectives

1. Learn about the work historians do and the types of source material they consult.
2. Describe the reasons some histories are hidden.
3. Describe the many foci of historical research in our multicultural world.
4. Practice history-centered intercultural communication skills.

It was a warm day in Denver, midsummer, 1862. Mary Eliza Walden was just 4 years old, with her blond hair in ribbons and curls. She was playing in the trading post and her 13-year-old brother, William, had been left in charge. An old Indian man came in and, after a few minutes he asked William "How much for the golden haired angel." Being 13, William thought it would be funny to put a price on his sister. So, he began a very long list: 44 beaver pelts, 14 bear skins, 37 mules, and so on . . . The old Indian man shook his head in disappointment and went on his way. William had a good laugh about it and thought nothing more of it until . . .

. . . just after the Spring thaw. He was on the edge of town when, in the distance, he saw a long ox-drawn wagon train weighed down with furs with dozens of mules in tow. As the wagon train got closer he recognized the driver, the old Indian man, and his folly dawned on him. He ran to the trading post and confessed everything to his parents. His mother picked up Mary Eliza and ran her over to the Sherriff's office. When the old Indian arrived at the trading post to buy the "golden haired angel" he was told that she had died of diphtheria over the winter.

Mary Eliza was sent to Michigan to stay with relatives until she no longer looked like the golden-haired angel. Her cousins had called her a common Michigan nickname, "Matie" (rhymes with Katie). Matie Eliza came home around the age of 9, a tall girl with brown hair whom the old Indian never recognized as the golden-haired angel he had worked so hard to buy.

Matie grew up, fell in love, married George Atwood Manfull, and had several children, the youngest of whom was Cyrus, my great-grandfather. The name, Matie, was my grandmother's name, my mother also named my middle sister, Matie. My youngest sister named her daughter Eliza.

In the early 1990s I was reading a book about urban legends by folklorist Jan Harold Brunvand. I was absolutely stunned to find that there is western pioneer folklore about Indian chiefs wanting to adopt young white girls with long blond hair. The story has been recounted to folklorists in Wyoming, Colorado, and Utah hundreds of times. The story is so common folklorists call it, "Goldilocks on the Oregon Trail."

Brunvand explains that folklorists are drawn to this story because it is a legend that is only popular in white folklore. There is no Native American corollary. The story, according to Brunvand, interests folklorists because it highlights the racism built upon the obvious fears the white settlers had regarding this new and, as they saw it, savage land (Brunvand, 1981).

Initially, I had trouble taking in Brunvand's words. My grandmother shared a bedroom with the "golden haired angel" while she was growing up. How could it be possible that the story was not true? It took me years to realize that Mary Eliza was only 4 when she was sent away. Perhaps there were big issues that her parents were dealing with that were inappropriate to share with the cousins back east. Could it be that the tale was a bedtime story told to a child who was living among strangers while she was far from home? Maybe the story was meant to assure her that she was sent away by loving parents who were doing their best to assure her safety? By the time Matie Eliza came home years later, the only truth she knew was her own.

I know my great-great grandmother's firsthand account of her experience. But I have no way of knowing what really happened.

—Helen Acosta

The above is my personal account of a family story that has been retold in my family for 150 years. This story was passed down through generations and still carries with it all the beliefs, biases, and fears of the original storytellers. While the story is set within an historical context and has been told as truth for over a century, the story is not what would be called history. My great-great grandmother's story is family folklore. In his Encyclopedia of American Folklore, Jan Howard Brunvand explains that "Folklore comprises the unrecorded traditions of a people; it includes both the form and content of these traditions and their style or technique of communication from person to person." Brunvand further explains that

"Folklore is the traditional, unofficial, non-institutional part of culture. It encompasses all knowledge, understandings, values, attitudes, assumptions, feelings, and beliefs transmitted in traditional forms by word of mouth or by customary examples" (Brunvand, 1996).

In this chapter we will discuss the primary sources, such as the above folklore, historians use to develop their historical narratives, hidden histories, the group histories that are taking their place beside the majority histories worldwide, and focus on some history-based intercultural skills that will help you succeed in your intercultural encounters.

Historians Make History

Historians have the difficult work of deciding what stories are important enough to tell to generations to come. Historians have to look back and decide what is valuable. Historians are, first and foremost, people. In the last few decades professional historical organizations have stressed that historians must embrace their own perspectives rather than pretending that humans have access to complete objectivity. Historians do not favor a single monolithic view or preferred account of events from the past. Instead, they value the multiple viewpoints that were present in every historical period that are uncovered only by people who are invested in knowing what happened to people who were like them. People of nearly every time and place have lived in a time of argument, controversy, and diverging viewpoints. The more we can learn about those viewpoints, the more we can learn about history. The "Shared Values of Historians" for the American Historical Association shows a focus on diligent inquiry (American Historical Association, 2011):

- improve our understanding of the past through a complex process of critical dialogue;
- honor the integrity of the historical record;
- leave a clear trail for other historians to follow;
- acknowledge your debts to other historians;
- acknowledge and voice your point of view;
- multiple, conflicting perspectives are among the truths of history;
- celebrate mutual respect and constructive criticism.

Historians look to a variety of materials to build their narratives:

- **The public record:** news articles, government documents and today, people's public internet presence.
- **Private records:** personal correspondence, family photos.
- **Oral histories:** firsthand accounts of historical events as told by the people who experienced them.
- **Folklore:** The stories, usually oral, told from generation to generation that transmit the experiences of earlier generations

Winston Churchill, prime minister of Great Britain through World War II (WW II), once said, "History is written by the victors." As a politician, Churchill was in the position to

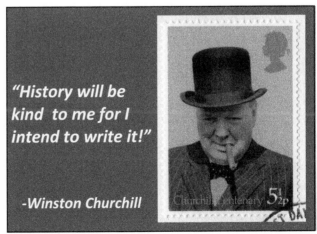

"History will be kind to me for I intend to write it!"

-Winston Churchill

© chrisdorney, 2014. Used under license from Shutterstock, Inc.

Figure 4.1 Winston Churchill quotation.

know the truth of his statement. Over the last decade much has been written about the "politics of memory." Politics, it seems, have a great deal to do with the stories we remember in our history. In their 2003 book, *Contested Pasts: The Politics of Memory*, authors and editors, Katharine Hodgekin and Susannah Radstone, brought together essays from 17 authors from around the world to examine the ways historical events, both distant and recent, are being remembered and talked about all over the planet today. Regardless of nation, historical events are still largely framed by the people in power. As a result, while many of today's leaders choose to "never forget" in order to avoid the dangers of the past, the history that we tend to honor is still the history of war, oppression, and victory (Hodgekin & Radstone, 2003).

Our Hidden Histories

"For most of history, Anonymous was a woman"
—Virginia Wolf (1882–1941)

When Kameron Hurley was in Grad School in South Africa she learned that women made up 20% of the African National Congress' military wing. She felt that this was a complete change in women's roles in the world and rushed to visit her thesis advisor. She felt like she finally had a topic she could sink her teeth into. She immediately explained to her advisor how exciting and important this change was because "Women have NEVER fought."

Her advisor did not mirror her excitement. Instead, he looked at her calmly and said, "Women have always fought." He explained that Shaka Zulu had an all-female contingent

Figure 4.2   Women have always fought.

of fighters and in every resistance movement throughout history there were women who fought beside men, sometimes making up 20% to 30% of the fighting forces.

When Hurley started doing her research she found that everything her advisor had said was true. Women have always fought side-by-side with men but their contributions have been lost to history. Among her many findings, Hurley found that it was only recently that the bones of Viking warriors dug up by archeologists in Eastern England have finally been DNA tested. It turns out that most of these Viking warriors who invaded from the north were women (Hurley, 2013).

If Kameron Hurley's research is to be believed, why do not we learn about the women warriors of the Revolutionary War in school? Why do not we learn about Sarah Shattuck and the women of Growton, MA dressing in their husband's clothes and successfully defending the Nashau River Bridge (Women in Military Service for America Memorial Foundation, 2013)?

According to many feminist scholars, we do not learn these stories because they do not fit the American narrative that we have learned in school, through books, films, documentaries, and television programs. Ann M. Little, Associate Professor of History and author of the 2007 book *Abraham in Arms: War and Gender in Colonial New England*, argues that even feminist scholars find themselves falling for a harmful narrative when they discount the work of nineteenth century women historians as amateur hobbyists. She explains that as humans we want to believe that all the work we are doing today has improved the lives of the people around us. As a result, we have constructed a powerful and inaccurate narrative that women lacked opportunity and resources back in the bad ol' days. This narrative sets women of today apart from "the bad times," giving the appearance that things are really better today. Little warns that this focus erases the contributions of women just as surely as the all-male histories of the past did (Little, 2009).

Figure 4.3 Feminist scholars are falling for a harmful narrative when they assume that nineteenth century women historians were just amateurs.

This propensity to assume that everyone is more civilized than they were in the past has also obscured our understanding of the way people have been treated throughout history. History Professor Rosanne Welch is the author of the 1998 Encyclopedia of Women in Aviation and Space and coauthor of *The Promise*, a children's chapter book based on the true story of a child who grew up in slavery. Dr. Welch explained in a recent appearance with her coauthor that before people from Africa were brought, against their will to the New World, slaves had always been the spoils of war. The historical record shows that slaves, prior to the New World, were treated as servants but not as less-than-human. It was only in the mass enslavement of hundreds of thousands of people who were brought to the New World against their will that an entire race of people were treated as less than human (Comer-Jefferson & Welch, 2014).

Historian Howard Zinn once said, "If history is to be creative, to anticipate a possible future without denying the past, it should, I believe, emphasize new possibilities by disclosing those hidden episodes of the past when, even if in brief flashes, people showed their ability to resist, to join together, occasionally to win. I am supposing, or perhaps only hoping, that our future may be found in the past's fugitive movements of compassion rather than in its solid centuries of warfare."

Multiple Histories for Multiple Perspectives

For thousands of years history was, as Churchill said, "written by the victors." This was partially due to the small number of people who could read the written histories. Royals employed people who wrote the official histories and, while there were millions of alternate experiences of these moments that were written about, only those with access to the written word and access to a large group of people to transcribe the writings held the power to control what was known and recorded as history. Gutenberg's printing press of the fifteenth century made it possible for a single person to reproduce thousands of pages of print in a matter of hours. The printing press was so inexpensive and easy to use that books, which had previously only been available to the very rich, became a part of the lives of merchants and the daily newspaper, an innovation of the seventeenth century, made the written word available to people in major cities in Europe. This expansion of access to knowledge expanded the interest in higher education.

Figure 4.4 Gutenberg's printing press made the knowledge and history accessible.

By the mid-1700s, the merchant class throughout much of Western Europe was highly educated and there was a cultural expectation that their children would go to universities. The founding fathers of the US were primarily of this merchant class, or what Ben Franklin called, "The middling classes." While there was a continued expansion in access to education and knowledge through the 1800s, the largest increase in access to knowledge came in the wake of WW II. In the US, the GI Bill, an enormous federal program to support or returning veterans, provided free and low-cost education, health care, and home loans to our returning veterans. This government program provided support to roughly 11% of the US population and their children. Within a generation the percentage of US citizens completing college jumped from 25% in 1940 to 50% in 1970. The appearance of historians also changed. In 1940, historians in the United States were almost all white males from traditional merchant class families. By the 1970s, their ranks had expanded to include women, Blacks, Latinos, Asian Americans, and Native Americans. This expansion of access to higher education and increase in diversity among all academics, including historians, was mirrored in Europe and developed across Asia. While some of these new historians were interested in the same work as the white, male historians of the past, these new historians held other interests and they began to study the hidden histories of their own backgrounds.

Today, we have a much wider view of history, thanks to the expansion of academic interest that began in the 1970s and continues today. In this section, I will discuss the different types of history that are most common today.

The Histories We Tend to Think of as "History"

In schools all over the world children learn about their **national history**. They learn about the great events and leaders that are important to the nation. They learn about the founding of the nation and the values and beliefs of the leaders who shaped the national identity. Stories about the major events and the choices leaders have made are often a vital part of a nation's identity. In the United States, the story of the Boston Tea Party is told and retold. The values of fairness and standing up against tyranny are ingrained in our national identity as a result of these stories.

In schools all over the world children also learn about the political histories of their nation. **Political histories** are concerned with the pivotal events in a nation that are connected to the governing bodies and officials of a nation. When we learn about how a particular emperor, monarch, or president shaped the direction of a nation through the choices they made, we are learning about political history. In the United States, when we learn about how the nineteenth amendment (guaranteeing women the right to vote) or the 1964 Civil Rights Act or the Voting Rights Act affect our lives today we are learning about political history.

We also have large repositories of history that are maintained by governments all over the world. These **federal histories** are curated by a wide variety of historians with different specialties. Many federal historians, for instance those who work for the Library of Congress or National Parks Service, tell the stories of our public history and work to share these stories with the public. However, there are others whose work is secret. I was surprised to learn that the CIA and NSA have historians with high-level

© Brian A. Jackson, 2014. Used under license from Shutterstock, Inc.

Figure 4.5   Some federal histories are top secret!

clearance whose job it is to provide accurate accounts of the work of these secret agencies for later generations of federal employees as well as the public in the eventuality that documents of events are later declassified.

The Histories of Conquest

As mentioned earlier, most history before the late twentieth century was political and focused on wars and conquest. However, as more people who are not from powerful families have become historians, the people whose lands have been taken from them have become historians. Their focus on learning about the conquered and dispossessed has led to greater understanding of how events unfolded.

Much of history seems to be made up of an elaborate game of duck-duck-goose. The people in power circle those who are not in power until everyone is disoriented then, when those without power least expect it, **BAM!** They are tagged to chase or be chased. This game of chase happens when people in power displace people who are born without power.

Today, **colonial histories** are centered on the expansion of nations beyond their own borders and the effects those expansions had on the indigenous people whose lives were impacted by the colonizers. Colonial histories tend to tell the stories of powerful people who reach outside of their own nations to colonize other lands where the people have less advanced weapons, governments, or immune systems. As Jared Diamond states in his 1997 book, Guns, Germs and Steel, "Much of human history has consisted of unequal conflicts between the haves and the have-nots."

Colonization is not the only way that powerful people have dramatically impacted the lives of the less powerful. Diasporic histories tell another story about the ways conquest affects those of us who are less powerful. As defined by Robin Cohen in his 1997 book, *Global Diasporas*, **diasporas** are dispersals of people from their homelands, often traumatically, to two or more foreign lands. Cohen lays out five types of diasporas (Cohen, 1997): victim diasporas, labor diasporas, imperial diasporas, trade diasporas, and deterritorialized diasporas.

Victim diasporas happen when people are banished from their place of origin usually as the result of conquest, persecution, enslavement, genocide, or exile. The Trail of Tears was part of a 1,000 mile forced migration of an estimated 60,000 Native Americans from the Southeastern US to Oklahoma prompted by the Indian Removal Act of 1830. Historians estimate that roughly 8,500 people died on the unrelenting 1,000 mile walk to Oklahoma (History.com, 2014). Americans who are not part of the indigenous population are often unaware that 14% of the Native American population of the Southeastern United States died in this forced move. As a result, they tend to think that Native American's use of the term "genocide" to describe the forced migration is an exaggeration. However, with such great losses to the population, genocide is likely the appropriate term.

© Frnando Cortes, 2014. Used under license from Shutterstock, Inc.

Figure 4.6 The Indian Removal Act of 1830 resulted in a victim diaspora that displaced 60,000 people.

Labor diasporas happen when people live in indentured servitude, enslaved, or work as migrant laborers in a foreign land. Before slavery was common in the United States, indentured servants were brought, primarily from England, to work for landowners. People in debtors' prison often found that their debts were sold to landowners in the colonies and children were often sold into indentured servitude. Beyond these methods, with a depressed economy in Europe after the Thirty Years' War many people signed on as indentured servants in exchange for the cost of the trip to the colonies. Between one-half and two-thirds of the people who arrived in the colonies between 1607 and 1680 arrived as indentured servants. Indentured servants who had completed their service sought the guarantees that they had signed on for. Many had been promised money and land at the end of their years of service. Often, these promises were not kept and there were several uprisings of freed servants who had fulfilled their side of the bargain but had been left empty-handed. As a result, land owners sought a new labor pool. Between 1640 and 1661, many of the colonies legalized the importation and permanent enslavement of people from Africa (History Detectives, 2014). For 200 years people were brought from Africa

Figure 4.7 Labor diasporas bring migrant workers who feed America.

and lived their entire lives in slavery. In most places it was illegal for slaves to learn to read and their records were not kept as people but as property. Americans of African descent often reach a wall in their genealogical research when they reach the civil war. While historians have worked for decades to provide families with links to their ancestry, the records available have often made identification impossible. Luckily, today there are inexpensive DNA tests that can, at the very least, pinpoint the area of the African continent people's ancestors were taken from. In the United States, today, the labor force on our farms is no longer in indentured servitude or enslaved for life. Instead, migrant laborers from Mexico and other Central American and South American countries come to the United States to harvest our crops. Once here, most stay and raise their families. Their children and/or grandchildren are born as US citizens.

Imperial diasporas happen when migrants go to another land that has been conquered by their own nation. These migrants enjoy a higher status as a result of their connection to the conquering power. Imperial diasporas do not adapt to local customs, and locals are expected to adapt to their customs. English people moved to India to live and work for the British East India Company during the 190-year British colonization of India (1757–1947). During colonization, Indians were barred from holding government office and all offices were held by the English.

The Indian people suffered as a result of high taxes and few government services, while the English, who had taken charge of their government, prospered. The same happened when the United States forced the King of Hawaii, in 1887, to sign a constitution that stripped him of his powers while simultaneously creating a system in which only landowners, primarily white US citizens, were allowed to vote.

Trade diasporas happen when a community goes abroad to trade in a host society. While they learn the customs of the host society for trading purposes they do not assimilate and tend to return to their home country. Today, diamond dealers from Dubai, UAE, spend their winters at cruise ship ports of call

Figure 4.8 King Kamehameha was not the last king of Hawaii, but he was the last king to rule, thanks to US imperial diaspora.

in the Caribbean and their summers at cruise ship ports of Call in Alaska. Their home is still Dubai but they live and work for months or years in the Americas.

Deterritorialized diasporas happen when people have been forced from their land so that a ruling elite can take possession. Throughout history powerful people have taken the land that less-powerful people have lived on for centuries. One of the most famous instances of "taking" happened in the United Kingdom in the enclosure acts of 1730–1860. During this period, over 4,000 individual enclosure acts passed through parliament. Most of these acts were initiated in the house of Lords (made up entirely of titled land owners), and these land owners passed a series of

Figure 4.9 The Enclosure Acts forced people off their land in a deterritorialized diaspora and created the labor force that fueled the Industrial Revolution.

laws requiring land that had, for centuries, been common lands for peasants to farm on free of charge, to be fenced with expensive stone in order to "protect" the land. The commons had to be fenced with strong, stone fences by dates set in law and, if the lands were not fenced by the peasants by the deadline then anyone who could afford to fence the land would be given the land. Inevitably, the only people who could afford to fence the land were already large land owners. The enclosure acts forced hundreds of thousands of people off of their ancestral lands in England, Wales, Scotland, and Ireland in the 100-year period that became the Industrial Revolution (McElroy, 2012). These desperate people flooded into cities and crossed oceans in their hopes to survive for the next generation. They became the cheap labor that fueled the Industrial Revolution creating the largest group of wealthy entrepreneurs in world history.

Occasionally, people are also deterritorialized by natural disasters that leave them without a land to call home. Most recently, the 2004 Indian Ocean earthquake and tsunami displaced nearly 2 million people from 15 different countries.

Diaspora: As defined by Robin Cohen in his 1997 book, *Global Diasporas*, diasporas are dispersals of people from their homelands, often traumatically, to two or more foreign lands. Cohen lays out five types of diaspora (Cohen, 1997):

- Victim diaspora: People who are banished from their place of origin usually as the result of conquest, persecution, enslavement, genocide, or exile.
- Labor diaspora: people who live in indentured servitude or work as migrant laborers in a foreign land.
- Imperial diaspora: Migrants who go to another land that has been conquered by their own nation and enjoy higher status as a result of their status as a conquering power. Imperial diaspora do not adapt to local customs, and locals are expected to adapt to their customs.
- Trade diaspora: A community that goes abroad to trade in a host society. While they learn the customs of the host society for trading purposes they do not assimilate and tend to return to their home country.
- Deterritorialized diaspora: People who have been forced from their land by natural disasters or a ruling elite.

Minority Histories

Most often, when we think of "minorities" in the United States we think of racial groups. In this section we will talk about racial group histories and we will also talk about many other histories that are also minority group histories.

In many parts of the United States when issues of race are mentioned, only two races come to mind: Black and White. As discussed earlier in this chapter, many Black Americans have great difficulty delving into their ancestry because once they get to 1860 they find that their ancestors were not only treated as property but their names were most often left out of the property records. As a result, for many Black Americans learning their histories becomes a process of reclaiming what was stolen from their ancestors. However, it is important to remember that not all people of African descent in the United States have a history of slavery in their ancestry. Avoid that blanket assumption.

I teach at a school where the majority population is Latino. Legally, we are considered a "Hispanic Serving Institution." I have been through 2 US Census cycles with my students and I am still baffled by the fact that the United States does not provide a racial group for these non-Asian, non-Black, non-White, non-Native American, non-Alaskan native or non-Pacific Islanders to check. In essence, in the United States right now, people from Central and South America, who have lots of native Central and South American genetic traits, have no race, which means that today over half of the population of California has no race. They must choose a race that is not their own when they fill out their census form. As a result, my husband, a fourth-generation American of primarily Mexican, Lebanese, and English descent, chose Native American in the 2010 census because, as he puts it, "I look more Native American than anything else!"

This erasure of race leads many darker complected Latinos to confusion. Their questioning has spurred a great deal of study among Latino historians. Mexican Americans whose families have lived in the places that are now called Texas, New Mexico, Arizona, and California since before these places were part of the United States often say that they did not come to America, America came to them. Because of the work of Latino historians the stories that are told today are not just the stories of the Spanish and Portuguese explorers, the Spanish Colonial System, and US Manifest Destiny. Today, the winning of half of Mexico to the United States in the Mexican American War is part of the story. The story of the San Patricios is part of our history. The San Patricios were primarily Irish Catholic immigrants who came to the United States during the potato famines. Upon arrival, many were recruited into the US military to go fight in the Mexican American War. The folklore and historical accounts converge regarding the reasons these soldiers deserted the US Army to fight for Mexico. The folklore is that these soldiers were not allowed to celebrate Mass as their American commanding officers were Protestant. The folklore is that these soldiers heard their Latin Mass across the Rio Grande and they knew that their true loyalties were with their fellow Catholics. The American histories look to the long tradition of Catholics who left their own nations to fight beside their fellow Catholics. Irish Catholics had fought in the Armies of both Spain and France for centuries and Ireland, under British Protestant rule, had suffered. The field reports of the officers and the letters

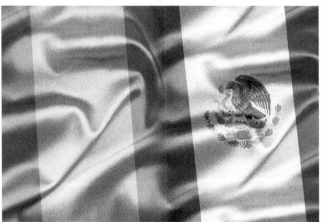

Figure 4.10   The San Patricios are seen as heroes in Mexico.

leader, John Riley, support this theory. While most of the San Patricios were eventually hung for treason, today, the San Patricios are celebrated as heroes in Mexico and, in the United States their story is gaining popularity. This story and many others are moving from folklore to historically verifiable events, thanks to the work of Latino historians.

While Asians make up over half of the world population, in the United States, Asians are a racial minority group that comprises just under 6% of the population. However, just an hour from my home in Delano, California, 38% of the population is Filipino. Filipinos are an Asian ethnic group. Like so many other immigrant groups, Filipinos find

© spirit of america, 2014. Used under license from Shutterstock, Inc.

Figure 4.11 Filipino Americans are the second largest group of Americans of Asian descent.

one another and create communities. Delano is a diverse town of just 53,000 people and Filipinos are the largest ethnic group. Filipinos have taken many different paths to come the United States. From 1898 to 1946, the Philippines were a territory of the United States. While there were anti-Chinese laws that stopped Chinese immigrants from immigrating to the United States, Filipinos were US nationals, just as Puerto Ricans are today. They were able to travel freely throughout the United States and relocate to any US state just as any other US citizen could. When the Philippines once again became an independent nation, Filipinos living in the United States were able to become naturalized citizens and they were able to bring over family members just as other US citizens can. Today, Filipinos are the second largest Asian population in the United States behind Chinese immigrants.

Ethnic histories often point out the inhumane treatment of the minority by the majority. Actor George Takai, known for his role as Sulu on Star Trek, has spent much of his life working to bring attention to the internment camps that he and other Japanese Americans were moved to during WW II. Takai recently funded the production of a musical based on the true story of a family that was interred in the camps. Takai's efforts and the efforts of other Japanese Americans have assured that this moment has been remembered. Other ethnic groups affected by internment in WW II have not had such success. At the same time the Japanese American citizens were being forced to leave their homes and live in camps, and German and Italian nationals in America and first-generation German-American citizens were also interred in camps. However, their stories are largely lost to history. Japanese Americans who were interred received an apology in 1976 from President Ford, and in 1992 each surviving detainee received $20,000 in reparations. The surviving Italians who were interred received an apology from President Clinton in 2000. To date, the US government has not issued an apology to the German Americans who were interred in the camps. The activism of Japanese Americans has assured that their ethnic history is told as part of mainstream history.

Gender histories, especially women's history, have been part of University curricula nationwide since the 1980s. During the women's movement of the 1970s, feminist scholars began uncovering the historic work of women and began asking why these historic achievements had been entirely left out of mainstream historical accounts. History text books through the 1970s and 80s only highlighted the successes of white men. Today, while women are represented in K-12 History textbooks, women's stories and accomplishments still make up only 2% to 3% of the stories. However, the work of women historians has been entirely successful in removing particular types of sexist language from K-12 textbooks. Now, when referring to the human race or job titles, gender-neutral language is universal in K-12 textbooks (Chiponda, 2011). Sadly, most narratives in textbooks today are still presented from a male perspective.

Gendered narrative portrayals create some clear themes that many feminist scholars claim are harmful to society as they diminish opportunities for women and diminish positive views of women. In their 2011 article for the History Journal, Yesterday and Today, Annie Chiponda & Johan Wassermann, professors in the department of History Education in the School of Education at the University of KwaZulu-Natal in South Africa, argue that the gendered assumptions in the most popular academic history texts from Taiwan, the United States, the United Kingdom, Russia, and South Africa promote three dangerous biases (Chiponda, 2011):

Figure 4.12   Does this little girl see people like her in her history textbooks?

1. **Women who make history are either exceptional or wicked:** Only women who are far more extraordinary than even the most successful men will make history, and women, outside the domestic sphere, are primarily responsible for negative contributions to history.
2. **Science is not for women:** Bad things happen to women in science; science is too dangerous for women and is the domain of men.
3. **Women belong in the home and if they leave they have to do double the work:** Women who do work outside the home are always expected to also do all of the work inside the home. This gives the impression that working outside the home is merely an extra burden for women.

Just as women have always fought, women have always worked. It was not until the Victorian era that women's roles were limited in the popular literature and the popular imagination to the domestic sphere. However, even when we look at the literature of the era, women's roles are far more diverse than the lady of the manor who spends her time reading and reclining on her fainting couch. All of the women who worked for the lady of the manor were working outside of their homes. The cooks, the housekeepers, the dress makers, the hat makers and the workers in the factories that made all of the tools used in the domestic sphere were primarily women workers. The myth that women have only recently worked outside the home is being torn away by gender historians and socioeconomic class historians.

Figure 4.13   Women have always worked.

Socioeconomic class histories draw attention to the class and wealth disparities that propel historic events. Many of the issues discussed in this chapter were propelled by class and wealth disparities: The enclosure acts, the Irish potato famine, the fight for Indian independence, the White landowner takeover of Hawaii, the levels of servitude we have kept our farm workers in for centuries, and the access to knowledge that, spurred by innovation, is today available to most people in the developed world.

As you can see, many possible histories are obscured or erased as a result of a lack of awareness that these stories and experiences have historic value. Experiences are also lost when social moirés change and the existence of cultural groups who do not fit those moirés is erased. The cultural groups are forced underground and their histories are lost. Nowhere is this loss more evident than in lesbian, gay, bisexual, transgender, and queer (LGBTQ) histories. People in these groups have been fighting for equal rights in the United States and many other countries since the 1960s. Sadly, there were Californians who pulled their children out of public schools in 2011 when the nation's first law required that LGBT history and the contributions of LGBT Americans should be included in age-appropriate history curriculum statewide.

Figure 4.14 LGBT history will be part of history textbooks in California beginning in 2015.

Dealing with History: Skill Building

Put Family Folklore in Its Historical Context

For nearly 30 years, the story of the old Indian and my great-grandmother was unquestioned truth in my mind. However, when confronted with the reality that this was a widespread legend I began to think about the motivations of the people in the story and I finally realized that this story was passed down through generations based on the memories of a 4-year-old girl. When faced with family folklore, question everything and check folklore books to find out if yours is a tale of the times.

Figure 4.15 Put family folklore in contex.

Act Like an Historian

Engage in thoughtful dialogue with others regarding your understandings of history. Search out public records, private records, oral histories, and folklore to gain a better

Figure 4.16 Act like an historian.

understanding of history. Never pretend that you are capable of complete objectivity. Instead, discover your biases and make sure to consider them when you learn about history. Accept that multiple, conflicting histories will always exist just as multiple, conflicting perspectives exist. Treat others' perspectives of history with respect.

Reveal Hidden Histories

When people in the United States say that women have never been allowed in combat, it is helpful to point out that Norwegian and Israeli women have been in combat roles since 1985. A global view of history is often helpful.

When you are learning about historic events and everyone seems to be of one gender, race, nationality, or socioeconomic class, ask yourself what other people of different genders, races, nationalities, and classes were doing while the historic events played out. If you are curious, do a web search. You will be surprised by the results.

Figure 4.17 Reveal hidden histories.

Search for the Diasporas in Your Own History

Most of us do not have a family heritage of wealth or power. As a result, when we study our ancestry, we learn that the people who came before us were often part of diasporas. Do a websearch on your religious, ethnic, or national background paired with the word "diaspora." Learn about the ways your ancestors have been "on the run." Find out if your ancestors were affected by victim diasporas, labor diasporas, imperial diasporas, trade diasporas, or deterritorialized diasporas.

Figure 4.18 Ellis Island.

Be Mindful of the Biases Historical Accounts Have Instilled in You

Historians are, first and foremost, people whose views of the world are formed by their time and place. We all tend to grow up thinking that the information in textbooks is the truth but, keep in mind that historians have biases just like the rest of us do. Question the choices historians make regarding what is worthy of inclusion in their work. Question the underlying

Figure 4.19 Do not assume I belong at home!

assumptions that come through in people's word choices. Are all things masculine considered positive? Are all things European/White preferred?

Be Mindful of the Histories of Others

We live in a multicultural nation and we work in a multicultural world. Everyone has different backgrounds. It is dangerous to assume anything about the histories that are important to others. You need to talk to people about the issues and periods of history that are most important to them before you make any assumptions. It is also dangerous to assume that

Figure 4.20   Learn about the histories of the people you care about.

others have the same understandings of history that you do. Go beyond the histories that are important to you. Learn about the histories that are important to the people around you.

We all have biases we are completely unaware of. The more you learn about other people's perspectives on the world the more you will notice your own biases and decide whether or not you want to maintain them as part of your identity. In the next chapter, we will explore the ways all of the factors discussed in these first four chapters come together to create the identities that make us who we are.

Glossary

Deterritorialized diasporas   Dispersals of people from their homelands as a result of people being forced from their land so that a ruling elite can take possession.

Diasporas   Dispersals of people from their homelands, often traumatically, to two or more foreign lands. Cohen lays out five types of diasporas (Cohen, 1997).

Folklore   The stories, usually oral, told from generation to generation that transmit the experiences of earlier generations.

Imperial diasporas   Dispersals of people from their homelands, by their own choice. These migrants go to another land that has been conquered by their own nation.

Labor diasporas   Dispersals of people from their homelands as a result of indentured servitude, enslavement, or need for work as migrant laborers in a foreign land.

Oral histories   Firsthand accounts of historical events as told by the people who experienced them.

Trade diasporas   Dispersals of people from their homelands, by their own choice, when a community goes abroad to trade in a host society.

Victim diasporas   Dispersals of people from their homelands as a result of being banished from their place of origin usually as the result of conquest, persecution, enslavement, genocide, or exile.

Works Cited

American Historical Association. (2011, January). *Statement on standards of professional conduct.* Retrieved from American Historical Association website: http://www.historians.org/about-aha-and-membership/governance/policies-and-documents/statement-on-standards-of-professional-conduct

Brunvand, J. H. (1981). *The vanishing hitchhiker: American urban legends and their meanings.* New York, NY: W W Norton and Company.

Brunvand, J. H. (1996). *American folklore: An encyclopedia.* New York, NY: Taylor and Francis.

Chiponda, A. W. (2011). Women in history textbooks—What message does this send to youth? *Yesterday & Today, 6*, 13–25.

Cohen, R. (1997). *Global diasporas: An introduction.* London, UK: Taylor and Francis.

Comer-Jefferson, D., & Welch, R. (2014, March 21). *Presentation on the promise and slavery.* Retrieved from The Promise website: http://www.welchwrite.com/promise/video-dr-rosanne-welch-speak-on-the-promise-and-slavery/

History Detectives. (2014, April 16). *Indentured servants in the U.S.* Retrieved from PBS: History Detectives website: http://www.pbs.org/opb/historydetectives/feature/indentured-servants-in-the-us/

History.com. (2014, April 16). *Trail of tears.* Retrieved from History.com website: http://www.history.com/topics/native-american-history/trail-of-tears

Hodgekin, K., & Radstone, S. (2003). *Contested pasts: The politics of memory.* London, UK: Routlege.

Hurley, K. (2013, May 20). *"We have always fought": Challenging the "women, cattle and slaves" narrative.* Retrieved from A dribble of ink website: http://aidanmoher.com/blog/featured-article/2013/05/we-have-always-fought-challenging-the-women-cattle-and-slaves-narrative-by-kameron-hurley/

Little, A. M. (2009, July 25). *Feminism and whig history: Why are we always fooled again?* Retrieved from Historiann website: http://www.historiann.com/2009/07/25/feminism-and-whig-history-why-are-we-always-fooled-again/

McElroy, W. (2012, March 8). *The enclosure acts and the industrial revolution.* Retrieved from The Future of Freedom Foundation website: http://fff.org/explore-freedom/article/enclosure-acts-industrial-revolution/

Women in Military Service for America Memorial Foundation. (2013, December 1). *Early years: American revolution.* Retrieved from Women in Military Service for America Memorial Foundation website: http://www.womensmemorial.org/H%26C/History/earlyyears(amrev).html

Chapter 5

Our Multifaceted Selves

Helen Acosta

"Every human being has hundreds of separate people living under his skin. The talent of a writer is his ability to give them their separate names, identities, personalities and have them relate to other characters living with him."
—Mel Brooks

Chapter Learning Objectives

1. Gain an appreciation of our multifaceted identities.
2. Learn about the pitfalls of stereotyping.
3. Understand the impact of privilege and appreciate the unearned benefits each of us receives as a result of membership in particular groups in our society.
4. Trace our majority and minority development within our own identities.
5. Learn to support other people's identities.

In 1973, I was 4 years old. I stayed home sick one day from my Huntington Beach Southern Baptist preschool. My mom took a sick day to take care of me. I was sitting at the kitchen table coloring when my mom asked me why I was trying to color with my right hand instead of coloring with my left hand as I had in the past.

I looked up and, in a matter-of-fact voice, said, "Because, I'm a devil child."

Suddenly, we were in the car and then I was sitting outside the preschool director's office. My mom was yelling on the other side of the door. Then, there was silence. The door opened, the preschool director stormed past me, and my mom stood in the doorway with her hands on her hips.

Figure 5.1   "Because, I'm a devil child".

Moments later, the preschool director marched in with my teacher in tow. My teacher, all white hair and wrinkles, glowered at me as she sulked into her boss' office.

At that point, I knew that I was in trouble. I did not know what I had done but I knew it was bad.

I remember sitting next to my mom listening to the angry voices on the other side of the door. Then, everything got very quiet.

My teacher walked past me without looking at me. The preschool director came out, crouched down so she could look at me eye-to-eye and said, "Helen, that woman won't hurt you anymore. You're going to have a new teacher tomorrow. There is nothing wrong with you. You are perfect as God made you. It makes God happy to see you color with your left hand."

From the perspective of a 4-year old, the whole incident was very confusing.

I remember thinking that being a devil child was something I could not change. It was part of who I was and that I could hide that part of me by coloring with my right hand. Over the next several weeks my mom convinced me that my teacher had been wrong and I was not a devil child. I went back to coloring with my left hand. I knew that my mom and the preschool director cared about me. I also knew that being left handed was a special gift.

Being left-handed is part of my identity. Even today, in my mid-forties, every time someone notices and, inevitably, says, "Hey, you're left-handed" I am reminded that I am not only left-handed but that I'm not a devil child.

—Helen Acosta

Each of us have experienced moments in our lives when an aspect of our identities is pointed out to us by others. These facets are pointed out in a number of ways when someone notices a difference between themselves and those they come in contact with. When a person who has noticed a difference points out an aspect of our identities, they might:

- **comment on the difference**
  - merely to verify that what they noticed is accurate
  - as a matter of curiosity
  - to celebrate what they see as your uniqueness

- **see the difference as an aberration, compelling them to**
  - call it out, using dehumanizing language
  - begin to work to change something in you so that you align with their expectations
  - try to come to terms with it, working to change something within themselves so they can accept the difference they see in the difference you.

We do not think much about our own identities unless we begin to notice, or are made to notice, how particular facets of our identities are similar or different from those around us.

In this chapter we will unpack the following:

- identity;
- stereotypes;
- privilege;
- majority/minority identity development;
- support for others' identities.

While in sociology and psychology "identity" is a person's conception and expression of their group affiliations and individuality, as used in this chapter, an **identity** is a person's conception and expression of a single facet of their individuality that is linked with a group affiliation.

When we think of our identities we tend to think of our self-image and our personalities. However, in order to gain more depth of understanding about our identities, rather than thinking of "identity" in the singular, it is helpful to think of "identities" in the plural. In essence, we all have multiple identities. It is the interplay of these identities that shapes the sense of self that becomes each person's self-image and personality. Over our lifetimes our identities shift, sometimes subtly, sometimes dramatically, based on our experiences of the world.

Our identities act as lenses through which we see the world. These lenses are constructed out of many of the experiences we have discussed in previous chapters:

- Our beliefs, values, and behavioral choices related to those beliefs and values;
- Our understandings and misunderstandings of our own histories and the histories of others;
- The mainstream and co-cultural influences that pervade our conscious and subconscious awareness;
- The mainstream as well as co-cultural groups to which we belong;
- The ways we navigate the social roles available within our cultures and co-cultures;
- The ways we interpret and enact the behavioral rules of our cultures and co-cultures.

Additionally, our identity lenses are also constructed of the following:

- The ways our physical presence is supported/negated by our cultures and the cultures within which we live.
- Our personal interests, abilities, and desires and the ways we see those interests, abilities, and desires reacted to within our cultures and/or the cultures within which we live.
- The ways people we care about treat us.
- Our personal awareness of all of the many internal agreements and contradictions created by all of our different identities.
- Our personal awareness of the blinders created by these identity lenses through which we view the world.

Unpacking Identity

In communication studies we often use the term "unpack" when we are going to separate out the component parts of a concept and analyze each on its own. To better understand "unpacking" concepts imagine that someone has just dropped a full grocery bag off at your home. You know that what is inside came from the market but, beyond that, you will have to unpack the bag and evaluate each item separately in order to figure out what to do with the contents.

Let us "unpack" the definition of identity . . .

Our identities are multiple.   Each one of us plays different roles in varying contexts in our lives. For instance:

Figure 5.2 Our identities are multiple. Each of us has many facets.

(Credit: © Jennifer Gottschalk, 2014. Used under license from Shutterstock, Inc.)

> In my family I am (in the order these happened in my lifetime): a daughter, a niece, a granddaughter, a great-granddaughter, a cousin, a sister, a wife, an aunt, and a great-aunt.
>
> In my personal life I am: a dog mom, a founding member of our local lesbian, gay, bisexual, and transgender (LGBT) chorus, an artist, an author, a communication and media trainer for social movement groups, an activist for progressive causes, a foodie who loves to cook, a really bad but enthusiastic gardener, an equally bad and equally enthusiastic home improvement attempter, a genre TV geek (science fiction and fantasy stories), and a Facebook addict.
>
> In my workplace I have been: an instructor, a forensics coach, a peer mentor, a department chair, a union representative, a mediator, a committee member (for many different committees), an academic senate representative, and a club advisor. Today, I am a communication professor, the Gender and Sexuality Awareness club advisor, the communication major advisor and a member of two other committees on campus.

Our identities act as lenses through which we see the world. Each of our identities focuses our attention just as the lenses in a pair of eyeglasses focus our ability to see when we look through the glasses. Lenses narrow our attention to what can be seen through that particular lens. Some lenses complement one another. For me, being a member of an LGBT chorus, Gender and Sexuality Awareness club advisor, and social movement communication and media trainer complement one another and focus my attention on issues that affect one particular community. There are times when the lenses create blinders that stop us from seeing experiences beyond the identity that we are focusing on in the moment. Because of my focus on LGBT issues there are times when I fail to understand the viewpoints of people outside of my community, especially when those viewpoints are not sympathetic toward the LGBT community. Sometimes our identities contradict one another, making our whole lives blurry. There were times when being a forensics coach and being anything else did not work well

From Chapter 1:
Beliefs are ideas and propositions that are held to be true. Beliefs are at the core of human culture because they generate the values, attitudes, and behaviors of human beings.

Values are important beliefs shared by members of a culture about what is good or bad, desirable or undesirable, important or unimportant.

Figure 5.3   Beliefs and values.

together. All of my time and focus, 10 months a year, was on speech and debate. My family, friends, and other interests lost out during this 9-year period of my life.

These lenses are constructed out of many of the experiences we have discussed in previous chapters:

Our beliefs, values, and behavioral choices related to those beliefs and values.   We can see how values and beliefs are learned and become imbedded in our identities in the 2004 documentary, *A State of Mind*. In the film, we are introduced to two North Korean preteen gymnasts as well as their families. Director, Daniel Gordon, shows us what it is like to live inside of North Korea, one of the most isolated nations in the world. In the film, we see how all information is controlled by the state. We see how the beliefs and values of these young girls are shaped by the state-controlled media and state-controlled schools. These two young girls' greatest wish in life is to please the dear leader with their performances in the Mass Games, an annual celebration of the birthday of their dear leader. Their families also believe that performing in the games is the highest calling in a young person's life and every choice the young girls and their families make becomes focused on this effort (Gordon, 2004).

Our understandings and misunderstandings of our own histories and the histories of others.   Our identities are deeply constructed by our connections with historical accounts related to our identities. As we grow, the historical stories we experience (through oral telling, viewing in films or documentaries or our own reading) create a context for who we are and how we see our role in the world. In our minds, we place our predecessors in these stories and make assumptions about the roles they played. These assumptions often reinforce the roles we see ourselves playing in the world today.

The first choice ever made in our lives, the name we were given at birth, often affects our view of ourselves from the very beginning. In many cases a name is passed down along with connected family stories. The people who tell us those stories reveal important values and dreams that are embodied in the names that they chose. I recently met a woman with a unique first name. I immediately asked if she was named after a family member. It turned out that she was named after her great-grand aunt who was a suffragette (a woman who worked in the social movement to gain the right of women to vote in the United States). Later in the conversation I learned that my new friend, who was named after her great-grand aunt, the suffragette, was a civil rights attorney. The name her parents gave her did not lead her to become a civil rights attorney but the values that her parents taught her through the oft-repeated story of her name and the values that led them to honor the name of a great aunt who was a suffragette likely influenced her career choices.

Figure 5.4 The name we are given at birth often affects our view of ourselves.

The mainstream and co-cultural influences that pervade our conscious and subconscious awareness.   Our identities are deeply influenced by the images and stories we encounter in print and electronic media. In 1954, sociologists Kenneth and Mamie Clark conducted an experiment that captivated the nation. In the experiment they showed Black children two different dolls that were identical in all but one way: One doll had peach skin tone (the white doll), the other had deep brown skin tone (the black doll).

While over 40% of the children said that the black doll looked most like them, over 60% of the children preferred the White doll and said that it was a nicer doll.

Since 1954, the experiment has been redone with many variations at least once a decade, all finding similar results. While children tested in 2009 would accept either doll, saying that the dolls are equal, when researchers ask deeper questions they still find that Black children have internalized negative stereotypes about people with dark skin. Black children still point out the black doll as "Ugly," "Bad," and "Mean."

So, while, in their own conscious thoughts, American children today believe that they are equal peers who, regardless of skin tone, have equal opportunities throughout their lives, they have subconsciously internalized the negative stereotypes about Black people that are still present in our television, film, video games, and print media (Ahuja, 2009).

The mainstream as well as co-cultural groups to which we belong.   We all live within a mainstream culture that impacts each of our perceptions of the world around us. In addition, many of us belong to several co-cultural groups that also impact our focus and perceptions.

The ways we navigate the social roles available within our cultures and co-cultures.   The Bugi people live in Sulawesi, Indonesia. The most revered members of their society are called "Bissu." Bissu act as their spiritual and community leaders. It is believed that the Bissu have special abilities to understand all kinds of different people because the Bissu are born both male and female. Most often Bissu are chosen at birth because they are born intersex (they have both male and female genitalia). Bissu grow up knowing that they have a special responsibility to give careful council, are trained by other Bissu, and are expected to lead wisely throughout their lives.

The Bugi's gender roles are not only different in the ways they treat people born intersex but also in the ways they treat the other gender roles. Unlike the United States where we have only two genders that are accepted in the mainstream, the Bugi have five: Bissu, oroané, makkunrai, Calabai, and Calalai. Calabai

Figure 5.5   Even today little Black girls in America think White dolls are nicer. We still have a long way to go before we reach true equality.

From Chapter 1:
Co-culture: An interdependent but equal cultural group that exists in a dominant or national culture. In intercultural studies, this term has come to replace the term "subculture."

Figure 5.6   Co-culture.

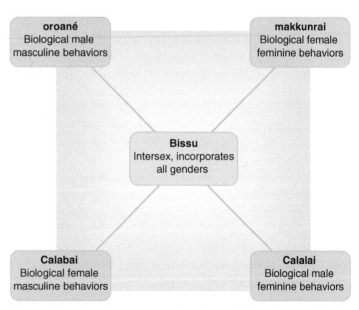

Figure 5.7   The five genders of the Bugi. (Helen Acosta, 2014).

are biologically female and act and dress in masculine ways, and Calalai are biologically male and dress and act in feminine ways. In Bugi society, the Bissu are the leaders. The other four genders are seen as equally important and are necessary in all spiritual matters. A good analogy to understand the importance of the five genders is to think of the genders as a pyramid. oroané, makkunrai, Calabai, and Calalai form the foundation of the pyramid while the Bissu are at the pinnacle (Graham, 2001).

The ways we interpret and enact the behavioral rules of our cultures and co-cultures.   Less than 100 years ago in the United States it would have been scandalous to see a woman wearing pants in public. In the war years of the 1940s, many women had worn pants to work in factories while the men were at war. However, they returned to their homes and their skirts after the war. Cultural rules about women wearing pants began to change in the late 1960s as a response to another war, Vietnam. Pants became part of the anti-war counter-culture. Blue jeans became symbolic of the movement for "peace, love, and rock and roll." In the wake of the peace movement, the women's movement of the 1970s also saw women in pants across the workforce. While part of the shift in cultural norms was practical, affording women the safety and comfort needed for a wide variety of industrial jobs, even women in white collar work began wearing pants to symbolize their equality with men in the workplace. Today, women and men in the workplace almost exclusively wear pants, though it is still culturally acceptable for women to wear skirts and dresses at work.

Additionally, our identity lenses are also constructed of:

The ways our physical presence is supported/negated by our cultures and the mainstream cultures within which we live.   In Fiji the standard for beauty has always been "bigger is better." Calling someone skinny is a traditional insult. However, in 1995, the standard began to shift. Not because Fijians began to suddenly shrink, but because of American satellite television. Dr. Anne E. Becker documented the shift in personal body image that occurred in Veti Levu, a province of Fiji's main island, from 1995 to 1998. While eating disorders had been unheard of in 1995, by 1998, the teen girls Dr. Becker interviewed were actively comparing themselves to the slender American and Australian actresses they saw on their TV screens. By 1998, over 60% of the girls were on a diet. The more TV the girls watched, the more negatively they viewed their own bodies. Girls who watched TV three or more nights a week were 50% more likely to view themselves as "too big or too fat" and they were 30% more likely to be on a diet (Goode, 1999).

Figure 5.8 This athletic Fijian woman is part of an internationally touring professional dance troupe. By traditional Fijian standards she would be considered quite petite.

Dr. Becker returned in 2007 and found that a decade later the young women of Veti Levu were still struggling with body image issues. Forty-five percent of the girls she surveyed had purged a meal within the last month and nearly 25% reported suicidal thoughts within the last year (Ireland, 2009).

In VetiLevu, American and Australian body image has colonized the minds of young women. These young women no longer love their thick bodies as they do not see images of themselves or people like them on their TV screens. Their physical presence has been negated in their own culture.

A wide swath of humanity, even here in the United States, shares a similar experience of the world. Only a small slice of "beauty" can be found in our TV programs. As a result, people who are not White, slender, or physically able rarely see themselves in the media they consume. They compare themselves to a standard that is, in most cases, entirely unreachable.

While people in any society are judged and tend to judge themselves regarding their levels of beauty, differences in physical ability tend to create far more dramatic distances between people. The bias toward physical ability is so strong in the United States that even though the Americans with Disabilities Act guarantees access to people who do not have the same abilities as those in the mainstream the default still tends to be discrimination rather than accommodation and inclusion. In 2012, complaints to the Equal Employment Opportunity Commission re-

Figure 5.9 This playground's universal design allows able-bodied and disabled people to enjoy the playground equally.

sulted in the single highest number of disability discrimination complaints in any 5-year period since the commission began (US Equal Employment Opportunity Commission, 2012a). These charges resulted in $103.4 million in payouts to the injured complainants (US Equal Employment Opportunity Commission, 2012b).

Our personal interests, abilities, and desires and the ways we see those interests, abilities, and desires reacted to within our cultures and/or the cultures within which we live.   In the United States, most of the top restaurant chefs have traditionally been male. It was not until TV programs, especially Iron Chef America, Top Chef, and Chopped made female restaurant chefs celebrities that the bias against women "on the line" began to change. Today, as the bias continues to shrink, larger numbers of women are seeking careers as chefs than ever before (Conrad, 2013).

The ways people we care about treat us.   The Family Acceptance Project is an organization that works to decrease mental and physical health risks for LGBT teens across the United States. The Family Acceptance Project has found that the number one indicator of risky behaviors by LGBT teens is the level of acceptance they enjoy at home. Teens who are rejected by their families are more than 8 times as likely to have attempted suicide, nearly 6 times as likely to report high levels of depression, more than 3 times as likely to use illegal drugs, and more than 3 times as likely to be at high risk for HIV and sexually transmitted diseases.

As long as the teen knows that their families or caregivers love them and will always protect them from people who would treat them cruelly for being LGBT, teens do not engage in the risky behaviors previously

The number one indicator of risky behaviors by LGBT teens is the level of acceptance they enjoy at home.

Teens who are rejected by their families are:

- more than 8 times as likely to have attempted suicide;
- nearly 6 times as likely to report high levels of depression;
- more than 3 times as likely to use illegal drugs;
- more than 3 times as likely to be at high risk for HIV and sexually transmitted diseases.

Figure 5.10 Family acceptance project.

thought to be part of the LGBT experience. The Family Acceptance Project has found this to be true even when the teens' families disagree with their LGBT status (Caitlyn, 2009).

Our personal awareness of all of the many internal agreements and contradictions created by all of our different identities.   There are times when parts of our identities come into conflict with one another and we have to choose which aspects of ourselves to favor. A friend of mine is both a Christian and a lesbian. She comes from a very devout conservative sect of her religion that does not accept LGBT experiences of the world. She has never given up either aspect of herself and she has spent the last 40 years struggling with how to balance these two seemingly contrasting identities. Now, in her 50s, she has found a Christian church that accepts and celebrates her as a whole person, without having to stop being a lesbian in order to be accepted. While she still feels more conservative in her beliefs and often critiques the pastor for his liberal tendencies she now feels more comfortable in her own skin, and less conflicted, than she has in years.

Our personal awareness of the blinders created by these identity lenses through which we view the world.   The rest of this chapter is dedicated to helping to gain an awareness of these blinders and finding ways to see beyond them.

Unpacking Stereotyping

While I was growing up, I idolized my great-grandfather's gardener. I barely knew Mr. Sanchez but one day I overheard my great-grandfather talking about him to one of his friends. They were talking about "the bullfighter" and it took me a few minutes to realize that "the bullfighter" was Mr. Sanchez. WOW. This totally normal looking guy led a remarkable double-life as a matador in the ring! After that, I always treated Mr. Sanchez with deference. I always brought him lemonade and bowed my head when I talked to him.

It was only in my teens that I learned that Mr. Sanchez, while a remarkable husband, father and provider, wasn't a bullfighter. After my great grandfather died we were visiting my great grandmother to help with Spring cleaning. My mom wanted a tree in the backyard pruned. Without thinking I said, in a perfect mimic of my great grand-father, "I'll call the bullfighter."

For a moment my mom stood in shocked silence. Then, very slowly, she said, "You know Mr. Sanchez isn't actually a bullfighter."

"Yes he is." I said in my most self-assured 15-year-old voice, "He is a matador on the weekends."

"No, Honey. He isn't. Your great-grandfather, bless-his-heart, called all of his Mexican workmen at the dairy bullfighters." Then she seemed to work it out. "But you were just three when he closed the dairy so you wouldn't have known that. Mr. Sanchez isn't a bullfighter and people will think you are racist if you call him that."

And then it dawned on me. My great-grandfather was a racist!

It took me several years to work through my feelings about that experience and I never called Mr. Sanchez a bullfighter again.

—Helen Acosta

We all stereotype. **Stereotyping** is a subconscious short-hand in which we make snap judgments without even thinking about the fact that we are making a decision. Often we are not aware that we have judged someone based on stereotypes until someone points the stereotype out to us. While we would like to believe that we are blank slates open to everyone unless they individually prove that they are not worth our trust, the reality is that we have biases and often we are not even aware of these biases, much less that we act based on them.

From Chapter 2:
Distinguishing valid generalizations from stereotypes:

1. Valid generalizations are qualified with words and phrases such as "most," "many," "the majority of," "often," and "generally," whereas invalid stereotypes use or imply universal terms such as "all," "every," "always," and "never."
2. Valid generalizations are based upon evidence, whereas invalid stereotypes are assumed and applied without evidence.

Figure 5.11   Distinguishing stereotypes from valid generalizations. (Staller, 2014).

Subconscious Bias

Subconscious biases are preferences that have built up in our minds based on our experiences. These preferences are the foundations of the snap judgments that we rely on when we stereotype. Often we are completely unaware of the ways our subconscious biases affect our thoughts about ourselves or our behaviors toward others. A friend of mine who is 4′10″ was cast in a sensuous role in a play at a local theater. When she showed me and a group of other friends the promo shot for the play, I had a reaction that I am still a little ashamed of. I blurted out, "But you're a pocket person! It just seems wrong for you to be so . . . exposed!" The room went silent. Everyone was staring at me. Then, my husband said, "I can't believe you just said that. It's so wrong!" That moment unraveled a subconscious bias that I had never considered. Somewhere in my past experience I had equated being petite with being forever cute and childlike, a complete sexual neuter. It took me a while to come to terms with my bias and the experience sensitized me to the fact that there are biases lurking in my subconscious that I am totally unaware of. For over a decade Tony Greenwald (University of Washington), Mahzarin Banaji (Harvard University), and Brian Nosek (University of Virginia) have been measuring our subconscious biases in their online Implicit Assumptions Project. Over the years they have found that everyone has subconscious social biases. These subconscious biases affect every aspect of our lives. To take an Implicit Awareness Test, visit www.projectimplicit.net.

Our biases are imbedded in our language and the choices we make. To better understand how these biases impact our ability to connect with people whose life experiences differ from our own, let us look at some historical stereotypes that have become so common in our language that we do not even recognize them as the painful labels they are:

"I got gypped": People tend to use this phrase to mean "I got conned." It is actually a slur against the Romani people, aka gypsies or travelers. Anti-Romani laws throughout much of Europe have existed for centuries. Today, there are still European cities where it is illegal for the Romani people to live or work.

"Jew down": People tend to think this means to negotiate a lopsided deal. This is a slur against the Jewish people that originated in Europe, centuries before the Holocaust.

© Ronald Sumners, 2014. Used under license from Shutterstock, Inc.

Figure 5.12   "Hooligan" is a slur against the Irish that began with accounts of a single Irish immigrant family in London, the Hoolihans.

"Hooligan": A term for rowdy antics, "hooligan" has become more common in the United States with the increase in popularity of British TV and film, and "hooligan" is actually a slur against the Irish that began with accounts of a single Irish immigrant family in London, the Hoolihans.

"Vandal": Today, a vandal is someone who tags your car. Initially, it was a Roman slur against the Germanic tribe of the same name.

"Redskin": A racial slur against Native Americans. In 1963, the National Council of Indians first filed against Trademark protection for the Washington team because "Redskin" is a racial slur against Indian people. Today, the bite of this racial slur has not lessened. According to Ray Halbritter, the Oneida Nation representative and CEO of Oneida Nation Enterprises, "It's an offensive term; it's a racial slur. It's a name you wouldn't use in casual or everyday conversation" (Schumacher-Matos, 2014).

In all of the above cases, the slurs originated at times when one group was dehumanizing another. So, they gave the group they were dehumanizing a label and that separated the group from the rest of humanity, making it easier to treat them differently from people they considered similar to themselves.

What About Positive Stereotypes?

"Positive stereotypes" are just as harmful as negative stereotypes. When we assume that all people of a particular group excel, then people who are part of that group who do not excel tend to disappoint us, just for being themselves. As a result, we treat them as failures because they did not measure up to our unrealistic expectations.

Figure 5.13 If you assume that she will throw off the curve in your calculus class that is a potentially harmful "positive stereotype".

Stereotyping Feels Like Aggression

While stereotyping is often just a mental shortcut for the user, the stereotype feels a bit different to the person being stereotyped. Stereotyping, especially when thoughtlessly used by a person from a majority group, can be described as little stab wounds or "microaggressions." Even when people in the majority do not mean to be cruel, these pin pricks build up over time and create festering wounds.

To measure the wounding effects of the use of stereotypes, the work of Dr. Derald Wing Sue is helpful. Dr. Sue has developed three terms that help us to categorize and clarify these microaggressions:

Microassaults: Deliberate harmful actions and language choices like displaying a Confederate flag or willfully using slurs against a particular group.

Microinsults: Words and actions that subtly convey rudeness and insensitivity while demeaning a person's identity. For

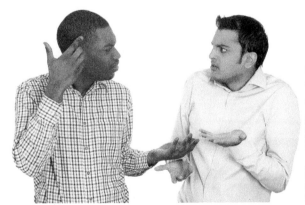

Figure 5.14 To avoid offending people who are different from you, learn about their histories and backgrounds, as well as the negative and positive stereotypes that have been used to categorize them.

instance, thoughtlessly asking a person of color how she got her job might imply that she only got it because of affirmative action. In addition, the unknowing use of stereotypes that are in common use by one group but are harmful to another group also falls into this area. Currently, the trans*women across the United States are working to stop people from using the term "tranny," a term that has been used in the gay community since the 1970s to refer to drag queens, often with an affectionate tone. However, people who are neither gay nor trans* who feel that being trans*gender is unnatural have, since the early 2000s, used the term "tranny" as an angry slur against trans*women. The term has moved from being a harmless, often affectionate identifier to hate speech that is often accompanied by physical violence. While trans*people and gay men have traditionally been friends and allies, many in the gay community are still unaware that the use of a term they consider their own is causing pain to people in another group.

Microinvalidations: Words and actions that exclude or negate the experiential reality of a person. Microinvalidations are the most common of the three "micros." For instance, people often ask my husband where he is from. He always gives the same answer, "Los Angeles." Then people get a little flustered and rephrase, "What country are you from?" he replies, "The US." For many people, even though my husband is a third-generation American and speaks only English, it seems that, because of his dark skin and Portuguese surname, he will never be a real American to them.

Dr. Sue explains that, in order to reduce the microstings that we unintentionally inflict on others, it is important to learn about the histories, backgrounds, negative stereotypes, as well as positive stereotypes that have been used to categorize a wide variety of people. Otherwise, you are doomed to continuously and unintentionally sting others with whom you interact (DeAngelis, 2009).

The Tunnel Vision Created by Stereotyping

In his 2008 eBook, unleashing the Idea Virus, Seth Godin explains Zipf's law. Named after its creator, Harvard professor, George Kingsley Zipf (1902–1950), Zipf's law explains why we have such extreme tunnel vision. It appears that we only have room in our heads for the #1 item in any category we have created so, when we are asked to think of a famous painting 95% of us will say "The Mona Lisa" (Godin, 2008).

While we like to think that it is not that important to come in first place it appears that, when it comes to the marketplace of ideas, being first place is the only place that our brains will hold on to.

What complicates issues further is that when we think of experiences of the world we will think of our own experiences first (#1 position, takes up 95% of our awareness) before any experience that we perceive to be its polar opposite (#2 position…holding about 3% of our awareness) and we rarely think beyond that. When we have to think beyond our own experiences we tend toward the "single story," which leads us to stereotyping that can damage our relationships with the people who we thoughtlessly stereotype.

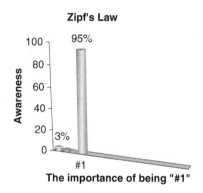

Figure 5.15 Zipf's law blinds us to ideas that are not in first place in our minds.

A note on the ever-changing terminologies preferred by people who are minorities in a larger majority culture: Stereotyping is one of the primary reasons the terminologies are constantly changing. Once the majority group begins using any minority self-naming terminology in a pejorative way, people in the minority group begin to test new terminologies that do not have the stigma attached. An example of this is the change in terminologies from "hermaphrodite" to "intersex" and from "androgynous" to "gender queer" or "gender fluid."

The Danger of a Single Story

In her October 2009 TED Global talk, Chimamanda Adichie, a best-selling Nigerian novelist, talks about the tunnel vision created by stereotyping. She explains that we tend to only see small slices of the world and every experience we have is filtered through the stories we have heard plus the stories we tell ourselves. So, if we read a single story (or watch a single film) about an experience of one person within a group, we tend to generalize that experience to the entire group. It is as though we say to ourselves: "I've walked in this one person's shoes for a tiny snapshot of their lives so now I know the experiences of everyone from that person's world". What is worse, Adichie explains, is that we tend to think of that single story as the true, or authentic, story that best explains the experiences of people from that group. Adichie explains that the only way to remove the blinders is to experience multiple stories of people from every group so that we do not fall into the trap of the single story (Adichie, 2009).

Prejudice

Prejudice is an unfair feeling of liking or disliking not based in logic or reason. Stereotypes are often based in prejudice though some stereotypes have nothing to do with affinity (liking or disliking), so they are not really prejudicial. For instance, the stereotype that people who wear glasses tend to be "bookish" is merely a blanket generalization that many people make without feeling any positive or negative feelings about the person wearing glasses. However, when the stereotype turns ugly and people who wear glasses are mocked for having "four eyes" and assumptions are made about them being unattractive to the opposite sex and that they have no lives and live with their parents well into adulthood, those assumptions tend to be based in prejudice.

Unpacking Privilege

Privilege is hard to understand until we begin to think of **privilege** as "the intangible, unearned benefits people get as a result of membership in a majority group." People do not plan on having privilege, most of us are born into our privileges and have no idea that we are getting advantages that other people do not have access to.

As a student, who may barely survive month-to-month, it may be difficult to imagine that you have anything resembling privilege. If you are part of a majority group, however, it may be easier for you to:

- get approved for an apartment;
- get roommates;
- get a job to help you get through school;
- get scholarship recommendations from your professors.

Keep in mind that there are many kinds of privilege in our society:

© donskarpo, 2014. Used under license from Shutterstock, Inc.

- **Male privilege:** Men in the United States have privileges that women do not have access to (discussed in-depth on page 123).
- **White privilege:** White people in the United States have privileges that people of other racial and ethnic groups do not have access to (discussed on page 124).

Figure 5.16   Privilege: the intangible, unearned benefits people get as a result of membership in a majority group.

- **Heterosexual privilege:** Heterosexuals in the United States have privileges that homosexuals, bisexuals, and asexuals in the United States do not. Until recently, only heterosexuals in the United States were ever allowed to get married, granting access to over 1,000 rights and responsibilities that are available only to married people under federal law. Sexuality tends to be an invisible identity. Today, it is still assumed that everyone is heterosexual until they prove otherwise. Having to prove your identity over and over again, sometimes on a daily basis, creates a great deal of tension for people in the United States who are not born heterosexual.

- **Christian privilege:** Christians in the United States have privileges that Muslims, Jews, Buddhists, Hindus, Sikhs, Native American beliefs, other theistic beliefs, and nonbelievers do not have access to. No non-Christian has ever been elected as President of the United States and unless you are Christian or Jewish, your faith will always make headlines if you are elected to office. Currently, only 8% of our Congress identifies as non-Christian and there is not a single member of Congress who identifies as an Atheist (Pew Research, 2013). In fact, in seven US states it is still illegal for Atheists to hold public office: Arkansas, Maryland, Mississippi, North Carolina, South Carolina, Tennessee, and Texas (Bulger, 2012).

- **Class privilege:** People who are rich have privileges that middle class and poor people in the United States do not and middle-class people have privileges that poor people do not (this idea is discussed in-depth later in the discussion of majority identity development in this chapter).

- **Cisgender privilege:** People whose gender identity matches the gender they were assigned at birth have privileges that transgender and other gender nonconforming people in the United States do not. People who do not feel comfortable presenting themselves as the gender they were assigned at birth make up between 2% and 5% of the US population. This minority group experiences extreme discrimination. The 2011 Transgender Discrimination Survey had some shocking findings regarding transgender Americans: 78% have experienced harassment at school, 15% experienced harassment so severe that they left school, 90% report having experienced discrimination or harassment at work, 47% said that they had lost a job or a promotion due to their transgender status, and transgender Americans experience homelessness at 4 times the rate of the general population. Sadly, all of this discrimination leads to a staggering statistic: 41% of the transgender respondents to the survey had attempted suicide (Grant et al., 2011).

- **Neurotypical privilege:** People whose neurology is the most common have privileges in the United States that people who are born with any of the autism spectrum conditions, dyslexia, developmental coordination disorder, bipolar disorder, ADD/ADHD, OCD, or any one of the many other neuroatypical differences do not. People in this group experience a wide variety of discriminations. The most common form of discrimination neuroatypical people experience is limited access to an education that actually meets their needs. Academic accommodations tend to be considered special add-ons that might be taken away at any time. Most parents of neuroatypical children have to fight for their children to have access to equitable educational opportunities.

- **Able-bodied privilege:** People who are able-bodied have privileges in the United States that people who are disabled do not have access to. Often people who are not able-bodied do not have access to public or private spaces because these spaces are not built with the needs of non-able-bodied people in mind. Imagine that you live in a wheelchair and you want to visit a friend's house. If the home has front steps and a porch as most US homes do, then you will have no way to enter the home without being assisted. Non-able-bodied people who are blind or deaf or must live life in wheelchairs report that people treat them like every kindness is an act of charity and that people often assume, when they do get a good job, that the non-able-bodied person only got the job because of affirmative action.

- **Citizen privilege:** People born in the United States or born to parents who are US citizens have privileges in the United States that people born outside the United States do not. In surveys of undocumented people, over 90% of respondents say that they would have come to the United States legally if they could have. However, there are not legal pathways available for immigration. This is especially true for the low-skilled workers who clean our dishes in restaurants, make our beds in hotels, and pick our food on farms. Each year there are nearly 800,000 farm labor jobs alone in the United States and it is estimated that over 50%, over 400,000 farm laborers, are undocumented people. Only 5,000 green cards per year are provided for farm labor jobs. This number is dramatically lower than the actual need (American Immigration Council, 2013). Undocumented people in the United States pay taxes but never have access to the services they pay for, are often separated from their children in deportation raids, are treated as less-than-human with distancing language (illegal alien), and their children who were brought here still have no pathways to citizenship (though, by executive order, they currently can apply for temporary resident status for 2-year periods while they are in school).

Beyond the larger majority categories listed above, there are a number of smaller minority groups that also suffer from a lack of privilege in the United States. For instance, even something as simple as the hand you write with confers rights to people who are in the majority. Right-handed people get the privilege of using tools (from computer mice to scissors to heavy equipment) that are built to fit their grips, driving vehicles that are oriented to their handedness and never having people comment on the hand that they write with.

While handedness is one of the lesser areas of privilege there are still issues for the minority population it affects. Left-handed people still have salaries that average 10% less than right-handed people's salaries and are underrepresented in neurological brain imaging studies because their brains are wired differently. As a result, less is known about how left-handed people's brains actually work (Tsuei, 2011).

Check Your Privilege: Gender

Regardless of gender, please complete the below checklist.

To avoid being sexually assaulted I:
_____ check my clothing to make sure it is not provocative
_____ carry pepperspray
_____ never/rarely walk alone at night
_____ always walk with purpose
_____ always note where the nearest exit is
_____ always tell someone where I am going
_____ keep my keys between my fingers in parking lots and on the street
_____ check the backseat of my car before I get in
_____ never park next to vans
_____ avoid wearing headphones so I can remain alert at all times
_____ always make sure my cell phone is charged
_____ have 911 on speed dial
_____ immediately turn and lock my door as I enter my home
_____ never go on a date with anyone I do not know well
_____ always take friends with me to social events, and stick with them throughout the evening
_____ never leave my drink unattended
_____ have taken self-defense classes

Everyday, I:

_____ worry that I might be sexually assaulted

If you checked more than five items on the above list you likely identify as a woman. If much of the list seemed overly sensitive and a little unbelievable, you may have just experienced male/masculine privilege. Women in the United States, especially feminine women, have been trained to believe that they are in constant danger from sexual predators and men have been taught none of the above (except to watch their drinks so they do not get robbed). This is just one area in which men tend to have intangible benefits that they are unaware of.

Sadly, gender still has an impact on earning power in the United States. The American Association of University Women's Fall 2013 report, _The simple truth about the pay gap_, shows the following:

- The pay gap has not improved in the last decade.
- The pay gap exists in every state in the United States.
- The pay gap is worse for women of color. Hispanic women find themselves with the largest pay gap, making only 53% of what men in the same professions make.
- The pay gap exists in nearly every occupation, women average about 77% of what men are paid.
- The pay gap grows with age.
- At every level of academic achievement, women's median earnings are less than men's earnings, and in some cases, the gender pay gap is larger at higher levels of education.
- The pay gap also exists among women without children.

(American Association of University Women, 2013)

Check Your Privilege: Race

The below checklist is adapted from Peggy McIntosh's _White Privilege: Unpacking the Invisible Knapsack_ (McIntosh, 1988).

When I go shopping:

_____ I can shop anywhere without someone following me around the store or accusing me of theft
_____ I can walk into any hairdresser's shop knowing that someone there will be able to deal with my hair
_____ I can walk into any supermarket and find the foods I grew up with
_____ When I ask to speak to the person in charge, I am usually greeted by someone of my own race
_____ I can buy "flesh colored" band-aids that do not contrast with my skin.

In the media:

_____ I can see people of my own race anytime I turn on the TV or open a magazine
_____ When I watch children's programs I always see people of my own race

In school:

_____ I learned about histories that taught me about my own heritage
_____ I was taught about the founders of our country, all of whom were of my race
_____ I learned that my race exists
_____ I learned that people of my race made this country what it is today
_____ I saw pictures of people of my race in all of my textbooks

_____ I was never asked to speak for people of my racial group

_____ I can walk into any classroom on campus and know that the majority of students share my race

_____ I can enroll in almost any class on campus and be assured that most of my professors will share my race

Financially:

_____ I can walk into any bank and, as long as I have a good credit and banking history, be assured that I can get a loan

_____ I can rent an apartment anywhere as long as I have good credit.

Personally, I am not made to feel that it is a reflection on my race if:

_____ I have body odor issues

_____ My body shape is different from mainstream expectations

_____ I am late to a meeting

_____ I openly discuss race

_____ I excel in a challenging situation

When I drive:

_____ I can drive anywhere I want to without the police pulling me over for being in the wrong place

_____ I do not get pulled over regularly just because there is an APB out for someone of my description

_____ I can drive a 5 to 10 MPH over the speed limit most of the time without fear of being pulled over

If you checked most of the above you quite likely identify as White (and you might come from a middle-class background).

Does Whiteness really matter? While it is uncomfortable to talk about and hard to wrap our minds around, just being White does tend to provide an economic boost, especially as we get older and attain higher education. To see how race and gender combined with level of education equate to economic inequality in the United States visit http://inequality.is/personal. You will be able to provide your personal information for gender, age, race, and education, then compare your income with people who differ in any of the four categories.

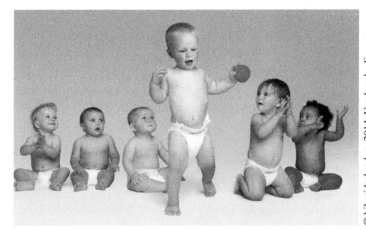

Figure 5.17 Being born White in the United States still provides an advantage.

© bikeriderlondon, 2014. Used under license from Shutterstock, Inc.

Majority/Minority Identity Development

The grid at Figure 20 adapted from Martin and Nakayama's discussion of minority and majority identity development outlines four stages of development (Martin & Nakayama, 2007). We can better understand our own identities if we take the time to evaluate the many paths we took as we developed each aspect of our identities. For instance, if you are White and left handed, then, while your racial identity likely followed majority identity development, your physical ability identity likely followed minority development.

In this section of the chapter I will only provide my own personal examples. It is not okay to label other people's developmental stages as that would require us to make huge assumptions that may not be accurate. As a result, in this next section, I will only refer to my own experiences. I hope that my own admittedly privileged experiences will be helpful in this discussion.

We all begin life as babies. Our identities develop as we grow. We all begin with unexamined identities. We only begin to examine our own identities when we begin to recognize differences between ourselves and others. In the next few pages we will discuss first, minority identity development then majority identity development.

Before we begin it is helpful to make a distinction between the mainstream use of the term "minority" and our use in this chapter. In US popular culture when the term "minority" of "minority group" is used, the definition is almost always related to a racial or ethnic group that is not White. In this section of the

Figure 5.18 We all begin life with unexamined identities.

chapter, however, when we refer to **minority identities** we are talking about identities that, regardless of your racial or ethnic group, diminish your privilege in the United States today.

People who are born with minority identities begin as we all do, with no awareness that differences exist. In the United States this means that people who are born into any of the following conditions are unaware of their differences initially: not male, not White, not heterosexual, not cis-gender, not Christian, not middle-class, not neurotypical, not physically abled, or not US citizens. Since they are not really aware of their differences they tend to accept the values and attitudes of the majority, including negative views of their own group. This is the **unexamined identity stage.** When I was very young, before the term "Native American" came into use, I remember playing Cowboys and Indians with my friends. The Indians were always the bad guys and the Cowboys were the good guys. No one ever wanted to be a brutal, callous Indian. One day I came home crying because my friends had made me be the Indian. My mom listened to all my complaints and my cruel racist assumptions about Indians. She paused for a moment and then said, "Honey, are you a brutal, horrible beast who kills everyone?" I thought a moment, "No. Why?" She smiled, "Because you're an Indian. You are part Cherokee, Seneca and Blackfoot." I would like to say that I immediately stopped being upset when I had to play the Indian. I would like to say that I told my friends that Indians were just people like us and that I was part Indian. But, instead, I did not tell my friends. I wanted to be just like them. I accepted the negative views of Indians for a time, just so I could keep fitting in with my friends. I was trying to conform to the majority culture.

Minority identities tend to develop when people realize that some aspect of their identity differs from the identities commonly seen in the larger culture. Once a person begins to examine their minority identity they may try, as I did above, to conform to the majority culture. In the **conformity stage,** people who have minority identities try to become part of the majority. In the conformity stage people tend to internalize the values and norms of the dominant group and have a strong desire to assimilate into the dominant culture. They tend to have negative attitudes toward themselves and their group and they tend to criticize other members of their own group. They may even be given negative labels by their own group. I have always been a big girl and I come from a family full of larger people. When I was in third grade other children began making fun of my weight. Everywhere I looked everyone was more slender than I was. There were no girls or women on TV who looked like me. So, I began to think that I should look more like them. I wanted to look like them. When I was 11 my mom enrolled me in a summer aerobics class because she did not know what else to do to help me in my quest to conform. The class was full of big girls who looked just like me. Instead of feeling like these girls were in the same situation I was in, I remember thinking that they must eat a lot more than I did and they must be really lazy. I had internalized the biases I saw in the weight-loss ads on TV. I, like the other girls, despised the class. We all acted like this was the worst thing that had ever happened to us. A few weeks into the ordeal, we were all sitting on the curb after class, sweating and waiting for our parents. One of the girls said that she hated the class. We all agreed. Then she said that she was ugly and fat. We all disagreed with her. She had gorgeous long black hair and big brown eyes and she even had a butt (something this White girl has had to work for her whole life). She laughed. She said that she thought we were all pretty. We all talked about what we liked about each other until our moms picked us up. Classes after that were much more fun. We had accepted ourselves and began coming to class to hang out with one another. We were no longer taking the class to get skinny like all the girls at school and on TV.

Figure 5.19 In the conformity stage, people try to make themselves fit majority culture ideals—it is healthier to learn to love yourself as you are.

Often, when people emerge from the conformity stage they find themselves fighting against their former conformity as well as the larger culture. When this happens, people enter the resistance and separatism stage. People in the **resistance and separatism stage** actively question majority beliefs and attitudes. They have a growing awareness that not all dominant group values are beneficial to minority groups. This may have been triggered by negative interactions with the majority culture. They tend to be motivated to learn about their heritage and to join clubs and groups in which they can discuss common interests and experiences and find support. Often people in this stage tend to focus on the values and norms of their minority group as being superior to the values and norms of the dominant group. I experienced this stage, in relation to my left-handedness, in my early years of college. On day while attempting to take notes in a chair desk with a right-handed armrest with a small jutting desk portion, I had had enough. I was suffering from constant back pain because every classroom was outfitted with these right-handed desks and I, as a left-handed person, had to twist awkwardly just to take notes in class. I was starting to feel persecuted. I went to the library and checked out all the books about left-handed people and left-handedness. I found out that, according to the Americans with Disabilities Act, 10% of the desks in each classroom are supposed to be left-handed. I became an outspoken advocate for left-handed seating in all classrooms. I took trips to the Southpaw stores in Los Angeles and San Francisco. I began making lists of all the left-handed people who had been famous throughout history and I began trying to connect all of my best attributes with theirs. I noticed that many left-handed people were artists and thinkers and I wanted to be just like them.

While I was stuck in the resistance and separatism stage I learned to speak out for the needs of people who were like me, which would soon help me speak out for the needs of people who were not like me. One day on the way to class, I met a young woman in a wheelchair. The elevator was broken and she could not get to class. Since I had done all that reading about the Americans with Disabilities Act, I knew that the school was out of compliance. I went to her classroom, on the second floor, and asked her instructor what the plan for that day's class session was. The instructor explained that they were doing mostly discussion and group work. I explained that her student could not come to class because the elevator was broken. I mentioned that it was a lovely day and that the outdoor group discussion area seemed to be available and shaded from the afternoon sun. The instructor sent her students downstairs, went and called maintenance to fix the elevator, and held class outside so that the young woman in the wheelchair would not miss an important day of class. That day, I emerged from the resistance and separatism stage into the integration stage. People in the **integration stage** of minority development tend to have a strong sense of their own group identity (based on gender, race, ethnicity, sexual orientation, and so on) and an appreciation of other cultural groups, realize that racism and other forms of oppression occur, but anger is redirected toward positive ends and they show a desire to eliminate all forms of injustice, not just oppression aimed at their own group. Once I entered the integration stage I began to notice all of the injustices many other physical and neurological minorities faced. I began learning more about them and eventually began learning more about people of other minority groups as well. I began standing up against injustice when I could because I knew what it felt like to be on the outside looking in.

Members of minority groups experience many of the above stages as they come to grips with different aspects of their identities. As you can imagine, most of us not only have minority identities but we also have majority identities that follow similar but different developmental stages.

Minority Identity Development	Majority Identity Development
Unexamined Identity	**Unexamined Identity**
For both majority and minority identities the unexamined identity stage is characterized by lack of exploration of identity.	
1 People in the unexamined identity stage of minority development tend to: • accept the values and attitudes of the majority, including negative views of their own group; • have a desire to assimilate into the dominant culture and express positive attitudes toward it; • be disinterested in or not concerned with their identity.	People in the unexamined identity stage of majority development tend to: • have some awareness of differences, but they do not fear other groups or feel superior to them; • base communication and relationships on similarities rather than differences.
Conformity	**Acceptance**
2 People in the conformity identity stage of minority development tend to: • internalize the values and norms of the dominant group and have a strong desire to assimilate into the dominant culture; • have negative attitudes toward themselves and their group; • criticize other members of their own group and may be given negative labels by their own group. This stage may continue until the individuals encounter situations that cause them to question their culture attitudes.	People in the acceptance identity stage of majority development tend to: • internalize and accept the basic inequities in society; • have no conscious identification with being in the majority; however, some assumptions based on an acceptance of inequities in society are subtly elitist; • be seen as individuals with no culture, group identity, or shared experiences of privilege; • avoid communication with minorities and/or take patronizing tone toward minorities. Some people never move beyond this stage, and if they do it is a result of a number of events, such as becoming good friends with minorities or taking a class or workshop that deals with issues of elitism or privilege.

Resistance and Separatism		Resistance
3	People in the conformity identity stage of minority development tend to: • have a growing awareness that not all dominant group values are beneficial to minority groups. This may have been triggered by negative interactions with the majority culture; • be motivated to learn about their heritage and to join clubs and groups in which they can discuss common interests and experiences and find support; • a blanket endorsement of one's group and its accompanying values and attitudes, and a subsequent rejection of the values and norms of the dominant group.	People in the resistance identity stage of majority development tend to: • blame the social system for inequalities; • resist elitism: this may take the form of passive resistance, with little behavior change, or active resistance—an ownership of elitism; • feel embarrassed or ashamed and may avoid or minimize their communication with people of their own group and seek out interactions with people of minority groups.

Integration		Redefinition and Reintegration
4	People in the integration identity stage of minority development tend to: • have a strong sense of their own group identity (based on gender, race, ethnicity, sexual orientation, and so on) and an appreciation of other cultural groups; • realize that racism and other forms of oppression occur, but anger is redirected toward positive ends; • show a desire to eliminate all forms of injustice, not just oppression aimed at his or her own group.	People in the redefinition and reintegration identity stage of majority development tend to: • refocus their energy on redefining dominant group status in non-elitist terms and are able to integrate being part of the dominant group into other facets of their identity; • realize that they do not have to accept the definition of their dominant group that society placed on them and can see positive aspects of being in their dominant group; • recognize their identity as a member of the dominant group but also appreciate other groups; • recognize that prejudice and racism exist in society and that blame, guilt, or denial does not help eliminate these types of elitism; • show awareness of the importance of understanding what comes with being part of the dominant group such as "Whiteness" and White identity.

Figure 5.20   Minority/Majority identity development stages. (Adapted from Martin & Nakayama, 2007; Helen Acosta, 2013).

People with majority identities are far more likely to experience the **unexamined identity stage** well into adulthood than people with minority identities. The reason for this is simple: If you are one of thousands who share your identity then you think that you are just like everyone else. You do not realize that there is anything to examine because that aspect of your identity is never brought into question. For instance, I never realized how much I took for granted when I was growing up. I never realized how many benefits I had that others do not: benefits of class that came to me because I had parents who were educated and I grew up in a middle-class home. I was 40 years old when I attended a campus staff development activity called "The Privilege Walk—Class Issues." In the activity the facilitator asked about 30 questions. For each question, we were told to take one or more steps forward or backward. Some of the questions that sent me forward were:

- If you ever attended a private school, take two steps forward.
- If you parents were able to help you with your homework take one step forward.
- If your parents took you to art galleries, museums, sporting events, or plays as a child take one step forward.
- If you have family members who are doctors, lawyers, or "professionals" take one step forward.
- If you ever got a good paying job because of a friend or family member take one step forward.
- If you were given a car by your family take one step forward.
- If you grew up in a home with lots of books for both adults and children take one step forward.
- If your parents completed college take one step forward.
- If you were raised in a home where a newspaper was read daily take one step forward.
- If you went to a sleep-over summer camp while you were growing up take one step forward.
- If you had private lessons or a private tutor while you were growing up take one step forward.
- If you did not have to get a job in high school to help with family finances take one step forward.
- If you have ever inherited money or property take one step forward.
- If your family took vacations outside of your state or nation while you were growing up take one step forward.

There was only one question that sent me backward: "If you have ever had to rely only on public transportation take 1 step back"

There were other questions related to class that sent other people in the room backward:

- If there were times in your childhood when you had to go hungry because your family could not always afford food take one step back.
- If your family ever lost their home when you were growing up take one step back.
- If your family car broke down and there was not enough money to fix it or get a working vehicle take one step back.
- If one of your parents was unemployed or laid off, not by choice, while you were growing up take one step back.
- If you were often embarrassed by your clothes or home while you were growing up take one step back.
- If you were raised in a single parent household take one step back.
- If you were raised in an area where there was crime or drug activity take one step back.
- If you were raised in a rural area take one step back.

By the end of the activity I found that I was the second most privileged person in the room. Before that day I had never considered how lucky I was to be born into a middle-class family to educated parents. I never thought of myself as anything but poor because we had shopped at the "Canned Food Warehouse" and my sisters and I only wore hand-me-downs for years. After the privilege walk I realized how lucky I was. Had I been born into another family I might not have had access to the reading specialist my parents paid to meet with me twice a week for a year to teach me the tricks that would make my dyslexic mind work for me instead of against me. I might not have had parents who could help me with my homework, who took vacations to unique and interesting places, and always went out of their way to enrich my childhood, whether it was an Angels' baseball game, the Army/Navy football game, a beautiful garden, or one of the many museums within a few hours of our home. In another family I might not have had the opportunity to go to music camp every summer during high school and I might have had to get a job instead. I might have had to work during the school year instead of enjoying my afterschool activities. Until I was 40 I had never examined this aspect of my identity. After the privilege walk my assumptions about my students and acquaintances changed. Instead of assuming that we were all pretty much alike when it came to class issues I found that the simple realization that I was tremendously lucky made me delve deeper and learn more about the people in my life.

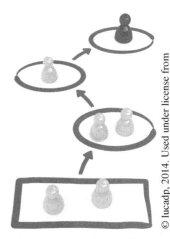

Figure 5.21   The accident of birth places those in a majority several moves ahead of those in a minority.

While I have spent my entire life in multicultural communities I was always "the White girl." There were always other White girls and White boys and for much of my childhood we were close to half the population in the schools that I attended. For part of my childhood I lived in the **acceptance stage** of Majority Identity development. While my Latino and Black friends had cultures that I could see, experience, and describe, I could never see my own culture. I knew that most of the White kids lived in the middle-class neighborhoods up the hill (though there were several Latino and Black families in my neighborhood) and most of the Latino and Black kids lived down the hill in a neighborhood that did not have curbs and gutters but instead just had dirt between people's yards and the street (there were hardly any White families who lived down the hill). I knew I had more than the kids who lived down the hill and about as much as the kids who lived near me. Beyond that basic understanding, I had no conscious identification with being in the majority; I did not realize that nearly everyone on TV had my skin color or that almost everyone my teachers ever talked about and almost everyone I ever read about was White. My parents worked hard to assure that I did not stay in this stage my whole life. My mom put me in the Camp Fire Girls, a group in which I was the only "White girl" and my parents consistently exposed me to cultures that were not my own (I still remember the Sikh blessing ceremony of a family friend's hardware store). Even through all of their efforts there was a time in fourth grade when I retreated from my Camp Fire Girls friends and sought friendships with the other White girls. It did not last long. I found that the other White girls tended to talk down to my old friends and acted superior to them. I felt uncomfortable with the way the White girls from my neighborhood treated my friends from Camp Fire Girls. The people from my neighborhood were deep in the acceptance stage of majority identity development. People in the acceptance identity stage of majority development tend to internalize and accept the basic inequities in society, and have no conscious identification with being in the majority; however, some assumptions based on an acceptance of inequities in society are subtly elitist. They also tend to be seen as individuals with no culture, group identity, or shared experiences of privilege and tend to avoid communication with minorities and/or take a patronizing tone toward minorities.

This story does have a happy ending. All of those White girls who had retreated into a clique in fourth grade grew out of their elitism by fifth grade. For a time we became a big, rowdy, fun group of girls who played together regardless of social class or race/ethnicity.

When people emerge from the acceptance stage they often enter the **resistance stage** of majority development. People in the resistance stage of majority development tend to blame the social system for inequalities, resist elitism: either in the form of passive resistance, with little behavior change, or active resistance—an ownership of elitism, feel embarrassed or ashamed, and may avoid or minimize their communication with people of their own group and seek out interactions with people of minority groups. I spent much of the early 2000s in the resistance stage in regard to my Whiteness. I had trouble dealing

Figure 5.22   Members of a majority group who enter the Resistance stage often protest for the rights of people who are in the minority.

with the historic actions of White people in regard to other groups of people and I did not like the fact that our society privileges people who are White. My resistance took the form of active resistance. I rallied and marched with people of color on a variety of issues. I joined the UFW and marched with farm workers, and I joined the Rainbow-PUSH coalition and picketed speeches made my people who had diminished the humanity of African Americans through their words and actions. I signed petitions and spoke in a variety of settings in my hopes of fighting the system that had given me gifts that were not made available to others.

I was angry for a long time. I was angry at our mostly-White government and a system that perpetuated power by mostly-White people. It was not until 2005–2006 that I finally ran out of anger and started to find a way to come to terms with my Whiteness. At that point I entered the redefinition and reintegration stage of identity development. People in the **redefinition and reintegration stage** of majority development tend to refocus their energy on redefining dominant group status in non-elitist terms and are able to integrate being part of the dominant group into other facets of their identity, realize that they do not have to accept the definition of their dominant group that society placed on them and can see positive aspects of being in their dominant group, recognize their identity as a member of the dominant group but also appreciate other groups, recognize that prejudice and racism exist in society and that blame, guilt, or denial does not help eliminate these types of elitism, and show awareness of the importance of understanding what comes with being part of the dominant group such as "Whiteness" and White identity. This was certainly my experience. I redefined myself as an advocate and ally, a role that I work daily to maintain today. I know that, as a member of the dominant culture, sometimes my voice can be heard more loudly than members of non-White groups. I know that I have a responsibility to listen and only

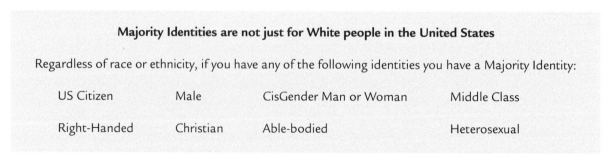

Figure 5.23   Common majority identities.

speak when people of a minority group want a megaphone to shout about their issues. It is tricky because there are times when I think that I know what to say or do but I still make huge mistakes and I have to say "I'm sorry, could you help me figure out how to avoid what I said/did so that I can avoid making that mistake again". To live in redefinition and reintegration I have had to learn to support others' identities by listening with my ears, eyes, and heart.

Support for Others' Identities

Once we begin to recognize that people who experience minority development in any area often find themselves at a disadvantage in mainstream culture we may feel a need to help or support, especially when we find ourselves in the last two stages of majority development. However, there are times when we want to be supportive but we forget to follow the Platinum Rule (Do to others what *they would have done to them*) rather than the Golden Rule (Do to others what *you would have done to you*). As a result, there are times when we are trying to help but we fail. A friend of mine wrote about a time when he really needed help but the first person to offer it was following the Golden Rule rather than the Platinum Rule.

Patrick RichardsFink wrote the following blog entry September 9, 2013 (used with permission)

Allies who are not Allies

Ten or more years ago, I was driving towards one of the most dangerous intersections in the state (according to the Department of Transportation! No shoulder, extremely busy, tons of semis and people not paying attention to what they are doing). My station wagon abruptly died. I had no cash on me, and about $40 in the bank that had to last for two weeks no matter what — I could not spend it on anything but the things it was budgeted for.

So there was a guy walking across the intersection, and he asked if I needed help. I said, yes, please, we need to push the car around the corner and about half a block to a parking lot where I could figure out what I was going to do. He said "Sure, I'll help."

He started trying to flag down cars. I said "What are you doing?" He said "I'll see if someone has a cell phone so they can call you a tow truck."

"I have a cell phone," I said. "I can't afford a tow truck. I just need to get me and my car out of this intersection."

He ignored me, and proceeded to flag down a semi. The driver leaned out and asked what the problem was, and the dude who thought against all evidence he was being helpful told him to call a tow truck.

At this point I came unglued. I said, loudly, "I don't need a tow truck, I can't afford a tow truck, please don't call a tow truck because I have no way to pay for one! Thanks for stopping but I just need a push."

The guy who was not really helping, who was actually distracting me from the task, looked hurt, and then he said "But you need a tow truck."

At this point? I'd had enough. I was tired, stuck in a dangerous position, not a little humiliated. I said "Are you going to help me push?"

He said "I tried to get you a tow truck."

I told him to f* off if he wasn't going to help me push my car.

About that time a friend of mine happened to be driving by. She's about 2/3 the size of the guy who couldn't figure out that I knew exactly what help I needed. She pulled into the parking lot, ran back, and at no small risk to herself helped me push my car out of the dangerous intersection, to a place where I could get under the hood and figure out what I needed to do to get it running and get home.

So: Were both of these people Allies?

There was no ideological test going on here, it was purely practical. Person X could not internalize what my problem was, so all he did was work on a "solution" that was actually more harmful than if he had just walked on by. Person Y actually jumped in and helped me do what needed to be done.

And that's what's going on here. This isn't about passing a purity test. This is about actions. Is someone helping? They are an Ally. Is someone complaining that their feelings are hurt because they are doing what they think I need and I am telling them it isn't? Not an Ally.

If a hundred people had come by and all of them had not only suggested a tow truck but told me that it was the best and correct solution to my problem, even though it was a solution that I considered and rejected for perfectly rational reasons (because if I had had access to a couple hundred bucks, I would have called a tow truck myself and had it towed to my mechanics), by the hundred and first I would be saying "Can you help me push? A tow truck is out of the question" and if they stood there and argued with me about how a tow truck was indeed the best solution, I would then be saying "Help me push or f* off."

I've caught some flak (not a lot, but a little) from some people for "not recognizing that you need Allies."

I know that I need Allies.

What I don't need are people who get upset when I get angry because they are calling a tow truck I cannot afford when what I really need is a quick push that will be easier if more of us are pushing.

Oh, yeah. I never finished the story. The not helpful guy? When he finally quit trying to get me a tow truck? He walked away. He didn't help push. He never intended to give me the help I needed, only the help that he decided I needed. He took his ball and went home.

—*(RichardsFink, 2013)*

There are times in all of our lives when we need a little help. Sometimes, we need support because of our minority status, at other times we just need support because we are in a tough situation. Often, when we reach out to give help to others, we are seen as "Allies." When we try to help we have the best intentions but, if we forget to put the other person's experiences first we end up stereotyping. When we stereotype we become microaggressors, we fall into the danger of the single story, and the blinders of privilege lead to tunnel vision that we must be mindful of if we want to avoid unintentional harm to people we wish to help.

There are times when we reach out to help, thinking that we are providing what is needed, but instead, because we can only see the solutions and opportunities we have access to (as a result of privilege) we are just wasting another person's time. That is usually when the person we are trying to help gets frustrated or angry. Then, to make matters worse, we get upset because we were just trying to help. We, then, fall into a whole new set of assumptions and stereotypes that just worsen the situation. Stick with the Platinum Rule (treat others as they want to be treated) to avoid falling into this cycle of negative regard.

Figure 5.24 Follow the Platinum Rule: Do to others what they would have done to them.

To learn more about ways to act with empathy, read Chapter 8: Adaptation and Empathy.

Glossary

Cisgender   People who identify as the gender they were assigned at birth.

Identity   In sociology and psychology, "identity" is a person's conception and expression of their group affiliations and individuality, as used in this chapter; an identity is a person's conception and expression of a single facet of their individuality that is linked with a group affiliation.

Majority Identity   An identity that, regardless of race or ethnic group, is the mainstream identity. Majority identities benefit from privileges that minority identities do not.

Microaggressions   The umbrella term for the emotional stab wounds of stereotyping people from a minority, these become more painful when someone from a majority uses the stereotype.

Microassaults   Deliberate harmful actions and language choices like displaying a Confederate flag or willfully using slurs against a particular group.

Microinsults   Words and actions that subtly convey rudeness and insensitivity while demeaning a person's identity. For instance, thoughtlessly asking a person of color how she got her job might imply that she only got it because of affirmative action. In addition, the unknowing use of stereotypes that are in common use by one group but are harmful to another group also falls into this area (see the discussion of historical stereotypes above).

Microinvalidations   Words and actions that exclude or negate the experiential reality of a person.

Minority Identity   An identity that, regardless of your racial or ethnic group, is not the mainstream identity. Minority identities do not benefit from the privileges of majority identities.

Privilege   The intangible, unearned benefits people get as a result of membership in a majority group.

Stereotyping   Is a subconscious short-hand in which we make snap judgments about other people without even thinking about the fact that we are making a decision.

Subconscious bias   A preferences that has built up in our minds based on our experiences. These preferences are the foundations of the snap judgments that we rely on when we stereotype.

Zipf's law   The tunnel vision that blinds us to ideas that are not in the first place position in our minds.

Works Cited

Adichie, C. N. (2009, October). *The danger of a single story*. Retrieved from TED website: http://www.ted.com/talks/chimamanda_adichie_the_danger_of_a_single_story.html

Ahuja, G. (2009, March 31). *Good Morning America: What a doll tells us about race*. Retrieved from ABC News website: http://abcnews.go.com/GMA/story?id=7213714&page=1&singlePage=true

American Association of University Women. (2013, September). *The simple truth about the gender pay gap*. Retrieved from American Association of University Women website: http://www.aauw.org/files/2013/03/The-Simple-Truth-Fall-2013.pdf

American Immigration Council. (2013, March 13). *Why don't they just get in line*. Retrieved from Immigration Policy Center website: http://www.immigrationpolicy.org/just-facts/why-don%E2%80%99t-they-just-get-line

Bulger, M. (2012, December 1). *Unelectible atheists: US States that prohibit Godless Americans from holding public office*. Retrieved from American Humanist Association website: http://americanhumanist.org/HNN/details/2012-05-unelectable-atheists-us-states-that-prohibit-godless

Caitlyn, R. (2009). *Supportive families, healthy chidlren: Helping families with lesbian, gay, bisexual and transgender children*. San Francisco, CA: Family Acceptance Project, San Francisco State University. Retrieved from Family Acceptance Project website: http://familyproject.sfsu.edu/files/FAP_English%20Booklet_pst.pdf

Conrad, K. (2013, October 31). *Rise of the female chefs*. Retrieved from Bespoke Magazine website: http://bespokemagazineonline.com/rise-female-chefs/?doing_wp_cron=1385314342.2606470584869384765625

DeAngelis, T. (2009). Unmasking "racial micro aggressions". *Monitor on Psychology, 40*, 42.

Godin, S. (2008). *Unleashing the idea virus*. New York, NY: Do You Zoom.

Goode, E. (1999, May 20). *Study finds TV alters Fiji girls' view of body*. Retrieved from New York Times website: http://www.nytimes.com/1999/05/20/world/study-finds-tv-alters-fiji-girls-view-of-body.html?src=pm

Gordon, D. (Director). (2004). *A state of mind* [Motion Picture].

Graham, S. (2001, April). *Sulawesi's fifth gender.* Retrieved from Inside Indonesia website: http://www .insideindonesia.org/weekly-articles/sulawesis-fifth-gender

Grant, J. M., Mottet, L. A., Tanis, J., Harrison, J., Hermann, J. L., & Keisling, M. (2011). *Injustice at every turn: A report of the national transgender discrimination survey.* Retrieved from National Gay and Lesbian Taskforce website: http://www.thetaskforce.org/downloads/reports/reports/ntds_full.pdf

Ireland, C. (2009, March 19). *Fijian girls succumb to Western dysmorphia.* Retrieved from Havard Gazette website: http://news.harvard.edu/gazette/story/2009/03/fijian-girls-succumb-to-western-dysmorphia/

Martin, J., & Nakayama, T. (2007). *Intercultural communication in contexts.* New York, NY: McGraw Hill.

McIntosh, P. (1988). *White privilege: Unpacking the invisible knapsack.* Retrieved from New York Model for Batterer Programs website: http://nymbp.org/reference/WhitePrivilege.pdf

Pew Research. (2013, January 2013). *Faith on the hill: The religious composition of the 113th congress.* Retrieved from Pew Research Religion and Public Life Project web site: http://www.pewforum.org/2012/11/16/ faith-on-the-hill-the-religious-composition-of-the-113th-congress/

RichardsFink, P. (2013, September 9). *Allies who are not allies.* Retrieved from Eponymous Fliponymous website: http://fliponymous.wordpress.com/2013/09/09/allies-who-are-not-allies/

Schumacher-Matos, E. (2014, March 19). *Ethics, morality and a ticking clock for how to report on The R**skins.* Retrieved from NPR website: http://www.npr.org/blogs/ombudsman/2014/03/19/291479274/ ethics-morality-and-a-ticking-clock-for-how-to-report-on-the-r-skins

Tsuei, C. (2011, December 6). *The health risks of being left-handed.* Retrieved from The Wall Street Journal website: http://online.wsj.com/news/articles/SB10001424052970204083204577080562692452538

US Equal Employment Opportunity Commission. (2012a). *Americans with Disabilities Act of 1990 (ADA) Charges (includes concurrent charges with Title VII, ADEA, and EPA), FY 1997–FY 2012.* Retrieved from US Equal Employment Opportunity Commission website: http://www.eeoc.gov/eeoc/statistics/enforcement/ ada-charges.cfm

US Equal Employment Opportunity Commission. (2012b). *Charge statistics: FY 1997 through FY 2012.* Retrieved from US Equal Employment Opportunity Commission website: http://www.eeoc.gov/eeoc/statistics/ enforcement/charges.cfm

Chapter 6

Verbal Communication

Helen Acosta

"To have a second language is to have a second soul."
—The Emperor Charlemagne (748–814 AD)

Chapter Learning Objectives

1. Identify the levels of language.
2. Learn about the many languages on our planet.
3. Gain an awareness of the ways linguistic relativity shapes our perceptions.
4. Learn ways to avoid misunderstandings and what to do when we offend.

When the Midwest chain store, Osco drugs, bought out Sav-on drug stores in California in the early 1990s, my husband could not stop laughing. Every time we passed one of their stores he would hold his stomach and make retching sounds and say, "Oh! I feel so ahhhhhhsko!" While my husband, a fourth-generation American born in East Los Angeles, does not speak Spanish, he has lived in Spanish-speaking communities his entire life. There are many Spanish phrases that he consistently uses. In context I surmised that "osco" must mean "to feel unwell." Much later I learned that "asco" in combination with other Spanish words has meanings that Osco drugs should have been more careful to research before opening their stores in Southern California. "Coger asco a" means "to become sick of," "dar asco" means "to sicken or disgust," "ser un asco" means "to be disgusting or worthless." Not surprisingly, many Osco drug stores located in Spanish-speaking communities failed within 5 years.

Figure 6.1   It is a good idea to check the languages of any area you plan to expand your business to. Otherwise you might "dar osco" your potential customers.

—Helen Acosta

In the United States, today, 214 different languages are spoken. The two most common languages are English and Spanish. As of the 2010 Census 34 million Americans spoke Spanish as their first language. That means that over 10% of the US population spoke Spanish as their first language.

The United States is not unique. Every nation in the world that has welcomed diversity or shifted its national boarders finds that they must accommodate a wide range of languages.

In this chapter we will identify the functions of language, explore the language diversity found in the world today, discover how the languages we speak affect our perceptions and behaviors, delve into the difficulties of translation, and learn what we can do to avoid confusion when we speak with people whose first language differs from our own.

The Levels of Language

Language is the primary mode of transmission humans use to share experiences and stories with other humans. Cultural values and beliefs are coded into each language as it grows. Language allows us to interact with deeper understandings of other people's experiences of the world. Language allows us a window into the mind of another.

There are four primary levels of language that exist across the many languages of the earth:

- Phonetics is the basis of most languages. Phonetics, the sounds of words, is the easiest to understand.
- Semantics are the meanings of words and sentences and the relationships between the meanings of words and the meanings of the sentences they exist within.

- Syntactics are the rules of language. Most often we think of these rules as "grammar."
- Pragmatics are the most difficult to understand because they are so complex. Pragmatics deal with the language ambiguities that can only be explained through contextual understandings of time, place, relationship, and manner of utterance.

Phonetic understandings of language are derived from the sounds of words as well as the way we transcribe the sounds of words. There are a number of sounds that are present in some languages that are not present in others. In the eighteenth and nineteenth centuries, explorers attempted to transcribe the sounds of languages that were not their own by merely approximating the sounds from their own languages in transcription. However, these approximations did not approach the actual sounds of the languages in many cases. For instance, the city we now know as Beijing was for centuries called "Peking" by English speakers because a British explorer attempted to transcribe the unfamiliar sounds using sounds that were part of his own language. Sadly, the lack of a "zhuh" sound in English at the time gave the explorer no way to notate the sound. It was only later that words like "pleasure" and "vision" came to English from their French origins. Today, the International Phonetic Alphabet (IPA), established in the late 1800s, allows linguists to more accurately transcribe and learn to speak sounds from languages that are not their own. While the IPA takes some effort to learn, once you are comfortable with all of the sounds of the IPA, learning languages that have sounds that are not in your first language is simplified.

Tonal languages are languages in which meaning is dependent on the combination of word and tone. Tonal languages complicate English speakers' understanding of phonetics. English is not a tonal language. As English speakers we use modulation of the voice in order to add meaning to phrases. For instance, we raise the pitch at the end of a question phrase. In many languages words are inflected rather than phrases and a change of inflection changes the word. An example of this, from Mandarin Chinese: mā means mother and mǎ means horse. In Mandarin Chinese there are four basic inflections or tones: flat and high (mā means mother), rising (má means "to bother"), dipping (mǎ means horse), and sharp down (mà means "to scold"). When English speakers initially encounter Mandarin speakers, the inflections sometimes sound angry as a result of the flat and high tone, rising tone and especially the sharp down tone which English speakers generally use only when they are frustrated or angry. The Chinese languages are just one group of thousands of tonal languages in the world. Most of the African languages are tonal and the Scandinavian languages are tonal as well.

While phonetics is concerned with the sounds of any language, **semantics** deal with the coded meanings of words and phrases in a language. Exploration of the differences between denotation (the dictionary definitions of words) and connotation (the many experiential meanings of words beyond their dictionary definitions) are just the tip of the iceberg that is semantics. While semantics help us uncover the literal, decontextualized meanings of words and phrases in a sentence, semantics can also help us understand how languages organize and express meaning. Through semantics we learn that when someone says, "He's a dog!" when referring to a male human they are saying that the male human tends to sleep around and lacks any interest in a monogamous relationship.

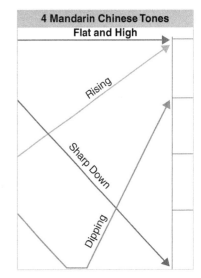

Figure 6.2 Mandarin Chinese is a tonal language. (Helen Acosta, 2014).

THE INTERNATIONAL PHONETIC ALPHABET (revised to 2005)

CONSONANTS (PULMONIC)

	Bilabial	Labiodental	Dental	Alveolar	Post alveolar	Retroflex	Palatal	Velar	Uvular	Pharyngeal	Glottal
Plosive	p b			t d		ʈ ɖ	c ɟ	k g	q ɢ		ʔ
Nasal	m	ɱ		n		ɳ	ɲ	ŋ	N		
Trill	B			r					R		
Tap or Flap		ⱱ		ɾ		ɽ					
Fricative	ɸ β	f v	θ ð	s z	ʃ ʒ	ʂ ʐ	ç ʝ	x ɣ	χ ʁ	ħ ʕ	h ɦ
Lateral fricative				ɬ ɮ							
Approximant		ʋ		ɹ		ɻ	j	ɰ			
Lateral approximant				l		ɭ	ʎ	L			

Where symbols appear in pairs, the one to the right represents a voiced consonant. Shaded areas denote articulations judged impossible.

CONSONANTS (NON-PULMONIC)

Clicks		Voiced implosives		Ejectives	
ʘ	Bilabial	ɓ	Bilabial	ʼ	Examples:
ǀ	Dental	ɗ	Dental/alveolar	pʼ	Bilabial
ǃ	(Post)alveolar	ʄ	Palatal	tʼ	Dental/alveolar
ǂ	Palatoalveolar	ɠ	Velar	kʼ	Velar
ǁ	Alveolar lateral	ʛ	Uvular	sʼ	Alveolar fricative

OTHER SYMBOLS

ʍ Voiceless labial-velar fricative
w Voiced labial-velar approximant
ɥ Voiced labial-palatal approximant
H Voiceless epiglottal fricative
ʕ Voiced epiglottal fricative
ʡ Epiglottal plosive

ɕ ʑ Alveolo-palatal fricatives
ɺ Voiced alveolar lateral flap
ɧ Simultaneous ʃ and x

Affricates and double articulations can be represented by two symbols joined by a tie bar if necessary. k͡p t͡s

VOWELS

	Front	Central	Back
Close	i • y	ɨ • ʉ	ɯ • u
	ɪ ʏ		ʊ
Close-mid	e • ø	ɘ • ɵ	ɤ • o
		ə	
Open-mid	ɛ • œ	ɜ • ɞ	ʌ • ɔ
	æ	ɐ	
Open	a • ɶ		ɑ • ɒ

Where symbols appear in pairs, the one to the right represents a rounded vowel.

SUPRASEGMENTALS

ˈ	Primary stress
ˌ	Secondary stress ˌfoʊnəˈtɪʃən
ː	Long eː
ˑ	Half-long eˑ
˘	Extra-short ĕ
ǀ	Minor (foot) group
‖	Major (intonation) group
.	Syllable break ɹi.ækt
‿	Linking (absence of a break)

DIACRITICS
Diacritics may be placed above a symbol with a descender, e.g. ŋ̊

̥	Voiceless	n̥ d̥	̤	Breathy voiced	b̤ a̤	̪	Dental	t̪ d̪
̬	Voiced	s̬ t̬	̰	Creaky voiced	b̰ a̰	̺	Apical	t̺ d̺
ʰ	Aspirated	tʰ dʰ	̼	Linguolabial	t̼ d̼	̻	Laminal	t̻ d̻
̹	More rounded	ɔ̹	ʷ	Labialized	tʷ dʷ	̃	Nasalized	ẽ
̜	Less rounded	ɔ̜	ʲ	Palatalized	tʲ dʲ	ⁿ	Nasal release	dⁿ
̟	Advanced	u̟	ˠ	Velarized	tˠ dˠ	ˡ	Lateral release	dˡ
̠	Retracted	e̠	ˤ	Pharyngealized	tˤ dˤ	̚	No audible release	d̚
̈	Centralized	ë	̴	Velarized or pharyngealized	ɫ			
̽	Mid-centralized	e̽	̝	Raised	e̝ (ɹ̝ = voiced alveolar fricative)			
̩	Syllabic	n̩	̞	Lowered	e̞ (β̞ = voiced bilabial approximant)			
̯	Non-syllabic	e̯	̘	Advanced Tongue Root	e̘			
˞	Rhoticity	ɚ a˞	̙	Retracted Tongue Root	e̙			

TONES AND WORD ACCENTS

LEVEL			CONTOUR		
e̋ or ˥	Extra high		ě or ˩˥	Rising	
é ˦	High		ê ˥˩	Falling	
ē ˧	Mid		e᷄ ˧˥	High rising	
è ˨	Low		e᷅ ˩˧	Low rising	
ȅ ˩	Extra low		e᷈	Rising-falling	
↓	Downstep		↗	Global rise	
↑	Upstep		↘	Global fall	

Figure 6.3 IPA Chart, http://www.langsci.ucl.ac.uk/ipa/ipachart.html, available under a Creative Commons Attribution-Sharealike 3.0 Unported License. Copyright © 2005 International Phonetic Association.

Semantics deal with the meanings of words and sentences and the relationships between the meanings of words and the meanings of the sentences they exist within. Many jokes in English are based in semantic confusion. Some examples of jokes that work because of semantic confusion are as follows:

- I went to the bookstore and asked the clerk, "where is the self-help section." She replied, "If I told you that would defeat the purpose!"
- Would a fly without wings be called a "walk"?
- Can vegetarians eat animal crackers?
- Why is there an expiration date on sour cream?

While US English and Canadian English share most words, you will see some semantic differences in Figure 6.4. You will notice that some of the Canadian terms such as "Chesterfield" and "Loonie" feel like an entirely different language even though both terms are, technically, English.

Some semantic differences between Canadian English and US English		
Term	Canadian	US
Knitted hat	Toque	Beanie, Hat
The shoes you wear to go jogging	Runners	Sneakers, Kicks, Tennis shoes
The room where the toilet is located	W.C., Washroom	Bathroom, Restroom
The letter "Z"	Zed	Zee
The cozy seating in the living room	Chesterfield	Sofa, Couch
Place of higher education where you pursue academics	University	College, University
Place of higher education where you learn a trade	College	Trade School
$1	Loonie	Dollar, Buck

Figure 6.4 Some semantic differences between Canadian English and US English (Helen Acosta, 2014).

Syntactics deals with the rules that govern the structure of any language—rules about ways in which words are put together to form phrases, clauses, or sentences. Linguist, Noam Chomsky often used the following example to show the power of syntax in creating meaning: Native speakers of English almost always have a sense that the nonsensical phrase, "colorless green ideas sleep furiously," is grammatically correct. Chomsky went on to show that another arrangement of the same words violates our language rules: "green furiously ideas colorless sleep." The rules of any language become second nature for fluent speakers of the language (Marcus, 2012).

Pragmatics considers the language ambiguities that can only be explained through contextual understandings of time, place, relationship, and manner of utterance. For instance, in most places and times in the United States when you ask someone, "Do you know what time it is?" they know that "yes" is not the expected answer. Instead, they give you the time of day. However, if you have gone to a Comic/ Science Fiction/Pop Culture Convention anytime between 2010 and today and ask almost anyone in attendance what time it is, the answer will almost always be the same (and often shouted by a crowd of people), "IT'S ADVENTURE TIME!" If you are not part of their co-culture you will be quite confused by their response, one that is embedded in their co-culture as a call-and-response based on the popular cartoon, *Adventure Time*. "IT'S ADVENTURE TIME" is a response based in a different context than the mainstream expected response, and thus, you might change the way you ask the question if you really want to know the time of day. You might adjust the way you ask to, "What is the time on your phone?" or "Do you have the time?"

Pragmatics also addresses the emotional content of a message as well as multiple meanings of a message. As such, the meaning of "Wow, awesome haircut" can only be discerned within the context of the experience. If the person delivering the message seems genuinely excited, happy, and maybe a bit surprised, then most likely the person who just got a haircut can be happy that their friend likes the outcome of their visit to the salon. However, if the person delivering the message says the same words but says them without facial expression and uses a flat tone of voice, then most likely the person who just got the haircut will feel pretty bad about the money they just wasted at the salon.

So Many Languages!

It is estimated that nearly 7,000 languages exist in the world today but according to the Endangered Languages Project 43% of those languages are in danger of dying out within one of two generations. Of the 280 known languages that were spoken by Native Americans when Europeans arrived, only 20 are still being learned and spoken by children today (University of Hawaii, Manoa, 2014).

In the summer of 1934, a small group of people met in Dallas, Texas, to explore some the world's lesser-known languages. This small group of people grew over the years into the Summer Institute of Linguistics. By the 1950s, the Institute had grown to a year-round nonprofit organization called SIL International. In 1954, they began publishing Ethnologue: Languages of the World, a publication that is, currently, updated annually. Today, Ethnologue is available free on the web. According to Ethnologue, world languages are broken into 136 different **language families** of common origin. However, 85% of people in the world today speak languages that are part of the six most common language families: Afro-Asiatic, Austronesian, Indo-European, Niger-Congo, Sino-Tibetan, and Trans-New Guinea. As you can see from Figure 6.5 one out of every five people in the world today speaks a language from the Sino-Tibetan language family. There are 461 languages in the Sino-Tibetan language family. Two hundred and ninety-eight different languages are spoken in China alone (Ethnologue: Languages of the World, 2014b).

However, many of the nearly 7,000 languages on the planet are in no way related to these 136 families. These languages are called **isolates**. These languages developed in isolation from other languages and share no common root. The Basque language is one such isolate. Basque country aka Euzkadi, politically situated in Northern coastal Spain, is surrounded by people who speak French to the north and Spanish to the south. However, the

Figure 6.6 Basque country (yellow on the map), today, is in Spain (in cream on the map) but historically Basque country has been bordered by France (gray on the map) and Spain.

Language family	Total speakers	Percent of world population	Countries in which a language in this family is a first language
Afro-Asiatic	362,281,758	5.81	Algeria, Bahrain, Cameroon, Chad, Cyprus, Egypt, Eritrea, Ethiopia, Georgia, Iran, Iraq, Israel, Jordan, Kenya, Libya, Mali, Malta, Mauritania, Morocco, Niger, Nigeria, Oman, Palestine, Saudi Arabia, Somalia, Sudan, Syria, Tajikistan, Tanzania, Tunisia, Turkey, United Arab Emirates, Uzbekistan, Yemen
Austronesian	345,818,471	5.55	Brunei, Cambodia, Chile, China, Cook Islands, East Timor, Fiji, French Polynesia, Guam, Indonesia, Kiribati, Madagascar, Malaysia, Marshall Islands, Mayotte, Micronesia, Myanmar, Nauru, New Caledonia, New Zealand, Niue, Northern Mariana Islands, Palau, Papua New Guinea, Philippines, Samoa, Solomon Islands, Suriname, Taiwan, Thailand, Tokelau, Tonga, Tuvalu, United States, Vanuatu, Viet Nam, Wallis and Futuna
Indo-European	2,916,732,355	46.77	Afghanistan, Albania, Armenia, Austria, Azerbaijan, Bangladesh, Belarus, Belgium, Bosnia and Herzegovina, Brazil, Bulgaria, Canada, China, Croatia, Czech Republic, Denmark, Fiji, Finland, France, Germany, Greece, Iceland, India, Iran, Iraq, Ireland, Isle of Man, Israel, Italy, Latvia, Lithuania, Luxembourg, Macedonia, Maldives, Myanmar, Nepal, Netherlands, Norway, Oman, Pakistan, Peru, Poland, Portugal, Romania, Russian Federation, Serbia, Slovakia, Slovenia, South Africa, Spain, Sri Lanka, Suriname, Sweden, Switzerland, Tajikistan, Turkey, Ukraine, United Kingdom, United States, Vatican State, Venezuela
Niger-Congo	430,784,205	6.91	Angola, Benin, Botswana, Burkina Faso, Burundi, Cameroon, Central African Republic, Chad, Comoros, Congo, Côte d'Ivoire, Cuba, Democratic Republic of the Congo, Equatorial Guinea, Gabon, Gambia, Ghana, Guinea, Guinea-Bissau, Kenya, Lesotho, Liberia, Malawi, Mali, Mayotte, Mozambique, Namibia, Niger, Nigeria, Rwanda, Senegal, Sierra Leone, Somalia, South Africa, South Sudan, Sudan, Swaziland, Tanzania, Togo, Uganda, Zambia, Zimbabwe
Sino-Tibetan	1,268,209,279	20.34	Bangladesh, Bhutan, China, India, Kyrgyzstan, Laos, Myanmar(Burma), Nepal, Pakistan, Thailand, Vietnam
Trans-New Guinea	3,536,267	0.06	East Timor, Indonesia, Papua New Guinea
Totals	5,327,362,335	85.42	

Figure 6.5   Adapted from Ethnologue: Languages of the World, Acosta, 2014.

Basque language is derived from neither. While linguists have hypothesized connections to other languages for decades, no actual connection has ever been found. Roughly 2 million people live in Basque country and speak the Basque language. Regionally the language is referred to by the following names: Euskara, Euskera, and Vascuense (Ethnologue: Languages of the World, 2014a).

The languages of the world vary so greatly that learning to speak a second language, especially one from a language family that is different from your own, is quite difficult. As a result, we tend to rely on translations and interpreters when we need to communicate with someone whose language is one that we do not speak.

Translation vs. Interpretation

In the United States many people tend to mix the terms "translator" and "interpreter." However, these particular jobs are very different from one another. A **translator** is a person who works to translate a text from one language to another. The best translators have a deep understanding of both the original language and the target language. They work with dictionaries and reference materials to effectively transfer not just words but to maintain the underlying meanings that are culturally bound. Most often, the best translations are translations into the translator's native language. If you have ever hit "translate" on a website you know how complicated the work of any translator is.

Interpreters must be able to translate in both directions fairly instantaneously. In most instances, interpreters work with the spoken word and have no access to reference materials while they work. The best interpreters not only know the words of two or more languages but understand the culturally bound meanings, colloquialisms, jargon, and slang common to any speaker's language choices.

While both translation and interpretation are, today, tremendously difficult, there are technologies on the horizon that might bring our science fiction fantasies to life. Ajit Narayanan began his career working with autistic children in India, a nation in which 122 native languages are spoken. Most of his work was with people who do not speak. As a result, he developed an app that allows nonspeaking people to use images to communicate their needs to people who speak. However, he found that without grammar (syntax) it was still impossible for a nonspeaker to fully communicate their needs. As a result, he continued adding to his app. He developed a visual grammar to connect the images into sentences and he developed a reader programmed with all of the rules of English. As a result, Avaz users can develop highly complex, completely grammatical sentences. And, according to Narayanan, in his February, 2013 TED talk, Avaz is not just helping autistic children to communicate their needs. Avaz is helping autistic children learn to speak and, in the future, he plans to program the rules of many more languages into Avaz to support autistic children worldwide. He hopes, to revolutionize second-language learning and app translators worldwide. Avaz is currently available in English, Danish, and six Indian languages: Hindi, Kannada, Malayalam, Marathi, Tamil, and Telugu.

Linguistic Relativity: The Languages We Speak Affect Our Perceptions, Behaviors, and Memories

In the early twentieth century a variety of thinkers began noticing that people who spoke different languages tended to focus their attention in different ways. These thinkers noticed that the language used by people influenced their thought processes and behaviors. There were several theories developed during this period to attempt to explain this apparent relativity in languages. The most famous is actually a test of one of these theories. The theory tested was initially developed by Edward Sapir who believed that language influenced thoughts and behavior in fairly superficial ways. However, Sapir's student,

Benjamin Lee Whorf, took this notion much further when he argued that a speaker's language influences the way the speaker perceives the world. Whorf made his theory popular through his engaging writing and speaking style. Since Whorf's ideas were the most famous these were the obvious choice for testing. Roger Brown and Eric Lenneberg, who were critical of the notion that language influences thoughts, behaviors, and perceptions, reformulated Sapir's theory into a testable hypothesis known today as the **Sapir–Whorf hypothesis** (Swoyer, 2010).

Figure 6.7 Linguistic relativity and linguistic universalism have struggled against one another for decades. (Helen Acosta, 2014)

The Sapir–Whorf hypothesis fell out of favor in the 1960s and 70s when linguists, the most well-known of whom was Noam Chomsky, were focused on principles of universality. Today the idea of **linguistic relativity**, first espoused by Edward Sapir and Benjamin Lee Whorf, is balanced with the **linguistic universalism** of the 1960s made famous by Noam Chomsky. As you saw in the chapter on Sameness and Difference we all struggle to find balance, and that is certainly the case among linguistic theorists. In the field of intercultural communication, since the mid-1990s, linguistic relativity had held more attention than universalism.

Language Influences Our Perceptions

Dr. Lera Boroditsky, a linguist at Stanford University, has found that about 1/3 of the world's languages provide a perceptual filter not found in English. This perceptual filter acts as a kind of human global positioning system (GPS). Rather than using general directional terms like "Left" and "Right," these languages use mapping terms in even the most basic communication. Instead of saying "Move your plate to the left," they might say "Move your plate to the North-northwest." Dr. Boroditsky spent some time in 2006 in Pormpuraaw, an aboriginal community on Cape York in Queensland, Australia. The people of Pormpuraaw use a language that has these "GPS filters." She explained that in Pormpuraaw even basic greetings included mapping functions. Instead of saying "Hi" or "How are you?" in Pormpuraaw, you say "Which way are you going?" Dr. Boroditsky explains that the expected answer is extraordinarily specific, and an example would be "North-northeast in the middle distance, how about you?" There are over 80 choices for your answer to this question. Each time someone shares a greeting you are expected to tell them your specific heading. Even young children are expected to share their heading each time someone greets them.

Here is the most exciting part: Dr. Boroditsky initially felt rather dim in the company of people, including small children, who always knew where they were on the map. She noticed after a few weeks that a little map appeared in her mind, and on the map in her mind, a little red dot that she knew was her. All of a sudden, she knew exactly what her own heading was no matter where she was, indoors or out. She asked a few of the people of Pormpraaw about the map that had appeared in her own head and they verified that they, too, had maps in their minds that they referenced constantly (Abumrad & Krulwich, 2011).

Figure 6.8 Dr. Broditsky eventually saw a map appear in her mind.

Location is not the only perceptual difference based in language. There are many others: Colors are perceived differently based on the variety of color choices found in any given language. Many African languages have 5 basic terms for colors, in comparison to the 11 basic terms for color used in most

European-based languages. When people who speak languages with only five color terms are asked to distinguish between colors that they have no terms to describe they find it harder to see the differences than people who speak languages with color terms that more closely approximate the colors shown (Greene, Boroditsky, & Liberman, 2010).

Many languages have no exact number words. In these cultures it is difficult to keep track of any quantity. The most recent numberless culture to be studied by American scholars is the Piraha tribe of Brazil. While the Piraha people have words for relative quantities that appear to have similar meanings to "smallest amount," "smaller amount," "larger amount," "much larger," and "largest amount," they do not appear to have any specific number words, thus invalidating Noam Chomsky's argument that every language shares universal characteristics including a counting system (Trafton, 2008).

There are differences even among languages that have exact number words. Children who speak Mandarin comprehend how the base 10 number system works much sooner than children using Anglophone number words (England and former English colonies like the United States). Why? Mandarin number words are more concrete and there are fewer words to learn in order to use the full system. There are only 18 words you need to learn in Mandarin in order to talk about all numbers. These 18 words are then compounded in order to make larger and larger numbers. Instead of "eleven" or "twelve," Mandarin number words translate to "ten-one" (shyr yi), "ten-two" (shyr erh). In contrast, English number words are more difficult to comprehend. The first 10 number words are simple but, once you get to eleven and twelve, meanings become oblique. Both eleven and twelve have original meanings that come from a root of "left over," twelve is two left over and eleven is one left over. Then thirteen is basically three-ten and everything begins to make sense again (Greene et al., 2010).

Many languages have gendered nouns that change perceptions of each noun. For instance, the German word for death is masculine and artists always portray death as a man, and the Russian world for death is feminine and artists always portray death as a woman. There are no gender pronouns in Finnish. Children learning Finnish as their first language take about a year longer to figure out if they are a boy or a girl than Israeli children raised with prolifically gendered language do (Greene et al., 2010).

Language shapes our perceptions of people from other cultures. Bilingual Hebrew/Arabic speakers were given an implicit association test. When tested in Hebrew bilingual speakers showed more favorable views toward Jewish people than they did when tested in Arabic. Same person + different language = different result (Greene et al., 2010).

> The languages we speak change our perceptions of
>
> - how to navigate terrain
> - numeric values
> - colors
> - genders
> - people from other cultures
> - time

Figure 6.9   The language we speak changes our perception in many ways. (Acosta, 2014).

Language shapes our perception of time. In English the future is ahead of us. For the Amayra people of the Andes the future is behind them and the past is ahead of them. In Mandarin, the past is above and the future is below (Greene et al., 2010).

Language Influences Our Behaviors

Economist and UCLA Professor, M. Keith Chen, has found that people who speak future time-focused (aka "futured") languages like English ("Tomorrow will be cold") have dramatically lower rates of personal savings than people who speak futureless languages ("Tomorrow is cold") like Japanese, Chinese, German, Dutch, Estonian, and Portuguese. Dr. Chen suggests that in futureless languages the future is always present so speakers of these languages are always reminded to take care of the future, while in futured languages, like English, the future is always far away and speakers have time to take care of it later (Chen, 2013).

Dr. Chen also found that this single variable in a language's approach to the future also impacted other behaviors as well. People who spoke futured languages were less likely to use birth control, more likely to smoke, less likely to be physically active, and more likely to be obese. So, while we, in America, believe that the future is ours we also tend to neglect the future as a result of the language we use.

Language Influences How We Remember Events

As English speakers we focus on individual people's actions. We describe not what happened but what the people did in any situation. We are focused on personal responsibility as well as personal culpability for actions taken. Conversely, according to Dr. Broditsky, in many languages the person involved in an action is less important than the action itself, and this difference appears to be most apparent in situations where the action was perceived to be an accident (Boroditsky, 2010).

Figure 6.10   English speakers tend to neglect the future because it seems so far away.

This linguistic difference seems to be most apparent here in the United States between English speakers and Spanish speakers. While the differences in memory of eye-witness events among these two populations are not huge, the differences are large enough to have lasting impacts in relationships and especially in the courtroom. Boroditsky and her associate, Caitlin Fausey, found that, when it comes to actions perceived to be accidents, Spanish speakers are far less likely to remember the actors and instead are more likely to remember the action. Instead of "The man dropped the vase" they might remember "the vase fell and broke." As a result, the placing of blame, when the action is perceived as an accident, is less likely when viewed by a Spanish speaker than an English speaker (Fausey & Boroditsky, 2011).

Figure 6.11   English speakers focus on the person who is to blame for an action while Japanese and Spanish speakers focus more on the action and tend to forget the person.

This difference in blame-placing was particularly apparent in the wake of the Fukushima meltdowns. While the American media continuously tried to get the Japanese government to focus on who was to blame for the incident, the Japanese government saw the meltdowns as an accident and seemed wholly disinterested in who was to blame. The American media began blaming the Japanese government for withholding information and burying the culprits. However, as an accidental event, blame was not the issue that mattered to the Japanese government. Instead, what mattered was the action itself and assuring that it never happened again. To date, Japan has idled all 50 of its nuclear reactors as they continue to debate whether it is possible to make them safe enough to use in the future. Currently, over 60% of the Japanese public is against returning to nuclear energy (Adelman & Suga, 2013). In the absence of nuclear energy they have had to rely on unsustainable fossil fuels. However, since the Fukushima disaster Japan has brought online roughly three reactors-worth of sustainable green energy, mainly through solar plants, with several more wind and solar projects in development. The green energy movement has also spurred "smart cities" plans that focus on integrated smart grid technologies that reduce overall energy consumption (Kingston, 2013).

So, while the government of Japan was seen in a negative light by the American media, perhaps their lack of focus on "who is to blame" actually allowed them to react far more quickly to make changes that would likely take decades in the United States.

Linguistic Relativity and High- and Low-Context Communication Styles

Edward T. Hall is considered the father of Intercultural Communication. Hall was an anthropologist and cross-cultural researcher. Hall was fascinated by the ways in which people interact with one another. In his work, first on Navajo and Hopi reservations in the 1930s then later in Europe, the Middle East, and Asia, Hall came to understand that people use language differently, based on the values and needs of their culture. In the 1950s while he was an intercultural trainer for the state department he developed the concepts of high- and low-context culture in order to help American Foreign Service personnel better understand the ways people use language and do not use language in their interactions.

Low Context

It is assumed that communicators do not share a previously established context. Thoughts and ideas must be explained clearly, and meanings must be fully expressed in order to assure that everyone in the communication encounter grasps the contexts. For low-context communicators communicating unambiguously is important. High-context communicators often find low-context communicators to be wordy or micromanaging.

Some Low-Context Cultures

Australian	Hebrews/Jews (Israel, Europe, North America)
Dutch (Netherlands)	New Zealand
English Canadian	Scandinavia
English	Switzerland
Finnish (Finland)	United States (other than parts of Southern US)
German	

High Context

It is assumed that communicators share a previously established context. As a result, it is unnecessary, and often annoying to explain every detail. For high-context communicators, shared contexts build mutual respect. High-context communicators respect the other person's understanding of situations and leave understanding to the other person. Low-context communicators often find high-context communicators to be confusing and ambiguous.

Some High-Context Cultures

African (most)	Greek	Japanese	Southern US
Arab	Hawaiian	Korean	Spanish
Brazilian	Hungarian	Latin Americans	Thai
Chinese	Indian	Nepali	Turkish
Filipinos	Indonesian	Persian (Iran)	Vietnamese
French Canadian	Italian	Portuguese	South Slavic
French	Irish	Russian	

High/Low Context is about
how we process information (what we value as important)
more than it is about behaviors.

High Context

is where much of the
meaning comes from
between the lines.

Low Context

is where much of the
meaning comes from what is
explicitly verbalized.

(KapplerMikk, 2012)

Both high- and low-context communication styles exist in US culture to varying degrees. Whenever we can depend on a previously established context, we tend to fall into the shorthand of high-context communication. Whenever we know that we do not share previous contexts with someone or a group of people, we rely on the explicit directness of low-context communication style.

Linguistic Relativity, Language Taboos, and Euphemisms

The word "taboo" was introduced to the English language in 1777 by Captain James Cook. When Cook was exploring in what are known today as the Polynesian islands, he visited the island that is today known as Tonga. In Tonga there were a number of forbidden foods and activities. These were referred to as "taboo." The term was popularized in England and America during the Victorian era, a time when many activities were seen to be forbidden.

Words become taboo in any language when they are used primarily in a provocative or subversive way. Words that are taboo are the words native speakers know they are not supposed to speak. Breaking a language taboo is an act of rebellion that always elicits an emotional response from native speakers. In most cultures, words that are used to refer to sex or elimination are taboo. Also, words that deviate from or challenge the accepted or expected moral or ethical codes within a society become taboo, and these are often words related to religious beliefs, especially words related to death. However, there are other words that also challenge moral or ethical codes within a culture as well. For instance, in the United States, we like to believe that we treat everyone equally. As a result, words that were traditionally used to describe people based on their race, ethnicity, nation of origin, sexual orientation, intelligence, or physical ability have become taboo because they were used to separate and diminish opportunities for people who might be described using those terms. In some other countries where equality is less important than order and hierarchies are common, many terms that we, as Americans, would think must be taboo are instead seen as mere descriptions.

Some of the most unsurprising yet newsworthy work on linguistic relativity in the last decade has centered on language taboos and the euphemisms people use to refer to these taboo terms.

Over the last decade, Richard Stevens of the School of Psychology, Keele University, Staffordshire, United Kingdom, has

Figure 6.12 Words become taboo in any language when they are used primarily in a provocative or subversive way.

done a number of studies with a variety of colleagues on the effect of swearing on pain tolerance. He has found that swearing produces both an emotional and physical response that leads to increased aggression and decreased pain response. The increase in pain tolerance is most pronounced for people who rarely swear (Stephens & Umland, 2011).

The knowledge that swear words increase pain tolerance led Jeffery Bowers and Christopher Pleydell-Pearce of the Department of Experimental Psychology at the University of Bristol to wonder if the more polite substitute words that we use to soften the swear words also provided any pain tolerance. Bowers and Pleydell-Pearce conducted experiments to better understand the power taboo words and their more polite euphemisms have in our lives (Bowers & Pleydell-Pearce, 2011). Bowers and Pleydell-Pearce attached a device to the fingers of the vol-

Figure 6.13   Swearing decreases pain. But if you swear all the time the swear words lose their pain-reducing superpowers.

unteers. The device would measure electrodermal responses to stimuli. Then they had volunteers read sets of four words aloud: a taboo/swear term (e.g., "fuck"), a euphemism for the taboo term ("f-word") and a neutral word ("drum"), and a euphemism for the neutral word ("d-word"). Bowers and Pleydell-Pearce found that the taboo terms, when spoken aloud, led to a big change in skin tension, the euphemism for the taboo term led to less than half the tension, the neutral word when spoken aloud created even less tension, and the euphemism for the neutral word created the least tension.

Bowers and Pleydell-Pearce suggest that these unsurprising findings tell why euphemisms are found in all languages. Taboo or swear words cause emotional stress (and increase pain tolerance), even to utter aloud. Euphemisms are language softeners that decrease the psychological toll on those who use them.

Surprisingly, Bowers and Pleydell-Pearce extended their findings to other situations where the emotional toll on the speaker was lessened as a result of the language choices they made. Bowers and Pleydell-Pearce suggest that speaking a second language has the same emotional effect as euphemisms have. Speaking of difficult subjects in a second language is often less painful than speaking about those subjects in a speaker's first language. Here are some examples the authors share from other researchers findings: 1) A young Chinese man, when confessing to a priest, finds it unbearable to talk about his transgressions in his native language but can speak about those transgressions in his second language. 2) When people write or speak taboo words in their native language the words produce far greater stress than when they write or speak taboo words in a second language.

Bowers and Pleydell-Pearce conclude that euphemisms allow people to create emotional distance from what would otherwise be emotion-provoking and it turns out that speaking in a language other than your native language also provides the same distance (Bowers & Pleydell-Pearce, 2011).

There are many taboo word forms that would be unfamiliar to people from the United States. For instance, there are words that are so sacred or dangerous that only certain people are allowed to speak them. It would be inappropriate to write an example of any of these words as the written example would likely offend people of these cultures.

In many languages other than English, there are very clear semantic codes, involving honorifics and speech-level rules that speakers are expected to use to honor the relationship and status levels of the people with whom they interact. In the Korean language there are seven different speech levels.

Each level must also be combined with honorific and nonhonorific noun and verb forms, based on the situation. This leads to 14 entirely different sets of semantic rules a person must follow for different situations. However, the highest speech level is disappearing from use in everyday speech because it was the level used to address royalty. Today, this level reserved for royal occasions is only found in Korean films and costume dramas.

> While speakers of US English are familiar with avoiding taboo subjects, we are not familiar with the following language taboos:
>
> - Words that are so sacred or dangerous that only certain people can speak them.
> - Honorific and speech-level syntax that changes the way people of different status may speak to one another.
> - Avoidance honorifics that require people to avoid all references to the people they are honoring.

Figure 6.14   Unfamiliar language taboos.

The most difficult type of taboo for native English speakers to understand is likely avoidance honorifics. In many languages around the world people who occupy particular roles in life show reverence for their direct relations and/or those above them through the use of avoidance honorifics. Avoidance honorifics are complex language choices that avoid any direct reference to anything related to the person they are honoring. For instance, the Oromo people (who live in the East African countries of Somalia, Ethiopia, and Suriname) have a complex language system in which a wife may not say any word that starts with the same sounds or syllable as the names of her husband, his male relations, his clan, and his two best men at any time during her life. Instead, she must substitute other, often more general, words in order to show respect for the family of which she is now a part (Tesafe, 2007).

Taboo Subjects

Like taboo words, every culture has taboo subjects. For instance, in most of the world, visitors to a nation are advised not to talk about the nation's politics, religious or social issues as outsider views often offend. However, throughout Nigeria these discussions are welcomed and encouraged along with joyful and spirited debate. What some cultures find taboo, other cultures embrace.

Subject	Where it is taboo	Where it is preferred
How much money someone makes/how much something costs	Croatia, Germany, parts of the United States	China, Equador
How much a person weighs	United States, Canada	Ecuador, Democratic Republic of Congo
Politics, religion and social issues	Most of the world	Nigeria
A person's age	United States, Indonesia, and Sierra Leone	Vietnam
Seeking/suggesting psychological therapy	South Korea, Japan, African American communities	Argentina

Figure 6.15   The appropriateness of a topic of conversation changes from culture to culture. (Helen Acosta, 2014).

Policing Language

The language we use shapes our perceptions, our behaviors, and even our memories. As a result, it is not surprising that people often argue about language use and appropriate words, and word forms and phrases. There are a number of different ways people police languages.

The most obvious policing of language comes in the form of governmental language policies. In France the Académie Française holds an annual ceremony to induct new words into the French language. For a time, the Académie had great difficulty holding back the onslaught of English words that began to permeate the French language. However, the Académie found greater success once they began holding an annual competition to find French-sounding words to use instead of the English words that were creeping in. As a result, "chatting" online became "éblabla" and "talk" became "débat." While the Académie has slowed the increase of English words and phrases within the French language many still likely cringe when they hear people talk about "les air bags" in their cars, and what their plans are for "le weekend" (Jamison, 2010).

In many countries around the world the government enacts language policies. These language policies exist to favor the use of a particular language or to preserve native languages. In 1992, the Council of Europe drafted the European Charter for Regional or Minority Languages in order to preserve the many regional languages across Europe. The Charter only applies to languages traditionally spoken within the 47 European countries that signed the treaty. However, in the United Kingdom alone, six minority languages are now protected: Cornish, Irish, Gaelic, Manx, Scots, Scottish Gaelic, and Welsh. As a result of the Charter, all children in Wales now study Welsh until the age of 16. Similar educational mandates exist in Ireland and Scotland to preserve the Gaelic and Scots languages. However, while Cornish is protected by the Charter this regional language has not become part of any government mandate (Committee of Experts, 2010).

In the United States we have no official, federally enshrined language, though most Americans assume that English is the official language. However, 28 States, including California, have adopted English as their official language (Crawford, 2012).

In many countries, including the United States, there are several languages in which government publications, signage, and corporate communication are provided in multiple languages. In the United States, most often, the languages are English and Spanish. In China, government publications, signage, and corporate communication are provided in 14 different languages, primarily based on the language spoken by people within particular regions (Ethnologue: Languages of the World, 2014b).

Even when governments do not police languages people who use the language tend to self-police. In the United States there are words that are so taboo that if the wrong person uses the word that person will be verbally shamed by those around them. In our media we see instances of that shaming on a regular basis. For instance, as a White woman who grew up in the 1970s I have never said the n-word (and cannot even bring myself to type it because that word is entirely forbidden. I even think "n-word" when I have to think about the word ... and I cringe when I even think that euphemism).

Political correctness is a term originally used in the early twentieth century by socialists who felt that Stalinist policies had gotten out of hand. In the 1970s, the term was adopted, humorously, by young liberal Americans. The term had transformed by the 1990s. The term and its acronym "PC" were used pejoratively by American conservatives in reference to all attempts by American liberals to promote policy that would provide equitable opportunities and support minority groups' choices in identifying themselves by the names they might prefer. Political correctness became synonymous with the oft-repeated term "The thought police." The 1990s were a time of extreme change and extreme revolt against change. Changes from gendered to gender-neutral job identifiers such as "fireman" to "fire fighter" were seen as examples of political correctness taking over. Changes in terminology used to identify minority groups such as a change from "Indian" to "Native American" were seen as the thought police taking over and changes from Christian-centric to value-free culture terms such as "Winter Break" instead of "Christmas Break" were seen as a "War on Christmas." Political correctness became a point of extreme controversy in the 1990s. It was a term that became a rallying cry in what many call the "culture wars." Today the term is no longer in vogue though it is occasionally used by radio talk show hosts in search of ratings. While the term is no longer common the arguments still live. Anytime people argue about the need to change sports teams whose names are racial slurs, anytime we correct an older relative who uses gendered job titles, and every winter when the TV and radio talk show hosts drag out the "War on Christmas" we know that these arguments about who has the right to police our language live on today.

Avoiding Misunderstandings and What to Do When You Offend

Beyond all other advice in this section be aware that the most important thing to do when you offend because of your language choices or behaviors is to apologize and ask advice about how to avoid the offense in the future. When you are learning a second language it is a good idea to master the phrases that allow you to apologize and seek advice first, even before you learn how to ask where the bathroom is.

Phonetic Misunderstandings

Pronunciations differ from area to area, even among speakers of the same language. As a result, phonetic misunderstandings are common, and it also does not help that many people have their own idiosyncratic pronunciations of words. For several months after I met the man who would become my husband, I was confounded by a phrase that he used quite regularly. He would say what sounded to me like "I, Juan." I'd look at him, confused, and said "No, you are Enrique." He would laugh at me and we would go on with our day. Finally, it hit me. He was saying "I won!" To this day, I cannot get him to change the way he says the word "won," as it should rhyme with fun rather than pawn. While his pronunciation of the word is nonstandard, he would not change, so, I have had to adjust my expectations and occasionally give him a hard time about it, "What's that? You want a Korean dollar (also known as the "won" which rhymes with "yawn")." Beyond idiosyncratic differences, people who live in different regions of a country or share a language but live in different countries use different pronunciations of the same words. For instance, in parts of the American south, the word "creek" is pronounced like "crick." To avoid these confusions it is best to study the dialect that is most common to any community you plan to visit. Luckily, the internet is well populated with guides to help us avoid the phonetic misunderstandings that are most common across the English language.

When you are working with people from other countries it is important to be supportive when they are speaking in your language. Many languages do not have the same sounds and, as a result, learners of a language that has sounds not in their native language have tremendous difficulty even hearing the sounds that are not in their native language. For instance, Japanese people learning to speak English often have difficulty differentiating between "r" and "l" because these sounds are not present in Japanese. As a result, Japanese learners will often substitute the wrong sound, creating confusion for English-speaking listeners. Americans who are trying to learn to speak Chinese have a different perceptual difficulty. As English is not a tonal language, Americans have trouble learning the tones that go along with the words. If they say the word with the wrong tone they are saying an entirely different word but since American minds are structured through English, creating the connection of tone and word as necessary to create meaning is often a long-term challenge for Americans learning Chinese.

Semantic Confusion

Idiomatic expressions are phrases that, together, have a different meaning than the dictionary definitions strung together would provide. Idiomatic expressions are a daily part of every language. Unfortunately, these common but alternate uses of language are rarely found in dictionaries or other reference works. If I am in a meeting and someone says "Ugh . . . you're all over the map!" they are using an idiomatic expression. If I was not a native speaker, I likely would not understand that "It's all over the map" means that the discussion has been too wide ranging. Luckily, the internet provides us help with idiomatic expressions. If you hear an expression, in any language, that must be meaningful but the dictionary definitions are not helping you, type the phrase into a search engine. In most cases the meaning of the phrase will be found in one of the first few entries on the page.

When you are working with people whose first language is not English, it is a good idea to avoid idiomatic expressions whenever possible. However, these expressions are so common that we often do not notice when we are using them. As a result, pay close attention to the behaviors of the nonnative speakers you work with and, when they look puzzled, rephrase to avoid these types of confusion.

Figurative language also diverges from dictionary definitions by exaggerating or altering the meanings through the creative juxtaposition of words to form phrases that heighten sensory awareness of the word forms. Figurative language poses similar problems as idiomatic expressions do. In English, the seven categories of figurative language are imagery, simile, metaphor, alliteration, personification, onomatopoeia, and hyperbole. Imagery can be confusing when the image is one that is unfamiliar to the listener: "The black tree reached up toward the craggy orange slope." If the image is not true to the listeners' experience, you will lose them, even if the image is true to your experience of the world (as in figure 6.16). Similes can be confusing because they juxtapose two unlike things in order to create new meaning. No one knows if they are actually as "brave as a lion" because we do not actually know what it is like to be a lion. We also can only imagine being "as stiff as a board." Similes can be quite confusing for nonnative speakers. Likewise, metaphors can also be confusing. "Time is money," "He's a fat cat," and "You are my sunshine" can confuse when you are conversing with people whose first language is not English. Of all the types of figurative language hyperbole might be the most confusing for nonnative speakers. When we use hyperbole, when we exaggerate for effect, we know that we are exaggerating; however, people who are new to our language might not: "You could have knocked me over with a feather," "My dad is the smartest guy in the world," "That's the best idea ever." Again, as with idiomatic expressions as well as all of the other forms of figurative language, it is always a good idea to avoid these types of language when you are working with people who are new to the language. Be aware that, when you are learning a new language there will be other semantic differences that will lead to confusion. Make sure to look beyond the dictionary definitions to common usage in order to avoid continuous misunderstandings.

Figure 6.16 This dead tree in Dead Vlei, Namibia. seems surreal and sensory descriptions of it are hard to believe until you see it.

© Marcin Sylwia Ciesielski, 2014. Used under license from Shutterstock, Inc.

Syntactic Misunderstandings

Syntactic misunderstandings most often occur when we violate the rules of a language. If, for instance, we use only pronouns ("he," "she," "they," "it") in a conversation without ever referencing the associated nouns (Sam, Anna, supermarket), everyone involved gets confused. Another common issue related to pronoun use occurs because pronouns are not as prevalent in many languages. Many English learners use "he" to refer to men and women because their language does not rely on pronouns as English does. This is true for English learners whose first language is Portuguese, Japanese, Chinese, and many of the world's other languages. To avoid syntactic misunderstandings use shorter sentences with nouns rather than pronouns. All over the world for the last decade, people have experienced increased syntactic misunderstandings since the majority of people do not use punctuation when they use text messaging. So, in order to avoid confusion and frustration in the long run, consider using punctuation in your text messages.

Pragmatic Misunderstandings

Imagine that your phone just rang. Would you answer with "Hello," "What's up," "Yes," or your last name? In the United States we most often answer our phones with a greeting "Hello." However, Germans answer the phone with their last name and Greeks answer with "Yes" (ne). These are pragmatic elements of language use. The pragmatic elements of language use change over time based on changing contexts. Today, in the United States, an increasing number of people check the caller ID on their phones and address the caller by name when they answer, "What's up, Sis?" Pragmatics change based on social moirés. In the 1950s, it would have been inappropriate for a woman to go to coffee with a man she had just met. Today, people meet for coffee for business purposes, for academic purposes, and, on occasion, for romantic purposes. However, today, it is expected that an invitation to meet for coffee is not necessarily a request for a romantic encounter.

The pragmatics of any language are difficult to understand unless you have also studied the cultural etiquette of users of the language. Once you understand the cultural expectations across a wide variety of situations, it is easier to comprehend pragmatic usage. As discussed earlier, in some places in the world there are taboos about who can say what to whom in what situation. Some languages, like Korean, have very strict codes that require the most senior person to speak first and the more junior person to use less direct communication. Often in the plot of Korean dramas, when a less senior person speaks out of turn everyone in the room is shocked by the exchange. It is also helpful to understand other levels of directness that are common to the language. In the United States we have a tendency to soften criticism to such an extent that managers, supervisors, and teachers will often "suggest" changes. When these "suggestions" are made, it is important to understand that, pragmatically, the "suggestion" is really a directive. The expectation is that the change will occur.

To avoid pragmatic misunderstandings in English it is a good idea to monitor your interactions and take time to check with the people you are talking with to assure that their understanding of the discussion is the same as yours.

When you are learning a second language it is helpful to consume the popular culture of the country in order to gain understanding of the pragmatic elements that must be considered in day-to-day interactions. While you are learning the language, watch films and television shows created by and for people of the culture, read blogs, news articles, and books written in the language (for some languages you may have to learn a new alphabet or learn the pictographs that are the symbols used to communicate in writing). The more you can view the ways people interact within the culture the more well-prepared you will be for interactions of your own.

Summary

Language is the primary mode of transmission humans use to share experiences and stories with other humans. While all languages are different, most languages seem to share phonetic, semantic, syntactic, and pragmatic functions. While most languages on the planet are part of language families that share a common origin, there are many languages that developed in isolation and are not connected to any of the language families. Since languages are widely divergent translators and interpreters are often necessary for people who do not speak a language in which they want to communicate. The languages we speak dramatically affect our perceptions, behaviors, and memories. Since our languages are inextricably intertwined with our cultures, it is always a good idea to learn as much as we can about any culture in which we would like to speak the language of the locals while we visit.

Glossary

High-context communication style   It is assumed that communicators share a previously established context. As a result, it is unnecessary, and often annoying to explain every detail. For high-context communicators shared contexts build mutual respect.

Interpretation   The work of professional interpreters who must instantaneously hear, understand, and transfer information from one language to another.

Language families   Languages that share a common origin.

Language isolates   Languages that developed in isolation from other languages and share no common root.

Linguistic relativity   The school of thought concerned with the notion that language influences our perceptions in substantial ways.

Linguistic universalism   The school of thought concerned with the notion that languages are substantially similar and influence thought in similar ways.

Low-context communication style   It is assumed that communicators do not share a previously established context. Thoughts and ideas must be explained clearly, and meanings must be fully expressed in order to assure that everyone in the communication encounter grasps the contexts.

Phonetics   The sounds of words and the ways we transcribe the sounds of words.

Pragmatics   The study of the language ambiguities that can only be explained through contextual understandings of time, place, relationship, and manner of utterance.

Sapir–Worf hypothesis   Based on the work of Edward Sapir and his student, Lee Worf, the Sapir–Worf hypothesis was developed by Roger Brown and Eric Lenneberg who turned Sapir and Worf's notion that language influences thoughts and behaviors into a testable hypothesis.

Semantics   The study of the meanings of words and sentences and the relationships between the meanings of words and the meanings of the sentences they exist within.

Syntactics   The study of the rules that govern the structure of any language—rules about ways in which words are put together to form phrases, clauses, or sentences.

Tonal languages   Languages in which meaning is dependent on the combination of word and tone.

Translation   A text transferred from one language to another, with efforts made to maintain the underlying meanings of the original text that are culturally bound.

Works Cited

Abumrad, J., & Krulwich, R. (2011, January). *Birds-eye view.* Retrieved from NPR's Radio Lab website: http://www.radiolab.org/story/110193-birds-eye-view/

Adelman, J., & Suga, M. (2013, November). *Japan won't set dates for restarting 50 idled nuclear reactors.* Retrieved from Business Week website: http://www.businessweek.com/news/2013-11-18/japan-won-t-set-dates-for-restarting-50-idled-nuclear-reactors

Boroditsky, L. (2010, July 23). *Lost in translation: New cognitive research suggests that language profoundly influences the way people see the world; a different sense of blame in Japanese and Spanish.* Retrieved from Wall Street Journal website: http://online.wsj.com/news/articles/SB10001424052748703467304575383131592767868

Bowers, J. S., & Pleydell-Pearce, C. W. (2011, July 20). *Swearing, euphemisms, and linguistic relativity.* Retrieved from PLOS ONE website: http://www.plosone.org/article/info%3Adoi%2F10.1371%2Fjournal.pone.0022341

Chen, M. K. (2013). The effect of language on economic behavior: Evidence from savings rates, health behaviors, and retirement assets. *American Economic Review, 103*(2), 690–731. doi:10.1257/aer.103.2.690

Committee of Experts. (2010, April 21). *European charter for regional or minority languages: Application of the charter in the United Kingdom, 3rd monitoring cycle.* Retrieved from Council of Europe website: http://www.coe.int/t/dg4/education/minlang/report/EvaluationReports/UKECRML3_en.pdf

Crawford, J. (2012, February). *Language legislation in the USA.* Retrieved from Issues in US Language Policy website: http://www.languagepolicy.net/archives/langleg.htm

Ethnologue: Languages of the World. (2014a, Spring). *Basque: A language of Spain.* Retrieved from Ethnologue: Languages of the World website: http://www.ethnologue.com/language/eus

Ethnologue: Languages of the World. (2014b, Spring). *China.* Retrieved from Ethologue: Languages of the World website: http://www.ethnologue.com/country/CN/status

Fausey, C. M., & Boroditsky, L. (2011). Who dunnit? Cross-linguistic differences in eye-witness memory. *Psychonomic Bulletin & Review, 18*(1), 150–157.

Greene, R. L., Boroditsky, L., & Liberman, M. (2010, December 13–23). *Language: This house believes that the language we speak shapes how we think.* Retrieved from The Economist website: http://economist.com/debate/overview/190

Jamison, A. (2010, March 31). *French government picks new words to replace English.* Retrieved from The Telegraph UK website: http://www.telegraph.co.uk/news/worldnews/europe/france/7540588/French-government-picks-new-words-to-replace-English.html

KapplerMikk, B. (2012, July 12). *High vs low context communication.* Portland, OR: Summer Institute for Intercultural Communication.

Kingston, J. (2013, November 30). *Opinion: Imagining post-nuclear Japan.* Retrieved from The Japan Times website: http://www.japantimes.co.jp/opinion/2013/11/30/commentary/imagining-post-nuclear-japan/#.UpuWSsRDsa8

Marcus, G. (2012, December 7). *Happy Birthday, Noam Chomsky.* Retrieved from The New Yorker website: http://www.newyorker.com/online/blogs/newsdesk/2012/12/the-legacy-of-noam-chomsky.html

Stephens, R., & Umland, C. (2011). Swearing as a response to pain—Effect of daily swearing. *The Journal of Pain, 12*, 1274–1281.

Swoyer, C. (2010, Winter). *Sapir–Whorf hypothesis.* Retrieved from Stanford Encyclopedia of Philosophy website: http://plato.stanford.edu/entries/relativism/supplement2.html

Tesafe, W. (2007). Laguu in the Oromo society: A sociolinguistic approach. In A. Amha, M. Mous, & G. Sava (eds.), *Omotic and Cushitis language studies.* Collogne: Rüdiger Köppe Verlag.

Trafton, A. (2008, June 24). *MIT-led team finds language without numbers.* Retrieved from MIT News website: http://web.mit.edu/newsoffice/2008/language-0624.html

University of Hawaii, Manoa. (2014, March 9). *Endangered languages: Why so important?* Retrieved from The Endangered Languages Project website: https://docs.google.com/document/d/19MvWf22roO_egGdcma1rSAplMrQitKskxL3xn0gBgSU/edit).

Chapter 7
Nonverbal Communication

Mark Staller

"I speak two languages, Body and English."
—Mae West

"The most important thing in communication is hearing what isn't said."
—Peter Drucker

Chapter Learning Objectives

1. Clearly distinguish nonverbal communication from verbal communication.
2. Understand and describe five major characteristics of nonverbal communication in order to appreciate the importance of nonverbal communication for intercultural interactions.
3. List and describe 10 general functions of nonverbal communication.
4. Develop an awareness of and sensitivity to cultural differences in 10 specific areas of nonverbal communication.
5. Understand the functions of silence in different cultural settings.
6. Be aware of nonverbal messages related to dining in different cultures.
7. Develop effective habits and practices in order to improve your nonverbal communication.

© michaeljung, 2014. Used under license from Shutterstock, Inc.

Introduction

In Chapter 6 (Verbal Communication), we distinguished between "high context" and "low context" cultures. We Americans are primarily "low context" communicators who (when compared to people from other cultures) tend to focus more on the verbal messages travelling through the auditory channel. We expect people to communicate clearly with their words, and we try to interpret these verbal messages accurately.

"High context" cultures, in contrast, pay attention to multiple communication channels at once. In addition to the vocalized words traveling through the auditory channel, they also pay attention to the many nonverbal messages traveling through the visual, tactile, and olfactory channels. If we "low context" Americans want to communicate effectively with people from high context cultures, we need to develop an appreciation of, and sensitivity to, nonverbal communication and the many elements of nonverbal communication.

In this chapter, we will first clearly distinguish nonverbal communication from verbal communication, and we will point out five characteristics of nonverbal signals that make them such an important element of intercultural communication. Next, we will list and explain 10 general functions of nonverbal communication, and then we will explore 10 specific areas of nonverbal communication. After exploring two additional areas of nonverbal communication—the use of silence and nonverbal messages sent while dining—we will end the chapter with general advice and specific tips for improving your nonverbal communication.

Distinguishing Between Verbal and Nonverbal Communication

To clearly distinguish between verbal and nonverbal communication, we need to complicate these two categories a bit: communication can be verbal or nonverbal *and* vocal or nonvocal. Thus, there are four categories to distinguish between different types of human communication: communication can be 1) verbal and vocal, 2) verbal and nonvocal, 3) nonverbal and vocal, or 4) nonverbal and nonvocal.

	Verbal Communication	Nonverbal Communication
Vocal Communication	Speaking words and sentences	Laughing, grunting, sighing Paralanguage: voice rate, volume, pitch, etc.
Nonvocal Communication	Writing, texting, and signing	Body position and posture, body movement, facial expressions, eye contact, etc.

Figure 7.1   Nonverbal communication can be vocal or nonvocal.

Verbal communication is communication expressed in human language. If you are communicating with words (nouns, pronouns, prepositions, adjectives, adverbs, and verbs), you are communicating verbally. Words can be vocalized, but they can also be encoded in visual symbols, so verbal communication can occur through the visual channel as well as the auditory channel. You may decide that some verbal messages should be written out and shared in letters, emails, or text messages.

Vocal communication is communication expressed through the voice. Human beings use their diaphragms, vocal chords, and mouths to communicate vocally. Often we vocalize words, but sometimes we vocalize sounds that are not words. For example, you can communicate with people through the use of chuckles, grunts, exasperated sighs, and "oohs and aahs" of surprise.

If you use verbal, vocal communication, you speak words with your mouth that travel through the auditory channel. The vocalized sounds of these words are heard and decoded by your listeners. Be aware that when you vocalize words, you are also sending vocal, nonverbal messages at the same time. Your voice volume, your rate of speech, and your tone of voice also communicate messages to your audience. These vocal, nonverbal elements are called **paralanguage**. When you speak to people, you need to pay attention not only to *what* you say, but also to *how* you say it.

When you use nonverbal, nonvocal communication, you will usually forgo the auditory channel and send messages instead through the visual and tactile channels. You can communicate through your use of space, your posture, your touch, your body movement, and so on. Nonverbal, nonvocal communication is usually what people are referring to when they use the term "nonverbal" communication.

Nonhuman animals communicate almost exclusively through nonverbal forms of communication: they may make sounds, but they do not vocalize words. More accurately, if nonhuman animals vocalize words (like some parrots do), they do not comprehend what these vocalized words mean. Human language distinguishes human beings from other animals, and human language (we learned in Chapter 1) is largely responsible for human culture.

However, although human language and verbal communication are at the heart of human culture, we need to be aware of the large part that nonverbal communication still plays in human communication. In the next section, we present five characteristics of nonverbal communication that make nonverbal cues a very important element in intercultural interactions.

Figure 7.2 American sign language is a verbal, nonvocal form of communication.

Five Characteristics of Nonverbal Communication

1. **Whereas verbal communication is intermittent, nonverbal communication is continuous.** Nonverbal communication occurs 24 hours a day, 7 days a week. If people can see you, you are communicating with them through your nonverbals whether you want to or not. Nonverbal communication is why you cannot *not* communicate.

   Even if you do not share a common language with other people, there is a wealth of information you are sharing through your nonverbal behaviors. When you are interacting with people from other cultures, they are observing your nonverbal behaviors, and you are observing theirs. Since nonverbal communication is continuous, people from different cultures are constantly communicating as soon as they come into contact with one another.

2. **Whereas most verbal communication is conscious and intentional, nonverbal communication is often unconscious and unintentional.** We usually choose the words we use to express our ideas, but we are often unaware of our nonverbal behaviors. You need to tune in to the unintended messages that you are sending to others with your facial expressions, your body movement, and your paralanguage.

You also need to pay close attention to the nonverbal behaviors of your communication partners. You can learn a lot about people from other cultures just by tuning in to their nonverbal signals. Paying attention to nonverbal cues is a way to "go below the surface" of a culture. When you pay attention to the unconscious nonverbal behaviors of others, you can gain valuable insights into what they are thinking and feeling, even if you cannot understand the words that they are speaking.

3. **Nonverbal communication is more believable than verbal communication.** If there is a contradiction between your verbal communication and your nonverbal communication, people will most likely believe your nonverbal communication because "actions speak louder than words." For example, if you say, "I'm not angry," but your hands are clenched, your voice volume is loud, and your brow is furrowed, people will think you are angry despite your words.

Since nonverbal behaviors trump verbal messages, nonverbal communication is just as important as, and sometimes even more important than, your verbal communication. Low-context Americans need to pay special attention to the nonverbal messages that are being sent (and that need to be received) during intercultural interactions.

Figure 7.3   Nonverbal communication is more believable than verbal communication, but it is also more ambiguous and confusing.

© urobanks, 2014. Used under license from Shutterstock, Inc.

4. **Nonverbal communication is more ambiguous than verbal communication.** Although nonverbal communication is more believable than verbal communication, it is also more difficult to interpret. For example, is someone probably lying if they are speaking too slowly or too quickly? Is someone frowning because they are displeased with you, or because they are concentrating? Is someone scratching their nose to send you a message or to relieve an itch?

The ambiguity of nonverbal messages is increased in intercultural interactions. Although some nonverbal behaviors may be universal, many nonverbal behaviors differ from country to country and even from one co-culture to another. A head movement or a hand gesture can mean radically different things in different countries and cultures. Because the chance of misunderstanding increases when nonverbal cues are involved in communication, special care and attention must be given to nonverbal communication in intercultural contexts. Intercultural communicators must practice "nonverbal humility" and realize that they should not overestimate their ability to interpret the nonverbal cues of people from other cultures.

5. **Nonverbal communication is used more often than verbal communication to send relational messages.** You rarely interrupt a conversation to say to another person, "I do not find you very interesting," or "I respect and admire you." However, you are often sending these sorts of relational messages with your nonverbal cues. While your vocalized words will often relate to the subject of a conversation, your paralanguage, facial expressions, and body language will communicate how you think and feel about your conversational partner.

Since a major task of intercultural communication is to establish satisfying relationships with people from other cultures, the relational messages sent through nonverbal cues are a very important element of intercultural communication. Even if you have a very limited amount of words you can use to communicate with people from another culture, your body language and your paralanguage can communicate that you respect them and that you want to enter into a friendship or cordial relationship with them.

Five Ways Nonverbal Communication Differs From Verbal Communication
1. Nonverbal communication is continuous.
2. Nonverbal communication is often unconscious.
3. Nonverbal communication is more believable.
4. Nonverbal communication is more ambiguous.
5. Nonverbal communication is used more often to send relational messages.

Figure 7.4   Nonverbal communication is an important element of intercultural interactions.

Ten General Functions of Nonverbal Communication

In 1969, Paul Ekman and Wallace Friesen published an article in *Semiotica* (vol. 1.1, pp. 49–98) entitled "The Repertoire of Nonverbal Behavior: Categories, Origins, Usage, and Coding." In this article, they listed five functions of nonverbal behavior and created the five nonverbal categories of 1) affect displays, 2) illustrators, 3) emblems, 4) regulators, and 5) adaptors. We will present a brief explanation of these five categories in order to introduce to you these five now widely recognized functions of nonverbal behavior.

1. **Affect displays:** Affect displays are nonverbal displays that reveal the inner states—the attitudes and emotions—of communicators. In 1967, Dr. Albert Mehrabian published two research studies that claimed that 93% of human attitudes was communicated nonverbally (38% paralanguage and 55% nonverbal, nonvocal elements). Mehrabian's statistic has become a truism in the field of Communication Studies. Although his percentage may be a bit high, the fact that it has gained widespread acceptance indicates that people recognize the important role that nonverbal cues play in the communication of emotion, especially the nonverbal cues of posture, facial expressions, and paralanguage.

2. **Illustrators:** Illustrators are nonverbal cues that emphasize or reinforce verbal messages. If people in America say, "So pleased to meet you," they will usually reinforce this verbal message with a smile. If people in Japan say, "I am very sorry," they will usually bow deeply as they make their apology. Around the world, good storytellers will use their hands and appropriate hand gestures to bring their verbal stories to life.

3. **Emblems:** Emblems are nonverbal signs that replace verbal messages. Sometimes people communicate very clear messages without saying a word. In America, you can indicate that you agree or disagree with someone by shaking your head up and down or side to side; you can indicate that you approve or disapprove of someone by giving a "thumbs up" or a "thumbs down" sign; and you can indicate that you love or hate someone by giving them a hug or a slap. However, be aware that these nonverbal signs may have other functions and send other messages in different countries and cultures of the world.

4. **Regulators:** Regulators are nonverbal cues that regulate the flow of conversation: they indicate when someone is done speaking or when someone would like to speak. Sometimes we may indicate that we want someone to stop speaking by raising our hand and giving a "stop" signal.

Sometimes we use a very similar hand signal (but raise our hand higher) to indicate that we would like a turn to speak or to ask a question. Much more often, we regulate the flow of our conversations with our use (or nonuse) of eye contact.

5. **Adaptors:** Adaptors are nonverbal movements we make to adjust to either our inner or outer environment. If we are tired, we may yawn. If we are itchy, we may scratch ourselves. If we are hot, we may fan our face with our hands. If we are stressed or nervous, we may bite our nails or play with our hair. When trying to read the nonverbal cues of others, it is important that we do not interpret their nonverbal adaptors as illustrators or emblems: when people yawn or scratch their nose or play with their hair, they may not be trying to send any message at all to us.

Figure 7.5 A head scratch can be an emblem, an illustrator, or an adaptor.

In addition to the five functions of nonverbal communication noted by Ekman and Friesen, there are at least five other functions of nonverbal behavior. Nonverbals are also used to 6) create and communicate our identities, 7) indicate status, 8) arouse or indicate interest, 9) contradict verbal messages, and 10) send potentially unwelcome or embarrassing messages. Let us consider each of these additional functions of nonverbal communication.

6. **Nonverbals are used to create and communicate our identities.** Our identities as males and females, our identities as young people and old people, and our identities as members of specific people groups are created and communicated in part by the clothes that we wear. Our identities as members of specific people groups may also be created and communicated in part by our hair styles and our personal belongings, and by the particular hand gestures and signals that we employ.

7. **Nonverbals are used to indicate status.** People may send messages about how much power, authority, wealth, or prestige they have by the clothes they wear, the amount of space they use, and the amount of eye contact they make with their conversational partners. Status may also be indicated by grooming, jewelry, and personal possessions.

8. **Nonverbals are used to arouse interest or to indicate interest.** We may indicate interest in a conversational topic by our posture, our rate of speech, and our tone of voice. We may indicate our interest in developing an interpersonal relationship by our use of space and touch, our eye contact, and our facial expressions. We may indicate our interest in a romantic or sexual relationship by our clothing and grooming, our use of scent, our gait, our proximity, and our use of touch.

9. **Nonverbals are used to contradict verbal messages.** Although we may say one thing with our words, we may communicate the exact opposite with our nonverbal cues. We may say, "My, isn't that intelligent," when our paralanguage and facial expression indicate that someone has just done a very stupid thing. Nonverbal cues that contradict verbal messages are the essence of sarcasm.

10. **Nonverbals are used to send potentially unwelcome or embarrassing messages.** Instead of verbally telling your superiors that their public statement is incorrect, you might subtly signal that they should quickly retract or modify this statement. Instead of verbally telling someone that their pants are unzipped, you might want to send a nonverbal message that allows them to rectify the problem without undue attention. In cultures in which it is important to "save face," this function of nonverbal communication is especially important.

The last two functions of nonverbal communication—sending nonverbal messages that contradict verbal messages and sending potentially unwelcome or embarrassing messages nonverbally—are functions of nonverbal communication that are frequently exploited in high-context cultures.

People in high-context cultures often do not "say what they mean." Effective intercultural communicators are aware of the difference between high- and low-context cultures, and they develop their ability to send and receive both verbal and nonverbal messages.

Ten General Functions of Nonverbal Communication
1. Nonverbals are used to express inner states. (affect displays)
2. Nonverbals are used to reinforce a verbal message. (illustrators)
3. Nonverbals are used to replace a verbal message. (emblems)
4. Nonverbals are used to regulate communication interactions. (regulators)
5. Nonverbals are used to adjust to the environment. (adaptors)
6. Nonverbals are used to create and communicate our identities.
7. Nonverbals are used to indicate status.
8. Nonverbals are used to arouse interest or indicate interest.
9. Nonverbals are used to contradict verbal messages.
10. Nonverbals are used to send potentially unwelcome or embarrassing messages.

Figure 7.6 Nonverbals have many communicative functions.

Ten Specific Areas of Nonverbal Communication

We have noted that most nonverbal communication is unconscious. The unconscious nature of nonverbal communication is, in one important way, a blessing: if you had to consciously keep track of all the elements or areas of nonverbal communication, you would be facing a very daunting task. There are at least 10 areas of nonverbal communication that have been identified and studied by human communication researchers and theorists. We present to you now a list of these 10 areas of study:

Ten Areas of Study in the Field of Nonverbal Communication
1. **Chronemics**: the study of the way people and cultures view and use time
2. **Proxemics**: the study of the way people and cultures use space
3. **Haptics**: the study of the use of touch
4. **Personal appearance**: the study of the outward appearance of individuals
5. **Kinesics**: the study of body movement
6. **Hand gestures**: the study of the use of hand gestures
7. **Facial expressions**: the study of the use of facial expressions
8. **Oculesics**: the study of eye behavior, gaze, and eye-related nonverbal communication
9. **Olfactics**: the study of human smell and the use of scents
10. **Paravocalics** (or paralinguistics): the study of the nonverbal elements of vocal communication

Figure 7.7 The study of nonverbal communication can be divided into 10 different areas.

Technically, numbers 6, 7, and 8 (hand gestures, facial expressions, and oculesics) are subcategories of the broad category of Kinesics (body movement), but these areas of nonverbal communication are often separated out into their own categories. We will describe each of these 10 areas of nonverbal communication, paying special attention to the differences in nonverbal behaviors and expectations that exist in each of these areas in different countries and cultures.

At the end of each subsection that describes one of these 10 areas of nonverbal communication, we will provide a bulleted list of some specific examples that will help to sensitize you to different nonverbal rules, expectations, and behaviors that exist in different national cultures and different co-cultures. We have gleaned these specific examples from personal experience and through research.

However, cultures are changeable and individual communicators can deviate from dominant cultural norms, so these specific examples may no longer apply to a dominant national culture and may have never applied to particular individuals within a culture. Do not assume that the specific examples of nonverbal communication differences we offer will apply to your intercultural communication partners, or else you will be guilty of stereotyping others.

1: Chronemics

In Chapter 3, we introduced to you the monochronic and polychronic time orientations that exist in different cultures because these two time orientations cause people to value different things. On the one hand, people from monochronic cultures often view time as linear, and they think that time can be wasted or "spent" wisely. Consequently, they value their time highly, and they also value punctuality and promptness, adhering to plans, keeping schedules, following agendas, setting and meeting deadlines, and the completion of tasks.

On the other hand, people from polychronic cultures often view time as circular or reoccurring, so they think of time commitments as objectives that may or may not be achieved. Polychronic people change plans often and easily, and they value and are committed to people, relationships, and socializing.

The way that cultures view and use time is an important area of nonverbal communication because people with different time orientations can misinterpret or negatively evaluate one another's behaviors and motives. Monochronic people may think that polychronic people are not "serious about their work" when they arrive late for, or socialize at, business meetings. Polychronic people may think that monochronic people are rude and insensitive when they do not want to adjust schedules or modify agendas to allow for family activities or other social obligations.

Countries or regional cultures that are recognized as predominantly polychronic are China, Egypt, India, Indonesia, Mexico, Pakistan, the Philippines, and many other countries in Africa, Latin America, and South and Southeast Asia. Countries that are recognized as predominantly monochronic are Austria, Canada, England, Germany, Israel, Japan, Russia, South Korea, Switzerland, Taiwan, and Turkey.

After identifying particular countries that are predominantly polychronic or monochronic, we need to make two clarifications. First, some national cultures may combine both a monochronic and polychronic time orientation in different situations or social contexts, so it may be difficult to clearly place every country in one column or the other.

Second, although a particular time orientation may dominate in a national culture, a country may have co-cultures with different time orientations. For example, although the United States is predominantly monochronic, it has polychronic co-cultures in Hawaii, New Orleans, and many Native American communities. Americans speak of "Hawaiian time" and "Indian time" (and they speak of New Orleans as "The Big Easy") in order to acknowledge that different time orientations exist within US borders.

As you interact with people from other cultures, be sensitive to different time orientations, but do not use your preferred time orientation as an excuse for violating a host culture's time rules and expectations. If you know about monochronic and polychronic time orientations, with this knowledge comes a responsibility to negotiate appropriate uses of time with your intercultural communication partners.

Chronemics Around the World:

- Bus and train schedules in Germany are often kept down to the minute, and passengers will be upset if these schedules are not strictly followed.
- Local tour guides in Mexico and other Central American countries may not start or stop tours at the scheduled times.
- Monochronic Switzerland is famous for the accuracy of its watches and time pieces.
- American college classes typically begin and end on time, and students may be penalized for arriving late or leaving class early.
- College students in some Latin American countries typically arrive up to a half-hour late for a college class, but they are also willing to stay an hour after class to visit with their professor.

Figure 7.8 Monochronic people "watch the clock."   **Figure 7.9** Polychronic people enjoy socializing.

2: Proxemics

E. T. Hall, the founder of the field of proxemics, discovered that people have a "personal space bubble" that they occupy and think of as their own. The size of this space bubble, however, varies from culture to culture. Individualistic societies that value privacy generally require more personal space. These cultures include Australia, Canada, England, Germany, Sweden, and the United States. (Personal space is almost sacred in Germany.)

Collectivistic cultures tend to require very little personal space. These cultures include many nations in Asia, the Middle East, Latin America, and many US Hispanics. Generally, females need less personal space than males, and children need less personal space than adults.

Some of the situational factors that affect the amount of personal space required are status differences, cooperative vs. competitive endeavors, and the nature of the interpersonal relationship between two communicators. People with different status usually stand farther apart, whereas people with equal status stand closer together. People involved in cooperative endeavors often get closer together than people who are competing against one another.

However, the most important situational factor in proxemics is the relationship between two communicators: the closer the relationship, the closer people will usually stand or sit next to one another. In the late 1960s, Hall proposed that there were four interpersonal distances recognized in American culture, and he gave precise measurements for these distances. Many research studies related to proxemics in America have been carried out since then, and they confirm Hall's distances.

Americans recognize **intimate distance** (touching to 18 inches) reserved for romantic partners and immediate family members, **personal distance** (18 inches to 4 feet) reserved for extended family members and close friends, **social distance** (4–12 feet) reserved for coworkers and casual acquaintances, and **public distance** (12 feet or more) reserved for public speakers. The fact that closer proximity is used in America to signal relational intimacy is indicated by the expressions, "We are really close," "Let's keep in touch," and, "Stop being so distant."

Other cultures use interpersonal proximity in a similar manner, but the distances that signal intimate, personal, social, and public relationships may be shorter or longer than the distances recognized in America. For example, typical Arab and Israeli conversations, even among casual acquaintances, are at a very close range (1–2 feet), and good friends in the Middle East may stand close enough together when speaking that they can smell each other's breath. Close physical proximity, even among casual acquaintances, is also very common in Brazil. Brazilians may pass very close by you (a foot or less) without feeling a need to say "Excuse me."

It is important to be aware of differences in personal space expectations because invading someone's personal space and "popping" their personal space bubble can be interpreted as an act of aggression or as an attempt to establish relational intimacy. On the other hand, backing away from people because you think they are "too close" may be interpreted as signifying that you do not want to be their friend. What may be an appropriate amount of personal space in your culture may be considered "keeping your distance" in another culture.

Proxemics Around the World:

- In some Asian cultures, students do not sit or stand near their teachers as a sign of respect and deference.
- In India, there are elaborate rules for how closely people from one caste may stand to people from another caste.
- An Arab in an elevator may stand right next to you, even touching, even though no one else is in the elevator.
- In Brazil, even though there are high crime rates in urban areas, people riding public transportation will still sit close to, and converse with, strangers on a bus or train.
- People in France, Italy, and Spain (and in many Asian countries) do not usually stand in lines or "queues."

Figure 7.10   Standing too close.

© Howard Klaaste, 2014. Used under license from Shutterstock, Inic.

3: Haptics

All human beings need human touch to thrive. Babies who are never held and cuddled often die despite being clothed and fed. The official term for infant mortality due to lack of touch from caregivers is called "failure to thrive." Nevertheless, the amount of touch that is appropriate varies from culture to culture.

America is a low-contact culture. In the dominant US culture, people touch each other only in certain prescribed situations. Upon greeting, Americans often shake hands, but only for a few seconds, and then they step away. Same-sex touching among US men is fairly rare, except on the sports field. With the increase in sexual-harassment lawsuits in America, public touching in work or social situations has decreased even further. However, America is not the only low-contact national culture. Other low-contact cultures are found in northern Europe, North America, and East Asia. People touch infrequently in England, Germany, and Japan.

Low-contact Americans will need to adjust their haptic expectations and behaviors when traveling to high-contact countries or interacting with people from these countries. High-contact cultures can be found in South America, southern Europe, and the Middle East. Expect a lot more public touching to occur in Brazil, France, Italy, Greece, Mexico, Saudi Arabia, and Spain. In South America and Mexico, touch is routine. In Mexico, an abrazo, a physical embrace, is common among both males and females.

The brief American handshake greeting is inappropriate in some parts of the world. A firm handshake is considered rude and aggressive in Turkey. A limp handshake is appropriate in many parts of Africa, but pay attention to local handshake customs. The continent of Africa is the "handshake capital" of the world, with a wide variety of handshake variations. One interesting variation occurs in western Africa, where you are expected to slap your middle finger against the middle finger of your handshake partner. On the island of Fiji (and other places) you may be expected to shake hands during an entire conversation, especially when meeting someone for the first time. If you pull your hand away, you may offend your conversational partner.

In some countries, instead of a handshake, you usually greet people with an embrace and a kiss (or kisses) on or near the cheek. This greeting is common, for both men and women, in France, Italy, and Spain. Upon meeting, you and your conversational partner will often be expected to kiss each other's cheek at the same time, and then immediately kiss the opposite cheek. Although the Dutch are not especially "touchy," they are famous for the Dutch "triple kiss." When greeting someone in the Netherlands, you usually give three kisses on the cheek, right-left-right.

The Maori culture in New Zealand has a special formal greeting called a "hongi." When performing the hongi, you place your nose and forehead against the nose and forehead of your partner so that you can exchange the "ha," or breath of life. Similar nose-touching greetings are sometimes performed in Hawaii, Mongolia, and parts of the Middle East and Africa.

In addition to touching upon greeting, people in high-contact cultures will also touch much more frequently than Americans do throughout a conversation. Frequent touching in Arab societies replaces the bowing and handshaking rituals of other societies. Light touching and close proximity are a sign of general friendship in Brazil.

However, it is important to know about the same-sex and opposite-sex touching expectations of different cultures. Although touching is common in the Arab Middle East, it is only common among people of the same sex. Muslim women seldom touch or are touched by people outside of their family. Nonsexual, same-sex handholding, though, is common in the Middle East, as well as Algeria, China, and Indonesia.

In some countries and cultures, opposite-sex PDAs (public displays of affection) are almost never appropriate, not even between a husband and wife. Traditional Chinese men and women seldom show physical affection in public. In some Muslim countries, PDAs may even be illegal and punishable offenses. After spending several years in Indonesia, my American friend James experienced "reverse culture shock" when he returned to America and saw men and women kissing and touching in public. He was, he said, repulsed by this behavior, and it took him several months to adjust back to the American standards of appropriate PDAs.

You need to be especially aware of cultural touching taboos. Since the left hand is used to engage in basic biological functions in many parts of the world, it is almost always offensive to touch people or things with your left hand. In Thailand and Laos (and almost any Buddhist country) it is rude to touch either a child or an adult on the top of the head. In Nigeria, it is rude to touch an elder on the top of the head. Shaking hands with dignitaries is taboo in Great Britain.

When interacting with people from other cultures, pay attention to their haptic behaviors. If you are able to speak their language and you are not sure if touching is or is not appropriate in a particular situation, ask. In fact, asking permission before hugging, kissing, or touching someone is not a bad procedure to follow even in American culture.

Haptics Around the World:

- People in warmer climates near the equator tend to touch more often, whereas people in colder climates far from the equator tend to touch less often.
- Two Americans in a coffee shop might touch each other once or twice in an hour, whereas two French people in a coffee shop might touch each other 50 times in an hour.
- There was no word for "kiss" in Japanese, so the Japanese adapted the English word and now say "kisu."
- A British couple was sentenced to 1 month in jail for kissing in public while in the UAE.
- Compared to some other cultures, Americans and Brits are touch deprived.

Figure 7.11   Brazil is a high-contact culture.

Figure 7.12   There are many handshake variations in the continent of Africa.

4: Personal Appearance

When we first come into contact with other human beings, one of the first things we become aware of is their outward appearance. Although many cultures have a proverb similar to "Don't judge a book by its cover," we often make judgments and assumptions about others (either consciously or unconsciously) based on their physical appearance. People's physical appearance is comprised of their clothing, their grooming, and their body markings and adornments.

One function of clothing is to protect the human body from the physical elements. Inuit men and women wear parkas (hooded fur coats) to insulate themselves from the freezing temperatures of the northern climate. Russian men and women wear ushankas (fur hats with ear flaps) to protect themselves from the bitter Siberian winters. High in the Andes mountains, Peruvian men and women wear chullos, stocking caps with ear flaps woven out of llama wool. In Mexico and the Philippines, people protect themselves from the sun with wide-brimmed sombreros. In Eucador and Central America, they wear Panama hats. In the Middle East, Arab men wear keffiyehs, pieces of cloth fastened to their heads with leather cords called agals.

Sometimes head coverings have a more esthetic function. The French and Basque people wear berets. Scottish men wear caps called tams. In western Africa and Asia, men wear skullcaps called kufis. In Morocco and northern Africa, men wear the distinctive red fez.

Sometimes head coverings and clothing items have religious significance. Orthodox Jewish men and boys wear special skullcaps called "yarmulkes" in public, and other Jewish men may wear these yarmulkes when praying or during religious observances. Although turbans are sometimes worn in Southeast Asia and the Middle East, they have special religious significance to Sikhs. Sikh turbans, called dastaars, are mandatory articles of faith worn by all practicing Sikhs.

Figure 7.13 Panama hat.

Figure 7.14 Keffiyeh.

Figure 7.15 Ushanka.

Figure 7.16 Yarmulke.

Figure 7.17 Kufi.

Figure 7.18 Sombrero.

Figure 7.19 Turban.

Many cultures use clothing to signal sex differences: males and females often wear different articles of clothing. For example, even though America is an egalitarian society that promotes gender equality, males still usually distinguish themselves from females by wearing pants or shorts, rather than skirts or dresses. However, in other national cultures, males do wear skirt-like or dress-like clothing articles that are considered to be masculine or "male." In the Middle East, Arab males wear pull-over robes called "thobes." African males wear long, flowing shirts called "dashikis." Indonesia males wear sarongs. Samoan males wear lava-lavas. Irish and Scottish men sometimes wear kilts.

Figure 7.20 Thobe.

Figure 7.21 Dashiki.

Figure 7.22 Sarong.

Figure 7.23 Kilt.

Human beings also use clothing to cover the "private" parts of their body, but what parts of the body are appropriate for public and private display differs from culture to culture. Different states of dress and undress are appropriate in different countries.

In most Muslim countries and cultures, most of the human body is expected to be covered in public. Both men and women often wear long-sleeved shirts and pants or full-length robes or body coverings. Most Muslim countries require women to wear a head scarf called a "hijab," and some Muslim countries also require women to wear a facial veil called a "niqab." Some Muslim women wear a full-body covering called a "burka."

Figure 7.24 Hijab.

Figure 7.25 Niqab.

Figure 7.26 Burka.

In contrast, some cultures allow for more public exposure of the human body. Brazilians often have a relaxed attitude toward, and take pride in, their bodies. They often wear little clothing when at the beach or during carnival. Topless sunbathing by both men and women is common and acceptable in parts of Finland, France, Greece, and Spain. Some indigenous cultures in Africa and South America participate in some sports while unclothed below the waist. Families in Japan and Korea may bathe together at public bath houses.

Avoid making ethnocentric judgments or evaluations about people with different standards of modesty. Covering the body is not necessarily an act of prudishness or a sign of body hatred. Uncovering the body is not necessarily a sign of licentiousness or an act of seduction.

Clothing has many other functions in human cultures. It can be used to indicate social class or status. It can be used to indicate that a person is married or unmarried. It can signal a person's affiliation with a clan, tribe, or ethnic group. It can signal one's occupation or religious calling.

When visiting other national cultures, think carefully about the clothes you wear. You need to dress appropriately for the climate, and you need to dress appropriately for the culture you are visiting. If you are not sure whether it is appropriate to wear the local or native clothing of a culture, ask. Be aware that you may also need to remove your shoes when entering certain cultural spaces. You will usually need to remove your shoes when entering a Buddhist shrine, a Muslim mosque, or a Japanese home.

Figure 7.27 Many Native Americans find it offensive when nonnatives wear traditional Indian clothing.

Figure 7.28 You will be expected to remove your shoes upon entering a Japanese home.

In addition to clothing, personal appearance is comprised of grooming and body marking and adornments. Like clothing, hairstyles can indicate a person's sex, status, or group affiliation. Be aware that some cultures require people to cut their hair (or to not cut their hair) during times of mourning.

Body markings or tattoos are common in many cultures. Tattoos can be used as esthetic adornments, rites of passage, memorials to loved ones, talismans, acts of rebellion, or markers of group affiliation. In The Philippines, they are often used to indicate social ranking and accomplishments. In Latino cultures, they often carry religious significance. Tattoos have gone mainstream in modern American culture, but they are not usually placed on the face. However, the New Zealand Maori culture has distinctive facial tattoos called ta moko. In some national cultures (China, Japan, and Vietnam) tattoos are associated with criminal activities, so they may be taboo or even illegal.

Body adornment is especially common and prevalent among Indian women. There are 16 different articles of adornment for Indian women, including the bindi, a black or red dot placed on a woman's forehead. The bindi can be used for esthetic purposes, but it can also indicate marital status or carry religious significance for practicing Hindus. Indian body adornment also includes necklaces, nose rings, finger rings, ornamental belts, wrist bracelets, and ankle bangles, many times made out of gold. For Indian women and Indian families, jewelry is not just an adornment: it is also a sign of status and a method of ensuring financial security.

A special ornament often misunderstood by Westerners is the Kirpan, the small ceremonial sword worn by baptized Sikhs. The Kirpan is neither a functional weapon, nor is it a mere cultural or ethnic symbol. It is an essential article of the Sikh religion that has a very special significance to devout Sikhs, similar to the significance that the cross symbol has to some Christians.

Just as you need to avoid ethnocentric judgments in regard to the clothing worn by people from other cultures, you also need to keep an open mind about the grooming habits, body markings, and body adornments used by people in different cultures. To form satisfying intercultural relationships with people in other countries and cultures, you need to look beyond their outward appearance that may or not be acceptable according to your own cultural standards.

© paul prescott, 2014. Used under license from Shutterstock, Inc.

Figure 7.29   Indian woman wearing a bindi.

© ChameleonsEye, 2014. Used under license from Shutterstock, Inc.

Figure 7.30   New Zealander with ta moko.

Personal Appearance Around the World:

- People from traditional cultures in Samoa and Mauritania prefer large women, and they will even expect a young girl to gain weight when she is of marriageable age.
- The Kayan tribe in Thailand think that women with long necks are beautiful, so women stretch their necks with up to 20 pounds of brass rings.
- Young girls of the Karo tribe in Ethiopia practice self-scarification, and they signal that they have reached marriageable age when their concentric stomach scars are complete.
- Red is an auspicious clothing color in China, thought to bring good luck.
- Buddhist monks wear orange or saffron robes to signal the message of enlightenment to the world.

5: Kinesics

In the field of Communication, kinesics is the study of how people and cultures use and interpret body movements. Sometimes people communicate messages through their posture (the way they sit and stand). For example, In Saudi Arabia, Egypt, Singapore, or Thailand, ankle-to-knee leg crossing could be taken as an insult. In Thailand, feet are considered to be the lowest part of the body, so they should never be pointed in the direction of another person.

Instead of handshaking rituals or kissing rituals, low-contact cultures often have bowing rituals. The Indian *Namaste* bow is often performed when meeting or parting. You bow slightly while bringing both hands together in front of the heart as a sign that you recognize the deity in other human beings. The *wai* bow is ubiquitous in Thailand. Very young toddlers are taught to "wai" because this bow is used for greetings, farewells, to show respect, to show appreciation, and sometimes as an apology. To perform the wai, you place the palms of your hands together and hold them vertically pointing toward the chin followed by a slight head bow. The higher the hands and the lower the bow, the more respect you are showing.

Bowing is extremely important in Japan. The Japanese bow originates at the waist, with the back held straight. Men and boys often hold their hands at their sides, while women and girls clasp their hands in their laps. There are at least six different types of bows in Japanese culture. An acknowledgement bow is performed at about 5 degrees; a greeting bow is performed at about 15 degrees, a respect bow is performed at about 30 degrees, and a high respect bow is performed at about 45 degrees. Because bowing is so ingrained in Japanese culture, you can often observe a Japanese person bowing while speaking on the telephone. Bowing is not as formalized in other Asian countries as it is in Japan, but it still occurs during special occasions. For example, in China, bowing protocols are observed at weddings and funerals and during diplomatic apologies.

In addition to bowing behaviors, Americans should be aware of prostration behaviors. Prostration involves touching the ground with a part of the body above the knee. It is used as a gesture of reverence or submission in many major world religions, including Baha'i Faith, Buddhism, Hinduism, Islam, Jainism, and Sikhism. Sikhs prostrate themselves before their holy book. Muslims perform prostrations daily during their prayers. Some Zen Buddhists perform 1,080 full prostrations per day.

Genuflection is a partial prostration involving touching at least one knee to the ground. Genuflection was very common in several different cultures during the Middle Ages. However, people in the African Yoruba culture still practice partial prostration before their elders. Genuflection may seem very odd to egalitarian Americans, but it is still practiced in America as part of formal marriage proposals: a man will sometimes get down on one knee to formally propose to his potential marriage partner. Bowing has also survived in American culture in one particular context: although we would find it odd for two Americans to greet each other by bowing, we find it quite natural for an actor or singer to "take a bow" at the end of a performance.

We will end this section on kinesics with a reminder that head movements may signal different things in different cultures. Americans are sometimes very confused by the Indian "head wobble." People in India may wobble their head from side to side to indicate that they are paying attention, that they understand you, or that they agree with you. In other words, what looks like a "no" headshake to Americans may actually be a "yes" headshake in India.

"Yes" and "no" headshakes are also reversed from American headshakes in the country of Bulgaria. Bulgarians shake their heads from side to side to indicate that they agree and they shake their heads up and down to indicate that they disagree. To indicate "no," Bulgarians may also quickly duck their head while making a clicking sound. However, people in China may indicate opposition by tilting their heads back and sucking in air loudly through their teeth. When communicating with people from other cultures, even a simple nonverbal "yes" or "no" can be misunderstood.

Kinesics Around the World:

- In Samoa, it is rude for a standing person to sway their body while having a conversation.
- To most Europeans, Americans appear to "strut" while they walk, swinging their arms more widely and taking up more space than Europeans do when they walk.
- In Germany, people are usually expected to sit and stand up straight as a sign of good character. Slouching or slumping is seen as a sign of poor upbringing.
- Japanese companies often provide training in correct bowing to their employees.
- In many parts of the world, you will not sit down to use the restroom. Instead, you will use a "squat" toilet.

© EurngKwan, 2014. Used under license from Shutterstock, Inc.

© szefei, 2014. Used under license from Shutterstock, Inc.

Figure 7.31 Wai bow.   **Figure 7.32** Namaste bow.

Figure 7.33   Muslims prostrated in prayer on Friday.

Figure 7.34   Buddhist pilgrim performs full prostrations.

6: Hand Gestures

When using hand gestures in your intercultural interactions, you need to be aware of the amount of hand gestures and the size of hand gestures that are appropriate. Italians, Brazilians, Africans, and people from the Middle East employ hand gestures with greater frequency and intensity than people from many other cultures. Many Japanese, Chinese, Germans, Scandinavians, and Canadians are more restrained in their use of hand gestures, and they view bold hand gestures as ostentatious or ill-mannered.

More importantly, you need to understand that the meaning of hand gestures can be very different in different cultures. When hand gestures are used as nonverbal emblems, they do not necessarily have a universal meaning. In fact, the same hand gesture can have several different meanings. For example, in America, touching your thumb and index finger while holding your palm outward is used to make the "okay" sign. In Japan and Korea, the same hand gesture indicates money. In France, it means zero or worthless. In Tunisia, it means, "I'll kill you." In Brazil and some other Latin American countries, this same gesture is an obscenity.

In Hawaii, curling the middle three fingers into the palm, extending the thumb and little finger, and then twisting the hand back and forth means "hang loose." In some African countries, a similar hand gesture is a curse. In India, it sometimes operates as a blessing or talisman. In Italy, it indicates that a man's wife has been unfaithful. In Norway, it is a salute to Satan.

Sometimes different national cultures use different hand gestures to signify the same thing. To indicate admiration, French people will kiss their fingertips. Italians will twist an imaginary mustache, and Brazilians will curl one hand in front of the other as if they are looking through a telescope.

What Americans signify with an extended middle finger, Turks signify by placing the thumb under the index finger with a closed fist, Australians signify with a V sign and their palm turned inward, Brazilians signify with the American "okay" sign, Sicilians signify with a forearm jerk, Pakistanis signify with a closed fist, and Iranians signify with a thumbs up gesture. Knowing this particular list can enable you to nonverbally insult people in over half a dozen different cultures.

You must be very careful with your hand gestures when interacting with people from other cultures. A hand gesture that is perfectly acceptable in one culture may be totally offensive in another culture. In America, people often point with their index fingers. In Kenya, pointing with an index finger is very insulting. In China and much of the Arab world, pointing is rude and offensive. Germans point with their little fingers. The Japanese point with their entire hand and with their palm held upward.

In America, you may beckon for someone to come close by raising your palm to the sky and curling your fingers inward several times. In the Philippines, this same hand gesture is highly offensive. In many Asian countries, this gesture is used only when beckoning dogs.

A good "rule of thumb" when using hand gestures in intercultural interactions is to generally avoid the use of emblems. If you do not know the verbal language of the people you are communicating with, you may have to pantomime and use lots of hand movements to get your point across, but you should not assume that what a hand gesture signifies in America is what your intercultural communication partners will understand.

Hand Gestures Around the World:

- In Japan, people strike the palm of one hand with a clenched fist to show agreement. This is an obscene gesture in Indonesia.
- In America, you raise the index finger to indicate the number one. In Italy, this same hand gesture is used to indicate the number two.
- The open-palmed "stop" gesture commonly used in America is one of the worst nonverbal insults you can give in Greece.
- Crossed fingers that signify good luck in America signify a woman's genitals in Vietnam.
- In Japan, you must receive cards and gifts with both hands. It is considered very rude to use only one hand.

Figure 7.35 A "thumbs up" can get you in trouble in Iran and Afghanistan.

© racorn, 2014. Used under license from Shutterstock, Inc.

Figure 7.36 An "A okay" can get you in trouble in Brazil and other parts of Latin America.

© Andresr, 2014. Used under license from Shutterstock, Inc.

7: Facial Expressions

Along with body posture, facial expressions are the main nonverbal cue of the internal emotional state of a communicator. As soon as human beings see anything that looks like a face, they "read out" the emotional state of the "person." Hence, emoticons, small visual images of faces, are now included in online communication to help reveal the emotional state of the person sending a computer-mediated message.

Unlike hand gestures that vary widely among different cultures, facial expressions seem to have some universal similarities in all people groups. At least six basic emotions seem to be communicated with similar facial expressions in all cultures: 1) happiness, 2) sadness, 3) disgust, 4) fear, 5) anger, and 6) surprise. One "proof" for the universality of facial expressions is that children born blind seem to smile, frown, and make other facial expressions identical to the facial expressions of infants who can see and observe adults. Many basic facial expressions do not seem to be culturally transmitted behaviors.

The universality of facial expressions is good news for the intercultural communicator. Although hand gestures and head movements and other nonverbal gestures can convey very different messages, human facial expressions often reveal that the same human emotion is being experienced by communicators regardless of their host culture. If you become a perceptive observer of facial expressions, you can at least know what your intercultural communication partners are feeling even if you do not know what other messages they are trying to communicate.

Paul Ekman (the same Communication researcher who developed the five general categories for the functions of nonverbal communication) is recognized as the leading expert in human facial expressions. Ekman developed a Facial Action Coding System (FACS) that mapped out 43 facial muscles responsible for 7 micro-expressions. (Along with the six basic emotions listed above, Ekman also lists contempt as a universal basic emotion revealed by a common facial expression.)

Ekman has consulted with the FBI and the CIA, and he is the inspiration for the main character of Dr. Cal Lightman on the television show "Lie to Me" that originally aired on the Fox television network from 2009 to 2011. On the show, Dr. Lightman uses "scientific" knowledge about facial expressions to determine when people are or are not telling the truth.

Although Ekman and his alter-ego Dr. Lightman have done much to popularize the importance of facial expressions in nonverbal communication, the television show "Lie to Me" has had one unfortunate effect. Like television forensic crime dramas that have created unrealistic expectations about the capabilities of forensic science, the show "Lie to Me" and other "lie-detection" experts that publicly advertise their services have created unrealistic expectations about our ability to accurately read facial expressions. Remember that nonverbal communication is more ambiguous than verbal communication. No one can read facial expressions and know the internal emotional state or veracity of a human communicator with 100% accuracy.

When you are communicating with people from different cultures, you should observe their facial expressions carefully, but you should remember that it is difficult to interpret facial expressions accurately. Although smiles are often used to indicate happiness, people in Eastern cultures will often smile to hide embarrassment, anger, and other "negative" emotions that are not culturally acceptable. Thailand is called "the land of smiles." However, this does not mean that Thais are always happy. Thai people smile when they are happy, and when they are confused, and when they are embarrassed, and when they are angry, and when they are sad.

Some cultures train people to mask their emotions by keeping what Americans call a "poker face." In the East, this desired behavior is called "inscrutability." Inscrutability is the quality of being difficult to understand or hard to read. In China and Japan, it is considered immature to reveal your emotions to others, so people strive to maintain an "inscrutable" face.

Also, although facial expressions may be universal, that does not mean that what provokes an emotion and a corresponding facial expression is the same in all cultures. In other words, you may observe Koreans with looks of disgust on their faces at the dinner table and you will know that they are disgusted, but there are many different reasons why they may be experiencing disgust. You may think that they are disgusted by the kimchi that they are eating (fermented cabbage which many Koreans find delicious), while they may actually be disgusted by the way you placed your chopsticks on the dinner table. Facial expressions may reveal *that* your communication partners are experiencing an emotion, but they do not reveal *why* that emotion is being experienced.

Facial Expressions Around the World:

- Because inscrutability is so common in Japan, American fast food companies opening branches in Japan have had to provide special classes to teach their Japanese employees how to smile at customers.
- Many Americans think that Germans are "stern" or unfeeling because German culture is more reserved in its use of facial expressions.
- Many Germans think that Americans are too "glib" and that they smile inauthenticly to mask their true feelings.
- Some indigenous cultures practice "fierce" facial expressions to intimidate their enemies.

Figure 7.37 Some Asian cultures admire an inscrutable face.

Figure 7.38 Some indigenous cultures admire a "fierce" face.

8: Oculesics

Eye contact is important in human communication because eye contact is used to 1) convey emotion, 2) regulate the flow of conversation, 3) monitor nonverbal feedback messages, and 4) indicate interest and attentiveness. The amount of eye contact that is appropriate during a communication transaction differs from culture to culture.

A major function of eye contact in the United States is to regulate the flow of conversation. Americans typically only look each other in the eye for a little over a second: their gaze bounces around as they are speaking. When Americans are done speaking or want verbal feedback, they then look directly at the person they are communicating with to indicate that it is their turn to speak.

In the United States, if people avoid making eye contact, others may assume that they are shy, disinterested, untrustworthy, or they lack confidence. However, Americans avoid eye contact with strangers on buses, elevators, and other enclosed spaces.

Some cultures use much more eye contact than the dominant American culture. In Middle Eastern cultures, men may stare intensely at each other to show sincerity. Sustained eye contact is used to indicate "I am telling the truth." Germans engage in very direct eye contact, much more than Americans. Whereas eye contact is made for about 1 second in America, it may last for 4 or 5 seconds in Germany. Like Middle Easterners, Germans think that a direct gaze indicates honesty and truthfulness.

Some cultures use much less eye contact than the dominant American culture. In African, Asian, Latin American, and Native American cultures, direct eye contact may be considered rude and disrespectful, especially if a younger person is establishing eye contact with an older person, a woman is establishing eye contact with a man, or if a subordinate is establishing eye contact with a superior. In Latin America, direct eye contact for a sustained length of time may be interpreted as aggressive and offensive.

Just as you need to be sensitive to cultural rules concerning same-sex and opposite-sex touching, you need to be sensitive to cultural rules about eye contact between the sexes. Generally, direct eye contact between different sexes and ages is expected in the United Kingdom, Australia, the United States, and Western Europe. However, in the Middle East, it is very inappropriate for men and women who are strangers to look each other in the eye in public.

In France and Spain and some Middle Eastern countries, direct eye contact between the sexes may be interpreted as indicating romantic or sexual interest. In North American gay male co-cultures, direct, sustained eye contact also often serves a similar function.

Oculesics Around the World:

- People in some cultures believe in the "evil eye" or "mal de ojo." They believe that people can transmit damaging thoughts merely through their gaze.
- Deaf co-cultures emphasize the importance of direct eye contact. Turning your back on a deaf person using sign language is essentially ignoring them completely.
- Many South Korean women pay to have "eyelid surgery" where a permanent crease is stitched into the upper eyelid.

© violetblue, 2014. Used under license from Shutterstock, Inc.

Figure 7.39   Many in Japan expect an indirect gaze.

© auremar, 2014. Used under license from Shutterstock, Inc.

Figure 7.40   Many in Germany expect a very direct gaze.

9: Olfactics

Since the 1990s, olfactics, the study of the way different cultures view and use smell and scents, has been expanding rapidly in America. Overall, the sense of smell has been underappreciated in American culture. For many westerners, the sense of smell is "brutish" and animalistic. There are no common positive terms for a keen sense of smell in the English language, nor are there any common negative terms for those who have a poor sense of smell. In America, we do not usually praise someone for having a keen sense of smell, nor do we criticize someone for having a poor sense of smell.

When we Americans say that something "smells," we usually mean that it smells bad. Modern American culture (and many other modern western cultures) have been programmed by American businesses to have a fear of "offensive" natural odors. We are ashamed of natural body odors, and we often mask or neutralize these odors with perfumes, deodorants, and other products.

When interacting with people from other cultures, Americans need to realize that people from some cultures value the sense of smell in general, and they may appreciate very strong or very subtle scents. In some cultures, smell is "emperor of the senses." The calendar of the Ongee people who live on Andaman Island off the southeast coast of India is based on the smell of flowers that bloom at different times of the year. Andaman Islanders will point at their nose to signify "me" or "my smell," and they consider body smell to be part of the life force.

Many people in France are less aware of body odor than Americans, and Arab cultures find body odors natural and normal. In Arab countries, breathing on people can signal friendship and goodwill, and the smell of people's breath is sometimes used to gauge their health.

Arab cultures, however, also use a wide range of scents to perfume the body: musk, rose, saffron, walnut oil, sesame oil, ambergris, and sandalwood. If you partake in a traditional Arab dinner, you may also be asked to participate in an after-dinner perfuming ceremony, when both men and women are sprayed with several different scents.

A smell that one culture finds offensive may be pleasurable to another culture. The Dassanetcha tribe in Ethiopia thinks that the smell of cow is most pleasing. The Dogon of Mali find the smell of onions very attractive. Some cultural spaces are permeated by strong food odors such as curry or garlic.

Avoid making ethnocentric judgments about the bathing habits or preferred odors of other cultures. Some Americans think that people in France and the Middle East do not bathe often enough. However, many Asian cultures bathe very frequently, and some of them think that Americans do not bathe often enough! When interacting with other cultures, keep an "open nose" as well as an open mind. Over time, you can develop an appreciation for scents and odors that you may have initially found strange or unwelcome.

Olfactics Around the World

- Over 10,000 compounds can be recognized by the human sense of smell.
- The Desana who live in the Amazon can only marry people with different smells.
- Researchers have been unable to find a smell that is repellent to all people. What smells repellent to people in one culture may smell pleasant to people in another culture.

10: Paravocalics

Paravocalics or paralinguistics is the study of the nonverbal elements of vocal communication. When people speak a human language, they must speak words, but they also must speak these words in a certain way. Some of the elements of paravocalics related to intercultural communication are

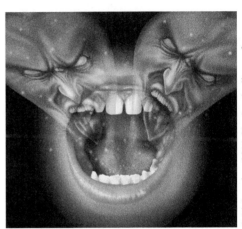

Figure 7.41 Americans have been programmed to think of natural mouth odor as "disgusting."

pitch, rate, volume, enunciation, pronunciation, accent, and vocal clutter. Pitch (also called intonation or inflection) is how high or low a person's voice is. Rate is how fast or slow a person speaks. Volume is how soft of loud a person's voice is. Enunciation (also called clarity or articulation) is how clearly a person voices their word sounds. Pronunciation is how correctly a person pronounces their words. Accent is regional variations in word pronunciation. Verbal clutter (also called vocalized pauses) are the filler words that a person uses in between sentences.

When you learn another human language, be aware that people in different countries and cultures may not speak this language with the same pitch, rate, volume, enunciation, or pronunciation. The Spanish language spoken in Mexico may have very different variations in paravocalics than the Spanish language spoken in Spain. Some claim, for example, that people in Mexico tend to speak Spanish with a higher pitch and a louder volume than people in Spain.

If you learn British English, you are not necessarily fully prepared to speak American English. Americans have very lax enunciation: they clip off the end sounds of their words, and they run their words together. Someone who is comfortable with crisply enunciated British English may be surprised to learn that they can hardly understand typical American English.

In Chapter 6, you learned that English speakers from different countries may use totally different words to signify the same thing or concept. When you learn about paravocalics, you come to understand that even if people do use the same word for a thing or concept, they may not pronounce this word the same way if they belong to different cultures or co-cultures. On the west coast of the United States, you will "park the car." However, if you are in Boston, you will have to "pahk the cah." Be prepared for regional differences in pronunciation and for regional accents or dialects when you visit another country.

In regard to verbal clutter or vocalized pauses, Americans use filler words like "uh," "uhm," and "ya know." Be aware that people speaking other languages also have commonly used filler words. Some common Spanish filler words are "bueno," "como," "entonces," "pues," and "o sea." French filler words are "eh bien," "euh," "quoi," and "tu vois." If you want to sound more fluent in a foreign language, drop the English filler words and learn to use the common native filler words.

In addition to paralanguage that accompanies verbal language, you also need to consider the paravocalic elements that are separate from human language. Human beings can also communicate by booing, gasping, giggling, hissing, laughing, moaning, sighing, yawning, and so on. There are many cultural variations in the particular sounds that are appropriate for specific situations. To show displeasure, Americans may boo or hiss, but in Rwanda, Rwandese people often hiss to gain the attention of others. To show they are enjoying themselves, Arabs in the Middle East may use a "zaghareet," a high-pitched vocal ululation with a trilling quality. There is no equivalent sound in western cultures. When listening to nonverbal, vocalized communication in an intercultural setting, expect variety.

Paravocalics Around the World:

- In the United States, people in the northeast speak more quickly than people from the South.
- The common voice volume in America is usually way too loud for Swedes and many other Europeans.
- In Zulu society, a slow speech tempo is used to indicate respect and sincerity.
- The Spanish language really is spoken at a faster rate than other languages. Researchers have discovered that it has a lower information density compared to other languages, so it is spoken at a faster rate compared to these same languages.

The Use of Silence

Whereas the study of paravocalics makes you focus on the nonverbal sounds used by people in different cultures, you also need to consider the fact that people can also communicate by making no sounds at all. Americans value speech and making their voices heard, but they need to realize that some cultures value silence and use silence to communicate important messages.

In America, silence is often used to put pressure on another person. Interviewers and interrogators remain silent to draw a person out. Often silence is used in America to indicate hostility or disagreement. Sometimes it is used to indicate agreement: "Silence means consent," or "Speak now or forever hold your peace." Silence is also used in America as a form of intentional rudeness, a way to ignore others. Italians and Greeks, like Americans, often value speech and devalue silence.

However, some cultures are much more comfortable with silence, and they use silence to send positive messages. Silence is valued in Asian and Indian cultures, as well as in Swedish, Finnish, and Native American cultures. Silence may be used to show respect or awe, to create a listening space, and to indicate that one is listening deeply and intently. Silence may also be used to mark important occasions. For example, two Navajo friends who have not seen each other for a long time might sit together in silence. Also, some Jewish mourning rituals involve sitting in silence to show respect for the family of the departed.

The following list of proverbs shows how differently cultures value silence. These proverbs also help to explain why silence is avoided or sought for in different countries and cultures.

Proverbs about Silence

"Barking dogs seldom bite." (American)
"Beware of silent men and still waters." (American)
"Dumb dogs are dangerous." (American)
"The squeaky wheel gets the grease." (American)
"Silence is medication for sorrow." (Arab)
"Take a man by his words and a bull by his horns." (Finnish)
"Silence was never written down." (Italian)
"A flower does not speak." (Japanese)
"It is the duck that squawks that gets shot." (Japanese)
"The silent man is the best to listen to." (Japanese)
"Health is quietly keeping silent." (Swedish)
"Talking is silver, silence is golden." (Swedish)

Nonverbal Messages and Dining

One of the most difficult aspects of intercultural communication to master is learning to send the appropriate nonverbal messages while dining with people from another culture. People from different countries and cultures may use very different nonverbal signals while dining, so you can avoid some confusion and some embarrassing situations by doing some research before dining with people from other cultures.

In some cultures, you are supposed to bring a gift for your host. However, you can send inappropriate nonverbal messages by bringing the wrong kind of gift. When giving a gift to a Japanese host, avoid gifts wrapped in white and that come in groups of four because the color white and the number four are both associated with death. When giving a gift to a Chinese host, avoid knives or sharp implements that can imply the severance of a relationship. Be aware that gift giving is very important in China and Japan, so it is important to know about gift-giving etiquette and taboos.

In Germany, India, Japan, and Turkey, you are expected to completely clean your plate. However, in other cultures you are expected to leave a little food on your plate to indicate that your host has satisfied your appetite. Cleaning your plate might indicate to them that you want more food.

In some cultures, when you want to indicate that you have had enough tea to drink, you turn your teacup upside down. However, if you are in a bar in Australia and you turn your glass upside down, you are indicating that you are ready for a fight. Clearly, knowing the nonverbal messages sent by specific drinking and dining behaviors is important!

Figure 7.42   Had enough to drink, or . . .

Figure 7.43   Ready for a fight?

Improving Your Nonverbal Communication

Keeping track of the different nonverbal communication expectations and behaviors of the many cultures of the world can be difficult, but your efforts to be sensitive to cultural differences in nonverbal cues will pay off in the long run. We will end this chapter with a short list of general tips for improving your nonverbal communication skills in intercultural situations. We have made these tips very general so that you can use them almost anywhere and for any communication situation.

Some Final Tips for Improving Your Nonverbal Communication:

- Practice observing people and their nonverbal behaviors. Watch an undubbed foreign movie.
- Place nonverbal cues in context. Think about who is speaking to whom, where, and why.
- Become a high self-monitor. Pay attention to your own nonverbal cues, and get feedback on your own nonverbal behaviors.
- Remember that nonverbal communication is ambiguous—keep open to multiple interpretations.
- Know your own cultural rules for nonverbal communication.
- When interacting with a particular people group, study up on their common nonverbal behaviors.
- Do not stereotype. Remember to make room for individual, idiosyncratic behaviors.
- Practice communicating only by using nonverbal cues. Interact with people who speak a different language that you do not know.
- Think of an intercultural communication transaction as an "improvised performance." Work with your conversational partner to create a communication transaction that works for you both.

Summary

If you read this chapter carefully, you can now clearly distinguish between vocal and nonvocal and verbal and nonverbal communication. You also understand five important ways that nonverbal communication differs from verbal communication: compared to verbal communication, nonverbal communication is 1) continuous, 2) often more unconscious, 3) more believable, 4) more ambiguous, and 5) used more often to send relational messages.

You now know 10 general functions of nonverbal communication. Nonverbal communication is used to 1) reveal emotions, 2) substitute for verbal messages, 3) reinforce verbal messages, 4) regulate the flow of communication, 5) adapt to the environment, 6) create and communicate personal identity, 7) indicate status, 8) arouse or indicate interest, 9) contradict verbal messages, and 10) send potentially unwelcome or embarrassing messages.

Now you also know 10 specific areas of nonverbal communication studies. When analyzing or discussing nonverbal communication, you can speak about 1) chronemics, 2) proxemics, 3) haptics, 4) personal appearance, 5) kinesics, 6) hand gestures, 7) facial expressions, 8) oculesics, 9) olfactics, and 10) paravocalics. Now you also have some general knowledge of how people and cultures may have different nonverbal expectations and behaviors in these 10 areas.

You also now realize that people and cultures may value and use silence differently, and you understand that you must be aware of the nonverbal messages that you send by your dining and drinking behaviors. Finally, you now know some general tips for improving your nonverbal communication in a wide variety of communication situations.

Glossary

Adaptors   Nonverbal behaviors that help people adapt or adjust to their environment.

Affect displays   Nonverbal cues that signal the emotional state of a communicator.

Attire   A person's clothing, apparel, or outfit.

Chronemics   The study of how people and cultures view and use time.

Emblems   Nonverbal symbols that take the place of verbal symbols.

Eye contact   Direct visual contact with another person's eyes; when the gaze of two people meet.

Facial expressions   A nonverbal gesture executed with the facial muscles usually indicating the emotional state of the person.

Hand gestures   Movements of the hands used to reinforce or substitute for verbal language.

Haptics   The study of how people and cultures view and use touch as a form of nonverbal communication.

High-contact cultures   Cultures that prefer and are comfortable with a high degree of physical contact and touching.

High-context cultures   Cultures that focus not only on verbal messages sent through the auditory channel, but also on other messages sent simultaneously through paralanguage and the visual and tactile channels.

Illustrators   Nonverbal symbols that emphasize or reinforce a verbal message.

Inscrutability   The quality of being difficult to understand or hard to read. Inscrutability is a desired personal trait in some Eastern cultures.

Kinesics   The study of the way people and cultures view and use body movement and gestures as a form of nonverbal communication.

Low-contact cultures   Cultures that prefer a low degree of physical contact and that require personal space.

Low-context cultures   Cultures who focus primarily on verbal messages sent through the auditory channel. They require a high amount of information in the words that people use.

Monochronic cultures   Cultures which view time as a linear entity that can be segmented into precise units.

Nonverbal communication   Any communication that occurs through means other than human language.

Nonvocal communication   Communication that occurs through means other than the human voice.

Paralanguage   Vocal, nonverbal communication elements such as pitch, rate, volume, and voice quality.

Personal appearance   The way people dress, groom, and adorn themselves.

Personal space   The area surrounding a person that is perceived as private by that person and who may regard movement into that space as intrusive.

Polychronic cultures   Cultures who view time as circular and repeatable and who tend to do several things at once.

Posture   The way people hold their body when standing or sitting.

Proxemics   The study of how people and cultures view and use space.

Regulators   Nonverbal cues that help control the flow of communication.

Relational messages   Verbal and nonverbal messages that communicate how we think and feel about others.

Territoriality   How people use space and other objects to indicate ownership or occupancy of areas.

Verbal communication   Communication expressed in human language.

Vocal communication   Communication expressed through the human voice.

Chapter 8

Adaptation and Empathy

Helen Acosta

"It's not so much the journey that's important; as is the way that we treat those we encounter and those around us, along the way"
—Jeremy Aldana

Chapter Learning Objectives

1. Gain an understanding of historical perspectives regarding adaptation.
2. Identify and explain the Bennett Scale for cultural adaptation.
3. Develop skill in the use of empathy across a variety of situations.

© adirekjob, 2014. Used under license from Shutterstock, Inc.

From the time I was four until I was six we lived in a little rented house-behind-a-house in Costa Mesa, California. Our next door neighbors, Carmen and Phil, were Filipinos who spoke a mix of American English and Tagalog, one of the primary languages spoken in the Philippines. When my parents had to work evenings or weekends, Carmen took care of me. I loved my Ninang (Tagalog for Godmother). We always went to the market and the park, sometimes we took the bus to the big hotel on the beach where Phil was a Chef and she watched while I played in the tide pools. I remember that I loved the little fried squid she made on special occasions. I loved the way they would crunch in my mouth.

That single experience is one I held onto as I grew. I made assumptions about the Filipinos I met based on that experience and tended to hold, mainly "positive," stereotypes about Filipinos throughout my childhood and young adulthood. It was only when I became close friends with a young woman who came to the United States from the Philippines when she was 6 that I began to realize that I had failed to adapt and empathize. The more I learned about her life, the more I learned how little I really knew. Luckily, she was very forgiving and corrected my flawed stereotypes with good humor rather than being offended or annoyed. Instead of operating from accurate assumptions based in knowledge of the culture and its rules I had been viewing Filipinos and their experiences in the US through the flawed lenses of a five year old who had loved her Ninang but knew very little else about the culture.

—Helen Acosta

In this chapter we will:

- unpack a few historical notions of adaptation;
- view adaptation through an interculturalist's lens;
- explore the skills that will help us develop empathy.

Historical Perspectives on Cultural Adaptation

When in Rome . . .

As early as St. Ambrose's advice to St. Augustine in 387AD, travelers have been given advice on how to adapt. Ambrose's famous, "When I am at Rome I fast as the Romans do; when I am at Milan I do not fast. So likewise you, whatever church you come to, observe the custom of the place, if you would neither give offence to others, nor take offence from them" (Hoyt, 1922), has, over millennia, morphed to the oft-repeated cliché "When in Rome, do as the Romans do."

Figure 8.1   When in Rome, enjoy slower daily dining experiences with friends . . . as the Romans do.

© ChameleonsEye, 2014. Used under license from Shutterstock, Inc.

Melting-Pot Assimilation Metaphor

Popular in the United States from the 1780s through the 1970s, the melting-pot metaphor of how immigrant groups become "real" Americans is an example of cultural assimilation. In the assimilation model, new immigrants are absorbed into the mainstream culture, leaving their previous culture and beliefs behind, and everyone becomes the same over time.

Integration and Desegregation

In the United States from the 1940 through the 1980s, integration and desegregation referred to the act of incorporating, primarily, racial groups into the larger, white majority. This did not imply that the racial groups would have to give up anything in order to be integrated into the larger population. Integration in the United States sought to create shared and equal access to governmental and social structures through judicial reforms like Brown vs. The Board of Education and legislative reforms such as the Civil Rights Act of 1964.

While there is no longer forced segregation, poor communities are now more segregated than ever before and climbing out of poverty is becoming far more difficult. Dr. Boyce Watkins, Scholar in Residence in Entrepreneurship and Innovation at Syracuse University, attributes this lack of upward mobility to the loss of community that occurred when segregation ended. Higher-income blacks from segregated communities moved their homes and businesses to integrated communities leaving enclaves of poverty where vibrant communities had once flourished (Watkins, 2013).

Learning to Adapt

To connect more fully with the experiences of others we need to learn to question our own viewpoints and become open to perspectives that differ from our own.

In 1968, Milton Bennett joined the Peace Corps. For 2 years he lived and worked with people in Micronesia. When he returned he sought out a doctoral program where he could examine his experiences more fully. He chose the doctoral program in intercultural communication and sociology at the University of Minnesota. Today, Dr. Bennett continues to be one of the leading voices in Intercultural Communication.

The Bennett Scale aka the Developmental Model of Intercultural Sensitivity has been used internationally for nearly three decades in order to help people question their assumptions and become more open to experiences unlike their own (Bennett, 1986).

The scale helps people understand the developmental stage they have reached and aids them in moving to the next level of development.

As with all tools developed by humans for human use, the Bennett Scale was developed by a

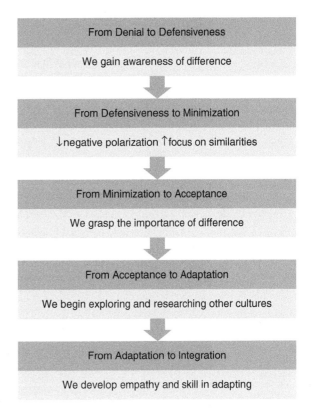

human whose perspectives influence his approach. Milton Bennett sees the ability to live and work within other cultures as a primary focus and an ultimate good. His scale helps people develop the skills to be effective communicators who live in and work in other cultures as well as their own.

WARNING: The Bennett Scale is a developmental scale in which skills are developed over years rather than weeks or months. If you are student who is new to intercultural communication skills, do not expect yourself to leapfrog to the highest level just because you work hard over a short period of time. Instead, focus on the stage you are in and work to move to the next level. Development of these skills requires huge adaptations that lead to major cognitive restructuring over several years. Your instructors have experienced this restructuring in a variety of ways and can act as guides as you enter this journey.

Growing Beyond Denial

Before we become mindful of differences we tend to ignore them. When we ignore the differences between ourselves and others we assume that everyone we meet shares our perspectives. If our experience of the world has been safe and friendly we assume that everyone shares that experience. As a result, we are wholly unaware of experiences that are unlike our own. When we are confronted with those experiences we are either confused by them, unsettled by them, or are wholly blind to them. As a result, we sometimes make errors that are painful to people whose experiences of the world are different from our own.

When we deny difference we might use phrases like the following:

- *"I don't see race."*
- *"It's just another city, what's the big deal?"*
- *"Hey, as long as they speak English, we're good."*

When we remain in **denial** our lives are sometimes hindered because we intentionally avoid interactions with people who look or sound different, we avoid places that feel different, and we skip opportunities because they feel uncomfortable. Unfortunately, with the blinders of denial in place we also tend to dehumanize people whose experiences differ from our own.

To grow beyond denial of differences:

- Do a web search of taboos and etiquette in different cultures (kwintessential.co.uk is a great resource). Choose one behavior, such as "greeting behaviors," list the preferred behaviors by country on sticky notes, and put them on a wall map. Which behaviors are the most different from ours? Imagine visiting that place and enacting the behavior in order to operate effectively within their culture.
- Watch subtitled films made by people from other cultures for consumption in their own countries. Watch the movie twice. The first time you view the film write down behaviors, choices, customs, or references that did not make sense to you. Read about the cultural values and behaviors that are most prevalent in the culture (again, kwintessential.co.uk is a great resource). Look for clues that explain the behaviors, choices, customs, or references that did not make sense to you.

Figure 8.2   A little research, a wall map, and some sticky notes can help you move beyond denial of difference.

© verything possible, 2014. Used under license from Shutterstock, Inc.

Once you have found answers to most of your questions watch the movie again. The behaviors, choices, customs, or references enacted by the characters should make more sense now that you understand why their behaviors, choices, customs, or references are different from your own.

Growing Beyond Defensiveness

When we begin to notice differences, we sometimes become defensive and become protective of our own experiences of the world. At times, we will value our own experiences as superior or as the "truth" and devalue the experiences of others. This is often hurtful to the people whose experiences are being devalued.

When we are defending against difference we might use phrases like the following:

- *"They are all so rude!"*
- *"They could learn a lot from us!"*
- *"Why can't they just speak English?"*

When we are in the **defense** stage we create a confrontational environment in which interactions become frustrating. Our interactions are complicated by the "us vs. them" attitude we adopt when we are feeling defensive toward different places. We tend to view our home culture and its ways above all others. At these times we may find ourselves exhibiting disdain for the ways of others. When we are in this defensive mode our interactions are quite stressful and we feel as though we are under siege. We sometimes retreat from these stressful interactions and avoid situations where we have to engage.

To grow beyond defensiveness:

- Find the similarities between your culture and the culture you find yourself being defensive toward. List the similarities by country or by the individual person you are feeling defensive toward. If you are feeling defensive toward a culture, challenge yourself to be adventurous. Try one of the foods of the culture, visit a community, find a friendly person and talk to them. If you are feeling defensive toward an individual person ask yourself if you would feel defensive if the person was of your own culture. Read about the behaviors, choices, and customs that are generally common to people of that culture to see if you are misunderstanding some aspect of your interactions. If cultural differences are the only reason you are feeling defensive, understanding the differences and similarities in their communication choices will help you to overcome your internal bias. If the defensiveness stems from issues other than cultural differences perhaps some of the advice provided in Chapter 9 of this text will help you work through your defensiveness.

Figure 8.3 When you catch yourself defending against difference challenge yourself to break out of your thought patterns.

© PathDoc, 2014. Used under license from Shutterstock, Inc.

- Talk with someone whose beliefs differ from your own. Focus on your similarities initially, then seek to understand the cultural factors that create the differences.

Growing Beyond Minimization

Once we have gained an appreciation of differences we sometimes find that we begin to focus only on the similarities. This tendency holds its own dangers. When we focus only on similarities we miss the differences that are often important parts of the identities of the people we work with. By focusing only on our similarities we erase, sometimes central, parts of who people are. This is especially harmful when we make assumptions that because people are similar to us in some ways they are obviously similar in the ways that are most important to our own identities.

When we are minimizing difference we might use phrases like the following:

- *"We're all human."*
- *"Smiling is a universal language."*
- *"I just have to be myself. As long as I'm honest and open they'll get that!"*

When we are in the **minimization** stage we tend to emphasize the similarities between people and minimize the differences. This can create confusion in our interactions because we might fail to understand what motivates others whose life experiences differ from our own. If we assume that people are working from the same understanding as we are, we might miss the essential differences that explain behaviors and choices. This becomes especially harmful when, in our minimization of difference, we focus on our own personally perceived universal truths and attempt to place those truths onto people whose own beliefs differ from our own.

To grow beyond minimization of difference:

- Refer to the discussion of privilege in Chapter 5. When we are in minimization we tend to assume that because people are like us in some ways they also enjoy the same intangible benefits that we enjoy. Review your majority identities and make a list for each identity of the intangible benefits you did not ask for but you have as a result of being part of that majority. If you are unsure of the intangible benefits do a web search under "[the majority identity] privilege." Then, circle the identity with the greatest number of benefits. Imagine that you were born into an identity that did not provide all of the benefits of the identity you circled. What opportunities and benefits would you lose? If we can imagine our lives in other people's shoes we are far more likely to honor rather than minimize their experiences.

Figure 8.4   When we minimize the differences caused by privilege we often negate the most wonderful aspects of another person.

© lucadp, 2014. Used under license from Shutterstock, Inc.

- Make a list of your characteristics that you like the most. Put a star next to the items that you think make you "unique." List the ways the starred items help you to succeed in your endeavors. Then, imagine what it would be like if people always ignored those starred items and assumed that you were "just like them."

Growing Beyond Acceptance

Once we have begun to appreciate difference and stop erasing other people's experiences of the world, we are done, right? Nope. **Acceptance** of difference is only the beginning of an exciting adventure that will expand your world for the better. When we begin to accept difference our curiosity may be aroused and we begin focusing on the ways difference and diversity improve situations.

When we begin accepting difference we say things like the following:

- *"Our diversity is our strength."*
- *"I respect their values and I work to maintain my own."*
- *"I need to learn a little more about their culture before my next visit."*

There are still drawbacks to merely accepting difference. The good: we recognize and respect cultural differences between people and we tend to work from the assumption that behaviors are best understood within their cultural context. The problematic: we tend to become overwhelmed and focus on learning about other cultures rather than learning how to successfully negotiate our interactions with people from these cultures.

To grow beyond acceptance of difference:

- Begin focusing on the specific skills that illustrate your understanding of the beliefs, values, and cultural expectations of people from the cultural group you are interacting with.
- Review the following terms and decide which best describes you as an intercultural communicator (if none of these fit then you quite likely have not reached acceptance of difference yet):
  - **Cultural relativists** believe that our ideas and understanding of the world are only true within our own culture. Concepts of right and wrong are culture-specific. Cultural relativists believe that we do not have the right to judge the actions of people from other cultures because our viewpoints are limited by our own cultural blinders.
  - **Ethnorelativists** believe that while there is no absolute position to judge another's actions from, our assumptions and behaviors are logically connected to our beliefs and values (which spring from our home culture/s). This does not imply that all cultural practices are above reproach. It just implies that ethnorelativists suspend judgment and learn about cultural contexts when they encounter unfamiliar cultural practices.
  - **Social justice advocates** believe that, regardless of the society into which a person is born, everyone should have equitable access to social resources. Social resources are the resources of a culture that are made available to people within a society. For instance, driving a motor vehicle is a social resource. Social justice advocates working in Saudi Arabia have found that many women in Saudi Arabia would like to drive. However, in Saudi Arabia, while it is not against the law for women to drive, women are simply not issued drivers' licenses. Since mid-2013 women all over Saudi Arabia have

Figure 8.5 While social justice advocates have long wanted to help Saudi women gain the right to drive they knew it was wrong to take action until Saudi women began standing up for their rights.

© Antonio Guillliem, 2014. Used under license from Shutterstock, Inc.

been arrested for driving without a license. Social justice advocates working in Saudi Arabia are assuring that the women arrested are treated with dignity and in accordance with international laws. Social justice advocates work within cultures and cultural groups, especially within marginalized populations to create equitable access to social resources. Social justice advocates actively struggle to avoid placing their own beliefs above those of the marginalized people they work with. They mindfully work to support the beliefs of the people they work with.

Growing Beyond Adaptation

When we learn to adapt to differences we learn to empathize, to shift frames of reference, and to enact the skills we have gained as intercultural communicators. We begin to adapt our behaviors based on who we are talking to and we begin to better understand people whose experiences differ greatly from our own.

When we begin adapting to difference we say things like the following:

- *"I chose to use their expected behaviors and my work was accepted."*
- *"To resolve the dispute I thought about what their approach would be and used it."*
- *"I'm working to meet them halfway."*

When we are in the **adaptation** stage there are times when we are acutely aware of the choices we are making and we shift back and forth between our home culture/s frames of reference and the frames of reference of the host culture. There are also times when the host culture becomes second nature, and we no longer have to think about what is appropriate or acceptable. At times we can see from both perspectives at once. However, in this stage people have also reported an increase in confusion and sometimes, the polar opposite of the defensiveness against difference stage. In other words, if we are not careful in the adaptation stage, we may end up holding the host culture up as superior to our home culture/s....at that point we need to return to the tools for overcoming defensiveness so that we do not end up treating people from our home culture/s badly.

To grow beyond adaptation to difference:

- Begin consuming the comedy of the host culture. It is true, you do not fully understand a culture until you appreciate its comedy.
- Develop a network of cultural informants (people who are part of the culture and are willing to assist you in understanding contexts and behaviors that do not seem to fit your previous understanding of the culture) to ease you through any difficulties you might encounter within the culture.
- Enjoy a fully immersive experience within the culture. Whether it is a several week-long business trip, a vacation, a semester abroad, or just a move across town to live in a neighborhood where another culture is more dominant, the quickest way to further build your intercultural communication skills at this point is to have a completely immersive experience. While you are there, consult the W-curve theory of culture shock and chart your progress.
- Develop boundaries and strategies to protect parts of your identity that you value. Identities are malleable and it is easy to lose yourself as you become fully immersed within any cultural group.

Figure 8.6   The quickest way to move beyond adaptation to difference is to have a fully immersive intercultural experience: TRAVEL!

Continuing to Grow Through Integration

When we reach **integration** we tend to see ourselves as always learning and becoming. We work to maintain mindfulness, increase skills, and continuously see multiple perspectives.

When we begin integrating difference we say things like the following:

- *"I finally understand where they are coming from and I find myself seeing things from their perspective."*
- *"Now that I know how things work it is beginning to feel like home."*
- *"I find it helpful to look at the situation from multiple points of view."*

Integrating our understandings of difference into our daily routines and into our interactions with people from a culture different from our own seems seamless at first but, we reach a point where we begin to feel like outsiders in the host culture and outsiders in our home culture(s). Bennett called this a "marginal identity" (Bennett, 2000). This new identity holds deep awareness of both home and host cultures. This stage, as well, can be confusing.

To continue to grow through integration of difference:

- Seek out people who have also developed marginal identities. Gain deeper understanding of this unique type of identity formation through your interactions with individuals who share this unique experience of the world.
- Keep a journal or blog to track your experiences and share them with people from your home and host cultures. You can also do the same with your favorite social network.
- Stay connected with your home and host cultures in order to stay current. Cultures are dynamic. You may experience a culture for a few decades but when you leave the culture keeps changing. Maintain connections when

Figure 8.7 Stay connected and share experiences with people from your home and host cultures. Online social networks make this easy.

you are away so that you maintain awareness of the changes that have occurred since you left. This will diminish the feeling of alienation that happens to many when they return to a culture after an absence.

A Reminder for Type A Students Who Expect Perfection of Themselves

This process is not one that anyone experiences overnight. The amount of growth that occurs in the Bennett Scale happens over years rather than days or even months. Do not feel bad if you see yourself in an earlier stage. Just focus on building your skills to move to the next.

Milton Bennett's Developmental Model of Intercultural Sensitivity

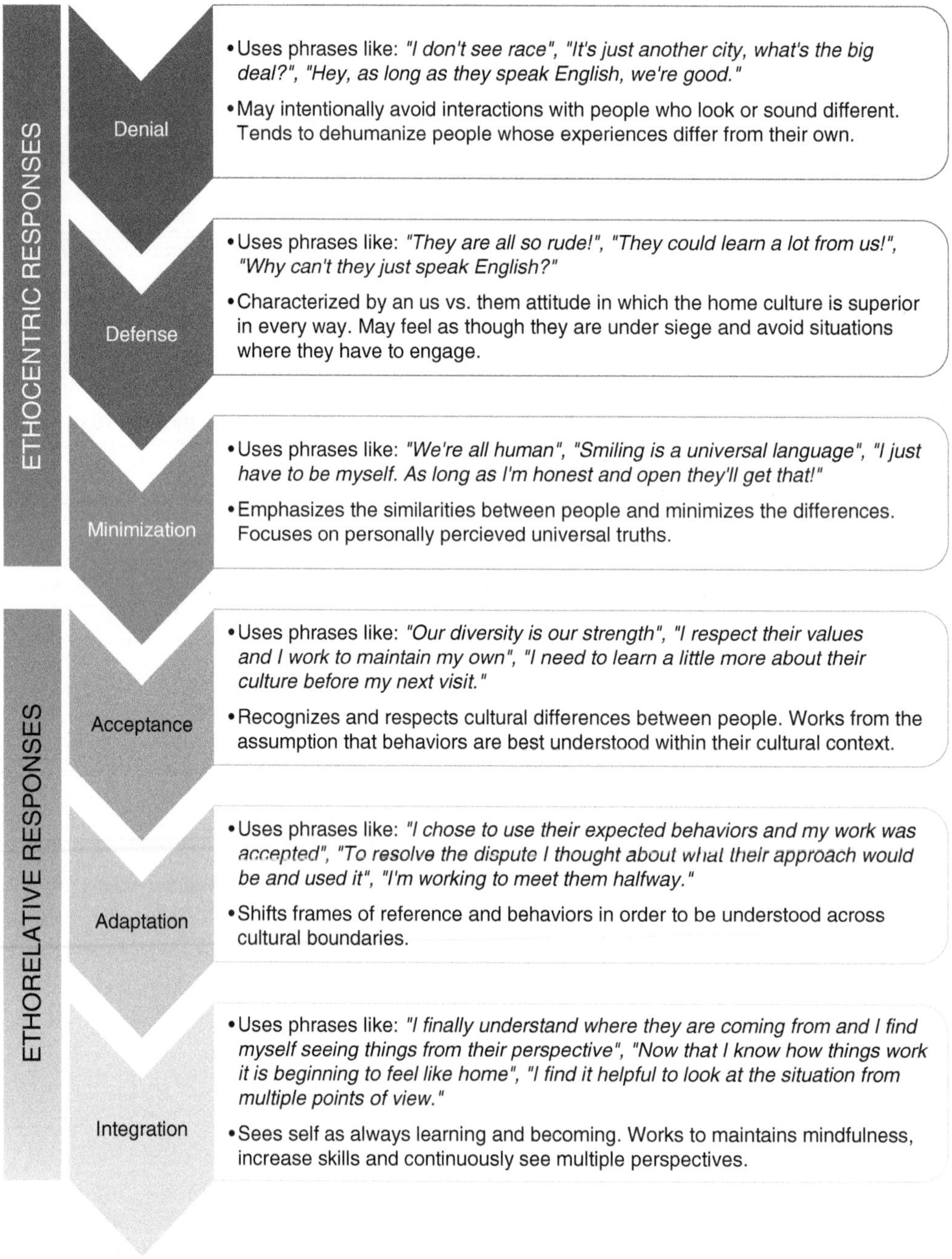

ETHOCENTRIC RESPONSES

Denial
- Uses phrases like: *"I don't see race"*, *"It's just another city, what's the big deal?"*, *"Hey, as long as they speak English, we're good."*
- May intentionally avoid interactions with people who look or sound different. Tends to dehumanize people whose experiences differ from their own.

Defense
- Uses phrases like: *"They are all so rude!"*, *"They could learn a lot from us!"*, *"Why can't they just speak English?"*
- Characterized by an us vs. them attitude in which the home culture is superior in every way. May feel as though they are under siege and avoid situations where they have to engage.

Minimization
- Uses phrases like: *"We're all human"*, *"Smiling is a universal language"*, *"I just have to be myself. As long as I'm honest and open they'll get that!"*
- Emphasizes the similarities between people and minimizes the differences. Focuses on personally percieved universal truths.

ETHORELATIVE RESPONSES

Acceptance
- Uses phrases like: *"Our diversity is our strength"*, *"I respect their values and I work to maintain my own"*, *"I need to learn a little more about their culture before my next visit."*
- Recognizes and respects cultural differences between people. Works from the assumption that behaviors are best understood within their cultural context.

Adaptation
- Uses phrases like: *"I chose to use their expected behaviors and my work was accepted"*, *"To resolve the dispute I thought about what their approach would be and used it"*, *"I'm working to meet them halfway."*
- Shifts frames of reference and behaviors in order to be understood across cultural boundaries.

Integration
- Uses phrases like: *"I finally understand where they are coming from and I find myself seeing things from their perspective"*, *"Now that I know how things work it is beginning to feel like home"*, *"I find it helpful to look at the situation from multiple points of view."*
- Sees self as always learning and becoming. Works to maintains mindfulness, increase skills and continuously see multiple perspectives.

Figure 8.8   Ethnocentric vs. Ethnorelative responses. (Helen Acosta, 2013)

Learning to Empathize

Empathy is often misconstrued as simply being able to mirror the feelings of others. Empathy, when we refer to it in intercultural communication, is a set of skills that allow you to not only mirror the emotions of others but also view the world as they see it. The University of California, Berkeley Greater Good Science Center describes two kinds of empathy: affective empathy and cognitive empathy.

Affective empathy is what we normally think of when we think of empathy. **Affective empathy** is the emotional response we feel when we witness someone experiencing emotions. We may mirror the person's emotions or feel stressed and overwhelmed by their emotions. For most of us, affective empathy is biological and instantaneous. Interesting note: we experience hormonal changes when we experience another person's emotions.

Cognitive empathy is often referred to as "perspective taking." Cognitive empathy is the ability to imagine what someone is thinking or feeling. To build cognitive empathy we have to understand people's motivations and frames of reference. Many of the skills related to cultural literacy and global engagement that we focus on in intercultural communication help build your ability to step into the perspectives of people whose experiences are vastly different from your own.

In western culture much of the research regarding empathy development comes out

Figure 8.9 Affective empathy is the emotional response we feel when we witness someone experiencing emotions.

Figure 8.10 Cognitive empathy, perspective taking, requires learning about other people's motivations and frames of reference.

of the field of Nursing as well as Parenting Science. Parenting Science is a multidisciplinary field inclusive of elements of Sociology, Psychology, Neuroscience, Ethnopediatrics, and more. The primary skill groups that are focused on in both Nursing and the Parenting Sciences are the following:

- developing self-awareness and the ability to distinguish your own emotions from the emotions of others;
- perspective taking;
- regulating your own emotional responses.

Initially, learning to empathize may seem like a soft or weak skill set. However, research suggests that people who have skills in empathizing with others enjoy benefits that others do not.

Some proven benefits of empathy:

- Managers who are seen as empathetic have greater longevity and their employees take fewer sick days.
- People who act with empathy in their marriages feel greater intimacy and satisfaction in their relationships.
- Doctors who show empathy have healthier patients and enjoy better health themselves.

(Greater Good Science Center, 2013)

There are a number of simple ways to increase your empathy skills:

- develop greater self-awareness;
- improve perspective taking;
- regulate your emotional responses.

Build Empathy by Developing Self-Awareness

Maintain In-the-Moment Mindfulness

If you grew up in the United States you likely spend a lot of time focused on the future rather than focusing on what is going on right here, right now. When we are focused on what will happen in the future we tend to neglect the experiences that are right in front of us. As a result, we forget to connect with the people around us. Here are six tips to help you find in-the-moment mindfulness:

© Gregory Johnston, 2014. Used under license from Shutterstock, Inc.

Figure 8.11   Make time and space in your life to live in the moment.

1. Focus on what is going on around you right at this moment. When you catch yourself carrying on an internal dialogue refocus your attention out of your head and on something outside of yourself.
2. Savor great moments. Do not think about getting a great shot of the moment to share later, instead experience the moment in the moment.
3. Lose track of time. When you find that you forget about the clock and everything else other than the task at hand you have found a flow state. People who find flow states on a regular basis live longer, happier lives.
4. Make time to experience your feelings and accept what needs to be done. When you avoid a task, large or small, you create extra stress about avoiding the task. Instead, accept that the task has to be done and make the time to complete the task. Additionally, do not avoid feelings about major issues. Instead, make the time to work through your feelings and experience them in the present.
5. Make a habit of noticing new things in order to avoid going on autopilot.
6. Make time for nothingness. Give yourself space to breathe and merely observe your internal state.

(Dixit, 2013)

Build Empathy by Increasing Your Emotional Intelligence

Emotional intelligence is the ability to recognize our own emotions, discern what our emotions are trying to tell us, and understand the impact our behaviors related to our emotional states have on others. Here are six tips to help increase your emotional intelligence:

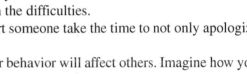

1. Pay attention to how you react to others. Be honest with yourself about how you tend to think and interact with others. Imagine yourself in their place before you act.
2. Shine a spotlight on the great work of others. Let your work speak for itself.
3. Accept your weaknesses. Be honest with yourself about both your strengths and weaknesses. Bring people into your life whose strengths compliment your weaknesses.

Figure 8.12 Build your emotional intelligence (EQ) for better relationships.

4. Learn to stay calm in stressful situations. Rather than deflecting your stress onto others, work to focus your attention on the problem at hand and work through the difficulties.
5. Take responsibility for your actions. When you hurt someone take the time to not only apologize but find ways to repair the damage done.
6. Before you act on your emotions imagine how your behavior will affect others. Imagine how you would feel if someone approached you acting the way you are about to act.

(Manktelow, 2013)

Watch Out for Those Moments When You Forget to Empathize

Empathy leaves us when we are focused on ourselves and our own needs or interests. Several studies have shown that:

- Our own internal states such as momentary hunger, temporary discomfort, heightened arousal, or afternoon blahs can turn off the empathy we normally feel for others. This phenomenon is called the hot/cold empathy gap (Loewenstein, 1996).
- Focusing on monetary concerns, especially gambling and speculation about the monetary value of anything, turns off our altruistic/empathetic impulses (Brafman & Brafman, 2008).
- When we are required to engage in activities that clash with our moral values, especially when we are required to harm others, we separate ourselves from our empathetic responses as a method of protecting ourselves from the pain we may be causing. This process is called moral disengagement (Reich & Laqueur, 1990).
- We are less likely to feel empathy when we are in groups or crowds than when we are alone. This tendency has been termed "The Bystander Effect" (Darley & Latané, 1968).

Figure 8.13 Empathy leaves us when we are focused only on ourselves and our own needs or interests.

Build Empathy Through Perspective Taking
Step Into Their Shoes, Not Onto Their Toes!

Actively imagine what another person is experiencing. Rather than reacting immediately think about how the other person might feel in a given situation. Consider the other person's experiences, their difficulties, the rules for behavior that they follow, as well as their beliefs/values.

Develop Your "Empathy Reflex"

In his book *Brain Rules,* developmental molecular biologist, Dr. John Medina, gives advice to couples in order to defuse emotionally charged moments. He calls this simple two-step process **"the empathy reflex."** He suggests, rather than mirroring volatile emotions and reacting with equal force, instead, to follow these two simple steps:

1. **Describe the emotions you think you are seeing**: "Wow, you look angry enough to throw something."
2. **Make a guess as to the cause of all of the emotions**: "You had to go into work 2 hours early today and you probably had to work all day on that project that is due next week. I'll bet you had to work with that guy from accounting who always pushes your buttons! To top it off you had to work late and that threw you right into the rush hour traffic. I'm sorry you had to go through all that! No wonder you're so upset!"

In most cases these two steps will diffuse the emotionally charged situation and create an opening for sharing of difficulties and experiences (Medina, 2008).

Read Fiction, Especially "Literary" Fiction

Over the last decade a number of studies have shown the positive link between reading fiction and empathy. These studies have looked at short-term effects in which a person reads a 15-minute empathy-provoking story then interacts with another person to reading whole works of fiction.

After over a decade of published results the findings seem to suggest that readers of fiction:

- tend to show more empathy for others;
- are better at reading people's nonverbal behaviors;
- arc better at predicting the actions of others.

Figure 8.14   Literary fiction builds empathy through complex characters who have a well-developed inner world in which they grapple with deep dilemmas.

The type of fiction that seems to build the most empathy is what is called "Literary Fiction" (Chiaet, 2013). Literary fiction tends to be more complex, multileveled, and universal. In literary fiction the characters tend to grapple with deep dilemmas, have a well-developed inner world and the stories are less focused on the plot and more focused on the motivations of the characters. To find contemporary literary fiction look up the list of current PEN award and O'Henry award winners.

Make a Face

Did you know that Botox makes it difficult to empathize with others? One of our basic human traits is to mirror the facial expressions people show on their faces when they are talking to us. When we mirror their expressions we feel their emotions. Until recently, many researchers thought that the facial expressions were merely an indicator of listener's emotional reactions. However, new research on people who have had facial Botox has verified that the facial expressions come first and they lead to emotion connections. Since people who have had Botox cannot mirror the emotions of those they come into contact with, they actually feel less emotion and have more trouble empathizing with others (Paul, 2007). To improve your ability to empathize actively, mirror facial expressions while you are listening.

© Djomas, 2014. Used under license from Shutterstock, Inc.

Figure 8.15 If you cannot move your face, you lose your ability to empathize with others. Keep the wrinkles to keep your empathy.

Do Not Depend on Your Gut

Gut reactions are personal and nonuniversal. Instead, check your perceptions by asking what the other person is thinking or feeling.

Validate Others' Experiences

Even when you disagree with someone, you can maintain a personal connection by validating their experiences of the world. Recently, the power of validating and accepting the experiences of others has gained new attention through the groundbreaking work of the Family Acceptance Project.

Dr. Caitlyn Ryan is a clinical social worker who has been working with lesbian, gay, bisexual, and transgender (LGBT) youth and their families since the 1970s. When she began as a young social worker in Atlanta, Georgia, she was shocked by the number of LGBT youth who were living on the streets because their parents had rejected them. Over the next 40 years she interviewed thousands of parents and families of LGBT youth and she learned a surprising truth: Whether accepting or rejecting, every parent she spoke with had acted from the same motivation for their children. That motivation was love. The problem Dr. Ryan faced was that young people from rejecting families were at enormous risk for poverty, disease, and, most of all, suicide. She changed her approach and began sharing the frightening statistics with families that had rejected their LGBT children. When confronted with the dangers they unknowingly placed their children in, rejecting families immediately changed. They wanted their children home where they

© mpokcik, 2014. Used under license from Shutterstock, Inc.

Figure 8.16 Even if you do not agree, validate the experiences of others for their happiness as well as your own.

were safe. They wanted their children to know that they were loved, and, even if their parents could not understand or did not approve of their LGBT status, their parents, most of all, wanted them safe and whole.

Dr. Ryan has followed up with thousands of families. The previously rejected families that she works with now have healthy, whole young people who are back at home and no longer at risk for dangerous behaviors. Even in families where there are still religious or cultural barriers to acceptance of the child's LGBT status, the children have stayed home and have rebuilt their relationships with family members.

The mere recognition that it is difficult to be LGBT in this country and that families are important to the survival of LGBT youth has allowed young people and their families to reconcile (Ryan, 2013).

Build Empathy by Regulating Your Own Emotional Responses

We cannot achieve empathy without first building our own ability to weather difficult situations. **Hardiness** is a term used to describe people who deal well with stressful situations. People who have high levels of emotional hardiness tend to avoid physical and mental illnesses often related to stress.

According to behavioral psychologist Dr. Susan Kobasa, hardy individuals share three basic outlooks on life:

Challenge: Hardy individuals tend to see stressful situations as challenges or puzzles to overcome rather than overwhelming misfortunes that have befallen them.

Personal control: Hardy individuals accept challenges and work to master them. Even when they cannot master the challenge they find the elements that they have mastered and work to optimize the successes in those areas. Hardy individuals do not get mired in what others might brand "failure." Instead, they search for new options and keep moving forward.

Figure 8.17 Emotional hardiness: challenge, personal control, and commitment.

Commitment: Hardy individuals are committed to living active, engaged lives. They believe that their lives have purpose. Their purpose leads them to try to influence their surroundings. Even when they experience setbacks they continue forward because they can see the broader purpose they are committed to.

(Kobasa, Maddi, & Kahn, 1982)

Each one of us has the capacity to develop emotional hardiness. In the next few pages you will experience some methods you can use to increase these capacities within yourself.

Build Empathy by Following the Platinum Rule

On August 17, 2013, Islan Nettles left her apartment, ready for a night on the town with some girlfriends. As they walked toward a club in Harlem, a group of men began shouting racial and transphobic slurs at them. Nettles was attacked, thrown to the ground, and beaten so badly that she was raced to the hospital, survived for a few days in a coma, and then slipped away.

At her memorial service Islan's girlfriends, who had been with her that night, were told this was not a political rally and they should be respectful of Islan's family's wishes. Islan's family and a string of *community leaders spoke, one after the other. Several speakers referred to Islan as "Vaughn" and spoke about her as "him." Her girlfriends, who, like Islan, were trans*women, cried on the sidelines, occasionally attempting to correct the speakers. Each time a speaker erased Islan's identity it felt to them like she was being killed again. Islan had given everything to be the woman she knew she was and it was not until Laverne Cox, a trans*woman who has recently gained fame on the Showtime Series,* Orange is the New Black*, took the stage, that Islan's girlfriends felt that Islan's memory was being honored. In her speech, Cox acknowledged the pain these thoughtless erasures were causing, "I know there are lots of people out there who are upset that she's been called by the wrong pronoun. That hurts me, too. I stand here as a trans*woman of color and my heart aches for this loss. I think that what the trans*community needs to hear is that our lives matter." (Shapiro, 2013).*

Islan's family treated Islan and her girlfriends the way the family wanted to be treated. Were they following the golden rule? Most likely, yes. "Do to others as you would have done to you," was reflected in the choices of the Nettles' family. They were treating the attendees the way the family would want to be treated. But the question is: Is the golden rule good enough in a world where people who are so diverse interact with one another on a regular basis?

Many thinkers from the last century, such as George Bernard Shaw and Karl Popper, thought that the golden rule was not good enough. The golden rule only asks you to consider your own preferences and apply those preferences to your interactions with others. In the early years of this new century a new rule is emerging: **the platinum rule**. People all over the world have begun to advocate the platinum rule as an upgrade to the golden rule. The platinum rule is deceptively simple: "Do to others as they would have done to them." Most agree that the platinum rule is much harder to live by than the golden rule.

The platinum rule makes us take responsibility for our choices. Rather than thoughtlessly enacting our own personal preferences in the assumption that everyone would prefer the same, we, instead, have to consider the other person and, rather than merely asking ourselves what the best way to treat another person is, we need to ask the other person how they would prefer to be treated.

The Platinum Rule

Do to others what they would have done to them

Figure 8.18 Rather than asking ourselves how we would want to be treated we need to ask the other person how they would prefer to be treated. (Helen Acosta, 2014).

So, instead of saying that someone is being overly sensitive, cruel, rude, and so on . . . for reacting differently than we might in the same situation, the platinum rule asks us to ask why another person has a different reaction than we would, to delve deeper and work to understand rather than dismiss the experience of someone who is different from us.

Build Empathy: Use Ting

The Chinese character, **ting**, "to listen" sheds some light on how to listen with empathy.

Think about your last interaction with another person. Were you scrolling through messages on your phone while simultaneously half-listening to the other person? Maybe if your phone is in your pocket, you were trying to listen but your imagination ran away with you and you missed half of what the other person was saying. Either that or something they said sparked an argument that you wanted to make about what they were saying so, instead of listening, you began waiting until they stopped talking so you could make your comment. These are all very common predicaments in the western world. We do not tend to value listening as much as we value speaking. As a result, we have a tendency not to listen empathetically. Imagine that you listened with your ears, eyes, and heart, and full attention every time you interacted with another person. You might react more slowly, pause more often before responding, and take more time to consider how your response would impact the other person. Ting helps us to listen with empathy because it adds space and time to focus on the other person.

Figure 8.19   The Chinese concept, ting, differs from our Western concept of listening. (Helen Acosta, 2014).

Build Empathy: Develop Nondefensive Communication Skills

In September 2012, a user posted a picture in the "funny" section of reddit.com with the heading "I don't know what to conclude from this." He had taken the photo without permission and, apparently, he found it to be very funny. The subject of the stolen photo was Balpreet Kaur, a student from Ohio State. She, like so many other Ohio State students, was out shopping in flip flops, yoga pants, and a T-shirt. What confused the user who posted the picture? Ms. Kaur's Turban and beard. To their credit, most reddit readers did not think that ridiculing someone for looking different was funny. The least expected response came from the young woman herself (used with permission from Balpreet Kaur):

Hey, guys. This is Balpreet Kaur, the girl from the picture. I actually didn't know about this until one of my friends told [me] on facebook. If the [original poster] wanted a picture, they could have just asked and I could have smiled :) However, I'm not embarrassed or even humiliated by the attention [negative and positive] that this picture is getting because, it's who I am. Yes, I'm a baptized Sikh woman with facial hair. Yes, I realize that my gender is often confused and I look different than most women. However, baptized Sikhs believe in the sacredness of this body—it is a gift that has been given to us by the Divine Being [which is genderless, actually] and, must keep it intact as a submission to the divine will. Just as a child doesn't reject the gift of his/her parents, Sikhs do not reject the body that has been given to us. By crying 'mine, mine' and changing this body-tool, we are essentially living in ego and creating a separateness between ourselves and the divinity within us. By transcending societal views of beauty, I believe that I can focus more on my actions. My attitude and thoughts and actions have more value in

Figure 8.20   Balpreet Kaur showed reddit users how to communicate nondefensively.

them than my body because I recognize that this body is just going to become ash in the end, so why fuss about it? When I die, no one is going to remember what I looked like, heck, my kids will forget my voice, and slowly, all physical memory will fade away. However, my impact and legacy will remain: and, by not focusing on the physical beauty, I have time to cultivate those inner virtues and hopefully, focus my life on creating change and progress for this world in any way I can. So, to me, my face isn't important but the smile and the happiness that lie behind the face are :-). So, if anyone sees me at OSU, please come up and say hello. I appreciate all of the comments here, both positive and less positive because I've gotten a better understanding of myself and others from this. Also, the yoga pants are quite comfortable and the Better Together T-shirt is actually from Interfaith Youth Core, an organization that focuses on storytelling and engagement between different faiths.:) I hope this explains everything a bit more, and I apologize for causing such confusion and uttering anything that hurt anyone.

While Ms. Kaur likely experienced defensive reactions when she saw her own image used as the butt of a joke on reddit.com, she knew that a defensive response would not resolve the situation. Instead, she chose not to share that reaction with the world. She constructed a more empathetic nondefensive response that received thousands of positive responses and was shared worldwide. Additionally, the young man who initially posted the photo apologized for his thoughtless cruelty and thanked Ms. Kaur for her gentle approach. He said that she inspired him to learn more about Sikhs and that he was impressed by the Sikh focus on building a legacy rather than always focusing on the external as he had (West, 2012).

Nondefensive communication skills are discussed at length in the Conflict chapter. For the moment, it is helpful to note that defensive style shuts down reasoning and instead signals to those we are communicating with that we are ready to stand our ground and fight. Nondefensive communication choices actually help people to open up and begin to listen with ting.

Build Empathy: by Strengthening Your Emotional Resilience

Emotional resilience allows us to survive, and sometimes thrive, in difficult situations. To understand resilience, think of a balloon. When you blow it up, a balloon will stretch several times its original size. When you let the air out, depending on the materials used to make the balloon, it will sometimes shrink back to its original size, unharmed by the stressful experience of being stretched entirely out of shape. However, if the stress of being blown up is severe and the balloon is about to pop, usually the balloon will lose its shape entirely because it has lost its elasticity, also known as resilience.

Emotional resilience strengthens our ability to bounce back after we have experienced difficult situations. But more importantly, emotional resilience helps us to avoid exploding in the midst of stressful situations.

Figure 8.21 The elements of emotional resilience. (Helen Acosta, 2013).

We can build our emotional resilience by building some specific skills that are discussed below.

Anticipating Contexts

We can only anticipate the situations we might face when we prepare ahead of time. While we are preparing for a difficult situation we need to consider the following:

- where the situation will occur;
- what environmental factors might influence the outcomes of the situation;
- differences in personal experience among the participants;
- differences in cultural expectations among the participants;
- differences in expected outcomes among the participants.

Openness

We gain the skill of openness when we remind ourselves that ours is just one experience of the world and we begin to focus our attention on learning about the experiences of others. Once we begin learning how to effectively support the experiences of others, without losing ourselves in the process, we gain openness. Becoming open to others' experiences of the world is an ongoing process that requires mindful attention.

A second aspect of openness that most of us neglect is the skill of being open to our own errors. It does not mean that you are a bad person if you make a mistake. Just apologize, learn from the mistake, and repair any damage that may have resulted from your own error/s.

Meaning-Focused Coping

Positive psychology is the newest area of study in the field of psychology and "meaning-focused coping" has garnered a lot of attention as an indicator of resilience. When we find ourselves in difficult situations and we focus, not on how hard things are but instead, on what we will learn from the experience, we are engaging in **meaning-focused coping**.

Other elements of meaning-focused coping include the following:

- drawing on personal beliefs or values to find meaning in a difficult situation;
- reminding ourselves of what we have learned from previous difficult situations;
- shifting our life goals and priorities as a result of a difficult situation;
- finding the good in every situation, from the most mundane to the most complex.

(Folkman, 2008)

Figure 8.22   Develop strong social connections with at least a handful of people. Strong networks of support make us feel better about ourselves.

Social Coping

Social coping is a skill that can only work within social networks. So, the first step toward social coping is building strong social connections with at least a handful of people. These social connections provide support in trying times (friends and family allow us to cry on their shoulders, vent, talk through tough times) and, even when these connections are not immediately available they bolster our sense of self and help us to remain resilient in trying times. In simple terms, when times are tough, we know we have people we can turn to who understand, accept, and care about us. These networks of support make us feel better about ourselves. When we feel better about ourselves we are better at dealing with difficult situations.

Physical Health

Our mental health is deeply connected to our physical health. When we do not get enough sleep, do not eat properly, and do not take preventative care of ourselves, our mental health tends to deteriorate along with our physical health and we lose the ability to bounce back from difficult situations.

Build Empathy: Practice Positive Regard

When we treat others as though their motives are pure we tend to have better experiences with them.

For instance, if you cannot find your phone and your first assumption is that your roommate stole it, more than likely, you and your roommate will have a rough time getting along with one another. However, if your first assumption is that you misplaced your phone and that, more than likely, your roommate will help you find it you will have a much more positive experience. Most of us like to reflect back what others see in us. When you ask your roommate to help you find your phone, you will get the help you need . . . and, if your roommate did take your phone you have just shown your roommate who you hope they are and given them a moment to think about who they want to be. Usually, when you treat people as though they are good, kind, and helpful, they tend to fulfill your expectations. The same is true when you assume the worst.

Example: Several years ago, I lost a friend who was from Iran because of a misunderstanding. I lost

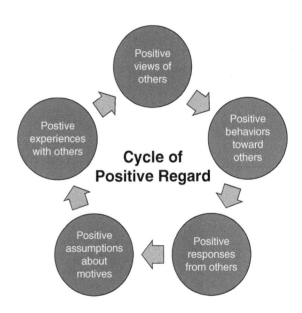

Figure 8.23   The cycle of positive regard. (Helen Acosta, 2013)

my positive assumptions about his motives when we entered into an agreement regarding money. I thought his demand to negotiate a better deal for himself was unfair and completely out-of-line with our friendship and, as a result, my cycle of positive regard shifted to a cycle of negative regard. Within a few weeks our friendship ended. A few years later I learned that, when it comes to monetary transactions there are very specific cultural expectations and behaviors that my friend was enacting that I misunderstood.

His cultural expectation as an Iranian was that when dealing with monetary issues a friendly negotiation would begin as a sign of my respect for his intelligence. For my friend, my refusal to negotiate was a sign that I did not respect him and did not value him as a person. If I had assumed the best about him and chosen to learn about his motives and cultural expectations, I would not have lost my friend.

In intercultural situations **positive regard** can be lost and regained. To jumpstart the cycle here are a few methods you can use:

- Remind yourself to withhold judgment.
- Assume positive intent among the people you are interacting with.
- Learn about cultural expectations that may be informing the behaviors of the people with whom you are interacting.
- Learn and enact the behaviors that the people you are working with will expect of you. People appreciate it when you make an effort.

Test Your Empathy and Resilience

Neuroscience and Learning columnist, Annie Murphy Paul, explains that one of the best ways to test your hardiness and build empathy skills is through face-to-face competitive game play.

Tabletop Gaming to Improve Empathy

She explains that when we compete in tabletop games we have to pay close attention to our competitors, their facial expressions, body language, and strategic choices. She interviewed Kyle Mathewson, who was a lead author in a UC Berkeley study in which the authors found that people use entirely different parts of their brain when they are playing a game against a computer than when they are playing a game against a live opponent sitting across the table from them. Mathewson explained that we create a mental model of our opponent's intentions so that we can anticipate how they will play.

Figure 8.24   Table top gaming improves empathy as well as emotional hardiness.

© Iriike, 2014. Used under license from Shutterstock, Inc.

Tabletop Gaming to Improve Hardiness

Annie Murphy Paul also discusses the benefits of tabletop gaming in learning to regulate your emotional responses. Competition of all kinds tests our emotional resilience and tabletop games are no exception. Learning to win and lose gracefully requires all the skills of emotional resilience and positive regard (Murphy Paul, 2012).

Glossary

Acceptance   The fourth step of the Bennett model of intercultural sensitivity, acceptance, is an ethnorelative response in which we accept both the similarities and differences in others.

Adaptation   The fifth step of the Bennett model of intercultural sensitivity, adaptation, is an ethnorelative response in which we learn to empathize, to shift frames of reference, and to enact the skills we have gained as intercultural communicators.

Affective empathy   The emotional response we feel when we witness someone experiencing emotions.

Cognitive empathy   The ability to imagine what someone is thinking or feeling.

Defense   The second step of the Bennett model of intercultural sensitivity, defense, is an ethnocentric response in which we become protective of our own experiences and devalue experiences that are not like our own.

Denial   The first step of the Bennett model of intercultural sensitivity, denial, is an ethnocentric response in which we ignore differences and, when confronted by differences, we are either confused by them, unsettled by them, or are wholly blind to them.

Emotional hardiness   A term used to describe people who deal well with stressful situations.

Emotional intelligence   The ability to recognize our own emotions, discern what our emotions are trying to tell us, and understand the impact our behaviors related to our emotional states have on others.

Emotional resilience   Our ability to bounce back after we have experienced stress.

Empathy reflex   Rather than mirroring volatile emotions and reacting with equal force, instead describe the emotions you are seeing and make a guess as to the cause of all of the emotions.

Ethnocentric response   As described in the Bennett model of intercultural sensitivity, an ethnocentric response is one in which the communicator relies solely on their own experiences of their own culture to interpret new experiences and make behavioral choices.

Ethnorelative response   As described in the Bennett model of intercultural sensitivity, an ethnorelative response is one in which the communicator relies on experiences of both their home and host cultures to interpret new experiences and make behavioral choices.

Integration   The sixth and final step of the Bennett model of intercultural sensitivity, integration, is an ethnorelative response in which we develop a marginal identity, an identity that includes behaviors and beliefs of the home and host culture.

Meaning-focused coping   When we find ourselves in difficult situations and we focus, not on how hard things are but instead, on what we will learn from the experience.

Melting-pot assimilation metaphor   Popular in the United States from the 1780s through the 1970s, the melting-pot metaphor of how immigrant groups become "real" Americans is an example of cultural assimilation. In the assimilation model, new immigrants are absorbed into the mainstream culture, leaving their previous culture and beliefs behind, and everyone becomes the same over time.

Minimization   The third step of the Bennett model of intercultural sensitivity, minimization, is an ethnocentric response in which we focus solely on the similarities between ourselves and others.

Nondefensive communication   Reacting to difficult situations without allowing your emotional reactions to impede effective communication.

Perspective taking   Actively imagine what another person is experiencing. Consider the other person's experiences, their difficulties, the rules for behavior that they follow, as well as their beliefs/values.

Platinum rule   Do to others as they would have done to them.

Positive regard   When we treat others as though their motives are pure we tend to have better experiences with them.

Social coping   Social connections provide support in trying times (friends and family allow us to cry on their shoulders, vent, talk through tough times) and, even when these connections are not immediately available they bolster our sense of self and help us to remain resilient in trying times.

Ting   The Chinese character, to listen. The character includes listening with your ears, eyes, full attention, and heart.

Works Cited

Bennett, J. M. (1993). Cultural marginality: Identity issues in intercultural. In R. M. Paige (Ed.), *Education for the intercultural experience. Intercultural Press: Yarmouth. Maine.*

Bennett, M. J. (1986). A developmental approach to training for intercultural sensitivity. *International Journal of Intercultural Relations*, 10, issue 2179–196.

Brafman, O., & Brafman, R. (2008). *Sway: The irresistible pull of irrational behavior.* New York, NY: Doubleday.

Chiaet, J. (2013, October 4). *Novel finding: Reading literary fiction improves empathy.* Retrieved from Scientific American website: http://www.scientificamerican.com/article.cfm?id=novel-finding-reading-literary-fiction-improves-empathy

Darley, J. M., & Latané, B. (1968). Bystander intervention in emergencies: Diffusion of responsibility. *Journal of Personality and Social Psychology*, 8, 377–383.

Dixit, J. (2013, September 20). *The art of now: Six steps to living in the moment.* Retrieved from Psychology Today website: http://www.psychologytoday.com/articles/200810/the-art-now-six-steps-living-in-the-moment

Folkman, S. (2008). The case for positive emotions in the stress process. *Anxiety, Stress and Coping*, 21, 3–14.

Greater Good Science Center. (2013, November 11). *Empathy.* Retrieved from UC Berkeley Greater Good Science Center website: http://greatergood.berkeley.edu/topic/empathy/definition#why_practice

Hoyt, J. K. (1922). *Hoyt's new cyclopedia of practical quotations, 1820–1895.* Retrieved from Bartleby.com website: http://www.bartleby.com/78/710.html

Kobasa, S. C., Maddi, S. R., & Kahn, S. (1982). Hardiness and health: A prospective study. *Journal of Personality and Social Psychology*, v42, 168–177.

Loewenstein, G. (1996). Out of control: Visceral influences on behavior. *Organizational Behavior and Human Decision Processes*, 272–292.

Manktelow, J. (2013, November 11). *Emotional intelligence.* Retrieved from Mind Tools website: http://www.mindtools.com/pages/article/newCDV_59.htm

Medina, J. J. (2008). *Brain rules: 12 Principles for surviving and thriving at work, home, and school.* Seattle, WA: Pear Press.

Murphy Paul, A. (2012, February 9). *Beyond strategy and winning, how games teach kids empathy.* Retrieved from Mind Shift website: http://blogs.kqed.org/mindshift/2012/02/beyond-strategy-and-winning-how-games-teach-kids-empathy/

Paul, P. (2007, June 17). *With botox, looking good and feeling less.* Retrieved from New York Times website: http://www.nytimes.com/2011/06/19/fashion/botox-reduces-the-ability-to-empathize-study-says.html

Reich, W., & Laqueur, W. (1990). *Origins of Terrorism: Psychologies, Ideologies, Theologies, States of Mind .* Baltimore: Johns Hopkins University Press.

Ryan, C. (2013, November 7). *Family acceptance project: Families are forever.* Bakersfield, CA: PFLAG Bakersfield.

Shapiro, L. (2013, August 28). *Shouting disrupts vigil for murdered transgender woman Islan Nettles.* Retrieved from Huffington Post website: http://www.huffingtonpost.com/2013/08/28/islan-nettles_n_3832004.html

Watkins, B. (2013, March 12). *Dr. Boyce: Was integration a good thing for black people? Probably not.* Retrieved from Black Blue Dog website: http://www.blackbluedog.com/2013/03/news/dr-boyce-was-integration-a-good-thing-for-black-people-probably-not/

West, L. (2012, September 26). *Reddit users attempt to shame sikh woman, get righteously schooled.* Retrieved from Jezebel website: http://jezebel.com/5946643/reddit-users-attempt-to-shame-sikh-woman-get-righteously-schooled

Chapter 9

Approaches to Conflict

Mark Staller

"The reality today is that we are all interdependent and have to co-exist on this small planet. Therefore, the only sensible and intelligent way to resolve differences and clashes of interests, whether between individuals or nations, is through dialogue."
—Tenzin Gyatso, the 14th Dalai Lama

Chapter Learning Objectives

1. Realize that there are different definitions and views of conflict and different cultural approaches to conflict.
2. Understand the different types of conflict.
3. Identify the sources of intercultural conflict.
4. Gain a general knowledge of some of the international conflicts that have occurred.
5. Use an American approach to conflict management based upon five conflict management strategies.
6. Develop other approaches to managing conflict based upon four conflict management styles.

© ChameleonsEye, 2014. Used under license from Shutterstock, Inc.

Introduction

© Attila jANDI, 2014. Used under license from Shutterstock, Inc.

Figure 9.1   A Medieval Japanese Kabuki scene.

A good dramatic story, especially a melodramatic story, needs a good conflict. Sometimes the main character in the story faces an internal conflict. Sometimes the main character must overcome nonhuman forces, like technology or the supernatural. Most often, however, a conflict arises between the main character (the protagonist) and a human opponent (the antagonist). The dramatic climax usually occurs when the conflict presented in the story is resolved. Conflict is an essential component of most fictional genres.

But what about conflict in real life? Is conflict an essential element of human life and social interaction, or is conflict an unnecessary and unproductive component of human experience? Should conflicts among human beings be acknowledged and faced directly, or should conflicts be avoided? This chapter will reveal that cultures have very different views of conflict and very different approaches to dealing (or not dealing) with conflict.

First, we will present a positive view of conflict and a negative view of conflict, and we will point out how these two different views of conflict can cause people in different cultures to take very different general approaches to conflict management. We will also point out several other specific differences among cultural approaches to conflict.

Next, we will deepen your understanding of conflict by listing and describing about a dozen different types of conflict and about a dozen different sources of intercultural conflict. We will also sensitize you to the different international conflicts that have occurred between the United States and other countries of the world, and we will note some other international conflicts that have occurred between different nations of the world.

Next, we will present in some detail the American approach to dealing with conflict by presenting five popular conflict management strategies, and then we will contrast the American conflict management approach to other approaches by presenting four conflict management styles that are used in different parts of the world. We will end this chapter with a few specific tips about personal approaches you can take to conflict management.

A Positive View of Conflict

Generally, a positive view of conflict is often held in America and in many modern western nations. Although people in modern western cultures recognize that poorly managed conflicts can lead to very negative consequences, they often think that conflict is not the problem, but, rather, poor "conflict management." If people just manage their conflicts properly, many Americans and westerners believe, they can resolve their differences and solve most interpersonal and international problems that arise.

A typical American textbook definition of "conflict" will describe conflict in neutral terms. A conflict may be defined as an "incompatibility" between two or more parties. Two people or two people groups may have different goals or objectives, so they will have to discuss these incompatible goals or objectives in order to resolve their conflict. If the correct techniques and strategies are used during the conflict resolution, it is often assumed, a positive solution will be found that will satisfy the people and parties involved in a conflict.

Many Americans believe that conflicts of opinion should be directly addressed and discussed, and they often encourage people to "speak up" if they disagree with someone or something. This expectation arises in part from the American democratic political process. Democratic decision-making relies on the voicing of different opinions and upon strong advocacy for competing ideas and positions. People in democratic countries are encouraged to make their voices heard and to participate in healthy political debates so that the best policies can win out in the "marketplace of ideas."

The sharing of dissenting opinions and the expectation of a fair amount of "healthy conflict" is also present in the American legal system. American jurors are expected to listen to the arguments and examine the evidence provided by the prosecution and the defense, and then they are expected to debate the merits of the evidence and arguments provided. If a jury returns a verdict too swiftly, they might be accused of "groupthink" and of not taking their jury duty seriously. Jurors are expected to express their opinions (especially dissenting opinions) and to raise questions so that the best, most just decision can be reached.

Democratic decision-making that encourages "healthy conflict" is also part of American business and industry. When working in problem-solving or decision-making groups, American employees are encouraged to share their ideas, even though (or especially when) these ideas might conflict with ideas proposed by others. The prevailing view in American business is that the best ideas will win out when they are tested against other ideas, and the best decisions will be made when dissenting opinions are considered. Sometimes a small group will even appoint someone to be a "Devil's Advocate" to express dissenting opinions if there is too much agreement within a group.

One other factor that contributes to the positive view of conflict in modern western cultures is the value of individualism. Individualistic cultures that value self-expression and self-actualization will often view conflict as necessary and appropriate. When people come into conflict with their society or with others, in order to be "true to themselves" (it is believed), they must have the courage to speak up and express their individual needs, desires, goals, and opinions. In an individualistic culture like America, expressing a conflict, and even insisting that a conflict cannot be resolved because it would violate an individual's autonomy, may be viewed as heroic.

Figure 9.2 Modern democratic countries encourage "healthy conflict" and political debate.

© 360b, 2014. Used under license from Shutterstock, Inc.

A Negative View of Conflict

In contrast to the positive view of conflict held by many Americans and by several other modern western cultures, a majority of traditional collectivistic cultures have a very negative view of conflict. Collectivistic cultures that value group cohesion and group harmony often view conflict as a "disharmony" that threatens the very existence of the collective. When conflict arises in a collectivistic culture, people may become very uncomfortable and even frightened. They have no well-developed notion of "healthy conflict," and they tend to view all conflicts as unfortunate occurrences that should be avoided.

People in cultures with a "high-uncertainty avoidance" orientation are not comfortable with the expression of many different opinions, especially when these opinions clash or conflict. People in these cultures prefer to have one "official" voice or opinion expressed, and they may view the expression of "dissenting opinions" as embarrassing and inappropriate social faux pas. Whereas a typical American boss might encourage and appreciate a "healthy debate" of a proposed company policy, a typical German boss might expect the company policy to be implemented without question.

People in cultures with a "high power distance" orientation are not comfortable with subordinates disagreeing with their superiors. People in these cultures expect that those in authority will be respected, and they think that questioning a superior is disrespectful and inappropriate. Whereas an American teacher might be pleased when students voice their disagreements because they are "thinking for themselves," a Chinese teacher might be offended by such behavior because the students are being "rude and disrespectful."

In many cultures of the world, conflict is almost always viewed as inappropriate, disruptive, harmful, and dangerous. Conflict is actively avoided, and if a conflict does occur, it is a matter of shame and embarrassment, not pride. The expression of dissenting opinions is discouraged, and those who help to maintain the harmony of a group are appreciated and rewarded.

© Arcady, 2014. Used under license from Shutterstock, Inc.

Figure 9.3   Many cultures view conflict as inappropriate, disruptive, harmful, and dangerous.

Some Specific Cultural Differences

Now that we have introduced you to two very different cultural views of conflict, we will provide some other, more specific differences in the ways that cultures view or approach conflict. Besides having a very general view of conflict as "positive" or "negative," people in different countries and cultures may also expect different behaviors when a conflict arises. We will focus on the behaviors that are least familiar and most perplexing to an American audience.

Negotiating a Price

Although America is classified as a "low uncertainty avoidance" culture, there is one area where most Americans like to avoid uncertainty: Americans usually prefer to have set prices and fees for goods and services. We usually expect items in stores to be clearly marked with a price, and we expect people who are providing us services to have clearly set fees. We might be suspicious of the motives of store owners and service providers who do not provide a set dollar amount up front.

However, in many countries, negotiating the price of an item or service is the expected and normal behavior. The bargaining or negotiating process is a way for both parties involved in the transaction to demonstrate their intelligence and good sense. If you refuse to bargain or negotiate a price, not only may you end up paying much more money for a product or a service than you should, but you may also end up offending people. Do not assume that someone who

Figure 9.4 When shopping in some countries, you will be expected to negotiate a price.

wants to negotiate a price is "trying to take advantage of you," and realize that your refusal to negotiate a price may send the message that you think a person is untrustworthy or unintelligent.

Setting Deadlines

Sometimes people from monochronic cultures involved in conflict resolution or negotiation feel compelled to set a deadline for resolving a problem or completing a negotiation. However, if they are negotiating with people from polychronic cultures, setting a deadline has little effect on their negotiation partners, and it only serves to put pressure on the monochronic party that feels compelled to set a deadline.

Since polychronic people view time commitments as objectives that may or may not be reached, and since they change plans and schedules often and easily, time deadlines have little influence on them. If you are trying to resolve a conflict or complete a negotiation with a polychronic person, forget about time deadlines. If you have a monochronic time orientation, you will only get more nervous and agitated as the deadline nears, and you will feel compelled to make unnecessary concessions as your self-imposed deadline approaches.

Short-Term Dispute Settlement vs. Long-Term Relationship Development

People from modern western cultures often focus on the short-term settlement of disputes. They view conflicts as problems related to impersonal goals or objectives, and they even encourage those involved in a conflict to "separate the people from the problem." In other words, they want to focus on the incompatible goals or objectives of the parties involved, and they do not want to focus on or refer to the specific people involved in a dispute. If different goals or objectives can be reconciled, they think, then a conflict or problem is "solved."

However, for many cultures, when a conflict arises, you cannot "separate the people from the problem" because the relationship between the people involved in a conflict is more important than the different goals or objectives that they might have. The reason a conflict is dangerous is that it threatens to disrupt the harmonious relationship between people.

When engaged in intercultural conflict, people from western cultures need to understand that the people involved in a conflict, and the relationship between these people, is often of paramount concern to people from particular cultures. Instead of focusing primarily on the short-term settlement of a dispute, westerners need to also pay attention to the long-term relationship development that is or is not occurring during the conflict resolution or negotiation.

Saving Face

"Face" is a very important concept in some cultures. "Face" involves a person's standing or reputation in their community. To be dishonored or disrespected is to suffer a loss of face. To allow someone to maintain their honor or dignity is to help them save face. In many high-context cultures, people allow others to save face by avoiding direct verbal disagreements in public. They may not directly tell someone "no," but their nonverbal behaviors signal their disagreement.

Americans using a competitive conflict management approach are sometimes oblivious to the importance of "face" for some people and cultures. Competitive Americans may boast that they "won" a conflict without realizing that they have caused others to "lose face." When involved in a conflict with people who care about "face," make sure you do not publicly draw attention to "winners" and "losers" in a negotiation.

Figure 9.5 A Thai shows respect for the King of Thailand. To publicly criticize the King is a great error.

Outsider-Neutral Mediation vs. Insider-Partial Mediation

When seeking to mediate a dispute between two parties, Americans and people from modern western cultures often assume that the parties involved in a conflict would prefer neutral third-party outsiders who can mediate a dispute without bias. Since outside mediators have no connection to either party, they assume, the disputants will view the mediators as credible and trustworthy.

However, some people and cultures prefer to have mediators who are partially involved in a conflict. They view third-party outsiders with suspicion because these third parties have nothing at stake in the conflict. Instead of a "neutral" outsider, some people and cultures prefer a respected insider as mediator of a dispute. Since these insiders have something to gain or lose in the resolution of the conflict, they are looked upon as more credible and trustworthy than an outsider.

Different Types of Conflict

Although some cultures avoid conflict and even talking about conflict, we believe that you can become better at managing intercultural conflict when you have a well-developed vocabulary for talking about the different types of human conflict that arise. One important goal of the study of Intercultural Communication is to decrease international tensions, to promote international understanding, and to advance international peace initiatives. To decrease or resolve conflicts more effectively, we need to clearly distinguish the different types of conflict that exist:

Armed conflict: A political conflict in which armed combat involves the armed forces of at least one state or factions within a state seeking autonomy or independence.

Class conflict: Conflict between people of different social or economic classes.

Escalating conflict: Conflict that becomes more confrontational, destructive, or serious over time.

Ethnic conflict: Disputes between contending groups whose members identify themselves primarily on the basis of ethnicity.

Historical conflict: Conflict based on past events and memories of past events.

Internal/Intrapersonal conflict: A psychological struggle created by incompatible or opposing needs, drives, wishes, or demands.

International conflict: A conflict between two or more nation states.

Internecine or intragroup conflict: Conflict within a group or country.

Interpersonal conflict: Conflict between two individuals.

Pseudo conflict: A perceived incompatibility that does not actually exist.

Serial conflict: Conflict that occurs repeatedly.

Simple conflict: An actual incompatibility between two or more interdependent persons or groups.

Figure 9.6   The harm caused by armed conflict cannot be ignored.

© Oleg Zabielin, 2014. Used under license from Shutterstock, Inc.

Different Sources of Intercultural Conflict

In addition to 12 types of conflict, we will now present to you 12 sources of intercultural conflict. People from different cultures and co-cultures may come into conflict for many different reasons. Knowing these sources of conflict can help you to reduce or better understand intercultural conflicts that arise at the interpersonal, national, and international level.

1. **Conflicting goals or objectives.** Sometimes people do engage in simple conflict when they really do have incompatible goals or objectives. A conflict may arise between you and another person that has very little to do with your cultures of origin and a lot to do with the fact that you both want different things. The rest of this list reveals, however, that the causes of conflict sometimes go much deeper.

2. **Desire to separate or nationalize.** Many armed conflicts are not conflicts between nations. Many armed conflicts are within national borders, and they involve people groups that want to separate or nationalize.

3. **Different criteria for making evaluations or judgments.** Sometime people disagree about what is good or bad, beautiful or ugly, right or wrong. However, in order to make these sorts of evaluations, people need to use "judging criteria," and sometimes they do not even agree on the judging criteria that should be used to make an evaluation. Judges in an international beauty contest, for example, may disagree about what cultural standards of beauty should be used in the beauty contest.

4. **Different/divergent evaluations or judgments.** If people do agree on the judging criteria for making an evaluation, they may still disagree about whom or what meets these judging criteria. You and a friend may both agree that "spicy" food is best, but you may think that an ethnic dish is "way too spicy" while your friend might judge it "not spicy enough."

5. **Different perceptions or interpretations of behaviors and events.** Sometimes conflicts arise when people have very different perceptions or interpretations of the very same event. A crime and an arrest involving people from majority and minority racial or ethnic groups may be viewed very differently by people from these two groups.

6. **Different standards of appropriate and inappropriate behavior.** What may be perfectly acceptable behavior in one culture may be perfectly horrible behavior in another culture. Conflicts can arise, for example, when standards of modesty in one country are violated by someone whose cultural standard of modesty is quite different.

7. **Disputes over borders, land, or territory.** Many times territorial disputes occur at the international level. Often countries come into conflict when a border marker is disputed. For example, tensions are currently high between the nations of China and Japan because of disputes concerning which nation possesses certain island territories.

8. **Opposing values.** Although you may be involved in an intercultural conflict that on the surface seems to be about appropriate or inappropriate behavior, sometimes the underlying issue is a disagreement about values. Ironically, people and cultures sometimes disagree about how a conflict should be handled because they value conflict differently.

9. **Past/historical injury or harm.** Although we often look for a present disagreement in an intercultural or international conflict, the heart of the conflict may be rooted in a deep-seated cultural memory of past injury or harm.

10. **Power struggles.** Power struggles can occur at the interpersonal, national, and international level. Some disputes are really about who has the most power. The resolution of a conflict is sometimes used as an opportunity to display "who is in charge."

11. **Violations of specific social norms or rules.** Unlike general standards of behavior, social rules or norms are sometimes very specific. If you do not know the specific social norms of a culture that you visit, you may unintentionally give offense. Sometimes specific social norms are only in effect at very specific times and places, like the ritual of "earning beads" at a New Orleans Mardi Gras event.

12. **Worldview clashes and differences in basic beliefs.** Some of the most difficult conflicts to understand and resolve are worldview clashes. Sometimes people from cultures with different worldviews come into conflict at a very basic, fundamental level that is often unconscious and hard to discover.

Figure 9.7 Intercultural conflict may be rooted in a deep-seated memory of past injury or harm.

International Conflicts

Although in this textbook we are focusing on building interpersonal relationships with people from other cultures, we do need to provide you with some general knowledge about the major international conflicts that have occurred in recent world history. To emphasize the seriousness of intercultural conflict, we will first present to you a list of major genocides of the twentieth century. Genocide is the systematic killing and extermination of a people group because of their race, ethnicity, religion, or cultural practices. The major genocides listed in Figure 9.8 involved the extermination of close to one million people or more.

Major Genocides of the Twentieth Century

1. **Armenian genocide:** Often listed as the first genocide of the twentieth century. ½ to 1½ million Armenians were killed by the Ottoman's of Turkey.

2. **Holodomor genocide:** 2 to 8 million Ukrainians killed or starved by the Soviet regime.

3. **Holocaust:** 6 million Jews exterminated by Nazi Germany.

4. **Nigerian genocide:** 1 to 3 million Igbo killed by Hausa and Yoruba.

5. **Rwandan genocide:** ½ to 1 million Tutsi killed by Hutu.

Figure 9.8   Intercultural conflict can result in horrific consequences.

The major genocides of the twentieth century are a sobering reminder that intercultural conflict can result in very serious human harm. People with a cosmopolitan outlook who want to be "citizens of the world" need to continually remind others that genocide is a possible consequence of ethnic prejudice and discrimination.

Whereas genocide cannot be justified, wars are sometimes classified as "just" or "unjust." Regardless of your personal views about war and America's historical involvement in war, you need to be aware of the international conflicts that the United States of America has been involved in so that you can be sensitive to the attitudes people from other cultures and countries may have about America. Here is a list of wars that the United States of America has been involved since the Colonial era:

American Wars

Indian Wars	Colonial Era-1890	
Franco-American Naval War	1798–1800	US vs. France
Barbary Wars	1801–1805	US vs. Morocco, Algiers, Tunis and Tripoli
War of 1812	1812–1815	US vs. Great Britain
War of Texas Independence	1836	Texas vs. Mexico
Mexican-American War	1846–1848	US vs. Mexico
Civil War	1861–1865	Union vs. Confederacy
Spanish-American War	1898	US vs. Spain
Philippine-American War	1898–1902	US vs. Philippines
World War I	1917–1918	US joins forces with Britain, France, and Russia against Germany, Italy, and Austria-Hungary

(Continued)

World War II	1941–1945	US joins forces with Britain, France, and Russia against Germany, Italy, and Japan
Korean War	1950–1953	US and South Korea vs. North Korea
Vietnam War	1955–1975	US and South Vietnam vs. North Vietnam
Bay of Pigs Invasion	1961	US vs. Cuba
Grenada	1983	US intervention in Grenada
Panama	1989	US vs. Panama
Persian Gulf War	1990–1991	US vs. Iraq
Invasion of Afghanistan	2001	US vs. Taliban
Invasion of Iraq	2003	US vs. Iraq

When you interact with people from other cultures, you must understand that your interpersonal relationships with these people will be influenced by America's international relationships. Some people are from countries that are or have been militarily allied with the United States, and they may be favorably predisposed to you just because you are an American. Some people are from countries that are or have been in armed conflicts with the United States, and they may be negatively predisposed to you just because you are an American.

However, be aware that people's thoughts and attitudes about America are influenced by much more than America's military history. America is a major player in world political events. America is a major importer of goods and services from around the world. American popular culture is exported in large amounts to other countries. American tourists visit many of the countries of the world.

Figure 9.9   The United States has a history of sending soldiers to fight wars in distant lands and countries.

© Oleg Zabielin, 2014. Used under license from Shutterstock, Inc.

When people from other countries and cultures interact with you, their initial thoughts and feelings about you will be influenced by their general thoughts and feelings about America. If you want to communicate effectively with these people and build satisfying relationships with them, then you should be sensitive to these initial thoughts and feelings.

In addition, when interacting with people from other countries and cultures, in order to avoid conversational taboos and inappropriate comments and questions, you need a general understanding of international conflicts outside of the United States. What is your understanding of the international conflicts and tensions between the following countries?

International Tensions and Conflicts
ARAB–ISRAELI
BRITAIN–IRELAND
CHINA–JAPAN
CHINA–TAIWAN
CHINA–TIBET
INDIA–PAKISTAN
NORTH KOREA–SOUTH KOREA
NORTH VIETNAM–SOUTH VIETNAM
SUDAN–SOUTH SUDAN
UNITED KINGDOM–ARGENTINA

Figure 9.10 Knowing about international conflicts can help you avoid inappropriate comments and questions.

The American Approach to Conflict Management (Five Conflict Management Strategies)

Now that we have briefly gotten you to think about international conflicts and how they might affect your interpersonal relationships with people from other countries and cultures, we will focus in this section of the chapter on the American approach to conflict management.

In the 1970s, Kenneth Thomas and Ralph Kilman identified five main conflict management strategies.

According to Thomas and Kilman, the five main strategies people use to manage conflict are 1) avoiding, 2) accommodating, 3) compromising, 4) competing, and 5) collaborating. Thomas and Kilman's categories have proven to be a very fruitful way for Americans to think about conflict and conflict management. The following chart is based upon these five categories.

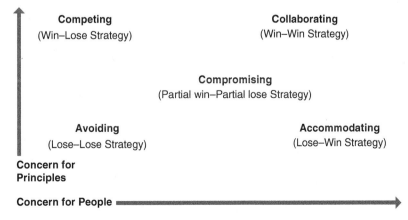

Five Conflict Management Strategies

| Competing (Win–Lose Strategy) | Collaborating (Win–Win Strategy) |

Compromising (Partial win–Partial lose Strategy)

Avoiding (Lose–Lose Strategy)   Accommodating (Lose–Win Strategy)

Concern for Principles

Concern for People

The chart of five conflict management strategies is a powerful tool for developing different responses to different conflict situations. If you tend to have one primary response to conflict situations, this chart can help you expand your repertoire of conflict management techniques.

While there is widespread agreement about how to label the different quadrants of the conflict management strategies chart, there are different approaches for labeling the x and y axes. We prefer to label the x or horizontal axis "Concern for Relationships" and the y or vertical axis "Concern for Principles."

We believe that one of the most fruitful ways of dealing with conflict is learning to balance your concern for the principles involved in a conflict with your concern for the relationships that you have with the people involved in the conflict. If you thoughtfully analyze and evaluate both the principles and relationships involved in, and impacted by, a conflict, then you will be able to choose the appropriate conflict management strategy. We will describe each conflict management strategy in turn and, paying attention to the x axis and y axis of the chart, we will point out when this strategy is most appropriate.

Avoiding Strategy: The "avoiding" quadrant is located in the bottom left corner of the conflict management chart. People who use the avoiding strategy disengage from discussion when a conflict arises, or they attempt to change the topic under discussion. When pressed to address a conflict situation, they may physically disengage by leaving the room or by engaging in another activity.

The avoiding strategy can also be labeled the "Lose–Lose" strategy: since the conflict is completely avoided, the different goals, opinions, or desires of the parties involved are never adequately addressed, so both parties "lose." People who constantly use the avoiding strategy are sometimes labeled "ostriches" because when conflicts arise they seem to stick their heads in the sand and refuse to address the concerns of others.

However, the conflict management strategies chart reveals a situation when the avoiding strategy is appropriate. When the principles involved in a conflict are not that important, and when you do not need to maintain a relationship with the person(s) involved in the conflict, then avoiding the conflict may be the best strategy.

Figure 9.11   Americans often think of a conflict avoider as someone with their "head in the sand."

Accommodating Strategy: "The accommodating" quadrant is located in the bottom right corner of the conflict management chart. People using the accommodating strategy "give in" and let the other parties involved in a conflict have their way. They give up their own wishes or desires in order to accommodate the wishes or desires of others.

The accommodating strategy can also be labeled the "Lose–Win" strategy. If you accommodate the other parties in a conflict and give up your wishes and desires, you "lose" and they "win." People who constantly use the accommodating strategy are sometimes labeled "doormats" because they always seem to let other people walk all over them. Since they always give in, excessive accommodators are not difficult to work with, but they may become unhappy people who think that others are constantly taking advantage of them.

However, the conflict management strategies chart helps us understand when the accommodating strategy may be a good response to a conflict. When the principles in a conflict are not that important but the relationships with the other parties involved in a conflict are important, then accommodating may be the best way to handle the conflict.

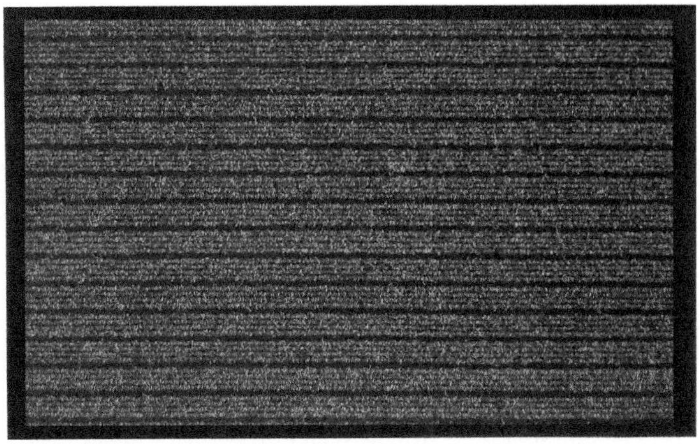

Competing Strategy: The "competing" quadrant is located in the top left corner of the conflict management strategies chart. People using the competing strategy strongly advocate for their goals or opinions. They seek to gain the compliance of others involved in a conflict so that their own opinions prevail and their own goals are reached.

Figure 9.12 Americans often think of accommodators as "doormats" that get walked all over.

The competing strategy can also be labeled the "Win–Lose" strategy. If you get others to comply with your wishes or desires, then you "win" and they "lose." People who constantly use the competing strategy view every conflict as a competition that they must win. Excessively competitive people who insist that others always bend to their will may "win" most arguments, but they often lose out on meaningful relationships. Most people get tired of constantly giving in to them, so super-competitors often find themselves with few friends.

However, the conflict management strategies chart indicates that the competing strategy is sometimes warranted. When you do not need to maintain long-term relationships with the people involved in a conflict and you think that they are asking you to violate an important principle, then you should "stick to your guns" and battle for what you believe is right.

Figure 9.13 Americans sometimes think that competitive conflict is warranted.

Compromising Strategy: The "compromising" quadrant is in the center of the conflict management strategies chart. People using the compromising strategy give up a bit of what they actually desire, and they expect the other parties involved in a conflict situation to do likewise. All parties in the conflict are expected to yield a bit so that everyone gets at least some of what they desire.

Many people think that the compromising strategy is the best strategy for conflict management because no one loses and everyone wins, but the compromising strategy is most accurately labeled the "Partial Win–Partial Lose" strategy because although there are no clear losers in a compromise, there are also no clear winners. No one involved in the compromise gets what they actually desired. When your concern for the principles and people involved in a conflict are moderate, the compromising strategy may be appropriate. However, there is one final conflict management strategy that can lead to a clear "Win–Win" result.

Collaborating Strategy: The "collaborating" quadrant is in the top right corner of the conflict management strategies chart. People using the collaborating strategy seek to negotiate a resolution to a conflict that provides both parties what they want. They ask the other people involved in a conflict to join them as partners seeking a mutually beneficial solution to a problem.

The collaborating strategy can also be labeled the "Win–Win" strategy. Since all the parties involved in a conflict work together to figure out how everyone can have their most important interests met, no one "loses" and everyone "wins." This "Win–Win" negotiation strategy is also called "interest-based bargaining." Rather than defending "positions" in a conflict, people share their interests and concerns. Instead of viewing the other parties involved in a conflict as opponents who will attack your bargaining position, you view them as collaborators who can help you protect your interests and address your concerns.

Thomas and Kilman's five conflict management strategies (avoiding, accommodating, competing, cooperating, and collaborating) are now widely recognized and endorsed by American negotiation trainers and practitioners. Americans especially like the idea of "win/win" collaborative strategy that directly addresses conflict while ensuring that all parties in a conflict benefit from the negotiation that occurs.

Figure 9.14   For Americans, compromise is a "partial win/partial lose" because no one gets exactly what they want.

Figure 9.15   Americans think that directly addressing conflict can lead to a "win/win" situation.

Other Approaches to Conflict Management

The American approach to conflict management (embodied in Thomas and Kilman's five conflict management strategies) has one glaring weakness: it does not take into account the importance that conflict avoidance has for other cultures. People in cultures that teach it is in everyone's best interest to avoid conflict must be perplexed when they see the avoiding strategy labeled the "lose/lose" strategy. In the American model of conflict management, avoiders are often labeled "ostriches" and accommodators are labeled "doormats." These labels are certainly not flattering to people who prefer to accommodate others during a conflict or who prefer to avoid conflict altogether.

In the early 2000s, Mitchell R. Hammer developed an intercultural "conflict management styles" chart that recognizes that some people and cultures do not like to address conflict directly. The four conflict management styles he identifies and describes are determined by two variables: first, whether a person prefers to address a conflict directly or indirectly; second, whether a person prefers to address a conflict with emotional restraint or with emotional expressiveness. Here is a brief description of each conflict management style:

Discussion Style: People who use the discussion style prefer to address conflict directly, but they avoid the open display of emotion. They want to "talk things out" in a "reasonable" manner. The discussion style of conflict management is the dominant style in England and the United States. Many British and American people value frank, direct discourse and cool, calm deliberation. They like to address problems head-on, but they may get uncomfortable if a conversation gets heated or emotionally charged.

Engagement Style: People who use the engagement style want to address conflict directly, but they also expect the people involved in a conflict to become emotionally engaged. A strong display of emotion, they believe, demonstrates that a person cares about the matter at hand. The engagement style of conflict management is the dominant style in Greece, Italy, and many Latin American countries. (It is also the dominant style of African-Americans in the United States.) Many Greeks, Italians, and Latin Americans value direct discourse that is animated and punctuated by strong emotional displays. They are willing to "get in your face" in order to make their point, and they expect you to be just as passionate when you express your viewpoint or position.

Accommodation Style: People who use the accommodation style do not like to address conflict directly, nor do they like strong displays of emotion. They prefer to address conflict indirectly in order to "save face," and they strive to maintain a calm, "inscrutable" demeanor that reveals little of their inward state, especially if they are angry or upset. The avoidance style of conflict management is the dominant style in Japan and many Southeast Asian countries. Many Japanese and Southeast Asians value verbal discourse that appears harmonious, and they expect people to pay attention to subtle nonverbal signals that indicate disagreement and dissatisfaction. They often find it very difficult to express an opinion that contradicts the opinions of others in their group, and they also find it very difficult to display an emotion that they think may threaten the cohesiveness of their group.

Dynamic Style: People who use the dynamic style avoid the direct discussion of conflict, but they expect people to express strong emotions. They want to signal sincerity and commitment to their principles through the strong display of emotions, but their interest in strong relationships also causes them to avoid conflicts that may threaten these relationships. The dynamic style of conflict is the dominant style in Saudi Arabia and many other Arab countries. Many Saudis and other Arabs value animated, emotional verbal discourse and nonverbal displays, but they avoid "spelling out" the precise issues or concerns that they think may destabilize their political or social relationships. Instead, they often work through third-party intermediaries.

	Preference for Emotional Restraint	Preference for Emotional Expressiveness
Preference for Directness	**Discussion Style** (Country: US)	**Engagement Style** (Country: Italy)
Preference for Indirectness	**Accommodation Style** (Country: Japan)	**Dynamic Style** (Country: Saudi Arabia)

Figure 9.16   Hammer's four conflict management styles.

Knowing about these four conflict management styles can make you a much more effective intercultural communicator, especially when conflict arises in an intercultural setting. Here are some tips for interacting with people using your knowledge of the four different conflict management styles:

- Identify the conflict management styles preferred by the people with whom you interact so you can better understand their attitudes and behaviors when a conflict arises.
- Do not stereotype people and automatically assume that they use the same conflict management style that is dominant in their national culture. There will always be deviations from a dominant style, so all four conflict management styles can be found in people from a particular country or ethnic group. You need to determine whether the individuals you interact with deviate from or conform to the dominant conflict management style of their home country.
- Recognize that all four conflict management styles are valid. One of these styles is not "right" while the other styles are "wrong." Conflict management styles, like clothing styles, are a matter of preference.
- Identify the conflict management style you prefer, and share this preference with the people with whom you interact. They will have a better understanding of where you are coming from when a conflict arises.
- Be especially sensitive to people who have a conflict management style most opposed to yours (in the quadrant of the conflict management styles chart that is diagonal to your quadrant). When people with opposing conflict management styles interact, there is greater potential for misunderstanding and confusion.
- Identify the negative thoughts and assumptions you tend to think and make when dealing with someone who has a different conflict management style. Recalibrate your thinking and recognize the strengths and benefits of their style.
- Stretch yourself and develop the ability to use all four conflict management styles. Just as you can use different conflict management strategies in different situations, you can also use these different conflict management styles for different interactions.

Figure 9.17   People can learn to express emotions appropriately.

© bikeriderlondon, 2014. Used under license from Shutterstock, Inc.

To use all four conflict management styles effectively, Americans who prefer the emotionally retrained discussion style must become adept at emotional expression. Conflict can generate strong emotions in people, emotions like frustration, anger, fear, and mistrust. Some people avoid conflict because they do not want to experience such emotions, nor do they want to "make" other people angry or upset.

However, emotional communication is one of the deepest levels of communication that exists. When strong emotions are expressed and acknowledged appropriately, this emotional communication is like glue—it helps to form strong relational bonds. Here are some tips for effective emotional communication during conflict situations:

- When very strong emotions are interfering with your ability to express yourself or listen to others, take a break. You can explain that you need some time to compose yourself and to process your strong emotions.

- Affirm your respect for, and relational commitment to, a person who communicates or displays strong emotion, especially if they prefer the discussion style or accommodation style of conflict management. They are likely to experience shame and regret when getting emotional. Assure them that they have done nothing wrong.
- Do not apologize for getting emotional or displaying strong emotions. An apology implies that you have done something wrong, and that others are doing something wrong, by displaying strong emotions.
- When dealing with people who are uncomfortable with strong emotional expression, "dial it down" and moderate your enthusiasm, especially if you prefer the dynamic style or engagement style of conflict management.
- "Own" your emotions. Take responsibility for them, and expect others to do so likewise. Do not blame others for your emotions. Do not use your strong emotions as a form of "emotional black-mail." Learn to say, "I am angry," and not, "You make me so angry." You have control over your thoughts and feelings. You can choose how you will perceive and respond to the behaviors of others—empower yourself and others to be in charge of their emotions.
- Explore the thoughts and perceptions that are creating your strong emotions. Emotions are outward signs of inward perceptions and thoughts. If others experience or express strong emotions, encourage them to examine and share why they are angry, or fearful, or upset.
- Determine if your strong emotions are justified and appropriate by identifying the perceptions and thoughts that are generating these emotions. If your perceptions and thoughts are accurate and true, then your strong emotions may be perfectly appropriate.
- Allow others to be emotional and to express their strong emotions appropriately. When you accept and respect other people's ability to express and communicate emotion, and when you reciprocate and share your feelings with others, you are forging deeper relationships with others and strengthening the cohesiveness of your relationships.
- Do not allow yourself or others to "express" strong emotions inappropriately. Strong emotions are no excuse for demeaning or abusing other people. Name calling, personal attacks, and other "dirty tricks" should not be condoned or tolerated just become someone is angry or upset.

Summary

You now know that there are two very different views of conflict that exist in the world: the positive view of conflict held by some cultures causes some people to promote and embrace conflict, whereas the negative view of conflict held by some cultures causes many other people to avoid any kind of conflict.

You have deepened your understanding of conflict by learning about a dozen types of conflict and a dozen different sources of intercultural conflict. You have also learned a bit about international conflicts related to the United States and a few other countries.

You have increased your ability to deal with different conflicts and different conflict situations by learning about five conflict management strategies (avoiding, accommodating, competing, cooperating, and collaborating) and four conflict management styles (Discussion Style, Engagement Style, Accommodation Style, and Dynamic Style). You have also learned a bit about expressing emotions effectively during conflict situations.

Glossary

Accommodating   One of the five conflict management strategies. A person using the accommodating strategy gives in and allows the other person to have their way.

Accommodation style   One of four conflict management styles. People using the accommodation style prefer indirect and emotionally restrained discussion of conflict.

Armed conflict   A political conflict in which armed combat involves the armed forces of at least one state or factions within a state seeking autonomy or independence.

Avoiding   One of the five conflict management strategies. A person using the avoiding strategy does not directly engage in a conflict.

Competing   One of the five conflict management strategies. A person using the competing strategy gains their goal or objective at the expense of the other party involved.

Collaborating   One of the five conflict management strategies. People using the collaborating strategy work together to create a "win/win" situation for both parties.

Conflict   A perceived incompatibility between two or more interdependent parties.

Class conflict   Conflict between people of different social or economic classes.

Discussion style   One of the four conflict management styles. People using the discussion style prefer direct and emotionally restrained discussion of conflict.

Dynamic style   One of the four conflict management styles. People using the dynamic style prefer indirect and emotionally expressive discussion of conflict.

Engagement style   One of the four conflict management styles. People using the engagement style prefer direct and emotionally expressive discussion of conflict.

Escalating conflict   Conflict which becomes more confrontational, destructive, or serious over time.

Ethnic conflict   Disputes between contending groups whose members identify themselves primarily on the basis of ethnicity.

Face   A person's standing or reputation in a community or society.

Genocide   The systematic killing and extermination of a people group because of their race, ethnicity, religion, or cultural practices.

Historical conflict   Conflict based on past events and memories of past events.

Internal/Intrapersonal conflict   A psychological struggle created by incompatible or opposing needs, drives, wishes, or demands.

International conflict   A conflict between two or more nation states.

Internecine or intragroup conflict   Conflict within a group or country.

Interpersonal conflict   Conflict between two individuals.

Pseudo conflict   A perceived incompatibility that does not actually exist.

Serial conflict   Conflict that occurs repeatedly.

Simple conflict   An actual incompatibility between two or more interdependent persons or groups.

Chapter 10

Intercultural Communication Across Contexts

Bryan Hirayama

"Travel brings power and love back into life."
—Rumi

"Live as if you were to die tomorrow. Learn as if you were to live forever."
—Mahatma Gandhi

Chapter Learning Objectives

1. Identify and distinguish between travel and different types of tourism.
2. Understand what it takes to be a good guest in foreign countries and a good host to travelers and tourists.
3. Understand the educational systems within the United States from primary school to postsecondary schools and higher education.
4. List and describe the different healthcare systems around the world.

© Anna Vaczi, 2014. Used under license from Shutterstock, Inc.

© Stuart Jenner, 2014. Used under license from Shutterstock, Inc.

© auremar, 2014. Used under license from Shutterstock, Inc.

© intellistudies, 2014. Used under license from Shutterstock, Inc.

My home growing up was always a site for unexpected guests. From friends and family to my mother bringing home financially struggling college colleagues, our home has always been a place for people to crash. This practice turned into tradition and a part of the way our family did business. However, when Naoyuki from Japan arrived, our first of many foreign exchange students, our lives were forever changed. Since opening this revolving door, a handful of international students, and their friends in many cases have made their way into my mother's home. These relationships have impacted everyone around me from my family and friends to the local community. I often reminisce with others about our past guests and how we miss certain behaviors now understood as cultural misunderstandings. It is these experiences with people that piqued my interest in intercultural communication and relationships and has led me to adopt a lifestyle of taking opportunities to interact with people who from all walks of life. Some of the jobs I held in college, the people I interacted with, and places I often found myself all offered a new insight into this very diverse and fascinating world we are a part of. I am so thankful to everyone who has crossed my path intentionally or unintentionally and has helped to deepen my understanding of people and cultures. It is because of the friends I have made throughout my life like Kirk and Chou helping me to understand Hmong culture within the United States or Simon and Jordan helping me to develop a deeper appreciate for rugby that writing this chapter about travel, health, and education such a joy. In addition to these experiences with travelers, international students, and friends, it is through the opportunities created through my education, that this chapter was inspired.

After graduate school and with my Master's Degree in hand, I accepted a visiting professorship position in Japan at a small private university. This was an important personal pilgrimage for me as a Japanese-American who had little experience with Japanese traditions and customs. It was in Japan that I discovered a great deal about myself, about the world and others traveling internationally, and just how much my curiosity for culture and people had been shaped by my childhood experiences of hosting international students and people. While in Japan, I was afforded many opportunities that helped me understand culture and people in ways I would have never imagined. Opportunities that I would not have been presented with without my travels. I not only taught at the University while in Japan but filled a long-term substituting position at a middle school and high school, visited countless but vividly memorable elementary schools, and gave numerous talks to a variety of audiences about American culture and communication. However, one of the most important relationships I was able to build was a relationship with a pupil that I taught as a private tutor. Our bond grew well beyond student and teacher and I regard Mr. Arisawa and his family as my second Japanese family. For a year-and-a-half of my stay in Japan I enjoyed a home-cooked meal every week with the Arisawa family and bonded with their only son at the time, visited with their extended family as they came into town, sang karaoke, and countless other moments where I was brought into the fold of the family. I was even lucky enough to be invited to the hospital for the birth of his second child, what an honor. Also, while in Japan, I opened up my home to others traveling. Through a popular social networking website for travelers I registered my home as a place to stop and I hosted people from countries such as France, Slovenia, Ukraine, Korea, and of course other Americans passing through. Now back in the United States it is my experiences connecting with people from all walks of life as a child in unique circumstances to more strategic moments of intercultural interaction through travel that my wonderment and passion to experience the world and learn from people grows. As my travels take me into other countries and my travel plans each year become more extensive, and expensive, I look back with the fondest of memories and look forward with great hope for new adventures.

Introduction

It is likely through the adventures of your personal and professional lives that travel, meeting people from different places including those from abroad, and having to communicate effectively with them will become a cornerstone of your interactions and business. From visiting hallmark locations, like the Bay Bridge in San Francisco, or just a random encounter while Outlet Mall shopping, the chances of having to interact with people from cultures outside of your own is highly probable. Whether this is negotiating who gets the last few seats on a tour bus to talking about local treasures and attractions, training in intercultural communication could change these potentially anxiety-ridden and awkward moments into opportunities to connect with others.

Training in intercultural communication does not have to be expensive workshops where leading researchers in a specific area of intercultural communication discuss skills and behaviors it takes to be effective within different cultural contexts. Those are great and useful beyond belief. If given the opportunity to attend a good training through school or work, by all means jump on that opportunity. But the access and feasibility of attending these types of trainings are sometimes out of reach for the financially strapped college student or developing professional. Training can simply be receiving reliable information about people and their cultures from a variety of sources, including your college courses, and making a conscious effort to use this awareness to make informed decisions when communicating with others. Communicators must also be reflective and dedicated to revising their current working model for understanding people to be effective during these planned or chance encounters. It is about disciplining the mind and body, in many ways, to both get a point across but to do so in a way that makes sense to those we share our ideas with, given that person's background and the situation we find ourselves communicating in. The path to being a competent communicator is a life commitment and it is through the skills learned through courses like this one and the information shared in this textbook that students can continue to work toward being ethnorelative versus ethnocentric in their communication behaviors.

Mere training, through workshops or college courses, is not enough to become a competent communicator or avoid ethnocentric communication behaviors. In my opinion, the label of competent communicator is one that is given when people perish and those left behind remember and reflect on the way the deceased communicated throughout their life. Communication competency in this respect is not a static place one achieves through specific acts of communication but rather it is a commitment one makes to constantly being conscious of their communication, communicate in the best way possible given the desired goal and the situation, and staying dedicated to always reflecting and revising communication behaviors when they prove ineffective or out-of-date. In this light, communication competency is a constant struggle and "a process of becoming" by working toward perfection but with a knowledge of the reality that people inevitably always fall short and make mistakes. Even the most educated and well-trained communication scholars and practitioners slip up and has to go back to the drawing board and think about how to handle people and situations differently in the future.

Communication competency is often defined by two characteristics: appropriateness and effectiveness. Inherent within each of these characteristics is that individuals will already have a wealth of knowledge about people and cultures to be both appropriate and effective. However, without some type of exposure to individuals and their cultures, being appropriate and effective would potentially be a very difficult goal to accomplish. It is for this reason that courses like Intercultural Communication and textbooks such as these are so important for people with limited knowledge about diversity among and between people and cultures. Figure 10.1 identifies some of the commitments people interested in becoming competent communicators must adopt to join this ongoing process.

Some of the skills involved with being a competent communicator takes a commitment to:

1. Being aware of the similarities and differences among and between people and cultures.

2. Reflecting on one's own behaviors and recognizing how bias and prejudice impacts communication with others

3. Observing and revising their current working models of what individual cultures look like given their experiences within and outside of those cultures.

4. Staying dedicated to these commitments in an effort to consistently communicate effectively within and between cultures.

5. Take responsibility for one's own behavior. Individuals are the only ones in control of themselves and if this is not the case, further inspection is necessary.

Figure 10.1 Commitments of a competent communicator.

It has been our intention throughout this textbook to help you develop many of the communication competencies necessary to be both appropriate and effective in intercultural communication. Individuals who are in-tune with their metacognition, also known as their awareness and understanding of the way they think, and their intrapersonal communication, how they communicate with themselves, would seemingly be a lot more prepared to make more informed decisions regarding how to communicate competently. The ideas shared in this text are hopefully helping you to build a working knowledge and understanding of what intercultural communication is so when you are put in situations, both by happenstance and by choice, you will have a repository of both theoretical knowledge as well as a more sharpened understanding of your previous experiences to successfully navigate your future interactions. This chapter will cover a variety of areas in regard to travel, education, and health, and hopes to continue to grow your working models of people and cultures, so you have the tools necessary to be successful both in your interpersonal and professional relationships.

In this chapter, we will first explore the idea and practice of travel and a number of the considerations and opportunities that people should be aware of when it comes to communicating with others. Second, we will have a deeper look into the educational system in the United States and discuss cultural difference within and outside the United States regarding education. Lastly, we will explore the different approaches to healthcare, the different health systems around the world, and the impact religion potentially has on medical treatment. It is through this material that your literacy about these three areas should further help prepare you to make more informed decisions regarding communication. It is through a richer understanding of travel, how the US education and health system works, and understanding the difference concerning the way other countries function that communicators cannot only discuss these topics with others but handle themselves more effectively in conversation given what they know.

Travel and Tourism

There is something very magical about travel. Traveling to new and foreign places gives people the opportunity to see what they are made of in a number of ways. A whole host of skill sets are tested when people travel including navigating skills, time management skills, money management, and of course communication skills to mention a few. For people who are traveling with others, additional skills are put into practice, which can involve conflict management, negotiating travel plans and sightseeing preferences, and testing one's patience with others. Traveling

Once the travel bug has bitten you, your passport will never be the same.

can also be the defining moment in a person's life when they are confronted with themselves, their preferences, bias, and their understanding of who they are and who they want to be. International travel especially creates these and many other opportunities that can shift an individual's life trajectory in both positive and maybe not so positive ways.

> **Impact Story:** One of the most famous examples of how travel impacted an individual and shaped the course of their life is that of Ernesto R. Guevara de la Serna or as most people around the world know him as Che Guevara. According to biography.com, while on a break from medical school, Che, along with a close friend, traveled Latin America. Through his travel, Che was exposed to suffering and poverty, which sparked a change in the way he saw the world and government and influenced him to get involved. Despite how people feel about Che and his actions in Cuba as revolutionary, it was through his travel that he was able to discover something about the world and something about himself that would define him as a person, a man, and a revolutionist. His story has been showcased in countless books and documentaries and inspired the 2004 dramatization in the movie "Motorcycle Diaries (Nozik et al., 2014)."

Initially, personal discovery and transformation are not the drive behind most travel. It is the lure of famous places, different cultures and practices, and the artifacts such as food, tapestry, and art that inspire people to get their passports and flight itineraries. Monumental museums like Le Louvre in Paris, France, and the Acropolis Museum in Athens, Greece, are but a few of the many attractions that may inspire travelers.

What motivates people to travel and visit new places? There are a myriad of reasons that can provoke people to get their passports and jet set to new and exciting places. For some it is the lust for adventure and a taste for the extreme that fuels their travels while for others it can be a great deal more practical in seeking medical attention and care. Travel and tourism are not mutually exclusive in that they can overlap and coexist but one does not have to partake in tourism to travel but one has to travel to participate in tourism. **Travel** is simply the act of going places by some means of transportation whether that is by walking or riding or by quicker methods such as by boat or by air. Travelers in this respect are people who go places. **Tourism** is traveling for a specific type of enjoyment and pleasure often times to see sites that have historical, political, social, religious, or esthetic significance. In essence, someone could travel to a very famous tourist area and not participate in touristy events or see renowned places others have solely traveled there for. Tourists, however, seek out these wonders and it is often the primary purpose of their trip. For example, the act of traveling to India simply means getting there by some mode of transportation while participating in Holi, also known as the Hindu festival of Colors, is an act of tourism.

Top Museums to Visit Around the World
1. Smithsonian Institution in Washington, DC (USA)
2. Le Louvre in Paris (France)
3. The Acropolis Museum in Athens (Greece)
4. State Hermitage in St. Petersburg (Russia)
5. The British Museum in London (England)
6. The Prado in Madrid (Spain)
7. The Metropolitan Museum of Art in New York City (USA)
8. The Vatican Museums in Vatican City (Italy)
9. The Uffizi Gallery in Florence (Italy)
10. Rijksmuseum in Amsterdam (Netherlands)

Figure 10.2   Popular Attractions from Around the World List adapted from: National Geographic's: The 10 Best of Everything. 3rd Edition: An Ultimate Guide for Travelers.

Figure 10.3   Children at a Holi festival in India.

Whereas tourism in general embodies stereotypical behaviors of visiting sites and purchasing local products and services, there are other more specified types of tourism. **Ecological tourism**, also referred to as eco-tourism, is one such reason that involves traveling for enjoyment and pleasure based on environmental attractions. One of these environmental attractions one might seek could be a World Heritage Site. According to the United Nations Educational, Scientific, and Cultural Organization, also known as UNESCO, there are approximately 981 prosperities from around the world that qualify as National Heritage Sites (UNESCO, 2014). Sites such as the Great Barrier Reef in Australia, the Classical Gardens of Suzhou in China, and Yosemite in California are but a few of these locations recognized by UNESCO.

Also, in more recent years, ecotourism has also come to represent ecologically responsible travel where travelers are conscious of the ecological footprint they leave behind. Websites addressing what it means to travel responsibly so travelers can learn about how to minimize their ecological footprint have gained popularity and are a valued resource for those seeking this type of travel. Lonely Planet's website, a popular publication and website for travelers, includes information about the importance and impact of traveling responsibly (Wheeler & Wheeler, 2014). Eco-tourists are mindful of their communication, especially nonverbally, with the sites they visit and the intentional and unintentional messages they send about what travel should and can look like. The goal of leaving a site the way they found it and removing any debris or artifacts left behind might also be ways travelers communicate with the site and the native people as they act to preserve these revered environments. Remember that everything a person can have meaning to others. In this sense, everything is communication. Eco-tourists have a heightened sense of this potential impact and are conscious of what they do and how they do it while traveling.

Another popular form of tourism is medical tourism. This type of tourism has boomed over the last decade. **Medical tourism** involves traveling to countries where the cost

Figure 10.4   Last light at Cathedral Lake in Yosemite National Park, California.

and accessibility of certain medical procedures are more feasible than in one's country of residence or origin. According to the Center for Disease Control and Prevention website (2014), it is estimated that up to 750,000 Americans travel abroad for care annually. Countless websites are now dedicated to advertising medical tourism and the services offered at hospitals and clinics around the world. Special handbooks including *"Patients Beyond Borders Dubai Healthcare City Edition"* offer resources for medical travel within a specific area (Woodman, 2012). This particular edition is just one of nearly 10 such guides published in the name of Patients Beyond Borders. Other manuals including a *"Complete Idiot's Guide: Medical Tourism"* offer comprehensive principles and practices to safe and responsible medical tourism. With speculative savings of 90% of the medical costs of the United States, it is no wonder people and patients alike are seeking cosmetic and plastic surgery and augmentation, oncology treatment, experimental treatment with stem-cell research, cardiology, and a whole host of other specialized areas abroad.

Common to the American milieu is a story of the elderly packing onto buses and going across the Canadian border to purchase prescription drugs for a fraction of the price they could purchase them in the United States. This billion-dollar industry of medical tourism does much more than sell grandma and grandpa their blood thinners. Every service imaginable to patients is available abroad and with a price tag that often justifies a passport and an extended vacation. Whether it is traveling to enjoy the sights and sounds of unique ecosystems or seeking out medical services or procedures, travelers and tourist alike will share many similar intercultural experiences as they interactive with the local peoples.

Whether tourism or travel, people will encounter the host culture of that country or area they visit. A **host culture** is the dominant culture within a society a person visits. The dominant culture or host culture is shaping the practices and behaviors regarding communication (language and behavior), their history, dominant religions, gender roles, and other cultural norms. In the best of circumstances, host cultures are just as interested in visitors as the travelers are of the local people and customs. In less than desirable circumstances, the host culture can be reluctant to foreign people or outright hostile toward an outsider's presence.

In most cases, host cultures are welcoming and open to foreign visitors. It many instances visitors translate into business and revenues and are often welcomed especially in impoverished and developing countries. However, travelers might encounter people or cultures that have **xenophobia,** otherwise known as extreme fear or hatred of strangers or foreigners. People in the American military services may understand this sentiment too well with the recent military occupations in foreign countries. Historically, residents on the island of Okinawa have stood in opposition to the American Military instillation on the island. In other cases over the past decade, Americans traveling and living abroad have found themselves in tumultuous times as inner-country conflicts have erupted. The social and civil unrest in places like Egypt, Benghazi, and Syria to name a few can illustrate how conflicts within host cultures can cause serious safety concerns for those visiting and living outside of their home country. Also, the 2014 Winter Olympics in Sochi revealed unthinkable safety concerns for LGBT Olympic athletes and what some might believe are the antiquated policies and practices of a country's view and treatment of a group of people. Russia as the host culture was neither very welcoming nor open for travelers to be themselves without the risk of being in harm. In moments such as these, travelers must be very cautious not only about how they communicate with local people but how they communicate with each other. A lesbian or gay couple showing affection toward each other in places that oppose this type of behavior could have unthinkable consequences for travelers. Competent communicators, gay or straight, must consider this within these types of dangerous cultural contexts.

Now that we have explored different types of tourism, let us turn our attention to travel. The wonderful world of travel has changed a great deal since the backpacking trips after college of Baby Boomers and the Generation X. Although many of the adventures talked about by retired hippies and beatniks still exist, travel has become much more cost efficient and connected through the worldwide web. Thrill-seekers

Five Tips to Responsible Travel and Tourism

1. Be informed—Do the appropriate and necessary research about places of travel. Not only look to travel books and websites, also find blogs, personal narratives, or talk to people who have traveled and/or traveled to your desired destination.

2. Be aware—When traveling, people should be aware of the dangers that are typical of the area they are traveling to. If travelers have traditionally been treated unfairly when visiting this area or region, a traveler should be aware of these potential dangers and plan accordingly.

3. Be prepared—It is not just the motto of the Boy Scouts of America but it is also good advice for travelers. By being prepared in the planning and traveling, travelers are likely to have more fruitful, rich, and memorable experiences without the stress of being without something or being ill prepared. No traveler can account for the unexpected circumstances that arise during travel but when travelers have done their research, are aware of what they need to success navigate a foreign place, and have planned accordingly they are in much better shape to deal with the joys of travel.

4. Be open—When traveling to new places, travelers must be open to the experiences they have planned and the ones that will present themselves naturally during their trip. There will likely be things people encounter during their travel that will challenge their moral, ethical, and value code back home. Without jumping to conclusions or putting oneself in a sticky situation, travelers should be open to the things they are likely to encounter during their adventures.

5. Be responsible—People must take responsibility for themselves and the people they travel with. Travelers should be conscious of the rules, legal and social rules, of the places being visited and try to respect them at all cost without sacrificing their own moral, ethical, value, and religious codes. Much like the etiquette for camping, travelers should leave the places they visit better than the way they found them or leave as if they were never there. The underlying message is that travelers should take ownership in the way they behave and act. The primary ways travelers demonstrate being responsible is by communicating effectively with respect to the culture and people they visit.

Figure 10.5   Tips to responsible travel.

and culture junkies who seek to experience authenticity when traveling often search to the edges of the world to find these experiences. **Authenticity** is a mindset to travel to have experiences within a host culture that are true to the lives of the people who live within that culture. Homestay and study abroad programs are but a few of the ways to gain access to these types of authentic experiences within a host culture, something we will explore later in this chapter.

Because of technology and the formal and informal networks available to travelers via websites and applications, connectivity is changing the way that people travel. From searching for the most competitive prices for flights and hotels to making contact with people from all over the world to set up more intimate travel arrangements, technology is widening our worlds and creating new pathways. Rollenhagen (2013) in an article entitled "8 Dynamic Social Networks to Meet People Abroad" points to the variety of resources travelers have to connect with others, make their trips more meaningful and personal, and how travelers can learn from others while planning their trips to make the most of their stay. Websites like couchsurfing.com, travbuddy.com, and bewelcome.org, just to name a few, are interactive and inviting websites that are taking travel and transforming this experience for both travelers and the people who host and/or help them. Hosting in this context refers to people opening up their lives and sometimes their homes to people traveling. Hosting can be as casual as meeting a traveler for coffee and showing them around and can be more personal when hosts allow travelers to stay with them as they work the way through their travel path. Another form of hosting is that of individuals and families opening up their home to international students through study abroad programs.

Two unique paths to travel are study abroad programs and volunteer opportunities. **Study abroad** programs, sometimes referred to as international exchange and global exchange, allow international students to visit and live in a foreign country for educational purposes. According to the Open Doors Report (2013), approximately 283,333 American students studied abroad in 2011–2012 (Institute of International Education, 2013). The number of students studying abroad has continued to grow and with the access to techno-

Figure 10.6 International students come from all over the world to study in foreign countries.

logical resources for students and educational institutions themselves offering more programs for students to study abroad, this trend is likely to continue in the future. Many opportunities for international exchange start in primary and secondary schools through programs such as Kiwanis, Rotary, Lions International, and Youth For Understanding. Programs like Youth for Understanding, one of the world's oldest and most respected exchange programs, send high school students from all over the world to study abroad. These opportunities to study and learn can continue into college. In California, for example, there are many California Community Colleges (CCCs), California State Universities (CSUs), Universities in the University of California (UC) system, as well as private schools that have study abroad programs available for enrolled students. Regardless of how students get involved, there are countless benefits to the study abroad experience.

What an individual has to gain through studying abroad and international travel is hard to truly measure. According to Dwyer and Peters (2012), there are a lifetime of benefits from living and studying abroad, which included personal development, intercultural development, and educational and career attainment,

to name a few. Figure 10.7 identifies several benefits for studying abroad for youth but can be extended in most cases to almost any instance of international study program (Youth for Understanding USA: International Exchange Program, 2013). Other research suggests that the Big Five Indicators (BFI) for personality are also impacted by people's experiences studying abroad. In one such study, students had increases in their levels of openness and curiosity to novelty (Openness scale of the BFI), were more sociable and preferred to be in the company of others (Extraversion scale of the BFI), and were more cooperative and displayed a more even temperament (Agreeableness on the BFI).

Benefits of Studying Abroad

Discover and develop personal strengths like independence, confidence, and tolerance

Gain a new, global perspective

Increase proficiency in another language

Meet remarkable people and build lifelong friendships

Immerse yourself in different cultures

Learn how to interact with people from different backgrounds

Qualify for preferred college admissions

Enhance global career opportunities

Figure 10.7 List of why global exchange is unique to people according to the Youth for Understanding website.

Participants also showed a decrease in their more unpleasant emotions such as anxiety, depression, and vulnerability (Neuroticism scale of the BFI) (McGrourty, 2014). There are also some very obvious benefits of studying abroad that include a grounded experience learning another language, becoming familiar with the way of life of other countries and cultures, and creating relationships that will expand, test, and enrich the lives of international students and the people they come in contact with. Needless to say the benefits to international travel and tourism, whether that be for ecotourism or a study abroad program, these experience can create memories that will last a lifetime.

Volunteerism is yet another reason that people travel abroad. These types of trips are often highly structured and are geared toward humanitarian effort, philanthropy work, or driven by religious causes. The Peace Corps is an international service organization that sends Americans to all parts of the world to address serious needs in other countries. There are countless other organizations, nonprofits, and religious groups, both of which give people opportunities to do work in other countries while giving back to the countries they visit through the services provided through their volunteer efforts. The final and one of the most important reasons for people to travel is to see family, friends, or the origins of one's family. Sometimes this is the sole purpose of people's travel abroad. Checking out the sites or participating in local traditions might just be a tertiary benefit to reconnecting with family abroad. Whether this is to see relatives who are in another country, connect with old college roommate, military buddy, or fellow service member, or simply to relax in the company of familiar faces, this type of travel is one of the most rewarding. Regardless of the type of tourism or travel individuals partake in, often it is their communication with others and the sites themselves that will dictate how memorable and enjoyable the trip will be. Let us now turn our attention to some considerations people should keep in mind as they travel and interact with people who do not come from the same places or share the same beliefs, values, and attitudes.

Focus: Travel and Communication

As shared in the earlier chapters of this textbook, communication is multifaceted, and before communicating with people, there is any number of considerations people should make. When traveling, these considerations are often magnified because people are immersed within a culture that is not only foreign to them but also a potential language barrier can make it difficult to communicate effectively. Below are five suggestions travelers should keep in mind as they interact while abroad:

1. <u>Do your research</u> and find out how people communicate within the country you are visiting. Look beyond mere language differences. It is likely you will travel to a country where English is not the national language. Try to find out what are the preferred ways of speaking and acting within that country. If, for example, you are visiting a country where there is a strict religious influence that separates the sexes, please make yourself aware of the rules and nuances for communicating with people from the opposite sex. These rigid rules may have consequences and as a visitor to any country, you want to avoid any and all negative consequences if it can be helped. For example, talking on public transportation in Japan, specifically buses and trains, it is considered very rude to talk or talk loudly. Even talking on mobile phones is a no-no. On some buses and trains this is clearly communicated through certain signage as well. Knowing this before traveling to Japan may help individuals avoid awkward and judgmental moments from the Japanese people. There are a few exercises in the workbook that may help travelers internalize some of the areas they should research before travel. Please complete the following:
   Communication Faux Pas starting on page 10.7.
   Top 10 Nonverbal Behaviors starting on page 10.16.

2. Remember that you are a visitor to their country and when interacting and communicating with native people, please keep this in mind and try to <u>error on the side of respectful</u>. To know what is understood as respectful again requires some research and digging. Not all cultures communicate respect in the same ways. Whereas a quick response to someone's question might be interpreted in the United States as common courtesy, in other cultures with a strict hierarchical system talking back to someone even if they have asked you a question might be considered disrespectful. When travelers do their research, attempt to take on the perspective of native people, as well as practice cultural empathy, they intellectually position themselves to understand what is happening around them as they travel. Please complete the workbook exercise entitled **Intercultural Communication Reflections for International Travel** on page 10.9 to practice recognizing other skills and concepts that might be necessary for upcoming trips abroad. However, people cannot be afraid to communicate when traveling either. Do not be afraid to <u>jump right into the culture</u>. Although the last suggestion was about respect, you cannot be so afraid of making mistakes that you miss out on valuable experiences and relationships because you have forced yourself to be shy. Get into the culture and try your best to communicate effectively with those around you. This includes trying to speak the national language of the places you visit. In my experience, people often feel honored and are pleased to see travelers attempt to speak their language. It nonverbally communicates a willingness to adapt to the culture travelers visit instead of everyone having to work around a person traveling. Take a tip from St. Augustine's playbook, "When in Rome, do as the Romans do." To prepare to jump right into another culture, travelers should familiarize themselves with common words and phrases used by local people from the workbook exercise entitled **Top 10 Words and Phrases** starting on page 10.20.

3. In the same light that travelers should be willing to jump into the cultures they visit, you also should <u>put yourself out there</u>. One of the great exchanges about travel is that often both parties learn from each other. Authenticity and sincerity go a long way when communicating with others. Be open to others when the opportunities are there. As much as travelers should be willing to show people who they are, where they come from, and the preferred way of communicating in their home country, travelers must always be aware and respectful to avoid negative consequences of sharing that information. Be careful not to perpetuate negative stereotypes about people from your country or contribute to someone's xenophobia through your words and actions.

4. <u>Be observant, reflective, and willing to make adjustments</u> when communicating during travel. Depending on how limited one's experience and knowledge is within a particular country, it will become very important to take mental notes, recognize when social norms and communication codes have been violated, and lastly and most importantly be willing and ready to change ineffective and/or offensive behaviors. This advice is not only helpful when thinking about traveling but is generally a good advice for any encounter interpersonally.

5. You <u>should avoid passing judgment on others.</u> This advice applies to a number of areas regarding travel and a person's travel experiences. First, people should avoid passing judgment on others' travel experiences or desire to travel. For those individuals who value travel, it can seem oxymoronic for someone to claim that they are a free spirit or worldly person if they have not traveled internationally. In the same light, people who do not have a desire to travel or value the experience of travel can be skeptical of others who travel and their motives behind such dangerous and expensive adventures. Regardless of your experience traveling, be open to others' perspective about travel and know that people are unique and are entitled to think, feel, and behave however they would wish when it comes to travel. In addition, when people travel they are likely to see different cultures behaving in ways that challenge their moral and ethical code. The legality of

certain behaviors within a certain country as well as the cultural acceptability of certain behaviors within other countries and cultures might stand in direct opposition to what a traveler is used to in their home country as well as what they think is universally right. For example, if traveling to a country or area where many of the inhabitants are practicing Hinduism, talking about eating beef might not be well received because of how sacred cows are within that religion and culture. This example illustrates customs not eating certain products that most Americans consider a staple in their diets. However, there are plenty other examples of countries and cultures outside the United States eating things such as whale in Japan that may create feelings of discomfort or in extreme circumstances disgust. To avoid being ethnocentric, you must avoid passing judgment on others and contextually ground the way people live and communicate in the larger macrostructures such as their social, political, historical, economic, and religious influences. It is of course easily said than done but with the proper research prior to trips and an open mind, travelers can free themselves from these types of judgments.

With these suggestions in mind, people traveling to see family or touring famous archaeological sites can avoid some of the complications miscommunication might produce. The information above regarding travel and tourism hopefully inspires future travel plans, educational opportunities abroad, or just encourages the avid traveler to see more passport stamps accumulate as you jet set across the world. Along with the information shared in the rest of this textbook, travelers and tourists alike have some valuable tools and skills that will undoubtedly help them communicate more effectively while traveling. Use this information to develop more effective working models on your path to become a competent communicator.

Education

Education is something that most Americans value. A person's educational level and attainment can say a lot about them not only within the United States but also within other countries, cultures, and co-cultures. Whether a person goes to school or not, which schools they attend, and the levels of achievement or types of degrees they earn can all say something about them as a person, as an aspiring professional, or their training and expertise. Students who attended private school versus public schools during their K-12 years might be potentially thought of differently than those students who were home-schooled or earned their high-school diploma online. A degree from an Ivy League school including the opportunities a student attending one of these prestigious institutions is given can speak volumes to company executives and hiring managers as these degreed individuals enter into the job market. Education can also have meaning in the dating world as well as the job market as people meeting through formal and informal networks often established their educational and professional experiences. Parents who want the best for their children and in certain social circles where last names, reputation, and alumni status matter, a college can speak about a person's legacy, status, and potential. The communication within and between each of these unique educational cultures can also be as diverse or homogenous as the students, educators, administrators, and board members.

It is not my intent here to perpetuate any stereotypes about the different types of schools or a hierarchy within the major sectors of higher education. I do not hope to promote students going to big name schools because of the image they can create in the minds of others. However, it is by no coincidence that this section finds its way into this chapter of your text on intercultural communication. It is important that students of intercultural communication understand the jargon of education, especially higher education, so their literacy and competence when communicating with others both within and outside these systems they were a part of. It is beyond the scope of this chapter to discuss school systems across the globe.

Discussing the educational systems in other countries would require a number of chapters. Instead the information shared below about the education should increase your awareness and understanding of the complexity of the educational structures as a whole. As you encounter international students and people educated around the globe, this foundational knowledge of educational can deepen ones understanding of the experiences of others. Let us first turn our attention to primary and secondary education and the different types of schools within this system before moving into the different sectors of higher education and the schools within this system both within the United States and beyond.

Primary and Secondary Schools

As a student grows up, many students are unaware of the types of schools, the network or districts a school belong to, as well as the differences between schools and school systems. It is important to understand these differences before exploring how the educational system differs from those in other countries. A **school district** can be understood as a network of schools within a geographically determined area that are grouped together based on their relationship to each other in the progression of a student's education from primary to secondary school or a group of schools focusing on either primary or secondary education and are governed by centralized administration. Districts act as the umbrella in which both primary and secondary schools are housed and are held accountable by state and federal mandates. Although preschool, also called nursery school or pre-k programs, are not a part of many school districts; they serve an important role in preparing children to enter primary education. **Primary education** also referred to as primary schools or elementary schools can include grades kindergarten through eighth grade depending on the district they are a part of. **Secondary education** also referred to as secondary schools can include both middle school and high school of a student's education depending on the district. Middle schools vary from district to district but can be responsible for students in grades sixth through ninth. High schools, which can be combined middle and high schools, often accommodate ninth through twelfth graders.

Figure 10.8 The path to success does not always begin the same way for everyone. People need to be open-minded with their own path as well as the path others take to achieve their educational and career goals.

Secondary schools can be identified as an academic, vocational, or a technical school or offer programs that can be categorized as one or more of these types. When people think of a high school it is likely ideas of a traditional academics focus that come to mind. Schools with an academic focus have newly established Common Core State Standards that concentrate on English Language Arts and Mathematics to improve the quality of education for American students and to promote the highest academic achievement possible (California State Board of Education, 2014). On the other hand, vocational and technical schools also called Career and Technical Education, or CTE, are educational programs that offer a series of courses geared toward preparing individuals to enter a specified field or career that requires skills, training, and knowledge beyond those that require a baccalaureate or advanced degree (U.S. Deparment of Education: Institute of Education Sciences). Vocational education has been evolving in America since the turn of the twentieth century and was solidified into educational doctrine through the Perkins Act of 1984. The Perkins Act sought to expand on the Vocational Education Act of 1963 to strength the American educational system. Since the rise of vocational and technical schools in the early 1990s, CTE credits in US public high schools have declined in comparison to the increase in other subject areas offered (Hudson, 2013).

Primary and secondary schools have been further categorized by the US Department of Education as **public schools**, **private schools**, or an alternative school such as a **charter** or **magnet schools**. **Public schools** are free, through state and local government funds, primary and secondary schools that fall under the jurisdiction of local school boards and districts. **Private schools** are primary and secondary schools where students, versus state and local support, pay to attend these educational institutions. Private schools can be, but are not necessarily, affiliated with religious organization. Although the decision-making structure such as a board of trustees of private schools do not have to confirm to the standards set by surrounding districts, private school students are still required to meet or exceed the standards for all students within that level from the state regarding graduation requirements. Students who are not enrolled in schools, which fall into one of these types, must be a part of another system. Alternative schools such as charter or magnet schools are also primary and secondary schools that function very similarly to that of regular public schools and private schools but their focus and composition of students differ.

Under the alternative schools label falls both charter schools and magnets schools. **Charter schools** are public schools put together by interested parties such as parents, community members, or other vested interest groups with special purposes in mind such as serving specific student populations or the implementation of certain pedagogical protocol. **Magnet schools** are also public schools with a specific mission, orientation, emphasis, or those that permeate other schools through self-selected curriculum and instructional policies. Magnet schools often outwardly demonstrate a dedication to equitable practices and expose the students and community to unique educational opportunities unlike those traditionally found in other public and private schools. Lastly, students who are homeschooled are taught outside of tradition primary and secondary schools within the public and private school system. Homeschooled students are often taught at home by family and are still held to the same academic rigor as both public and private schools for graduation requirements.

The merit of each of these categories of schools is beyond the scope of this chapter but it is important to think about the impact and the potential difference in values, beliefs, and educational and social opportunities afforded to students within the public, private, alternative, and homeschool systems. Within the public and private school systems there are further distinctions regarding whether a student attended an appointed public school or attended a chosen public school and whether a private school is religious or nonsectarian (Grady, Bielick, & Aud, 2012). The diversity and complexity of the primary and secondary school system with the United States should provoke students in this introductory intercultural communication course to begin thinking about how other countries implement their educational structure and how that both influences students within that system and impacts interactions with students from overseas.

Top Four Reasons Parents Identified for Homeschooling Their Children

1. A concern about the environment of other schools

2. A desire to provide moral instruction

3. A dissatisfaction with academic instruction at other schools

4. A desire to provide religious instruction

5. Other reasons

Figure 10.9 Top Reasons Parents Homeschool Their Children
Information taken from The National Center for Education Statistics: Institute of Education Sciences *Parent and Family Involvement in Education, from the National Household Education Survey Program of 2012: First Look* Report. (Noel, Stark, Redford, & Zuckerberg, 2013).

Outside of the most developed nations around the world, many countries do not have free education for their people. Education is a luxury for the privileged and wealthy. In the United States, for example, a student stating that he/she is in high school is taken for granted, given that student's age and the laws in place ensuring free public education for students under the age of 18. However, for children living in certain parts of the world like the Philippines or Africa, education is a luxury sometimes not afforded or guaranteed. Students who are lucky enough to go to school may have great obstacles regarding travel, access to technology, and reliable mentors to help them through their educational journey. Students within the United States should be very grateful for the opportunities they are given, but more importantly understand that education is not something that is guaranteed to everyone around the world currently.

Without sounding trite, there are a number of considerations that communicators must keep in mind when interacting both with people from different educational systems and with people who were educated in another country. First, do not assume that people's educational experiences are superior or inferior to the education provided in other systems. Whether private school students outperform public and homeschooled students in subjects such as English, Reading, Math, and Science does not necessarily say anything about one's own experience within a public school or being taught at home. Secondly, just because someone comes from another country and is now in the United States for whatever reason does not mean that the education received back home is somehow of lower quality, less rigorous, or less effective than attending school within the United States. According to Programme for International Student Assessment's (PISA) 2012 results looking at 15-year-olds from around the world, the United States does not rank among the top five in mathematics, reading, and science (PISA, 2013). The results of national ranking in each of these subjects in addition to equity in educational opportunity are shocking to most Americans who, for whatever reason, believe that education in the United States is superior to those in other countries. People should do the research before jumping to conclusions about the type of educational experiences in other countries. Third, within any type of system there are both costs and benefits and students within any system can be successful or unsuccessful despite the institutional barriers or opportunities afforded to students within that system. Statistical analyses only tell part of the story of students from within each system. Although students can have agency within their particular system, federal and state officials, board members, administration at the district level, administration within each individual school, staff and faculty, the involvement in Parent Teacher Associations, and parents of students should all be stakeholders in the practices and quality of education delivered at any school within any system. It is not really until everyone gets involved will there be real change that can positively impact the citizenry as a whole.

The communication between and among students from similar or different educational systems can create both opportunities for greater understanding and further entrench commonly held stereotypes. As important as it is to treat individuals as such without taking note of their educational path may be remise to gathering important information about them that might allow more effective intercultural communication. Understanding a person's field of experience, the types of opportunities they may or may not have been given within a given school system, as well as additional extracurricular activities may help others access a frame of reference that may offer insight into the communication process. No one should be treated a certain way based on where they come from and the experiences they have had; however, it is the information of where someone is from and what they have experienced that might help others communicate more effectively across educational, social, political, and economic barriers.

Postsecondary Schools and Higher Education

Each year numerous publications such as *U.S. News & World Report: Best Colleges* and *Fiske Guide to Colleges* share rankings of the top high schools, colleges, graduate schools, and online education programs (Fiske, 2013; U.S. News & World Report, 2013). As students graduate from high schools they often look toward college for answers concerning their professional future. Earning Associate (AA and AS), Baccalaureate (BA, BFA, and BS), and Post-Baccalaureate (MA, MS, PhD PsyD, MD, EdD, etc . . .) degrees from certain institutions can nonverbally communicate to others about an individual's social status, earning potential, intellectual talents, among a whole host of other characteristics both positive and negative depending on the reputation that college or university and how others interpret this information. In this section of the chapter, we will discuss the higher education system, key terminology and practices for college life, student culture, and the college and university experience outside the United States.

Much like the primary and secondary education system, higher education has a similar layout. Colleges and Universities can be categorized as public, private nonprofit, and private for-profit. In California, for example, public colleges and universities include colleges in 112 CCCs, 23 CSUs, and 10 Universities in the UC system. Within the private nonprofit and for-profit system sector there are a couple of hundred colleges. Approximately 75 nonprofit colleges and universities in California belong to the Association of Independent California Colleges and Universities (Association of Independent California Colleges and University [AICCU], 2014). The mission behind each type of college, their drive, and the emphasis placed on students and student learning are addressed differently within each system and it is important for prospecting students to research this, and other information, before deciding which college or university is right for them.

Students who begin their educational path at a community college have a great deal of options and opportunity when it comes to earning degrees and certificates, transferring to other colleges and universities, increasing their knowledge and skill base within a particular field, or simply taking courses to fulfill lifelong learning aspirations. The CCC system now offers an array of Associate Degrees for Transfer (ADT) prompted by the passing of Governor Schwarzenegger's signing of SB 1440. Students who earn an ADT degree are given priority consideration for students looking to transfer to a CSU. This streamlined and simplified process is similarly offered by the UC system through their

© Syda Productions, 2014. Used under license from Shutterstock, Inc.

Figure 10.10   The options available to community college students continue to grow as the landscape of higher education changes to meet the needs of evolving society.

Transfer Admission Guarantee or TAG. Private colleges can have different standards and course requirements for transfer and they can vary from university to university. The admissions process to colleges and universities can be a daunting task, so students who can take advantage of ADT and TAG can ease some of their stress as they work through the transfer process. Community College students interested in transferring to look into these paths further for a better understanding of what these paths offer and their potential limitations to transferring to the college of their choice.

Community Colleges also offer Career Technical Education (CTE) programs where students looking into entering a certain field where an advanced degree is not necessary may take full advantage of the courses offered within the college or district. CTE programs can range from courses and training to prepare students for work in the healthcare field, manufacturing, industry, technology, and culinary arts, to name a few. The skills gained through these programs are invaluable to people looking to move into or move up within their career field. Other students who enroll in courses offered at the college, especially the community college, may be people looking to take courses of interest or continue their learning beyond their career or retirement. These lifelong learners may be in an art class to develop a new understanding or skill or want to complete unfinished courses from the past. Regardless of the type of program or degree a student pursues at the college, it is the students and the college who create the college culture at any given site.

The composition of the student body on college campus can vary greatly depending on the number of factors including the demographics of the area, the types of degrees or courses offered, and the demographics indicative of that field or area, as well as the

Figure 10.11   Career and Technical Education (CTE) programs help train professors for the careers of today.

reputation of the institution and the types of populations it has traditionally served. College campuses are becoming more diverse, especially within the CCC system, and new student populations are emerging. Beyond the **traditional students,** who transitioned from high school to college and have continued their education since graduation, **nontraditional students** are often defined as students over the age of 25 who have life circumstances beyond that expected for a traditional student such as family matters, employment, parenthood, care-giving responsibilities to children and/or elders, and prior military service, to name a few. Nontraditional students could have been enrolled as a traditional student, seeking readmission after an absence, or are enrolling in college for the first time. There is also **returning students** who are students who at one time were enrolled in college but for whatever reason were dropped or removed from their courses. Readmission or reenrolling in the college is often necessary for returning students to get back into the system since being dropped. Whether a student is a traditional, nontraditional, or returning student, there are other identifying descriptors of students and student populations.

Undocumented students are foreign-born people attending schools within the United States who entered this country either legally or illegally but do not currently have a viable legal status to do so. Because of the bipartisan legislature of the DREAM Act, undocumented students, also called DREAMers, are eligible for deferred action regarding deportation and qualify for some financial assistance to attend college depending on the state. Undocumented students are just one of many types of students people will likely encounter within any college culture. Many undocumented students are likely to fall into another grouping of students labeled first generation. **First-generation students** are students who are the first in their immediate family to attend school beyond a secondary education (high school). There are other descriptions that are used to identify students such as the 1.5 generation, underprepared students, and transfer-ready students. The emphasis on data within college systems for internal assessment, budgetary decisions, and other important practice and policy change continue to drive colleges and universities to identify students based on certain descriptors.

Outside of the demographic information gathered by individual colleges, districts, and state-governing entities regarding race and economic status, students who are a part of **traditionally underrepresented student groups** are those who historically did not enroll in college, continue their college career once started, or have significantly been less successful in the completion and graduation in their educational experience. Colleges that serve traditionally underrepresented student groups, specifically certain minority groups, can apply and be granted money and given a status of being a Minority Serving Institution (MSI). Some of the designations outlined by the US Department of Education include Alaska Native-Serving Institutions, Asian American and Native Pacific Islander-Serving Institutions, Institutions of High Hispanic Enrollment, Hispanic Serving Institutions, Historically Black Colleges and Universities, and Native American Serving Institutions: Nontribal Institutions, and Predominately Black Institutions, to name a few. Not all minority groups on campus will be given this status and there are student groups such as international students who are foreign nationals on a temporary visa or student visa, taking courses at an educational institution. There are plenty other student groups that are not being represented here; however, it might now be clear that the diversity beyond race, ethnicity, and socioeconomic status colleges and universities has a variety of students that help to create unique college cultures.

Figure 10.12 Studying within a discipline helps a person train their brains and bodies to interact in the world in a certain way.

Another important characteristic to contribute to the uniqueness of individual colleges and universities is the disciplines and departments presented on campus. **Disciplines** are specific areas of study, branches of learning, or fields of research that share a mutual understanding of knowledge and knowledge acquisition. In everyday terms it is the way that people train themselves to see the world, understand the world, and study the world through a particular lens. When students pick a major, in essence, they are making important decisions regarding how they want to be trained during their educational experiences and the discipline they want to be trained in. Much like the disciplines of martial arts, pupils often select an area to master and dedicate their time and energy toward whether it is Shotokan, Judo, or Jiu-jitsu. People who major in International Relations want to train their minds to think through the resources provided to them through their discipline. **Departments** can easily be understood as either a collection of instructors and administrators within a particular discipline or a group of disciplines housed under an overarching label that describes the shared work of disciplines. Many colleges and universities have Arts and Humanities as a department on campus that may have a number of specific disciplines under that particular department. Additionally, colleges and universities can group disciplines and department by schools. Student must familiarize themselves with the lingo and practices of the campuses they are on, so trips to financial aid, counseling, or other important offices can run smoothly.

Understanding the different types of colleges and universities, how they are run and their funding sources, commonly used terminology for student populations, as well as information regarding areas of study and how that is organized within colleges and universities is going to raise a communicators' literacy of college culture and potentially create more effective and meaningful interactions on and off-campus. Colleges and universities do not all function the same way within the United States, so it would probably be safe to assume that schools outside the United States may also do things differently. As the world becomes more competitive in all aspects of life from industry to athletics, it is no surprise that education is also a benchmark for competition. As other countries improve access to education and insure equitable practices within their colleges and universities, the United States becomes more aware of their practices and procedures. Inequities exist around the world regarding access to education for many people. Through the United Nations Educational, Scientific, and Cultural Organization: Institute for Statistics webpage addressing gender and education, Internet users are able to create a profile that compares them to others within certain demographics identifiers and highlights the disparity between literacy and educational access for people around the world. Some of the more alarming statistics are that 64% of the illiterate population is women. In places like Mozambique only 43% of women know how to read. This is similar in Togo where only 44% of women know how to read. Additional statistics about adults in Cambodia reveal that approximately 24% of women and 46% of men will finish primary school (UNESCO Institute for Statistics [UIS], 2014). Access and equity are at the forefront of educational policy discussions both within and outside the United States. Achieving the Dream, an international nongovernmental organization, has been working within the United States for the last decade to reform practices and policies in higher education to address issues regarding access and equity in an effort to promote student success (Achieving the Dream, 2014). Students within different college and university systems could greatly benefit from understanding the data for student populations they are a part of whether that is first-generation students or nontraditional students to continue effective practices within a particular system or self-impose interventions such as extra-tutoring or lab time to avoid the trends evident in the data. Students by no means have a deterministic path based on the data of student groups they are a part of but the data may be able to reveal and warn students of the pitfalls of other students similar to them. The sooner students raise their awareness, literacy, and communication skills within the culture of higher education, the better equipped they will be to handle the evitable obstacles they will encounter along the way toward their educational and career goals.

Health and Medical Practices

As diverse as the foods, dress, celebrations, traditions, rituals, and customs are within any culture, there is also a myriad of medical practices and perspectives concerning health. From the way people treat common sicknesses, to healthcare system itself within a country, to how religion influences medical protocol, health is an important factor communicators must consider and understand when interacting within medical offices and with people concerning their health. What complicates this conversation a great deal is that within individual cultures, like American culture, the practices and perspectives concerning health are so diverse that it is difficult to generalize how people look at and treat health. First, we will turn our attention to the different approaches to medicine. Second, we will explore the different healthcare systems across the globe. Lastly, we will discuss how religion and medical protocols coincide and collide.

Approaches to Medicine and Treatment

Before discussing different types of healthcare systems around the world it is important to understand how people and cultures look at medicine, care, and health. **Western medicine**, also referred to as traditional or conventional medicine, is the predominate type of treatment provided in the United States but has seen an increase in other types of care. Medical care in the United States through this traditional approach is based less on preventive medicine, like that in other countries such as Cuba, and more on reactive care to sickness, illness, or ailments that patients encounter. When a person gets sick they go to the doctor to find answers, get prescriptions, and hopefully get better. Although there has been a rise in the discourse surrounding preventative care, Americans have yet to collectively embrace this approach to health and wellness. In addition to the Western approach to medicine, which is widely practiced around the world, is **complementary/alternative medicine (CAM)**. With its roots in antiquity or "eastern medicine," CAM can be broken into two separate definitions. **Complementary medicine** refers to unconventional medical practices and procedures that are used alongside or in combination with traditional medicine. **Alternative medicine** refers to unconventional medical practices and procedures that are used in place of traditional medicine. With acupuncture clinics, holistic doctors, and other offices offering cultural remedies, Americans have seen the rise of complementary and alternative medicine. In some cases insurance companies are covering CAM.

In addition to these types of medicine are two types of medicine and treatment that blur the lines between alternative medicine and religious practice because of the potential cultural and religious underpinnings. Many cultures around the world share within their histories the important role of healers. Whether it is a shaman who looks to the spirit world within Hmong culture to help people through troubled health, a Mexican curandero using their magical and native medical practices, or a "hand trembler" or "stargazer" with the American Indian culture to diagnose the cause of a certain illness, the healer has played a central role in the understanding of health and medicine since the beginning of mankind. In many cases healers provide **holistic medicine**, or healing and care that take into account an individual's mind, body, and spirit when considering diagnoses as well as treatment options to their constituents. Holistic medicine, which could easily be categorized as either or both CAM in many respects, has also gained popularity within the United States. Lastly, **home remedies** are also a type of treatment and healing provided to people within their own home or community through the use of herbs, spices, vegetables, and other commonly found items. The roots of these family or cultural elixirs can be traced through history and religious influences and in other cases they can be tried-and-true fixes or helpful placebos created by one generation and passed down to the next. For thousands of years, the Chinese and Korean people have believed in healing power of ginseng. As a holistic medicine and home remedy to many ailments, ginseng is commonly taken in teas, tonics, and with other herbs and foods.

Regardless of the approach to medicine any particular individual or culture practices, it is important to understand the difference between this perceptive and respect the choices of people regarding their health. The types of medicine described above are often embedded into a country's culture and healthcare system. Walking down the streets in a small midwestern town in the United States it may be difficult to find an apothecary or shop specializing in herbs and spices to treat ailments but in other countries where this type of medicine and treatment is valued it might be a staple to see bens of ingredients such as ginseng at a storefront. How do countries treat healthcare? Who is financially responsible for people who need care? The answers to these questions are important for individuals looking to have a better sense of people around the world and communicate effectively with people who have different experiences when it comes to medicine.

Healthcare Systems

Health is an important element of all human existence. Three of the eight United Nations Millennium Development Goals focus on health issues (United Nations, 2014). Individual countries have structured healthcare and healthcare services differently depending on a number of factors. Beyond the factors that have helped to create these systems and the histories behind them, Reid (2009) discusses the four most pervasive models for healthcare systems around the world. They are identified and discussed below:

1. **The Bismarck Model:** Both providers (hospitals and offices providing services) and the payers (patients) are privately funded. Patients must obtain

Figure 10.13 Ginseng is a highly sought-after product and has special meaning and healing power within cultures within and outside the United States.

their own insurance; however, the government closely monitors profits generated for care by private insurance companies and providers. Also, everyone within the system is covered through a network of funds collected through this multipayer system. The cost for medical care is controlled within this system because of the regulations enforced by the government in this profit-monitored system. Countries such as Germany have this type of healthcare system.

2. **The Beveridge Model:** Healthcare within this system is provided by and paid for by the government. When people think of "socialized medicine" they are likely thinking of this model, which is financed by the government through a combination of taxes collected from the people. With the government financing all the entities within the system including how and what providers offer, the cost of healthcare tends to be low per capita. Countries such as Great Britain, Italy, Spain, Cuba, most of Scandinavia, and Hong Kong have or have had a version of this system.

3. **The National Insurance Model (NHI):** This system, which has elements from both the Bismarck and Beveridge Models, has a government-run insurance program but providers are privately owned. The government collects a number of taxes, including sales tax that creates the funds for this single-payer system. In essence, then the healthcare providers bill the government for the services used by patients. There are some exceptions to what is covered such as dental, optometry, and prescriptions but for the most part healthcare is free. Countries such as Canada, Taiwan, Japan, and South Korea have or use versions of this system.

4. **The Out-of-Pocket Model:** Much like it sounds, this system is little to no government control and individual, or single-payers, must pay directly for the services they receive. This system is found in many of the poorest and developing nations around the world. The disparity between who gets care and who goes without medical care within a health system is great and the balance of access and quality of care is afforded to those who have the money to pay. Poor countries without the funds or resources to sponsor or fund government-run, government-monitored, or universal care are likely to have this system. Countries such as India, Cambodia, Egypt, South America, Africa, and parts of China have or use a version of this system.

According to Reid, most of the nations around the world fall into the out-of-pocket model outside a handful of the most industrialized nations (Reid, 2009). America is not listed among the countries that use any one of these systems. American has practiced parts of these models until recently.

With the passing of the Affordable Care Act in June 2012, the landscape and system of healthcare within the United States has and will continue to change. The Affordable Care Act mandates that all Americans are covered through some type of health insurance whether it is private or government based. Children and aging Americans have Medicare and Medicaid to ensure that they are cared for. The rest of Americans must be covered or face financial penalties, which begin and continue to increase yearly after 2014. Similar to the healthcare system in Germany, people are able to choose between healthcare providers. Germany's system differs in many ways from that of the United States and other developed nations around the world. Universal healthcare systems like those offered in France and Britain, which provides their citizens with, guaranteed care for most, if not all, of their healthcare needs. There are of course differences in the funding sources to provide for these services within each country, exceptions to healthcare needs like dentistry among others, and not all the costs are necessarily picked up by these countries requiring patients to have additional insurance plans like gap insurance or come out of pocket for the services and treatment received.

Countries like Taiwan and China have undertaken massive reform projects over the past decade to improve the healthcare systems within these countries. China, for example, has undergone foundational healthcare renovations in an effort to provide better access and services to the Chinese people. Construction of new hospitals and clinics is underway to reach traditionally underserved rural populations. Such program and innovation comes with a cost and sustaining these structural changes will create new obstacles for the Chinese to deal with in the future. Taiwan, who is under a national health insurance system, covers all of their citizens. One of the most thought-provoking tools used within this healthcare system is the use and implementation of the Smart Card. Smart Cards are encoded with a patient's complete medical record, which allows healthcare professionals to access these records immediately when considering options for treatment. Taiwan and China are but a few of many countries motivated to make changes to their healthcare systems. Other countries are not as fortunate due to economic, technological, and political barriers.

In many developing nations there are significant obstacles in providing the amenities of healthcare that Americans, and people from other developed countries, often take for granted. In places like Africa where access to feasible and reliable transportation can be an issue for rural people, even getting to healthcare facilities can be an insurmountable barrier to receive proper care. This is not to take anything away from the care and treatments they are receiving from tribal or cultural healers or local doctors. However, when considering the death rate in developing nations of curable illness, it is important that people have access to treatments that will allow them to live long and healthy lives.

Religion and Healthcare

Having access to healthcare facilities is one thing but there are also other considerations regarding religion that both individuals and healthcare providers must understand when caring for patients. Followers within different religions have a hierarchy of priorities revolving around their god or deity and in some cases "prayer over medicine" is the moniker that dictates healthcare decisions. In February 2014, Pentecostal preacher and reality-television show star Jamie Coots died after being bit by a poisonous snake and refusing medical treatment. Despite previously losing a finger, Coots believed that no harm could come from snakes being a man of god as suggested in the bible (Fantz, 2014). Coots' unfortunate story is an example of how religion can influence individual's healthcare and treatment. This story is not unlike others involving religion and belief systems. Fadiman's (1997) book, *The Spirit Catches You and You Fall Down: A Hmong Child, Her American Doctors, and the Collision of Two Cultures*, chronicles the struggle of assimilating Hmong refugees as they are asked and forced to violate their cultural beliefs to use western medicine to treat their daughter who has epilepsy. This moving story about the Lee family out of Merced County in California provides another example of how healthcare providers must be respectful to cultural difference without being neglectful with patients to provide the highest-quality care possible. Highest-quality care possible can mean very different things to different groups of people because on their religion and religious practices. Jehovah's Witnesses, among other religious groups, who follow literal interpretations of the Old and New testaments, may refuse blood transfusions and organ donations regardless of threats to their health. People, regardless of their relationship to the healthcare system, must understand that cultures approach and handle health and healthcare very differently if they want to be successful at communicating effectively. What also complicates this even further is people who fall within traditional religious frameworks who might normally refuse certain types of care because of religion may break the mold and choose different ones. Individuals have to be treated as such on a case-to-case basis within their larger cultural contexts.

Health Communication

The role of competent and effective intercultural communication is no more evident than that within the context of healthcare. Healthcare providers on all levels should be aware of the differences between religions and their religious practices as it influences healthcare procedure and protocol and develop more efficient working models to communicate effectively about the choices and consequences of refusing care or service. The **physician–patient relationship** is the interaction between physicians in providing care to patients and the patient receiving care from physicians, which is crucial. Physicians have responsibilities to their patients and patients have responsibilities to both themselves and their medical providers when seeking care. To be more effective in these interactions, patients need to consider the following when communicating about their health:

Figure 10.14 Patients must not be passive consumers of their medical treatment but rather active participants in how care is delivered.

1. Become familiar with **medical terminology**. No one expects the average patient to be an idiot savant for medical terminology but patients need to see their agency for their health and healthcare decisions. Medical terminology is the specific language and phraseology used within the healthcare field. It is a technical jargon used within this specialized context.
2. Patients should not pretend that they understand a physician if the physician is being unclear or using medical jargon in a way that is confusing to patients. Patients must take it upon themselves to let the medical provider know information regarding diagnosis and/or treatment is unclear.
3. When in fact things are unclear or confusing, patients must ask for clarification. Medical providers are likely to keep moving forward with the diagnosis or talk if everything looks like it is registering. Patients must have the confidence to speak up and ask for clarification. What may be viewed as a stupid question within the mind of a patient may in fact be the question that should be asked to get the answers a patient needs to understand what is happening or what should happen.
4. One way to check for understanding is for a patient to paraphrase to the medical provider what they just learned. Patients often walk out of doctors' offices displeased with their interaction or had unanswered question that they either regret not asking or did not think to ask.

It is important for everyone to get the most from their healthcare professions. In some cases coming to appointments with scripted questions regarding health concerns can be helpful. With the rise of accessibility to medical information regarding symptoms, diagnosis, and treatment, patients have more power over the knowledge they walk into clinics and hospitals with. Self-efficacy becomes an important concept when understanding the way patients approach physicians during their medical encounters. Self-efficacy is a person's belief or perception in their ability or capacity to succeed in certain situations. It is about getting what a person wants out of specific situations. Patients should also keep in mind that they are not medical professionals and questions should be asked to promote dialogue rather than show off or challenge professional diagnosis; although there is a time and place for that as well. Patients must not be passive consumers of their medical treatment but rather active participants in how care is delivered.

Conclusion

Being a competent communicator includes cultural competency in a whole host of areas. This chapter hopefully gives aspiring competent communicators' insights into three unique contexts that can help them on their path to being informed about people's travel, educational, and health as well as promote intercultural sensitivity to difference. Effective intercultural communication is an important life skill that takes knowledge, patience, and practice. Through this chapter we hoped to share some of the knowledge and skills necessary to help you as you meet and interact with people who are both the same and different. In this chapter we also discussed some of the unique opportunities are afforded to people who travel or host those who travel which all involve communication. These encounters can open up new perspectives and understandings about different cultures and their views about how the world works. By having a foundational understanding about both the education and healthcare systems can broaden communicators' understandings of their own experiences as well as those who have navigated other paths on their way to success and wellness. It is with this newfound knowledge or refined knowledge of travel, education, and health that this travel hopes to influence your literacy concerning these three important areas of people's lives. Let this information shape your working models of these contexts and like the advice shared throughout the chapter suggests, keep revising and updating these models as new information challenges available.

Glossary

Authenticity   When traveling it is a mindset to have experiences within a host culture that are true to the lives of the people who live within that culture.

Ecological tourism   Traveling for enjoyment and pleasure based on environmental attractions. Also in more recent years eco-tourism has also come to represent ecologically responsible travel where travelers are conscious of the ecological footprint they leave behind.

Embodied ethnocentrism   The preference people have for familiar places. We feel comfortable in spaces and places that we consider to be our own (discussed at length in Chapter 2).

Ethnocentrism   The belief in the inherent superiority of one's own ethnic group or culture (discussed at length in Chapter 2).

Faux Pas   Communication that creates moments of social awkwardness between people because of a person's unexpected or uncharacteristic behavior given the expectations of the social situation or context.

Host culture   The dominant culture within a society a person visits. The dominant culture or host culture is shaped by the expected and accepted practices and behaviors regarding communication (language and behavior), history, religion, gender roles, and norms among other influences.

International students   Foreign nationals on a temporary visa, student visa, taking courses at an educational institution.

Medical terminology   The specific language and phraseology used within the healthcare field. It is a technical jargon used within this specialized context.

Medical tourism   Traveling to countries where the cost and accessibility of certain medical procedures are more feasible than in one's country of origin.

Metacognition   An individual's awareness and understanding of the way they think.

National character   A group of characteristics or behavioral traits that apply to the majority population of a whole nation (discussed at length in Chapter 2).

Nationality   The country in which someone is born, has citizenship to, or is naturalized into.

Nationalism   The sense of pride, patriotic nostalgia, or devoted commitment to one's nation.

Nontraditional student   Students over the age of 25 who have life circumstances beyond that expected for a traditional student such as family matters, employment, parenthood, care-giving responsibilities to children and/or elders, and prior military service that impact their enrollment status.

Physician–patient relationship   The interaction between physicians in providing care to patients and the patient receiving care from physicians.

Primary education   Also referred to as primary schools or elementary schools, can include grades kindergarten through eighth grade depending on the district they are a part of.

Public school   Free primary and secondary schools that fall under the jurisdiction of local school boards and districts.

Regionalism   Devotion, sense of pride, and loyalty toward a specific area within a country.

School district   A network of schools within a geographically determined area that are grouped together based on their relationship to each other in the progression of a student's education from primary to secondary school or a group of schools focusing on either primary or secondary education and are governed by centralized administration.

Secondary education   Also referred to as secondary schools, can include both middle school and high school of a student's education depending on the district.

Self-efficacy   A person's belief or perception in their ability or capacity to succeed in certain situations.

Study abroad   Also referred to as International Exchange and Global Exchange: Participation in educational activities while living in a country outside one's original country of origin for the purpose of living abroad and studying.

Tourism   Traveling for a specific type of enjoyment and pleasure often times to see sites that have historical or esthetic significance.

Traditional student   A student who transitioned from high school to college immediately following graduation, has stayed in school, and is between the ages of 18 and 24.

Undocumented student A foreign-born person, who entered the United States either legally or illegally, who does not have current legal status within the United States and attends school.

Vocational or technical education Also called Career and Technical Education, or CTE, are educational programs that offer a series of courses geared toward preparing individuals to enter a specified field or career that requires skills, training, and knowledge beyond those that require a baccalaureate or advanced degree.

Western medicine Also referred to as traditional or conventional medicine, is the predominate type of treatment provided in the United States and is reactive care to sickness, illness, or ailments that patients encounter.

Xenophobia Extreme fear or hatred of strangers or foreigners.

Works Cited

Achieving the Dream. (2014). *Achieving the dream: About us.* Retrieved from Achieving the Dream website: http://www.achievingthedream.org

Association of Independent California Colleges and University. (2014). Retrieved from Association of Independent California Colleges and University website: http://www.aiccu.edu

California State Board of Education. (2014, April 15). *California State Board of Education: Standard & frameworks: Content standards.* Retrieved from California State Board of Education website: http://www.cde.ca.gov/be/st/ss/index.asp

The Center for Disease Control and Prevention. (2014, January 13). *Medical tourism—Getting medical care in another country.* Retrieved from Center for Disease Control and Prevention website: http://www.cdc.gov/features/medicaltourism/

Dwyer, M. M., & Peters, C. (2012). *IES: Abroad News: The benefits of study abroad.* Retrieved from IES: Abroad website: http://www.iesabroad.org/study-abroad/news/benefits-study-abroad

Fadiman, A. (1997). *The spirit catches you and you fall down: A hmong child, her American doctors and the collision of two cultures.* New York, NY: Farrar, Straus and Giroux.

Fantz, A. (2014, February 18). *Reality show snake-handling preacher dies of snakebite.* Retrieved from CNN U.S. website: http://www.cnn.com/2014/02/16/us/snake-salvation-pastor-bite/

Fiske, E. B. (2013). *Fiske guide to colleges 2014* (30th ed.). Naperville, IL: Sourcebooks.

Grady, S., Bielick, S., & Aud, S. (2012, April). *Trends in the use of school choice: 1993 to 2007: A statistical analysis report.* Washington, DC: U.S. Department of Education, Institute of Educational Sciences, National Center for Education Statistics.

Hudson, L. (2013, November). *Data point: Trends in CTE coursetaking.* Washington, DC: U.S. Department of Education, National Center for Education Statistics.

Institute of International Education. (2013). *Open doors 2013: Report on International Educational Exchange.* Bureau of Education and Cultural Affairs, U.S. Department of State. Washington, DC: National Press Club.

McGrourty, R. (2014, April). Does study abroad accelerate personal growth? *Trends & Insights: For International Education Leaders, 1–5.*

Noel, A., Stark, P., Redford, J., & Zuckerberg, A. (2013, August). *Parent and family involvement in education, from the National Household Education Surveys Program of 2012: First look.* Washington, DC: U.S. Department of Education, Institute of Education Sciences, National Center for Education Statistics.

Nozik, M., Tenebaum, E., Tenkhoff, K. (Producers), Guevara, E., Granado, A., Rivera, J. (Writers), & Salles, W. (Director). (2004). *The motorcycle diaries* [Motion Picture].

Programme for International Student Assessment. (2013). *PISA 2012 results in focus: What 15-year-olds know about what they can do with what they know.* Organisation for Economic Co-operation and Development, Programme for International Assessment.

Reid, T. (2009). *The healing of America: A global quest for better, cheaper, and fairer health care.* New York, NY: The Penguin Press.

Rollenhagen, L. (2013, July 21). *8 Dyanmic social networks to meet people abroad.* Retrieved from Mashable.com website: http://mashable.com/2013/06/21/travel-social-networks/

UNESCO Institute for Statistics. (2014). Retrieved from United Nations Educational, Scientific, and Cultural Organization website: http://www.uis.unesco.org/Education/Pages/mind-the-gap.aspx?SPSLanguage=EN

United Nations. (2014). *United Nations: Millennium goals*. Retrieved from United Nations website: http://www
.un.org/millenniumgoals/

United Nations Educational, Scientific, and Cultural Organization. (2014). *UNESCO World Heritage Centre*. Retrieved from United Nations Educational, Scientific, and Cultural Organization website: http://whc.unesco.org

U.S. Deparment of Education, Institute of Education Sciences. (n.d.). *National Center for Educational Statistics:
Career/Technical Education Statistics*. Retrieved from Institute of Education Sciences, National Center for
Educational Statistics website: https://nces.ed.gov/surveys/ctes/

U.S. News & World Report. (2013). *Best colleges: 2014 Edition*. Washington, DC: Author.

Wheeler, T., & Wheeler, M. (2014). *About lonely planet; responsible travel*. Retrieved from Lonely Planet website:
http://www.lonelyplanet.com/about/responsible-travel/

Woodman, J. (2012). *Patients beyond borders: Dubai healthcare city edition: Everybody's guide to affordable,
world-class healthcare*. Chapel Hill, NC: Healthy Travel Media.

Youth for Understanding USA: International Exchange Program. (2013). *Youth for understanding USA: Study
abroad*. Retrieved from Youth for Understanding USA website: http://yfuusa.org/study-abroad.php